Advances in Ubiquitous Computing:

Future Paradigms and Directions

Soraya Kouadri Mostefaoui
Oxford Brookes University, UK

Zakaria Maamar
Zayed University, UAE

George M. Giaglis
Athens University of Economics and Business, Greece

T0344529

IGI PUBLISHING

Hershey • New York

Acquisition Editor:	Kristin Klinger
Senior Managing Editor:	Jennifer Neidig
Managing Editor:	Sara Reed
Development Editor:	Kristin Roth
Copy Editor:	Brenda Leach
Typesetter:	Michael Brehm
Cover Design:	Lisa Tosheff
Printed at:	Yurchak Printing Inc.

Published in the United States of America by
IGI Publishing (an imprint of IGI Global)
701 E. Chocolate Avenue
Hershey PA 17033
Tel: 717-533-8845
Fax: 717-533-8661
E-mail: cust@igi-global.com
Web site: http://www.igi-global.com

and in the United Kingdom by
IGI Publishing (an imprint of IGI Global)
3 Henrietta Street
Covent Garden
London WC2E 8LU
Tel: 44 20 7240 0856
Fax: 44 20 7379 0609
Web site: http://www.eurospanonline.com

Library of Congress Cataloging-in-Publication Data

Advances in ubiquitous computing : future paradigms and directions / Soraya Kouadri Mostéfaoui, Zakaria Maamar, and George M. Giaglis, editors.
    p. cm.
  Summary: "This book investigates the technology of ubiquitous computing, emerging applications and services, and social issues vital for the successful deployment of a ubiquitous computing application. Providing high quality, authoritative content on such topics as device design, wireless communication, location sensing, privacy concerns, attention focus, multi-person interaction, and direct interaction, work patterns, it is a must-have in library collections"--Provided by publisher.
  Includes bibliographical references and index.
  ISBN 978-1-59904-840-6 (hardcover) -- ISBN 978-1-59904-842-0 (ebook)
  1. Ubiquitous computing. I. Mostéfaoui, Soraya Kouadri. II. Maamar, Zakaria. III. Giaglis, George M.
  QA76.5915.A395 2008
  004--dc22
                                    2007037380

British Cataloguing in Publication Data
A Cataloguing in Publication record for this book is available from the British Library.

Advances in Ubiquitous Computing:

Future Paradigms and Directions

Table of Contents

Foreword..vi

Preface...viii

Acknowledgment..xiii

Chapter I
Mobile Phone and Visual Tags:
Linking the Physical World to the Digital Domain.....................................1
   Marco Avvenuti, Università di Pisa, Italy
   Alessio Vecchio, Università di Pisa, Italy

Chapter II
Context-Aware Mobile Learning on the Semantic Web............................23
   Rachid Benlamri, Lakehead University, Canada
   Jawad Berri, Etisalat University College, United Arab Emirates
   Yacine Atif, Massey University, New Zealand

Chapter III
Model-Driven Development for Pervasive Information Systems...............45
   José Eduardo Fernandes, Bragança Polytechnic Institute, Bragança, Portugal
   Ricardo J. Machado, University of Minho, Guimarães, Portugal
   João Álvaro Carvalho, University of Minho, Guimarães, Portugal

Chapter IV
Device Localization in Ubiquitous Computing Environments 83
    Rui Huang, The University of Texas at Arlington, USA
    Gergely V. Záruba, The University of Texas at Arlington, USA
    Sajal Das, The University of Texas at Arlington, USA

Chapter V
Enabling Programmable Ubiquitous Computing Environments:
A Middleware Perspective 117
    Christine Julien, The University of Texas at Austin, USA
    Sanem Kabadayi, The University of Texas at Austin, USA

Chapter VI
Determinants of User Acceptance for RFID Ticketing Systems 150
    Dimitrios C. Karaiskos, Athens University of Business and Economics, Greece
    Panayiotis E. Kourouthanassis, Athens University of Business and Economics,
    Greece

Chapter VII
Designing for Tasks in Ubiquitous Computing:
Challenges and Considerations 171
    Stephen Kimani, Jomo Kenyatta University of Agriculture and Technology, Kenya
    Silvia Gabrielli, University of Rome "La Sapienza," Italy
    Tiziana Catarci, University of Rome "La Sapienza," Italy
    Alan Dix, Lancaster University, UK

Chapter VIII
Kinetic User Interfaces: Physical Embodied Interaction with
Mobile Ubiquitous Computing Systems 201
    Vincenzo Pallotta, University of Fribourg, Switzerland
    Pascal Bruegger, University of Fribourg, Switzerland
    Béat Hirsbrunner, University of Fribourg, Switzerland

Chapter IX
M-Traffic: Mobile Traffic Information and Monitoring System 229
    Teresa Romão, Universidade de Évora, Portugal
    Luís Rato, Universidade de Évora, Portugal
    Antão Almada, YDreams, Portugal
    A. Eduardo Dias, Universidade de Évora, Portugal

Chapter X
Towards Ambient Business: Enabling Open Innovation in a
World of Ubiquitous Computing 251
    Christian Schmitt, University of Cologne, Köln, Germany
    Detlef Schoder, University of Cologne, Köln, Germany
    Kai Fischbach, University of Cologne, Köln, Germany
    Steffen Muhle, University of Cologne, Köln, Germany

Chapter XI
Activity-Oriented Computing 280
>   *João Pedro Sousa, George Mason University, USA*
>   *Bradley Schmerl, Carnegie Mellon University, USA*
>   *Peter Steenkiste, Carnegie Mellon University, USA*
>   *David Garlan, Carnegie Mellon University, USA*

Chapter XII
Privacy Threats in Emerging Ubicomp Applications:
Analysis and Safeguarding 316
>   *Elena Vildjiounaite, VTT Technical Research Centre of Finland, Finland*
>   *Tapani Rantakokko, Finwe LTD, Finland*
>   *Petteri Alahuhta, VTT Technical Research Centre of Finland, Finland*
>   *Pasi Ahonen, VTT Technical Research Centre of Finland, Finland*
>   *David Wright, Trilateral Research and Consulting, UK*
>   *Michael Friedewald, Fraunhofer Institute Systems and Innovation Research*
>   *Germany*

About the Contributors 348

Index 358

Foreword

With increasing computing power in ever smaller form factor devices, and the growth of short range ad-hoc networking, the vision of ubiquitous computing that was sketched out in the early 90s is moving closer to reality. However, while the hardware and networking layers are seeing significant advances, software systems and applications for ubiquitous systems are still in their infancy.

As such, this book, which is comprised of papers selected from the 3rd International Workshop on Ubiquitous Computing and those obtained by an open CFP, represents a timely and useful contribution. The editors have put together a nice collection of papers that bring out key challenges in this field and present some interesting solutions.

Many of the papers describe interesting applications that can be very useful. For instance, there are papers describing traffic monitoring, visual tags on cell phones, and mobile learning. Other papers focus on technology, such as issues related to localization and middleware. There are also some interesting papers that deal with programming and system building paradigms, such as introducing the idea of activity oriented computing, or kinetic user interfaces. Finally, there is a group of papers that describe issues related to privacy and user acceptance of some of these technologies.

Between them, the chapters cover many of the key challenges faced by ubiquitous computing. The editors should be commended for producing a volume that brings together these interesting papers. The book will be a useful resource for both academic researchers and practitioners in the field.

Anupam Joshi

Baltimore, MD

June 2007

Anupam Joshi is a professor of computer science and electrical engineering at UMBC. Earlier, he was an assistant professor in the CECS department at the University of Missouri, Columbia. He obtained a BTech degree in electrical engineering from IIT Delhi (1989), and a Masters and PhD in computer science from Purdue University (1991 and 1993, respectively). His research interests are in the broad area of networked computing and intelligent systems. His primary focus has been on data management for mobile computing systems in general, and most recently on data management and security in pervasive computing and sensor environments. He has created agent based middleware to support discovery, composition, and secure access of services/data over both infrastructure based (e.g. 802.11, cellular) and ad-hoc wireless networks (e.g. Bluetooth). He is also interested in Semantic Web and data/web mining, where he has worked on personalizing the web space using a combination of agents and soft computing. His other interests include networked HPCC. He has published over 50 technical papers, and has obtained research support from NSF, NASA, DARPA, DoD, IBM, AetherSystens, HP, AT&T and Intel. He has presented tutorials in conferences, served as guest editor for special issues for *IEEE Personal Comm.*, *Comm. ACM* etc., and served as an associate editor of *IEEE Transactions of Fuzzy Systems* from 99-03. At UMBC, Joshi teaches courses in operating systems, mobile computing, networking, and web mining. He is a member of IEEE, IEEE-CS, and ACM.

Preface

Information Technology (IT) is at a critical junction. The end of the era where *computers* dominated our perception of what IT is has already come; instead, *IT artefacts*, embedded in almost every imaginable place, provide us with services unimaginable in the near past:

- The home is transformed with automated key operations such as lighting, tempera-ture, entertainment systems, kitchen facilities, washing machines, refrigerators, space monitoring, and so on.
- Business practices are redefined through wireless networking, RF tagging, and remote monitoring, thus increasing supply chain efficiency and adding customer value.
- Public places are augmented with sensors placed in, for example, airports, museums, entertainment parks, and exhibition environments, capable of identifying user loca-tions and actions, and providing assistance and services as needed.

More and more, the digital permeates the physical space in a seamless manner. Wireless and mobile communication technologies are already widely deployed and their capabilities are ever increasing. New technologies, such as WiMAX, ad-hoc wireless sensors (illustrated, for example, with smart-dust micro-sensors), ZigBee, Wireless Mesh Networks, and 4G Networks emerge giving rise to the notion of *ubiquitous computing*. The vision of Mark Weiser in his famous 1991 article "The Computer of the 21st Century", according to which *"the most profound technologies are those that disappear; they weave themselves into the fabric of everyday life until they are indistinguishable from it,"* is today a reality.

Ubiquitous computing was coined by Weiser and colleagues at Xerox PARC in the late 1980s. They promoted a new way of thinking about computers, one that takes into account the natural human environment and allows the computers themselves to vanish into the background. The motivating idea is to make computing power available through the physical environment invisibly. This concept of invisible computing is primarily concerned with how emerging technologies can be best integrated into everyday life. Invisible computing allows users to interact with information devices that are small and task-focused instead of the traditional big, complex, general-purpose personal computers. The term *disappearing computer* has been coined to characterize this phenomenon. Similar terms include *calm technology, augmented reality*, *proactive computing*, and *autonomic computing*.

Ubiquitous computing has become a reality through certain technological trends and developments, which differentiate ubiquitous systems from their older counterparts. These trends can be summarized to the following:

- **Ubiquitous Networking:** Networks represent the backbone infrastructure of any ubiquitous system, either at the micro, the local, or the remote mobility levels. *Micro mobility* supports interactions that relate to our bodily experience. *Local mobility* involves interactions within individuals and artefacts within a given space. *Remote mobility* supports both synchronous and asynchronous communications in distant locations. The different mobility levels are supported by different technologies. *Wireless Personal Area Networks (WPANs)* aim to connect different devices (sensors, actuators, PDAs, etc.) that a user carries or wears. Thus, they aim to connect short-range micro networks that ensure connectivity between a small number of devices, creating on-body networks. The most common WPAN technologies are Infrared (IrDA), Bluetooth, and ZigBee. *Wireless Local Area Networks (WLANs)* are capable of supporting medium-range connections among different devices. The most common WLAN technologies are the IEEE 802.11 family of protocols (such as IEEE 802.11b, 802.11g, 802.11n or IEEE 802.11e). *Wireless Metropolitan Area Networks (WMANs)* provide LAN-like services, but in a wider coverage extent, such as an entire city. Common WMAN technologies are IEEE 802.16, and Terrestrial Trunked Radio system (TETRA). Last but not least, *Wireless Wide Area Networks (WWANs)* support remote connectivity among individuals and corporate systems through mainly cellular (mobile) networks such as GSM (2G), GPRS (2.5G), and UMTS (3G).

- **Ubiquitous Sensing:** Wireless sensor networks (WSN) represent the necessary leap towards ubiquity, where the environment anticipates user needs and acts on their behalf. Sensors perform two operations--sensing and actuation. Whatever the sensed quantity (temperature, light intensity), the sensor transforms a particular form of energy (heat, light) into information. Actuation converts the information into action and enables better sensing.

- **Ubiquitous Access:** Access devices constitute the front-end of ubiquitous computing, comprising of a multitude of device types that differ in terms of size, shape, and functional diversity. In essence, these devices dictate the interaction between the user and the ubiquitous system. The most important feature of these devices is their nomadic nature; they move with their users all the time, and accompany them in many types of services. They can be classified into *wireless/mobile devices* (such as mobile phones, pagers, personal digital assistants, palmtops, and tablet PCs), *wearable devices*, *ambient displays* (such as autostereotropic 3D displays, volumetric 3D displays, and holographic projections), and *everyday life objects* that incorporate sufficient computing capabilities.

- **Ubiquitous middleware:** Middleware is necessary to manage the multiple networks, sensors, and devices that collectively define a ubiquitous system. Middleware may be considered as the 'shell' to interface between the networking kernel and the end-user applications. Typical middleware services include directory, trading, and brokerage services for discovery transactions, and different transparencies such as location transparency, and failure transparency.

The consequences of ubiquitous computing for business and society are significant. Companies redefine their business models by deploying new means to efficiently communicate with their value chain stakeholders and to rapidly reach their consumers. We witness the emergence of new forms of electronic business, in which IT lies hidden in the background, but is constantly monitoring end-users' needs and wants by being proactive and autonomous. This book brings together high-quality research investigating the emerging field of Ubiquitous Computing from a multi-perspective analytical lens. The book includes chapters that present the *technology foreground* of ubiquitous computing, the *emerging applications and services*, as well as *certain social issues* that are vital for the successful deployment of a ubiquitous computing application. In particular:

In **Chapter I** (*Mobile phone and visual tags: linking the physical world to the digital domain*), Marco Avvenuti and Alessio Vecchio, both with the University of Pisa (Italy), discuss how the growing ubiquity and usability of smart mobile phones can be exploited to develop ubiquitous computing applications. The authors propose an extensible and portable programming platform that, using bi-dimensional visual tags, can turn mass-market camera-phones into systems capable of capturing digital information from real objects, use such information to download specific application code, and act as a GUI for interacting with object-dependent services.

In **Chapter II** (*Context-aware mobile learning on the semantic Web*), Rachid Benlamri (Lakehead University, Canada), Jawad Berri (Etisalat University College, United Arab Emirates), and Yacine Atif (Massey University, New Zealand) focus on the theoretical and technological aspects of *designing mobile learning services* that deliver context-aware learning resources from various locations and devices. In doing so, they consider three types of context awareness--platform-awareness, learner-awareness, and task-awareness. These contextual elements are defined at the semantic level to facilitate discoverability of context-compliant learning resources, adaptability of content and services to devices of various capabilities, and adaptability of services to task at hand and interaction history.

In **Chapter III** (*Model-driven development for pervasive information systems*), José Eduardo Fernandes (Bragança Polytechnic Institute, Portugal), Ricardo J. Machado and João Álvaro Carvalho (both with the University of Minho, Portugal) focus on the challenge of designing ubiquitous computing applications. In particular, they examine *design methodologies for pervasive information systems*. These systems are characterized by a potentially large number of interactive heterogeneous embedded/mobile computing devices. The authors discuss how model-driven development (MDD) approaches offer potential benefits that can be applied to the design and evolution of such complex systems.

In **Chapter IV** (*Device localization in ubiquitous computing environments*), Rui Huang, Gergely V. Záruba, and Sajal Das (The University of Texas at Arlington, USA) study the *localization* problem in ubiquitous computing environments. Localization refers to the problem of obtaining (semi-) accurate physical location of the devices in a dynamic environment in which only a small subset of the devices know their exact location. Using localization techniques, other devices can indirectly derive their own location by means of some measurement data such as distance and angle to their neighbors. Localization is a main enabling technology for ubiquitous computing environments because it can substantially increase the performance of other fundamental tasks, such as routing, energy conservation and network security.

In **Chapter V** (*Enabling programmable ubiquitous computing environments: a middleware perspective*), Christine Julien and Sanem Kabadayi (The University of Texas at Austin, USA) discuss how *middleware* solutions can enable the development of applications for ubiquitous computing environments. The authors propose the DAIS (Declarative Applications in Immersive Sensor networks) middleware that abstracts a heterogeneous and dynamic pervasive computing environment into intuitive and accessible programming constructs. A fundamental component of the model is a hierarchical view of pervasive computing middleware that allows devices with differing capabilities to support differing amounts of functionality.

In **Chapter VI** (*Determinants of user acceptance for RFID ticketing systems*), Dimitrios C. Karaiskos and Panayiotis E. Kourouthanassis (Athens University of Economics and Business, Greece) take a stance informed by the discipline of information systems and discuss the ever-important subject of *user acceptance* in ubiquitous applications. The authors focus on a specific RFID-based application and investigate the factors that influence its user acceptance. The theoretical background of the study is drawn from the technology acceptance model (TAM) and the innovation diffusion theory (IDT) and enhanced with factors related to privacy and switching cost features.

In **Chapter VII** (*Designing for tasks in ubiquitous computing: challenges and considerations*), Stephen Kimani (Jomo Kenyatta University of Agriculture and Technology, Kenya), Silvia Gabrielli and Tiziana Catarci (both with the University of Rome "La Sapienza," Italy) and Alan Dix (Lancaster University, UK) return to the issue of *ubiquitous applications design* and propose design and evaluation considerations emerging from a deeper understanding of the nature of tasks in ubiquitous computing. The authors argue that there is huge gap between the real-world and the desktop settings. The move from the desktop to the real-world raises various issues in terms of the nature of tasks that the ubiquitous devices/applications would be expected to support and the real-world context in which they will be used. A careful study of the nature of tasks in ubiquitous computing can make some design requirements in the development of ubiquitous applications more evident.

In **Chapter VIII** (*Kinetic user interfaces: physical embodied interaction with mobile ubiquitous computing systems*), Vincenzo Pallotta, Pascal Bruegger, and Béat Hirsbrunner (University of Fribourg, Switzerland) discuss *user interfaces for ubiquitous applications* and present a conceptual framework for user interfaces in mobile ubiquitous computing systems. More specifically, the authors focus on the interaction by means of motion of people and objects in the physical space. The chapter introduces the notion of the Kinetic User Interface as a unifying framework and a middleware for the design of pervasive interfaces, in which motion is considered as the primary input modality.

In **Chapter IX** (*M-Traffic: mobile traffic information and monitoring system*), Teresa Romão, Luís Rato, and A. Eduardo Dias (all with the Universidade de Évora, Portugal), together with Antão Almada from YDreams (also in Portugal), present *a real-life application of ubiquitous computing*. More specifically, the authors introduce M-Traffic, a multiplatform online traffic information system that provides real-time traffic information based on image processing, sensor data, and traveller behavior models. The system has a modular architecture that allows it to easily be adapted to new data sources and additional distribution platforms. In order to estimate route delay and feed the optimal routing algorithm, the authors have developed a traffic microscopic simulation model and present simulation results from using it.

In **Chapter X** (*Towards ambient business: enabling open innovation in a world of ubiquitous computing*), Christian Schmitt, Detlef Schoder, Kai Fischbach, and Steffen Muhle, all with the University of Cologne, Germany, provide *an economic perspective* to the world of ubiquitous computing by discussing the impact of Open Innovation in this world. The authors then proceed to design an Open Object Information Infrastructure (OOII) that enables Open Innovation in the context of ubiquitous computing. They showcase the benefits of this infrastructure by presenting an innovative smart service, called the Federative Library, which represents a first instantiation of the OOII.

In **Chapter XI** (*Activity-oriented computing*), João Pedro Sousa (George Mason University, USA), with Bradley Schmerl, Peter Steenkiste, and David Garlan (Carnegie Mellon University, USA), return to the issue of *ubiquitous applications design* and introduce a new way of thinking about software systems for supporting the activities of end-users. The authors suggest that models of user activities are promoted to first class entities, and software systems are assembled and configured dynamically based on activity models. This constitutes a fundamental change of perspective over traditional applications; activities take the main stage and may be long-lived, whereas the agents that carry them out are plentiful and interchangeable.

Finally, in **Chapter XII** (*Privacy threats in emerging ubicomp applications: analysis and safeguarding*), Elena Vildjiounaite, Tapani Rantakokko, Petteri Alahuhta, Pasi Ahonen (all with VTT Technical Research Centre, Finland), David Wright (Trilateral Research and Consulting, UK), and Michael Friedewald (Fraunhofer Institute Systems and Innovation Research, Germany), present an analysis of possible *implications to privacy in ubiquitous computing scenarios* and the gaps in the current state of the art in privacy enhancing technologies. The authors discuss experiences with data collection which suggest that users do not fully understand the possible privacy implications when they give their consent to data collection in public ubiquitous applications.

All in all, the twelve chapters contained in this volume collectively address all main dimensions of challenges associated with ubiquitous computing: *technologies* (hardware and software alike, including middleware solutions), *applications* (including issues related to design and usability), and *social issues* (e.g., privacy and user acceptance). Moreover, many chapters illustrate how real-world applications of ubiquitous computing transform the world in which we live and our perception of computing itself. In doing so, the book is a major step forward in advancing our thinking regarding Ubiquitous Computing.

Soraya Kouadri Mostéfaoui

Zakaria Maamar

George M. Giaglis

July 2007

Acknowledgment

The editors would like to acknowledge the help of all involved in the collation and review process of the book, without whose support the project could not have been satisfactorily completed.

Some of the authors of chapters included in this book also served as referees for chapters written by other authors. Thanks go to all those who provided constructive and comprehensive reviews.

Special thanks also go to the publishing team at IGI Global, whose contributions throughout the whole process, from inception of the initial idea to final publication, have been invaluable. In particular, we thank Deborah Yahnke, who continuously prodded via e-mail to keep the project on schedule and to Meg Stoking, whose enthusiasm motivated us initially to accept the invitation to take on this project.

We would like to thank Prof. Anupam Joshi from the Department of Computer Science and Electrical Engineering, University of Maryland, Baltimore County for writing the foreword to this book. We would also like to thank Dr. Lyes Khelladi from Cerist Algeria, who read a semi-final draft of the preface and provided helpful suggestions for enhancing its content.

In closing, we wish to thank all of the authors for their insights and excellent contributions to this book.

The Editors,

Dr. Soraya Kouadri Mostéfaoui, Dr. Zakaria Maamar, and Dr. George Giaglis

June 2007

Chapter I

Mobile Phone and Visual Tags:
Linking the Physical World to the Digital Domain

Marco Avvenuti, Università di Pisa, Italy

Alessio Vecchio, Università di Pisa, Italy

Abstract

The growing ubiquity and usability of smart mobile phones can be exploited to develop popular and realistic pervasive computing applications. Adding image processing capabilities to a mobile phone equipped with a built-in camera makes it an easy-to-use device for linking physical objects to a networked computing environment. This chapter describes an extensible and portable programming platform that, using bi-dimensional visual tags, turns mass-market camera-phones into a system able to capture digital information from real objects, use such information to download specific application code, and act as a GUI for interacting with object-dependent computational services. The system includes a module for on-phone extraction of visual coded information and supports the dynamic download of mobile applications.

Introduction

Despite the significant progress in both hardware and software technologies, Weiser's vision (1991) of an almost invisible computing and communication infrastructure able to augment the physical world with human-centric, seamless services is still not completely realizable or economically convenient. However, the deployment of ubiquitous computing applications can be significantly eased if a personal device is included as the access medium. The most obvious candidates are mobile phones, as they are in constant reach of their users, have wireless connectivity capabilities, and are provided with increasing computing power (Abowd, 2005). Moreover, an always growing number of commercially available devices are equipped with an integrated camera; according to recent studies, over 175 million camera phones were shipped in 2004 and, by the end of the decade, the global population of camera-phones is expected to surpass 1 billion.

Camera-phones enable a very natural and intuitive model of interaction between humans and the surrounding environment. Instead of manually getting information or editing service configurations, one can just point at a physical object to express one's will to use it; taking a picture of the object would suffice to set up the link with the offered services. The locality, spontaneousness and ubiquity of such an interaction perfectly fit with the pervasive computing paradigm, allowing us to access *context-dependent* services anywhere, anytime.

Capturing digital information from images is not a trivial task, especially when resource-constrained devices are used. To ease the acquisition process, objects can be labeled with visual tags, that is, bi-dimensional barcodes that encode context data. A programmable camera-phone can execute an image processing routine to read and decode the visual tag, without the need for additional hardware. Extracted data directly can provide information about the resource or, if the amount of information is too large, the visual tag can encode a resource identifier that can be used to gather information from the network.

Research in this area has contributed to the design of several barcode recognition algorithms and to envisage new interactive applications. The growing interest in this topic is also demonstrated by the release of commercial systems, which mainly focus on exploiting visual tags to link products or services to specific Web pages on the mobile Internet. However, we observe that currently available systems either lack in flexibility, as the software must be already installed onto the mobile device and cannot be dynamically extended in order to interact with new classes of resources, or run on specific hw/sw platforms (e.g., Symbian OS), thus preventing the deployment of services on most of the camera-phones already shipped or in production in the near future. Finally, architecture insights of commercial systems are rarely documented.

The objectives of this chapter are to introduce the reader to the techniques based on bi-dimensional barcodes, and to describe the design and the implementation of a software architecture, called POLPO (Polpo is on-demand loading of pervasive-oriented applications) that, relying on visual tags attached to real-world objects, turns mass-market camera-phones into a general platform for dynamically deploying mobile applications (Avvenuti, 2006).

The innovative aspects of the presented approach are flexibility and portability. Flexibility concerns the possibility of accessing new resource-dependent services and relies on a mechanism for retrieving and installing ad-hoc application modules from the network. Portability was achieved through the compatibility with the Java Platform, Micro Edition (JME) environment and required the challenging implementation of a pure Java visual tag decoder.

To summarize, the system that we describe has the following distinctive characteristics:

- **On-demand downloadable applications:** Interaction with a given class of resources such as printers, public displays, and so forth, takes place through a custom application. New custom applications can be downloaded from the network and installed onto the user's device as needed. This brings two advantages: i) the classes of resources that can be used do not have to be known a priori; ii) the user's device, that is resource constrained, includes only the software needed to interact with the services actually used.
- **Compatibility with JME:** The system, including the visual tag decoder, is written in Java and runs on devices compatible with the micro edition runtime system. This environment is quite limited in terms of memory and execution speed, but also extremely popular (nearly all mobile phones produced).

This chapter also discusses the idea of embedding binary code into visual tags as a way to distribute software patches and updates.

Background

Ailisto et al. (2006) defined the physical selection paradigm as the sequence of actions taken by the user to select an object of the physical world with a mobile terminal. The first step of the selection concerns the discovery of objects by humans. People should be able to clearly identify objects that are linked to the digital domain within their physical environment. Also, the physical objects should provide some kind of information to users in order to make clear which is the nature of the offered service. The second step involves the object discovery by the device, and it is usually triggered by physical actions performed by the users. Examples of triggering actions include taking a picture of the desired object, moving the device closer to the object, and so forth.

The physical selection paradigm thus requires the presence of information tags that are attached to physical resources. This small amount of information is read by the mobile terminal and acts as a pointer (e.g., in form of an URL) to the offered service. Such information can be visually represented by optically-readable barcodes. Bi-dimensional barcodes improve the amount of stored data by using both dimensions.

The proliferation of camera phones makes visual tags an obvious solution for linking the physical world to the digital domain. Objects can be easily identified by users because of the presence of the visual tag, and the action of taking a picture of the visual tag represents the physical selection of the object. Furthermore, the point-and-click gesture resembles, in the physical space, the actions that are performed by users when they double-click an icon in a graphical user interface, or when they follow a link in hyper textual documents. The world-wide project called Semapedia (Semapedia, 2005) is an emblematic example of how barcodes can be used for bringing the right information from the Internet to the relevant place in physical space. The project involves people in sticking visual tags to or near landmarks like the Leaning Tower of Pisa. The barcodes link to the Wikipedia entries for the locations.

The benefits that can be achieved by the integration between visual tags and camera-phones have been assessed by Toye et al. (2007). The authors discussed a study of using camera-phones and visual-tags to access mobile services. The study was carried out by observing the interactions of a number of participants with a prototype, and collecting interviews about their experiences. The results confirmed that applications based on visual tags are positively accepted and easy to learn.

Radio frequency identification (RFID) can be an alternative technology to incorporate information into everyday objects (Weinstein, 2005). RFID tags are small devices that respond to queries coming from a dedicated reader. RFID tags can be passive or active. Passive tags do not have any internal power supply; the current induced in the antenna by the carrier of the reader's transmitted signal is used to provide the power to the hardware and to transmit the reply. The range of operation of passive tags is usually in the order of few tens of centimeters (even when using more expensive hardware it cannot be easily extended above few meters). Active tags include an on-board power supply, which significantly extends their operation range, but introduces the problem of energy management. Generally, the flow of information is unidirectional (tags are read-only). Nevertheless, some RFID tags also include the possibility of writing new data into the tag, which in this case is equipped with a small amount of EEPROM.

The optimal choice between visual and RFID tags depends on many factors such as application requirements and operating conditions, since both technologies have advantages and drawbacks. For example, production costs associated to visual tags are very low (even standard printers can be used), but stored information cannot be dynamically changed and data acquisition requires line-of-sight visibility of tags. On the contrary, RFID technology is more expensive, but it does not impose visibility of tags and, in some cases, information can be updated more easily. We decided to adopt a tagging system based on visual codes because we assume that interaction is mediated by mobile phones that are provided with a camera but lack the capability of reading RFIDs.

Existing Symbologies

The original form of barcodes (Figure 1) stores information along one dimension as a sequence of bars and spaces, and information is read through the use of laser readers. These kinds of codes are part of our everyday life, as they are used to store universal product codes (UPC), that is, the code associated with almost every item in a store (originally developed for grocery items). UPC codes contain information that is only numerical, generally codified as a sequence of twelve digits (one is used as check digit). One-dimensional barcodes are reliable because of the high amount of redundancy (actually one of the dimensions is not used).

Bi-dimensional barcodes can be divided in two subcategories—stacked barcodes (also known as multi-row barcodes) and matrix barcodes. Stacked barcodes are formed by grouping together several one-dimensional barcodes. The most well-

Figure 1. Different symbologies

One–dimensional   PDF417   QR Code

MaxiCode   Data Matrix   DataGlyphs

known example of this class is PDF417 that, according to its specifications, is able to encode up to 1100 bytes or 1800 ASCII characters in a symbol. The PDF417 symbology includes error correction capabilities. Matrix barcodes are made up of small modules arranged in a grid-like pattern, and each module encodes a bit of information. Examples of matrix barcodes, shown in Figure 1, include Data Matrix, MaxiCode, QR Code, and DataGlyphs.

Data Matrix symbols contain black and white square data modules. Each symbol includes a finder pattern composed of two solid lines (called handles) and two alternating black and white lines on the perimeter. According to the specification, the maximum amount of data that can be encoded into a symbol is equal to 2335 characters or 1556 bytes. Data is spread over the entire symbol and Reed-Solomon codes are used for error correction. Data Matrix has been released to the public domain and is now protected by an ISO standard. Organizations that use Data Matrix codes include Adidas, Boeing, Airbus, Deutsche Post, and Ford Motor Company.

QR Code is a symbology created by Denso-Wave. This symbology is characterized by large data capacity; the maximum amount of information that can be contained in a symbol is 7,089 digits, or 4,296 alphanumeric characters, or 2,953 bytes (symbol sizes range from 21x21 modules to 177x177 modules). QR Code includes error correction capabilities; up to 30% of the codewords (8 bit) can be recovered. Since QR codes can also encode Japanese characters (Kanji, Kana, Hiragana), this symbology is widely adopted in Japan where camera-phones able to natively decode QR symbols are available. Besides the management of inventories, this symbology is used to ease data entry on mobile phones, for example to facilitate input of URLs in advertisement pages. QR Code is an approved ISO standard, and the patent right owned by Denso-Wave is not exercised.

MaxiCode is a symbology mainly used by United Parcel Service Inc., and it is primarily intended for encoding postal addresses. MaxiCode symbols are fixed in size (approximately 2.5x2.5 cm) and can contain up to 93 characters of information. MaxiCode's modules are hexagonal, and symbols include a central finder pattern.

DataGlyphs (Hecht, 2001) is a technique developed by Parc Research that encodes information as a matrix of tiny glyphs. Each glyph consists of a small diagonal line and represents a binary zero or one, depending on its direction. Different from the other symbologies, information encoded using DataGlyphs can be embedded within images with little degradation of the image quality. DataGlyphs include error correction (different levels are available) and data randomization (data is appropriately dispersed across the area of the symbol in order to recover information if a part of the symbol gets damaged).

Besides the symbologies described above, many other formats are available. The selection of the best symbology should be done on the basis of technical and commercial reasons. The symbology that we adopted in our system is Data Matrix, which has proved to be spatially efficient; it is the most widely implemented matrix symbology in the greatest diversity of applications and industries, and it is available as an open standard.

Related work

Cybercode (Rekimoto, 2000) is a visual tagging system based on a bi-dimensional barcode technology. The system has been used to develop several augmented reality applications where the physical world is linked to digital space through the use of visual tags. Cybercode is one of the first systems where visual tags can be recognized using low-cost CCD or CMOS cameras, without the need for separate and dedicated readers. Each Cybercode symbol is able to encode 24 or 48 bits of information. The system has been tested with notebook PCs and PDAs.

Rohs (2004) presents a system that turns camera-phones into mobile sensors for bi-dimensional visual tags. By recognizing a visual tag, the device can determine the coded value, as well as additional parameters such as the viewing angle of the camera. The system includes a movement detection scheme which enables users to use the mobile phone as a mouse (this is achieved by associating a coordinate scheme to visual tags). The communication capability of the mobile phone is used to retrieve information related to the selected tag and to interact with the corresponding resource. Tag recognition and motion detection algorithms were implemented in C++ for Symbian OS.

The Mobile Service Toolkit (MST) (Toye, 2005) is a client-server framework for developing site-specific services that interact with users' smart phones. Services are advertised by means of machine-readable visual tags, which encode the Bluetooth device address of the machine that hosts the service (Internet protocols addressing could be supported as well). Visual tags also include 15 bits of application-specific data. Once the connection has been established, MST servers can request personal information to the client to provide personalized services. Site-specific services can push user interfaces, expressed with a markup language similar to WML (Wireless Markup Language), to smart phones. MST also provides thin-client functionality: servers can push arbitrary graphics to the phone's display which in turn forwards all keypress events to the server. The client-side is written in C++ and requires Symbian OS.

A similar approach is described by Iso et al. (2003), where the authors propose an architecture for a platform that supports ubiquitous services. Real-world objects are linked to services on the network through visual tags based on geometric invariants that do not depend on the viewing direction (Iso et al., 2003). But different from other solutions, image processing does not take place on the user's device; pictures are sent to a server where they are elaborated and converted into IDs.

The solutions presented above are not completely satisfactory. Some of the limits are due to the fact that, at the time when research was carried out, supporting technologies were not fully mature, or because of the lack of computing resources. For example, Cybercode cannot be executed on mobile phones, limiting its usage in a ubiquitous computing scenario. Similarly, the need for a specific operating system is a barrier, from a practical point of view, to the adoption of a system by a large number of users. Finally, architectures based on a centralized decoding engine are constrained by scale factors and economical reasons (because the decoding process requires transferring the image from the mobile phone to a centralized server).

Recently, some commercial systems based on visual tag recognition have been released to the market. This motivates research and discussion of software practices and experimentation in this field. SCANBUY Decoder SDK (Scanbuy, 2007) is a software package for companies interested in utilizing existing handheld devices to capture and transfer barcode information. Its flexibility (support for multiple barcode protocols) enables businesses to deploy a wider range of useful and value-added mobile applications seamlessly within their organizations. ShotCode (ShotCode, 2007) is a system based on circular markers that are used to encode URLs. Once the URL has been extracted from the tag, the user is redirected to the encoded Web site without the need to type an Internet address on his phone. The encoding/decoding procedure of data into/from visual tags is proprietary, and visual tags are obtained only through the company's Web site. Technical specifications of proprietary codes are unavailable and the usage of the system is limited by the functionalities provided by the vendor. In some systems, visual tags do not directly contain URLs; instead they contain identifiers that are translated into the real URLs by accessing a specific service provided by the vendor. This limits the design space, especially in a ubiquitous computing scenario. For example, a visual tag cannot be used to contain the bluetooth address of a device in the nearby or to embed binary code. Other commercial systems include Semacode (Semacode, 2007), based on the Data Matrix standard, and the Kaywa reader (Kaywa, 2007) that supports both Data Matrix and QR Code. With respect to these systems, our architecture defines a technique for accessing context-specific services in the form of downloadable applications.

Visual tags have been used also in other contexts such as building an indoor location system. TRIP (Lòpez de Ipiña, 2002) is a low-cost and easily deployable vision-based sensor technology; by using circular barcode tags and inexpensive CCD cameras, it supports identification and localization of objects in the cameras' field of view. Each room can be equipped with one or more cameras; then by applying geometrical transformations, the position of tagged entities is determined. Thus, in comparison to other technologies that are expensive to install and maintain, TRIP provides a trade-off between the price, flexibility, and accuracy of localization.

On-Demand Loading of Pervasive-Oriented Applications

We assume a scenario where real-world objects, called resources hereinafter, are labeled with visual tags. Users, while on the move, are willing to interact with re-source-dependent services, without having to deal with technicalities of any sort. When the user is in the proximity of a given resource, if the offered service is of interest, he just takes a snapshot of the visual tag and, after a while, a new application will start running on the phone.

The POLPO system enables such a scenario by providing support for downloading the specific service application from the network and installing it onto the user's device without the need for a-priori knowledge of the resource. Of course, a program providing access to POLPO functionalities must be installed on the user's device. However, this is the only program that must be pre-loaded on the device. Its primary functions are the following:

- **Decoding of visual tags.** The image captured with the built-in camera is processed to extract the data contained into the visual tag.

- **Management of custom applications.** The program downloads and installs the custom application required to interact with the identified resource. Usu-ally, resources of the same kind may share the same custom application (i.e., a single application may be used to interact with all printers, another may be used with public displays, etc).

- **Management of user's personal data.** In many cases, applications need in-formation about the user to provide customized services. For this reason, the software installed on mobile phones includes a module that manages user's personal data and stores them into the persistent memory. Managed data may include user's name, telephone number, email address, homepage, and so forth.

Most of the existing systems use visual tags to encode only the ID of a resource. In these systems, after having extracted the ID from the visual tag, the mobile phone must open a network connection to retrieve the information needed to interact with the resource. This is usually accomplished by sending a request to a well-known server where IDs are mapped to relevant information. On one hand, this approach requires a minimal amount of information encoded into the visual tag (just the ID). On the other hand, the mobile device has to contact a server, usually through a GPRS/GSM connection with related costs and communication latency.

In our system, a visual tag does not contain only an ID. Whenever possible, the visual tag acts as a sort of visual database that contains all information needed to interact with the resource. In particular, each symbol contains the tuple:

(AppName, RepoURL, InitMsg)

where *AppName* is the name of the custom application that must be used to interact with the selected resource, *RepoURL* is the location of the repository of applications, and *InitMsg* contains the initial parameters for the application. The format of *InitMsg* depends on the resource type. For example, if the resource is a printer, *InitMsg* may contain the model, printing capabilities, IP address, and port number.

If all needed information is directly encoded within the visual tag, the mobile device does not have to contact an ID server. This solution is not feasible when the amount of information is too large to fit within a visual tag, or because the decoding process may become too computationally intensive and less robust. In these cases, the visual tag contains an URL that points to the needed information.

The main components of the POLPO system are shown in Figure 2. *Main GUI* visualizes a viewfinder that is used to point to the visual tag and take a picture of it. Then, the image is passed to the *Tag reader* module that extracts the encoded information. *Application broker* is responsible for downloading the custom appli-

Figure 2. System architecture

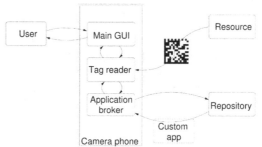

Figure 3. Interaction can be mediated by a manager

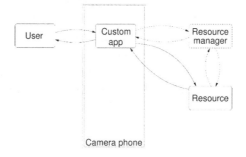

cation, and receives from *Tag reader* the name of the service, the location of the application's repository, and initial data.

Figure 3 shows the ways the downloaded *Custom application* interacts with the resource. Such an interaction may occur either through a direct network connection or, if the resource is not provided with computing/communication capabilities, through a resource manager. For example, let us consider the case where visual tags designate office doors. By taking a picture of the tag, users can stick a virtual post-it for the owner of the office. Since a door is not provided with any computing power, the custom application running on the phone communicates with an ambient-server that represents the resource.

System Implementation

POLPO is a software infrastructure that runs on Java-enabled (JME) camera-phones. The JME platform includes two configurations, several profiles, and some optional packages. JME configurations identify different classes of devices. The Connected Device Configuration (CDC) is a framework that supports the execution of Java application on embedded devices such as network equipment, set-top boxes, and personal digital assistants; the Connected Limited Device Configuration (CLDC) defines the Java runtime for mobile phones and pagers. Our system runs on top of the version 1.1 of the CLDC that provides support for floating point arithmetic (unavailable in version 1.0). The adopted profile is the Mobile Information Device Profile (MIDP) that, together with CLDC, provides a complete Java application environment for mobile phones.

Downloading Custom Applications

Java-enabled MIDP mobile phones can optionally install new applications using a GPRS/GSM connection according to a standard download procedure called *over-the-air provisioning* (OTA).

Applications for MIDP devices are packaged in form of jar archives. Each archive contains a *MIDlet suite*, that is, a set of one or more *MIDlets*, Java programs defined as extensions of the MIDlet class. A MIDlet's life-cycle is controlled by the application management software (AMS) that is part of the software operating environment of the device.

POLPO's custom applications are implemented as MIDlet suites downloaded and installed according to the OTA procedure. The only difference from standard MID-

Figure 4. Parameters passing

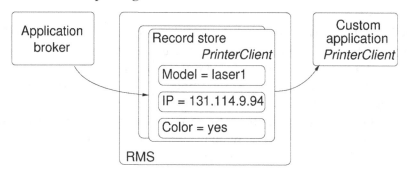

lets is in the way parameters extracted from visual tags are passed to applications, and it comes from the fact that the MIDP environment supports the execution of one application at a time, and does not allow method invocation between classes belonging to different suites. For example, a problem that arose while implementing POLPO was the impossibility of direct communication between *Application broker* and the custom applications, as they belong to different suites.

To overcome these constraints, we adopted a solution based on shared information stored in the persistent memory. In the MIDP programming environment, the basic storage abstraction is the *record store,* a collection of records. A record store is referred by a name, and a record is simply an unstructured array of bytes identified by a unique number. The *Record Management System* (RMS) is a set of classes that provides methods to create/destroy record stores and to save/retrieve records in a record store. As shown in Figure 4, the application broker creates a record store that has the same name of the custom application that is going to be installed, and writes into the record the initial parameters that have to be passed to the application. When the custom application is executed, it looks for a record store having the same application's name and, if any, it reads the data.

Apart from the initialization phase described above, POLPO custom applications can be designed according to the standard JME guidelines. Therefore, programmers can make use of all libraries provided by the Java runtime such as building graphical user interfaces, storing data into the persistent memory, and communicating with external components through the network or via SMSs.

It should be noted that the safe execution of POLPO applications is guaranteed by the Java security mechanisms. In particular, applications are executed in a sandbox and the JVM security manager grants access to specific APIs on the basis of levels of trust. Additionally, the bytecode verifier checks that newly installed applications do not perform any dangerous operation.

Lessons Learned

The portability of the Java language and the richness of the JME API allowed us to develop the POLPO system in a relatively short time. For example, the installation of a new custom application was achieved by calling the *platformRequest()* method of the *MIDlet* class and passing as argument the URL of the jar archive. This activates the AMS which starts the OTA installation procedure. However, in few cases we found the application model of the MIDP profile rather inflexible. In particular, the major issues came from two restrictions: *i)* a MIDlet has no way to know if a given MIDlet suite is already installed or not; *ii)* a MIDlet is not allowed to start a MIDlet that belongs to another suite.

The first restriction can be faced in two ways. Either *Application broker* always downloads and installs a custom application, possibly overwriting a previous installation, or it manages a list of already installed custom applications. Neither solution is completely satisfactory: the former leads to unnecessary traffic, the latter suffers from possible inconsistency of the application list (custom applications can be deleted by the user). The second restriction prevents *Application broker* from automatically starting a custom application after the installation procedure. Therefore, the user has to manually navigate through the set of installed applications and select the desired one.

During the implementation, we experienced some problems because of the Mobile Media API (MMAPI) optional package that enables access and control of device's multimedia resources. In particular, problems were due to the actual implementation of the *getSnapshot()* method, necessary to capture pictures through the built-in camera in a platform independent way. The two models of mobile phones that we used for building the demonstrator were equipped with VGA cameras, but they were able to capture images with a resolution of only 160x120 pixels, instead of 640x480 as it is possible with native applications. This problem is also described by Tierno et al. (2005).

The Visual Tag Decoder

POLPO uses Data Matrix visual tags to identify resources. We implemented an algorithm to decode Data Matrix tags that is compatible with the JME MIDP platform. Because of the constrained environment, we did not implement all the features of the Data Matrix symbology (e.g., the system does not support rectangular symbols or symbols with inverted colors). Also, we did not follow the reference decoding algorithm proposed in the Data Matrix specification since it is too resource-demanding for MIDP devices.

Figure 5. Recognition algorithm

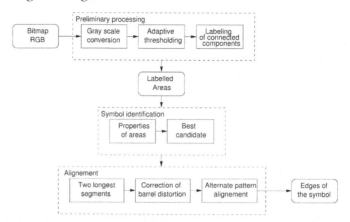

Figure 5 illustrates the main steps of the process that recognizes the visual tag within the image. First, the RGB color image is converted to a gray-scale image (Data Matrix symbols do not make use of colors). Then, the image is converted to black-and-white through an adaptive threshold. To limit the computational overhead, the threshold is set to the mean of the maximum and minimum values of luminance of the image.

The next phase determines all groups of neighboring pixels that have the same color. After the image has been divided into black or white regions, it is necessary to identify the handles, that is, the black solid bars that form two sides of the symbol. This is done by evaluating some metrical properties of each region and applying few empirical rules (the candidate black area must be contained in a larger white area, the perimeter of the candidate area must be larger than the others, etc.). The longest two segments in the selected area are considered as the best approximation of the handles, and a precision alignment technique is used to compensate the barrel distortion caused by the camera lens. To find the alternating pattern that forms the

Figure 6. Finding the alternate pattern

other two sides of the symbol, we adopted the following procedure. Let us call *P* the end point of one of the handles. A line is traced from *P* to each point of the border of a black area that is part of the symbol. Then, the line that has the highest value for *alpha* is selected, where *alpha* is the angle between the line and the handle (Figure 6). The same procedure is executed for the other handle, and the intersection of the two selected lines is used to determine the missing corner of the symbol.

Once the position of the symbol is known, the algorithm determines the number, dimension and position of modules. This is done by locating the center of the modules of the alternating pattern and building a sampling grid. Data modules are sampled at their predicted center where black is a one, and white is a zero. Groups of eight modules are converted into 8-bit symbol characters according to a positioning scheme defined by the Data Matrix specification. Finally, after Reed-Solomon error correction, data is converted according to a specific encoding scheme.

Performance

We carried out a simple experiment to evaluate the performance of the decoder on a real camera-phone. In particular, we measured the time needed to find and decode a symbol on a SonyEricsson k700i phone. To get beyond the 160x120 limit imposed by the implementation of the *getSnapshot()* method, images were acquired with the phone (from outside the Java environment), then they were transferred to a personal computer and back to the phone (this time within a MIDlet). The size of the symbol is 14x14 modules, and the symbol takes up to 25% of the image surface. Figure7(a) depicts the decoding time against the image size (the image is square sized).

Figure 7. Performance of the decoding algorithm

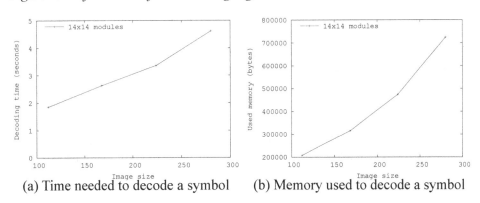

(a) Time needed to decode a symbol   (b) Memory used to decode a symbol

Figure 8. Video projector application

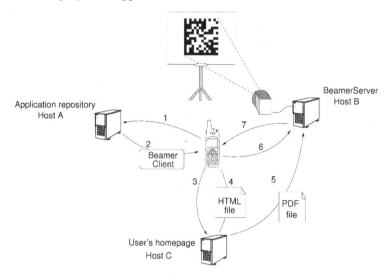

In the considered range, the decoding time is always acceptable and does not preclude the usability of the proposed approach. Figure 7(b) depicts the amount of memory needed to decode a symbol against the image size. Also in this case, the requirements of the algorithm fit the capabilities of currently produced phones (the size of the heap goes up to 4MB in some of the recent models).

Most mobile phones available today feature a fixed-focus camera and have no auto-focus or macro-mode capabilities. However, the focus range, which usually goes from 50-60 cm to infinity, is sufficient for the needs of ubiquitous computing applications. Such a range can be a problem only if the visual tag is very small, since in this case the phone should be very close to the tag. Note that the experiments described above have been carried out by using pictures acquired by the mentioned phone (SonyEricsson k700i, introduced into the market in 2004, maximum camera resolution 640x480, and macro-mode not available), without the need of additional lenses (the size of the tag was approximately 5cm x 5cm). The system is also able to decode successfully smaller tags, 3cm x 3cm and containing few bytes of information, when the distance between the phone and the tag is approximately 10 cm. Other devices may be provided with an auto-focus mode that, if available, enhances the recognition capabilities. In many cases, the auto-focus mode is automatically activated when the button is half pressed. In other cases, if the Advanced Multimedia Supplements (Java Specification Request 234) are implemented by the device, the auto-focus mode can be controlled by means of specific methods. Anyway, we believe that, while these features can make the system more efficient, they are not strictly necessary to have a properly working system.

Demonstrator Application

In this section, we describe a test application to demonstrate the architecture and the implementation of the POLPO system. The application allows a speaker to setup an impromptu slide show using a projector situated in a meeting room. We assume that user's presentations are available through the Web, for example, at his home page. After having entered the meeting room, the speaker selects the projector by taking a picture of its screen where a visual tag is displayed. He is then asked to choose the desired presentation from a list shown on the phone's screen. During the presentation, the mobile phone can be used as a remote control to select the displayed material.

Figure 8 shows the involved components and their interactions. The application that controls the projector is made up of two parts—a suite composed by a single MIDlet, BeamerClient that runs on the mobile phone and provides the graphical

Figure 9. Using POLPO to interact with a projector

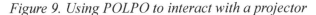

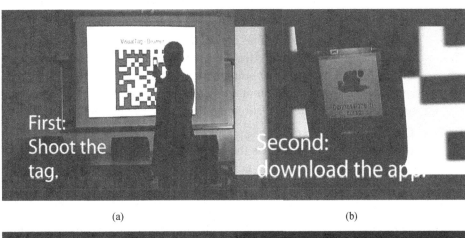

(a)   (b)

(c)   (d)

interface and a server, BeamerServer that is executed by the host that controls the projector. The system works as follows.

1. The Data Matrix tag that is initially displayed by the projector (Figure 9a) contains the URL of the repository of custom applications (Host A), the name of the custom application that must be used to interact with the projector (BeamerClient), and the set of initializing data (i.e. the name of the machine that controls the projector, Host B). When the tag is decoded, the application broker running in the mobile phone creates an RMS entry to store the address that BeamerClient must use to interact with the projector (i.e. Host B). The *BeamerClient.jar* archive is downloaded from Host A and installed (Figure 9b).

2. Once started, BeamerClient looks within the phone's RMS for an entry that contains the name of the machine that controls the projector. BeamerClient also needs the URL of the page that contains the links to the presentation files. To this aim it prompts the user for the address as shown in Figure 9c (to make this task easier, the field is pre-filled with the URL of the user's homepage that is part of the personal data so that a minimal amount of information has to be edited).

3. BeamerClient starts an HTTP connection and downloads from Host C the text of the page that contains the presentations. Then BeamerClient parses the HTML file; all *href* tags that point to files with a given extension (e.g. *pdf*) are interpreted as links to files containing a presentation. The list of available presentations is then built and shown to the user who selects the desired one.

4. The URL of the selected presentation is sent to BeamerServer, which in turn downloads the file and starts the presentation. Then, BeamerClient shows a GUI that allows the user to control the presentation; user's commands are forwarded to BeamerServer which acts consequently (Figure 9d).

The size of the Data Matrix decoder is approximately 4400 lines of code, while the size of the main GUI and the application broker together is less than 1000 lines of code. Once compiled, the size of the jar archive that includes the GUI, the decoder, and the application broker is approximately 70KB (without obfuscation). The jar of the BeamerClient is less than 10KB.

Future Research Directions

In the previous sections, we described how visual tags, which contain configuration information, can be used to provide a description of the selected resource and to load new software components from the network without manual input. In those cases, symbols contain only data, while code is retrieved using a network connection.

Alternatively, code fragments could be included into Data Matrix symbols. This way, the action of taking a picture would result in a program to be extracted from the symbol and installed onto the user device, for example to provide new functionalities or to update existing software without the need of accessing the network.

Because of the limited amount of information that can be contained in a visual tag, this technique is not always applicable. However, there are cases where it can be very effective. For example, a phone manufacturer that detects a software bug in a delivered phone model could distribute the patch that removes the malfunction by means of an advertisement page published in a popular newspaper. In this case, it would suffice to encode the single class, or the class fragment, into a visual tag. Another application is to use a visual tag to deploy new cryptographic modules on the user device.

In order to figure out the size and the complexity of visual tags containing code, we encoded the bytecode obtained from the compilation of the following class, which implements a trivial Caesar cipher:

```
public class ROT13 {
    public static String encrypt(String s) {
        char[] a = s.toCharArray();
        for(int i=0; i<a.length; i++)
            if(a[i] >= 'a' && a[i] <= 'm')
                a[i] = (char) (a[i] + 13);
            else
                a[i] = (char) (a[i] - 13);
            return new String(a);
    }
}
```

The size of the compiled class is 435 bytes that fits within the symbol shown in Figure 10.

Figure 10. Symbol that encodes the binary form of the ROT13 class

To recreate a class from its binary data, Java provides the following method:

Class defineClass(byte[] b, int offset, int len)

of the *ClassLoader* class: the returned *Class* object can then be used to generate instances of the represented class through given methods (reflection). Unfortunately, the reflection functionalities, as well as dynamic class loading, are unavailable in the CLDC/MIDP platform. Thus, the majority of currently available mobile phones are unable to incorporate direct code extraction from visual tags. Nevertheless, this technique can be successfully adopted on high-end smart phones, which often include a CDC Java platform.

Conclusion

Mobile phones will remain the platform of choice for the development of pervasive applications. Of course, the advent of new technologies will eventually modify the way users interact with the world that surrounds them. The work we presented starts from largely available, easy-to-use personal devices to demonstrate the technological feasibility of using camera-phones as a flexible platform for the ubiquitous access to context-dependent computational services.

Despite the availability of several systems that base context-data acquisition on visual symbologies, we believe that POLPO is a step forward in the direction of delivering site-specific services to the real-world. One reason is that POLPO supports dynamic downloading of new applications on mobile phones. The expandability of the software installed on the user's device is a key factor in a pervasive computing environment. In fact, the set of services available to users must grow as new devices or software systems are added to the environment. If the functionalities of the system are statically defined, users are forced to upgrade their devices continuously.

A second reason is that our system is based on the JME platform that eases the deployment of new services and makes it suitable, in the near future, for a much larger user base than the one afforded by other systems. As far as the mentioned implementation "bug" that, on many currently available mobile phones, limits the resolution of the images that can be obtained from the built–in camera only at a very low resolution, it is reasonable to say that it will be fixed soon. The expert group that defined the Java Specification Request 135 (Multi Media API) includes Nokia, Philips, Vodafone, Motorola, Siemens, and many other big players of the telecommunication industry. Thus, it is logical to suppose that in short time the Java implementation available on commercial products will be more adherent to the specifications.

References

Abowd, G. D., Iftode, L., & Mitchell, H. (2005). The smart phone—a first platform for pervasive computing. *IEEE Pervasive Computing. Special Issue: The Smart Phone: A First Platform for Pervasive Computing, 4*(2), 18-19.

Ailisto, H., Pohjanheimo, L., Valkkynen, P., Strommer, E., Tuomisto, T., & Korhonen, I. (2006). Bridging the physical and virtual worlds by local connectivity-based physical selection. *Personal Ubiquitous Computing, 10*(6), 333-344.

Avvenuti, M., & Vecchio, A. (2006). On-demand Loading of Pervasive-oriented Applications Using Mass-market Camera Phones, In *Proceedings of the 3rd International Workshop on Ubiquitous Computing* (pp. 39-48). Paphos, Cyprus.

Hecht, D. L. (2001). Printed embedded data graphical user interfaces. *IEEE Computer, 34*(3), 47-55.

Iso, T., Isoda, Y., Otsuji, K., Suzuki, H., Kurakake, S., & Sugimura, T. (2003). Platform technology for ubiquitous services. *NTT Technical Review, 1*(8), 82-88.

Iso, T., Kurakake, S., & Sugimura, T. (2003). Visual-tag reader: image capture by cell phone camera. In *Proceedings of International Conference on Image Processing (ICIP)* (pp. 557-560). Barcelona, Spain, IEEE Press.

Kaywa (2007). Retrieved from http://www.kaywa.com

López de Ipiña, D., Mendonça, P., and Hopper, A. (2002). TRIP: A Low-Cost Vision-Based Location System for Ubiquitous Computing. *Personal Ubiquitous Computing, 6*(3), 206-213.

Rekimoto, J., & Ayatsuka, Y. (2000). Cybercode: designing augmented reality environments with visual tags. In *Proceedings of DARE 2000 on Designing Augmented Reality Environments* (pp. 1-10). New York, USA. ACM Press.

Rohs, M. (2004). Real-world interaction with camera-phones. In *Proceedings of the 2nd International Symposium on Ubiquitous Computing Systems* (pp. 39-48), Tokyo, Japan.

Tierno, J., & Campo, C. (2005). Smart camera phones: Limits and applications. *IEEE Pervasive Computing. Special Issue: The Smart Phone: A First Platform for Pervasive Computing, 4*(2), 84-87.

Scanbuy (2007). Website: http://www.scanbuy.com

Semacode (2007). Website: http://www.semacode.org

ShotCode (2007). Website: http://www.shotcode.com

The Semapedia project (2005).Website: http://www.semapedia.org

Toye E., Sharp R., Madhavapeddy A., Scott D., Upton E., & Blackwell A. (2007). Interacting with mobile services: an evaluation of camera-phones and visual tags, *Personal Ubiquitous Computing, 11*(2), 97-106, Springer-Verlag.

Toye, E., Sharp, R., Madhavapeddy, A., & Scott, D. (2005). Using smart phones to access site-specific services. *IEEE Pervasive Computing, 4*(2), 60-66.

Weinstein, R. (2005). RFID: a technical overview and its application to the enterprise. *IT Professional*, 7(3), 27- 33, IEEE Press.

Weiser, M. (1991). The Computer for the 21st Century. *Scientific American, 3*, 94-104.

Chapter II

Context-Aware Mobile Learning on the Semantic Web

Rachid Benlamri, Lakehead University, Canada

Jawad Berri, Etisalat University College, United Arab Emirates

Yacine Atif, Massey University, New Zealand

Abstract

This chapter focuses on the theoretical and technological aspects of designing mobile learning (m-learning) services that deliver context-aware learning resources from various locations and devices. Context-aware learning is an important requirement for next generation intelligent m-learning systems. The use of context in mobile devices is receiving increasing attention in mobile and ubiquitous computing research. In this research work, context reflects timeliness and mobility to nurture pervasive instruction throughout the learning ecosystem. In this context of ubiquity that is supported by a new generation of mobile wireless networks and smart mobile devices, it is clear that the notion of context plays a fundamental role since it influences the computational capabilities of the used technology. In particular, three types of context awareness are being considered in this work —platform-awareness, learner-awareness, and task-awareness. In this research work, these contextual elements are defined at the semantic level in order to facilitate discoverability of context-compliant learning resources, adaptability of content and services to devices of various capabilities, and adaptability of services to task at hand and interaction history. The work presented in this chapter contributes towards this direction, making use of the progress in Semantic Web theory and mobile computing to enable context-aware learning that satisfies learning timeliness and mobility requirements.

Introduction

With the expansion of the mobile computing paradigm allowing users to access services anytime and anywhere, it becomes possible to deliver learning resources and services to nomadic learning communities. This form of mobile learning is being made more attractive with the recent advances in ubiquitous computing and Semantic Web. Mobile users equipped with wireless devices go through several contextual changes as they move around in physical and social surroundings. Context acquisition and management is therefore an important requirement for developing systems capable of sensing their environment and delivering ubiquitous services tailored to the learners' situation. Thus, context awareness is presented as a means of adapting learning services to provide 'just enough, just in time, and just for me' model of personalized learning (Low & O'Connell, 2006). Personalization is becoming increasingly important in the context of the Semantic Web (Aroyo et al., 2005). Existing techniques for learner modeling need to be enhanced to deal with the challenges created by the new form of mobile-user interaction. While the new forms of interactive multimedia and communication offer new possibilities for supporting innovative ways of learning, collaborating and communicating (Milrad, 2003; Mizoguchi & Bourdeau, 2000), the challenge is to develop new Semantic Web techniques that use well-defined standards and ontologies to deal with context and personalization at the semantic level, enabling hence intelligent handling of the dynamics of a user's conceptualization. Although, it is agreed that general-purpose modeling and reasoning with context is a complex problem, and much research work is needed before achieving any real progress in this field, we believe that there is a potential in the Semantic Web for developing such new context-aware intelligent learning systems. The research presented in this chapter contributes towards this direction, and is aimed at using the evolving Semantic Web and mobile computing to enable context-aware personalized learning services.

The main challenges in developing context-aware m-learning systems are related to the ability of such systems to model and consistently reason with high level contexts at the semantic level. Although some research attempts were made to solve some of these problems, the shortcoming of most of these efforts is their limitations to specific context elements and specific learning scenarios. In particular, a considerable amount of research in context-aware learning is now moving towards ontology-based context management for personalized learning (Mizoguchi & Bourdeau,

2000; Aroyo & Dicheva, 2002). The ontology approach to context awareness is top down, where human understandable concepts are defined. However, defining these concepts in terms of low-level contextual information using ontology rules and axioms is complex and is a major barrier to personalization. Most developed learning systems (Mizoguchi & Bourdeau, 2000; Aroyo & Dicheva, 2002, 2004; Alexander, 2004) restrict the use of ontology relations and rules to describing and adapting content and sequencing of learning material according to some predefined learning scenarios. Little contextual semantics however have been embedded in the ontology itself to enable dynamic context recognition and management. To address this shortcoming, our approach uses content ontology, learner ontology, and context ontology in an orthogonal way. This is due to the fact that learning content, learning styles, and users' context are semantically inter-related aspects of cognitive learning (Alexander, 2004). To deal with the distributed nature of contextual information (network/environment context, location, available time, learner profile, task at hand, and interaction history) and the heterogeneity of devices that provide services and deliver context, we partition context information into three categories —platform context, learner context, and task context. The three classes of contextual information are defined at the semantic level using ontology rules and axioms. These ontological structures are used to facilitate discoverability of context-compliant learning resources, adaptability of content and services to devices of various capabilities, and adaptability of services to task at hand and interaction history.

Another challenging aspect to the research community in the field of m-learning is the process of authoring and presenting learning resources (Chan, Sharples, Vavoula, & Lonsdale, 2004; Vavoula & Sharples, 2002). Mobile learning developers should take into account the features of the new medium (mobile devices and wireless networks), the operational environment, and the special requirements of mobile learners. This would require considerable efforts to develop new learning models dedicated to mobile environments for authoring, annotating, storing, and retrieving both Learning Object (LO) content and presentation features taking into account users' context. Furthermore, mobile learning induces other constraints related to the relatively short time required for a learning session and the depth of knowledge coverage. The goal is to allow learners to dynamically build a personalized learning path that is specifically adjusted to the learner's environmental, spatial, and temporal contexts. Hence, the target is to facilitate instruction for mobile learners by using mobile technologies for which presentation features are significantly restricted.

After highlighting the main challenges of mobile learning in the context of pervasive and ubiquitous computing, we describe in the next section the research efforts being made in the field. We then present our work to developing a framework for context-aware m-learning on the Semantic Web. The architecture of the proposed framework is described in section four. In particular, we show how our system enables intelligent context awareness, adaptability, metadata generation, and discoverability of lightweight learning resources. A case study showing the main functions of system is given in section five. Finally, conclusions from this work are drawn and further research work is suggested.

Related Work

Although much progress has been made in the field of mobile technologies and wireless networks, m-learning is still in its infancy. However, it is anticipated that ontologies and Semantic Web technologies will rapidly influence the next generation of context-aware mobile learning systems. This is motivated by the Semantic Web potential to solve the complex problem of context awareness. This section explores recent research work in the field of m-learning, emphasizing how ingredients from mobiles computing, e-learning standards, and the Semantic Web are being integrated to build context-aware personalized instruction. It should also be noted that some research attempts were made to develop m-learning systems outside the Semantic Web. For instance, in some research, unsupervised learning was used for modeling context (Flanagan, 2006), while another research used multicasting techniques for dissemination learning resources and services (Milrad, 2005). In this section, we also summarize current research efforts for developing e-learning standard for m-learning.

Wang, Li, Huang, and Wu (2006) proposed a personalized knowledge service framework for mobile learning leveraging Semantic Web services in support of context awareness. The system includes a number of modeling sources of context information as Web services that can be automatically discovered and accessed by a knowledge adaptation engine, which assist the mobile learners with different sets of learning tasks. Each source of contextual information is thus described by a profile that describes its functional properties in relation to one or more ontologies. Since these profiles are semantically annotated and wrapped as Semantic Web services, relevant sources of context information can be automatically discovered and accessed by the knowledge adaptation engine.

Tirellil, Laroussi, Derycke, and BenGhezala (2006) have adopted an approach based solely on Web services. The developed m-learning system is based on the so called fractal adaptive Web services and consists of reconfigurable and re-usable personalized elementary services. Web services are first composed and then adapted based on the user's preferences and profile, task at hand, device and environment features. The system was designed to be used in the context of mobile and collaborative learning scenarios.

Flanagan (2006) has introduced a different approach for context awareness based on unsupervised learning processes. He argued that ontologies are not well suited for context awareness because they are based on high level definitions of concepts and knowledge about their interaction. The author emphasized that while concepts may be understandable to people, defining contexts for each user using ontologies is a more complex problem. To solve the context modeling problem, the author proposed a solution based on the fact that user contexts can be easily classified and thus identified through unsupervised learning which processes the information available in the user's world and builds up a representation of the user's context. However, the efficiency of such an approach is solely dependent on the way labeling of the user requirements in a given context is performed. The author has dealt with labeling by attributing weights to the different user requirements, but no performance evaluation results were provided to evaluate such an approach.

Recently, another approach to m-learning using multicasting technology, called MUSIS, was developed at the Center for Learning and Knowledge Technologies (CeLeKT) in Sweden (Milrad, 2005). The system is based on multicast mobile services with multimedia information that are distributed over wireless networks. Multicasting services developed in MUSIS are organized as a range of content channels to which users can subscribe. User can build a personal portfolio of channels that interest them. Multimedia content is sent according to a predefined time schedule to subscribers over the cellular network using multicast technology. Users can then interact with the MUSIS client installed in the smart phone in order to look at the content. This approach differs radically from other mobile services based on streaming technology offered by most telecom industries. MUSIS relies on an existing commercial cellular network for transmitting its learning resources to learners. MUSIS services are not restricted to academic learning resources, but are of a general purpose with content related to TV news, music, entertainment videos, information related to student's activities, as well as lecture notes that may include video and sound.

The development of m-learning systems depends mainly on e-learning standard for mobile devices and wireless technology. Many research efforts have been made in the area of e-learning standards for m-learning. Veith and Pawlowski (2005) have demonstrated the need for extending existing e-learning standards to support the development of m-learning scenarios. They emphasized that the new standard should enhance the learning resources description such as Learning Object Metadata (LOM), didactics such as Learning Design (LD), and actor description such as Learning Information Packaging (LIP). In particular, they showed that new standards should handle issues related to location awareness, content packaging, and the concept of trusted computing. They argued that location information should be added to learner profiles, documents, and conceptions used in m-learning, as this is the key factor of m-learning. They also suggested that "the concept of trusted computing should be transferred to IMS Learning Information Packaging (LIP) repositories to enable trusted m-learning"(Veith & Pawlowski, 2005). The aim is to enable learners to work with one profile in different learning management systems. In addition, LMSs should be able to identify the target platform to which they have to serve documents and services. The work also shows how the concept of Content Packaging for learning resources can be extended to the end user. Thus, learners would be able to load these packages to their mobile devices and thus learn without being online. Many other research attempts were also made for adapting existing standards for m-learning. Capra, Emmerich and Mascolo (2001) propose a distinction between active and passive metadata for mobile systems: passive information, enabling an application to react to changes in the context; and active information, which delimits the context and the action required. Russell and Pitt (2004) propose metadata describing terminal capabilities; Friesen and McGreal (2005) addressed the specifics of specialized metadata for mobile devices proposing that key elements in mobile learning are indicators specifically of context and situation and these must be expressed as metadata including time and geographic location. Naito (2005) proposed the W3C's NaVigation Markup Language (NVML) for spatial information using latitude and longitude, and the 24-hour clock to indicate time.

Ontology-Based M-Learning

Although the stated goal of the Semantic Web is to enable machine understanding of Web resources, in a learning context, the conceptual structure of the content is an essential part of the learning material. Losing the contextual information of the content means that we will not be able to contextually integrate the concepts that we are trying to learn, which is vitally important in order to achieve an understanding of any specific subject area. In order to solve this problem, the Semantic Web is extended to provide not only semantic information for the machine, but also conceptual information for the human user. This form of extended Semantic Web, which is also sometimes called the Conceptual Web (Naeve, Nilsson, & Palmér, 2001) is the main goal of the educational Semantic Web. Thus, it is important to realize that the Semantic Web needs rich ontologies and evolving dynamic metadata that is not only for machine consumption, but also can support the evolution of human knowledge. To achieve such a goal, we often require formal representations for contextual information, learner modeling, and domain knowledge. These formal representations provide a backbone for context modeling and reasoning (Kay & Lum, 2005). Ontologies can play such a role by structuring the physical and virtual environment around the learner to elicit extended models of users and to deal with the dynamics of a user's conceptualization (Aroyo et al., 2005). Ontologies are structured in terms of objects, concepts, and relationships among them through axioms and relations. Thus, ontological structure provides a shared and common understanding that is intended to eliminate terminological and conceptual ambiguities. In addition to shared conceptualizations, ontology offers consistent semantic annotation of learning resources to enable better adaptation in specific contexts. Moreover, ontologies provide a basis for communication between learners, who have different contextual viewpoints (Ushold & Gruninger, 1996).

In the proposed framework, three ontologies are used to enable better learner modeling, efficient context acquisition and management, and reusable customized learning content. These are learner ontology, device ontology, and domain ontology. We have used the standard Ontology Web Language (OWL) for describing the above mentioned three ontologies. OWL offers a set of powerful primitives, mostly derived from description logic, and provides more expressive power than RDF (Resource Description Framework) and RDF-S schema. Although the used ontologies have a set of basic implicit reasoning mechanisms derived from the description logic which they are typically based on, we used other rules to make further inferences and to create useful relations on the ontological entities. The rules are employed to reason on the instances and to infer further information that cannot be captured by the used ontologies. These are implemented in the Rule Markup Language RuleML.

The learner ontology is mainly used to establish the user model vocabulary in the domain of interest (Kay & Lum, 2005). This is achieved in terms of metadata that is used to instantiate user models and to unify the terminology used for learner model interface. In addition, the learner ontology allows interoperability by enabling all client applications to understand, share, and enhance evolving learner models regardless the used software or mobile technology. Thus, the use of learner ontology in the proposed system facilitates sharing of learner's previous knowledge, temporal constraints, learner's preferences, and learner's interaction history across mobile devices and platforms. This ontology is used as the key to solving the personalization problem in the context of m-learning.

The device ontology deals with the technical aspects of mobile devices and their operational environment. In particular, it provides a shared terminology, shared taxonomy, as well as a conceptualization of mobile devices and wireless network technologies. This ontology allows generating metadata that can unambiguously communicate the technical and computational capabilities of the used mobile devices and their operational environment. This will greatly facilitate context acquisition, learning resource filtering and subsequent LO adaptations. The device ontology used in this work is described in Figure 1. Figure 1 also includes the set of basic axioms, and relations between the objects and concepts of the ontology. The ontology given in Figure 1, describes mobile devices in terms of their hardware, used software, network connectivity, customization features, and device type. Figure 2 shows a fragment of the OWL description of the mobile device ontology given in Figure 1. For space and readability purpose, only the operating system section of the ontology is presented in Figure 2.

The third ontology deals with the application domain knowledge. This is used to share a conceptualization of the domain of interest. It also allows semantic annotation of learning objects and thus enabling their discoverability, reusability, and interoperability across platforms. Moreover, ontology axioms and relations such as *Part-of*, *Necessary-Part-of*, *is-a*, and *is-pre-requisite* are used in this work to fulfill the *"just enough"* purpose of m-learning, by providing the learner with no more

Figure 1. Example of mobile-device ontology (numbers beside concepts represent concept Ids)

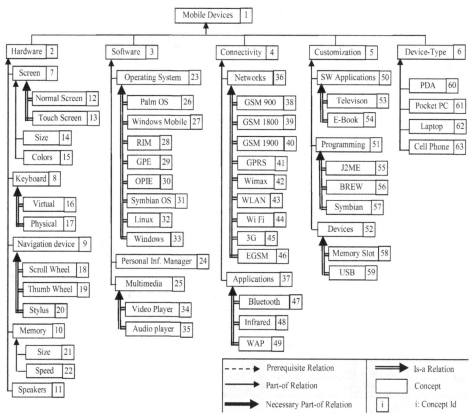

than the needed content. These rules are also used to build a learning sequence, called in this chapter, "*Learning Web (LW)*." LW is a sequence of Learning Objects (LOs) organized in a way to provide the learner with the most customized learning objects fulfilling his/her learning and contextual requirements. Granularity of the chosen LOs will depend on the available learning time set by the learner. Thus, the learning Web is planned so that it can be consumed within the learner's available time. The temporal constraint of the learning Web is satisfied by prioritizing for instance *Necessary-Part-of* over *Part-of* relation. For further details regarding the time constraints used in this work, we refer the reader to our previous work (Berri, Atif, & Benlamri, 2004; Atif, Benlamri, & Berri, 2005, 2006). Figure 3 shows a sample ontology in the photography domain (Long, 2004). This ontology is used in the case study presented in section 5. The OWL description of part of the photography ontology is given in Figure 4.

The explicit inclusion of the ontology in our framework aims at providing customized learning patterns which are delivered on-demand to the learner and/or com-

Figure 2. Fragment of the OWL description of the mobile-device ontology

```
<?xml version="1.0"?>
<rdf:RDF xmlns="http://www.owl-ontologies.com/mobile_devices_ontology.owl#"
 xml:base="http://www.owl-ontologies.com/mobile_devices_Ontology.owl#"
 xmlns:pl="http://www.owl-ontologies.com/assert.owl#"
 xmlns:xsd="http://www.w3.org/2001/XMLSchema#"
 xmlns:rdfs="http://www.w3.org/2000/01/rdf-schema#"
 xmlns:rdf="http://www.w3.org/1999/02/22-rdf-syntax-ns#"
 xmlns:owl="http://www.w3.org/2002/07/owl#">
<owl:Ontology rdf:about="Mobile_Devices"/>
<owl:Class rdf:ID="Software_3">
 <rdfs:subClassOf rdf:resource="#Mobile_Devices_1"/>
 <owl:disjointWith rdf:resource="#Hardware_2"/>
 <owl:disjointWith rdf:resource="#Customization_4"/>
 <owl:disjointWith rdf:resource="#Connectivity_5"/>
 <owl:disjointWith rdf:resource="#Device_Type_6"/>
</owl:Class>

(…)

<owl:Class rdf:ID="Palm_OS_26"/>
 <rdfs:subClassOf rdf:resource="#Operating_System_23"/>
 <rdfs:subClassOf>
  <owl:Restriction>
        <owl:onProperty rdf:resource="#is-a"/>
        <owl:allValuesFrom rdf:resource="#Operating_System_23"/>
        </owl:Restriction>
 </rdfs:subClassOf>
 <owl:disjointWith rdf:resource="#Windows Mobile_27"/>
 <owl:disjointWith rdf:resource="#RIM_28"/>
 <owl:disjointWith rdf:resource="#GPE_29"/>
 <owl:disjointWith rdf:resource="#OPIE_30"/>
 <owl:disjointWith rdf:resource="#Symbian_OS_31"/>
 <owl:disjointWith rdf:resource="#Linux_32"/>
 <owl:disjointWith rdf:resource="#Windows  33"/>
</owl:Class>
</ref:RDF>
```

bined with other patterns to form a self-adjusted learning route according to the learner's needs, context and available learning time. Knowledge resources consist in Learning Object Metadata (LOM) structured Learning Objects (LOs) tagged by their standard metadata attributes. The LO metadata attributes of interest in this study are *Classification*, *Typical Learning Time*, and *Relation*. The classification attribute categorizes a learning object for ontological indexation purposes. The typical learning time attribute reflects the duration of the enclosed continuous media or the length of time the learner would normally be allocated to complete the learning session communicated by the LO. Alternatively, this attribute could also reflect a timed test item. In the latter case, selected items may be composed together to build a time-limited test. The framework makes an explicit use of this attribute which temporally annotates the semantic of an LO to enable time-constrained instruction which is crucial in the context of m-learning. The relation attribute links an LO to other entities as defined by the ontology. This attribute is to be used as a means of interaction with the learner. In addition to the above mentioned metadata attributes, a number of mobile device metadata attributes as described in the device ontology are also considered. The device metadata attributes can be stored in the *meta-metadata* category of the LOM which is purposely reserved to accommodate any application-based metadata. The semantic of the ontological links is obtained by the applied rules. These rules are prioritized to reflect their importance or abstraction levels in a given knowledge taxonomy. For example, in a time-constrained learning environment, one would like to focus only on say "the necessary-part-of" rules of the ontology to get a quick abstraction on the general structure of the requested knowledge. In a less time-stringent learning environment, this abstraction could further include the "part-of," and/or "case-study" rules, and so forth. These knowledge-supporting rules generate additional concepts of the ontology in multi-level clusters which are used to infer a progressive knowledge based on learners' time constraints. In addition to the ontology rules, the system requires Web services to perform a number of tasks such as LO metadata generation, LO discoverability, time optimization, and content-presentation adaptations. More details about the used Web services are given in the next section which describes the system architecture and other Semantic Web technologies used by the system.

Figure 3. Fragment of the photography ontology

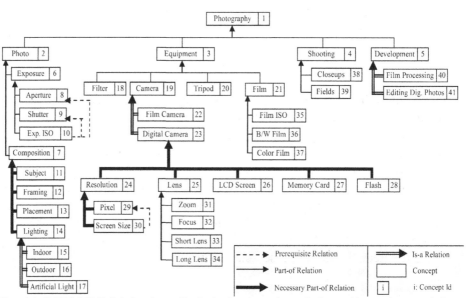

Figure 4. Fragments of OWL description of the photography ontology

```
<owl:ObjectProperty rdf:ID="NecessaryPartOf">
 <rdf:type rdf:resource="&owl;TransitiveProperty"/>
 <owl:inverseOf rdf:resource="#hasNecessaryPart"/>
</owl:ObjectProperty>
<owl:ObjectProperty rdf:ID="isPartOf">
 <rdf:type rdf:resource="&owl;TransitiveProperty"/>
 <owl:inverseOf rdf:resource="#hasPart"/>
</owl:ObjectProperty>
<owl:ObjectProperty rdf:ID="is-a">
 <rdf:type rdf:resource="&owl;TransitiveProperty"/>
 <owl:inverseOf rdf:resource="#has"/>
</owl:ObjectProperty>
<owl:ObjectProperty rdf:ID="isPrerequisiteOf">
 <rdf:type rdf:resource="&owl;TransitiveProperty"/>
 <owl:inverseOf rdf:resource="#hasPrerequisite"/>

<owl:Class rdf:ID="Resolution_24">
 <rdfs:subClassOf rdf:resource="#Lens_25"/>
 <owl:disjointWith rdf:resource="#LCD-Screen_26"/>
 <owl:disjointWith rdf:resource="#Memory_card_27"/>
 <owl:disjointWith rdf:resource="#Flash_28"/>
</owl:Class>

<owl:Class rdf:ID="Pixel_29"/>
 <rdfs:subClassOf rdf:resource="#Resolution_24"/>
 <rdfs:subClassOf>
  <owl:Restriction>
        <owl:onProperty rdf:resource="#isNecessaryPartOf"/>
        <owl:allValuesFrom rdf:resource="#Resolution_24"/>
  </owl:Restriction>
 </rdfs:subClassOf>
 <rdfs:subClassOf>
  <owl:Restriction>
        <owl:onProperty rdf:resource="#isPrerequisiteOf"/>
        <owl:allValuesFrom rdf:resource="#Screen_Size_30"/>
  </owl:Restriction>
 </rdfs:subClassOf>
 <owl:disjointWith rdf:resource="#Screen_Size_30"/>
</owl:Class>
<owl:Class rdf:ID="Screen_Size_30"/>
 <rdfs:subClassOf rdf:resource="#Resolution_24"/>
 <rdfs:subClassOf>
  <owl:Restriction>
        <owl:onProperty rdf:resource="#isNecessaryPartOf"/>
        <owl:allValuesFrom rdf:resource="#Resolution_24"/>
  </owl:Restriction>
 </rdfs:subClassOf>
 <rdfs:subClassOf>
  <owl:Restriction>
        <owl:onProperty rdf:resource="#HasPrerequisite"/>
        <owl:allValuesFrom rdf:resource="#Pixel_29"/>
  </owl:Restriction>
 </rdfs:subClassOf>
 <owl:disjointWith rdf:resource="#Screen_Size_27"/>
</owl:Class>
```

System Architecture

Figure 5 shows the architecture of the proposed system which is organized mainly in three conceptual layers in addition to a set of Web services achieving a variety of specialized learning services. The top layer includes the three ontologies described in the previous section and the associated axioms and rules. The three ontologies are coded in the Semantic Web ontology language OWL and their rules are written in the rule markup language RuleML. The middle layer includes the reasoning engine which represents the main component of the whole architecture. However, it should be noted that the structure and representation method of the ontology plays a crucial role in the implementation performance and accuracy of the reasoning (Kay & Lum, 2005). There are two methods for reasoning about the domains modeled in the ontologies. These are deductive and inductive reasoning. The deductive arguments are the ones that given a set of true premises, the conclusion must also be true. Inductive logic however, does not provide an assertion of truth to the conclusion. Instead, it provides a way to deduce that the conclusion is probably true based on the evidence supporting the premises (Copi, 1968). Deductive reasoning is used in our reasoning engine, mainly because our ontology representation supports a high degree of formality that can enable deductive reasoning. In addition, our ontologies are coded in OWL which represents ontologies through description logic. Thus, new facts about the domain can be generated using the true premises existing in the ontology as shown in the case study given in the next section. Different inference rules are used to reason about the knowledge embedded in the three ontologies. For instance, some inference rules associated with the learner ontology are used to infer pre-requisite knowledge and learner preferences, while rules for device ontology can infer information for content and presentation adaptation. Similarly, domain ontology rules are used to infer the necessary learning content, learning granularity, and the learning sequence. Rules from the three ontologies are applied in the order shown in the learning cycle given in Figure 6. Finally, the bottom layer includes the interaction manager which deals with the learner's queries and controls the learning sequence. The reasoning engine is also responsible for retrieving learning resources from distributed Web repositories. For that, it triggers agents that use a set of Web services to search for the resources required for a learning session, namely the learning objects, the user's learning profile and also learning experiences to build and adapt the learning web. The interaction manager (IM) authenticates learners and the devices in use for learning which can include any mobile computing device such as cell-phones, Personal Digital Assistants (PDAs), and Pocket PCs. IM uses natural language processing techniques to analyze learners' queries in order to extract keywords of interest. It also retrieves the mobile device profile and creates premises about them to be used by the inference rules associated with the device ontology. The interaction manager also performs other tasks such as learner profile

Figure 5. System architecture

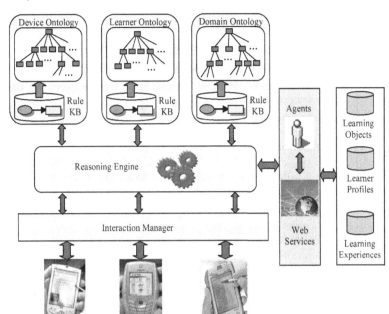

retrieval, and creation of premises describing the basic knowledge about learners for adaptation purposes.

The processing steps described in Figure 6 show the learning cycle adopted by the proposed system. Initially, the learner requests learning about a particular topic related to his current context. The learner formulates a query by using his mobile device. He then specifies the time he is willing to allocate to his learning session, if any. The query is then communicated to the server and is processed by the Interaction Manager which extracts the main keywords and noun phrases. Then the Interaction Manager retrieves device-type features from the mobile device, analyzes them, and initiates device premises for use by the reasoning engine for adaptation purpose. He then invokes the reasoning engine to work on the contextual elements gathered so far. First, the reasoning engine activates the ontology rules to extract the domain sub-ontology that fits the learner requirements. The extracted sub-ontology consists of all concepts and objects related to the learner query as described in the case study presented in the next section. The reasoning engine will then invoke further rules related to the learner profile and preferences, as well as those related to the used mobile device. The aim is to generate learner-device adaptation metadata, thus enabling automatic generation of contextual metadata for the three context categories (learner, device, domain). This metadata is to be mapped to a set of (lightweight) learning objects to retrieve only learning resources that meet contextual requirements. The mapping

Figure 6. Processing stages of a typical learning cycle

1.	Get-query from Learner (extract query keywords, and sense device type and environment).
2.	Retrieve metadata for mobile device features.
3.	Retrieve sub-ontology from the domain ontology using query-keywords.
4.	Generate metadata for the search engine based on the three contextual elements (learner, device, domain).
5.	Invoke the search Web service to search for context compliant LOs and return a list of LOs for each concept in the sub-ontology.
6.	Filter returned LOs using adaptation metadata.
7.	Add new facts to Knowledge-Base System (KBS) associating the retrieved LOs to their corresponding concepts (add facts of type *LOforC (LOi, Ci)*).
8.	Apply learning Web construction algorithm by invoking domain-ontology related axioms and rules and return a learning Web.
9.	Generate dynamically a Web service composition for the resulting learning Web by producing an OWL-S description of service composition.
10.	Invoke the Web service composition

process (i.e. ontology to learning objects) is geared by a search Web service which scouts distributed learning objects repositories in search of suitable lightweight learning objects. The search Web service will then return a set of context-compliant learning objects. At this stage of processing, new facts have to be added to the knowledge base associating the retrieved learning objects to their corresponding concepts. These premises are needed to build the right sequence of learning objects, hence, customizing the right learning Web. The learning Web construction process can then start by invoking a set of domain-ontology based rules as will be described in the case study below. Time constraints are used in the learning Web construction process to regulate and adapt learning granularity according to the prescribed time. Finally, a Web service composition process is invoked to implement the generated learning web. The Web service composition process consists in a dynamic generation of an OWL-S description of the learning Web.

Case Study

To illustrate the main functions of the proposed system, we provide the following simple scenario which uses the domain ontology given in Figure 3. In order to describe the different stages of reasoning engine, we provide below a description of some of the rules used in this case study. For clarity and readability purposes, the rules are coded in Prolog and describe the way the system deals with prerequisite learning concepts and the mandatory learning concepts that need to be scheduled for the learner respectively.

before(?LOi,?LOj) :- prerequesite(?Ci,?Cj), LOforC(?LOi,?Ci),LOforC(?LOi,? Ci).

In the above rule, ?LOi, ?LOj, ?Ci, and ?Cj represent variables, the commas separating predicates stand for the logical conjunction, and the symbol ":-" represents the condition if. The rule describes the fact that learning object LO_i is before learning LO_j if the following conditions are satisfied: concept C_i is a prerequisite of concept C_j, and LO_i and LO_j are the learning objects representing respectively concepts C_i and C_j in the learning web.

Figure 7. Example of ontology rules

```
<rulebase>                              <implies>
  <implies>                               <head>
    <head>                                  <atom>
      <atom>                                  <rel>isinLW</rel>
        <rel>before</rel>                     <var>LOj</var>
        <var>LOi</var>                        <var>LW</var>
        <var>LOj</var>                      </atom>
      </atom>                             </head>
    </head>                             <body>
    <body>                                <atom>
      <atom>                                <rel>necessarypartof</rel>
        <rel>prerequisite</rel>             <var>Cj</var>
        <var>Ci</var>                       <var>Ci</var>
        <var>Cj</var>                     </atom>
      </atom>                             <atom>
      <atom>                                <rel>isinLW</rel>
        <rel>LOforC</rel>                   <var>LOi</var>
        <var>LOi</var>                      <var>LW</var>
        <var>Ci</var>                     </atom>
      </atom>                             <atom>
      <atom>                                <rel>LOforC</rel>
        <rel>LOforC</rel>                   <var>LOi</var>
        <var>LOj</var>                      <var>Ci</var>
        <var>Cj</var>                     </atom>
      </atom>                             <atom>
    </body>                                 <rel>LOforC</rel>
  </implies>                                <var>LOj</var>
                                            <var>Cj</var>
                                          </atom>
                                        </body>
                                      </implies>
                                    </rulebase>
```

isinLW(?LOj,?LW) :- necessarypartof(?Cj,?Ci), isinLW(?LOi,?LW),
LOforC(?LOi,?Ci), LOforC(?Loj,?Cj).

The above rule however describes the fact that learning object LO_j must be included in the learning Web LW if concept C_j is a necessary part of concept C_i, and the learning object LO_i representing concept C_i is in the learning Web. Figure 7 shows the implementation of these two rules in the proposed inference engine.

Consider a situation involving a tourist visiting a museum; he would like to take memorable photos of art objects. The tourist needs to adjust his camera in order to obtain high quality pictures inside the museum. In order to have the necessary rudiments which allow him to fine-tune his camera, he requested using his Windows Mobile based PDA (Personal Digital Assistant), a disciplined presentation on photography and, in particular, on taking indoor quality photos. This case study uses the photography ontology given in Figure 3. The ontology includes a number of concepts related to photography which are linked with four ontology based relationships: *prerequisite*; *part-of*; *necessary-part-of*; and *is-a*.

Figure 8. From context-aware ontology production to learning Web composition

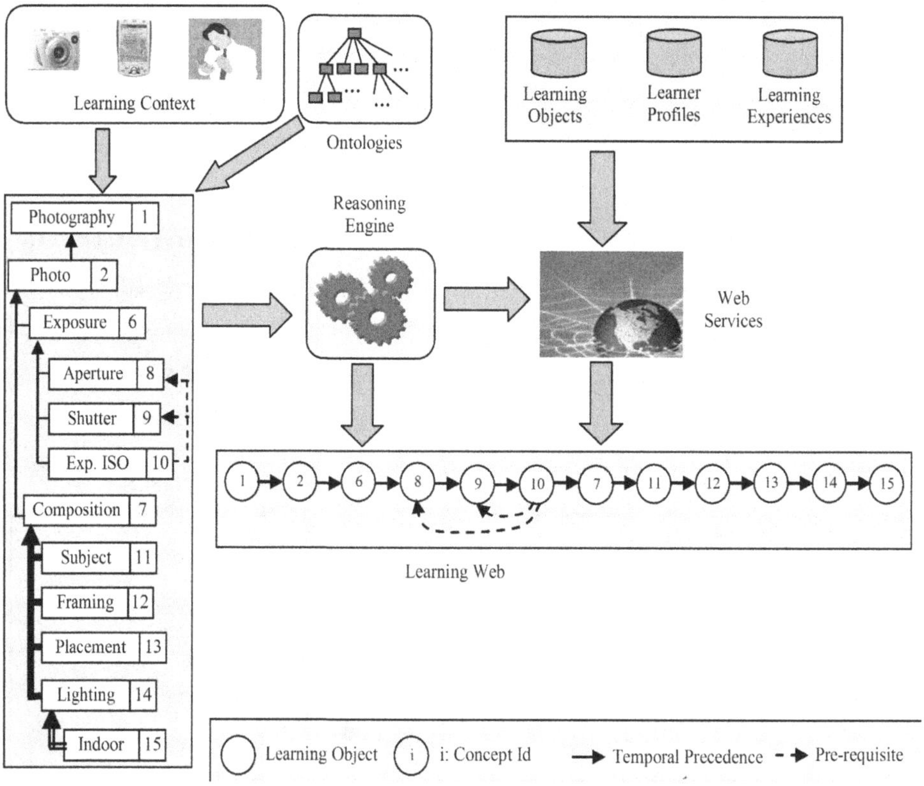

As described in Section 4, the system starts processing the query and attempts to match the keywords/noun phrases with the concepts in the ontology. The concepts are identified in the ontology to belong to the sub-tree *Photo* including two sub concepts *Exposure* and *Composition*. Concept *Exposure* is extracted with all its three Part-of sub concepts—*Aperture*, *Shutter* and *Exp. ISO*. Similarly, concept *Composition* is extracted with all its necessary sub concepts—*Subject*, *Framing*, *Placement* and *Lighting*. The concept *Indoor* is also extracted since it is specified in the learner query; however, concepts *Outdoor* and *Artificial Light* will not be included in the sub-ontology. These two concepts are not essential; they are kinds-of concept *Lighting* not of interest for our learner. Besides, the Interaction Manager retrieves metadata of the learner based on his profile and the learner ontology. Similarly, it will retrieve metadata of the mobile device based on the mobile device ontology and the technical specifications of the learner's PDA.

Figure 8 illustrates the steps leading to the production of the learning Web. The learning context includes the learner profile, the domain, in our case the photography, and the technical specifications of the device in use. The learning context is used along with the ontologies to extract the sub ontology, which represents the context compliant ontology.

Once the sub ontology associated with the learner query is derived, the next step consists of mapping the resulted ontology into a learning Web. To achieve this goal, first, the reasoning engine invokes a Web service that retrieves the lightweight learning objects for the concepts present in the context-aware ontology. A specialized agent which searches LO repositories distributed over the Web performs this task assuring that the learning objects retrieved match the technical requirements of the learner's PDA and its operational environment. The following step ensures that the retrieved LOs are compliant with the time constraints of the learner. The result of this step is the learning Web to dispense to the learner. Figure 8 shows the learning Web derived from the context-aware ontology. While the default mapping of the context-aware ontology to a learning Web is a depth-first traversal of the ontology, the rules need to be checked at each LO addition to the learning Web in order to comply with the relations' constraints. Consequently, since concepts *Aperture* and *Shutter* are pre-requisites of concept *Exposition ISO*, their corresponding learning objects LO8 and LO9 must temporally precede learning object LO10. More details about temporal sequencing of learning objects in ontology mapping can be found in (Atif, Benlamri, & Berri, 2003; Berri, Atif, & Benlamri, 2004; Benlamri, Berri, & Atif, 2006).

Prolog facts given in Table 1 are provided for readability purposes in order to allow readers who are not familiar with RuleML facts given in Table 2 to follow the case study. The facts describe the learning scenario explained above. They are derived from the relationships between ontology concepts before invoking the inference mechanism shown in the middle column, and facts inferred after the inferences, shown in the right column.

Table 1. Prolog facts

	Before Inferences	After Inferences
Prolog based facts for the photography sub-ontology	partof(C2,C1). partof(C6,C2). partof(C7,C2). partof(C8,C6). partof(C9,C6). partof(C10,C6). necessarypartof(C11, C7). necessarypartof(C12, C7). necessarypartof(C13, C7). necessarypartof(C14, C7). isa(C15, C14). LOforC(LO1,C1). LOforC(LO2,C2). LOforC(LO6,C6). LOforC(LO7,C7). LOforC(LO8,C8). LOforC(LO9,C9). LOforC(LO10,C10). LOforC(LO11,C11). LOforC(LO12,C12). LOforC(LO13,C13). LOforC(LO14,C14). LOforC(LO15,C15).	before(LO8,LO10). before(LO9,LO10). IsinLW(LO11). IsinLW(LO12). IsinLW(LO13). IsinLW(LO14).

During the inferences, when learning object LO7 is added to the learning path, the *isinLW(?LOj,?LW)* rule is triggered and learning objects LO11, LO12, LO13 and LO14 are added to the learning Web because they are all necessary parts of LO7. Moreover, since LO8 and LO9 are prerequisites of LO10, the *before(?LOi,?LOj)* rule is triggered to put LO10 after both LO8 and LO9 in the learning Web. Details of the reasoning process for the production of these inferences are shown in Table 1.

Conclusion

This chapter proposes a Semantic Web learning model to handle the specificity of mobile learning and the inherent constraints related to the introduction of mobile and wireless environments in education and training. In particular, the chapter provides a framework to deliver context-aware learning resources from various locations and devices. The aim of the chapter is to make use of the learning expertise

Table 2. RuleML facts

	Before Inferences	After Inferences
RuleML implementation	**Excerpt** ```<atom>
  <op>
    <rel>partof</rel>
  </op>
  <ind>C2</ind>
  <ind>C1</ind>
</atom>
<atom>
  <op>
    <rel>partof</rel>
  </op>
  <ind>C6</ind>
  <ind>C2</ind>
</atom>
...
<atom>
  <op>
 <rel>necessarypartof</rel>
  </op>
  <ind>C11</ind>
  <ind>C7</ind>
</atom>
<rel>isa</rel>
  </op>
  <ind>C15</ind>
  <ind>C14</ind>
</atom>

...
<atom>
  <op>
    <rel>LOforC</rel>
  </op>
  <ind>LO1</ind>
  <ind>C1</ind>
</atom>
...``` | ```<atom>
  <op>
    <rel>before</rel>
  </op>
  <ind>LO8</ind>
  <ind>LO10</ind>
</atom>
<atom>
  <op>
    <rel>before</rel>
  </op>
  <ind>LO9</ind>
  <ind>LO10</ind>
</atom>
<atom>
  <op>
    <rel>IsinLW</rel>
  </op>
  <ind>LO11</ind>
</atom>
<atom>
  <op>
    <rel>IsinLW</rel>
  </op>
  <ind>LO12</ind>
</atom>
<atom>
  <op>
    <rel>IsinLW</rel>
  </op>
  <ind>LO13</ind>
</atom>
<atom>
  <op>
    <rel>IsinLW</rel>
  </op>
  <ind>LO14</ind>
</atom>``` |

already adopted in desktop-based learning in order to suit mobile environments. The proposed system consists mainly of a rule-based reasoning engine and a set of Web services to contextualize learning content which is then mapped to a set of learning objects that meet the learner needs and the technical requirements of the used technology. We have used the Semantic Web to respond to the needs of mobile learners by providing ontological formulations that structure knowledge into meaningful content and creating an environment where software agents roaming around peer-to-peer learning object repositories can readily carry out sophisticated learning services discovery, filtering, and adaptation. The proposed system has demonstrated the utility of an ontology-based approach for communicating context information, and delivering just the right amount of knowledge learners can consume on the move using their mobile device. Our future research work focuses on extending the present system with a rich presentation layer that runs efficiently on a variety of platforms in a seamless way.

References

Alexander, B. (2004). Going Nomadic: Mobile Learning in Higher Education. *EDUCAUSE Review, 39*(5), 28–35.

Aroyo, L. & Dicheva, D. (2002). Courseware Authoring Tasks Ontology. In *Proceedings of the International Conference on Computers in Education* (pp. 1319-1321). Los Alamitos, CA.

Aroyo, L. & Dicheva, D. (2004). The new challenges for e-Learning: The educational Sementic Web. *Educational Technology and Society, 7*(4), 59-69.

Aroyo, L.M., Dimitrova, V. & Kay, J. (2005). Personalization on the Semantic Web: Editorial. Paper presented at the *Workshop on Personalization on the Semantic Web*. Edinburgh, UK, 25-26, July.

Atif, Y., Benlamri, R. & Berri, J. (2003). Dynamic Learning Modeler. *IEEE Journal of Educational Technology and Society. 6*(4), 60-72.

Atif, Y., Benlamri, R. & Berri, J. (2005). Knowledge Utility Optimization for Time Dependent Learning, In *Proceedings of the International Conference on Cognition & Exploratory Learning in Digital Age'05* (pp. 434-439). Porto, Portugal.

Atif, Y., Benlamri, R. & Berri, J. (2006). Can E-Learning Be Made Real-Time? In *Proceedings of the 6th IEEE International Conference on Advanced Learning Technologies (ICALT'06)* (pp. 314-318). Kerkrade, Netherlands.

Benlamri, R., Berri, J. & Y. Atif, (2006). A Framework for Ontology-aware Instructional Design and Planning. *Journal of E-Learning and Knowledge Society, 2*(1), 83-96.

Berri, J., Atif, Y., & Benlamri, R. (2004). Time-Dependent Learning. In *Proceeding of the 4th IEEE Conference on Advanced Learning Technologies (ICALT'04)* (pp. 816-818). Joensu, Finland.

Capra, L., Emmerich, W. & Mascolo, C. (2001). Exploiting Reflection and Metadata to build Mobile Computing Middleware. In *Workshop on Middleware for Mobile Computing. (Co-located with Middleware 2001)*. Heidelberg,

Germany. Retrieved on December 5, 2006, from http://www.cs.ucl.ac.uk/staff/c.mascolo/www/mmc01.pdf

Chan, T., Sharples, M., Vavoula G. & Lonsdale, P. (2004). Educational Metadata for Mobile Learning. Paper presented at the *2nd IEEE International Workshop on Wireless and Mobile Technologies in Education*.

Copi, I. M. (1968). *Introduction to Logic*. (3rd Ed.). New York, NY: MacMillan Company.

Flanagan, J.A. (2006). An unsupervised learning paradigm for peer-to-peer labeling and naming of locations and contexts, In *Proceedings of the 2nd International Workshop on Location and Context-Awareness*, Dublin, Ireland (Vol. LNCS 3987, pp. 204–221). Springer-Verlag.

Friesen, N., & McGreal, R. (2005). CanCore: Best practices for learning object metadata in ubiquitous computing environments. In *Proceedings of the International Conference on Pervasive Learning*, Kauai, Hawaii, *(PerEL '05)* (pp. 317-321)..

Kay, J. & Lum, A. (2005). Ontology based User Modeling for the Semantic Web. In *Proceedings of the International Workshop on Personalisation on the Semantic Web*, Edinburgh, UK (pp. 14-23)..

Long, B. (2004). *Complete Digital Photography*. Digital Photography Series. 3rd Ed. USA.

Low, L., & O'Connell M. (2006). Learner-centric design of digital mobile learning. In *Proceedings of the On-line Learning and Teaching Conference*, Brisbane, Australia, September, (pp. 71-82).

Milrad, M. (2003). Mobile Learning: Challenges, Perspectives and Reality. In Kristóf Nyíri (Ed.), *Mobile Learning: Essays on Philosophy, Psychology and Education* (pp. 25-38). Vienna.

Milrad, M. (2005, April). *Exploring New Ways to Support Learning and Communication Using Mobile Technologies*. Paper presented at Seeing, Understanding, Learning in the Mobile Age Conference, Budapest. Retrieved on December 22, 2005, from http://www.fil.hu/mobil/2005/

Mizoguchi, R. & Bourdeau, J. (2000). Using Ontological Engineering to Overcome Common AI-ED Problems, *International Journal of Artificial Intelligence in Education, 11*(2), 107-121.

Naeve, A., Nilsson, M. & Palmér, M. (2001). The Conceptual Web - our research vision. Paper presented at *the first Semantic Web Working Symposium*, Stanford. Retrieved on December 22, 2005, from http://cid.nada.kth.se/pdf/CID-156.pdf

Naito, H. (2005). Situated Information for Pervasive Computing. In *Proceedings of the Third IEEE International Conference on Pervasive Computing and Communications – PerCom*, Kauai Island, Hawaii (pp. 317-321). .

Russell, G., & Pitt, I. (2004). Visions of a Wireless Future in Education Technology. In *Proceedings of the Informing Science and Information Technology Education Joint Conference*, Rockhampton QLD, Australia, (pp. 747-752)..

Tirellil, I., Laroussi, M., Derycke, A. & BenGhezala, H. (2006). Fractal Adaptive Web Service for Mobile Learning. *International Journal of Emerging Technologies in Learning, 1*(2), 25-35.

Thornton, P. & Houser, C. (2004). Using Mobile Phones in Education. In *Proceedings of the 2nd IEEE International Workshop on Wireless and Mobile Technologies in Education (WMTE 2004)* (pp. 3-10).

Uschold, M. & Gruninger, M. (1996). ONTOLOGIES: Principles, Methods and Applications. *Knowledge Engineering Review, 11*(2), 93-155.

Vavoula, G. & Sharples, M. (2002). KLeOS: A personal Mobile Knowledge and Learning Organisation System", In *Proceedings of the 2nd IEEE Int. Workshop on Wireless and Mobile Technologies in Education,* Sweden (pp.152-157)..

Veith, P. (2005, October 25-28)). Conception and Development of Reusable and Modular Mobile Content. Paper presented at the *International Conference on Mobile Learning mLearn'2005*, Cape Town. Retrieved on December 5, 2006, from http://www.mlearn.org.za/CD/

Wang, J., Li, X., Huang, T. & Wu, B. (2006). Personalized Knowledge Service Framework for Mobile Learning. In *Proceedings of the Second International Conference on Semantics, Knowledge, and Grid (SKG'06)* (pp. 102-103).

Chapter III

Model-Driven Development for Pervasive Information Systems

José Eduardo Fernandes, Bragança Polytechnic Institute, Portugal

Ricardo J. Machado, University of Minho, Portugal

João Álvaro Carvalho, University of Minho, Portugal

Abstract

This chapter focuses on design methodologies for pervasive information systems (PIS). It aims to contribute to the efficiency and effectiveness of software development of ubiquitous services/applications supported on pervasive information systems. Pervasive information systems are comprised of conveniently orchestrated embedded or mobile computing devices that offer innovative ways to support existing and new business models. Those systems are characterized as having a potentially large number of interactive heterogeneous embedded/mobile computing devices that collect, process, and communicate information. Also, they are the target of technological innovations. Therefore, changes in requirements or in technology require frequent modifications of software at device and system levels. Software design and evolution for those require suitable approaches that consider such demands and characteristics of pervasive information systems. Model-driven development approaches (which essentially centre the focus of development on models, and involve concepts such as Platform-Independent Models, Platform-Specific Models, model transformations, and use of established standards) currently in research at academic and industrial arenas in the design of large systems, offer potential benefits that can be applied to the design and evolution of these pervasive information systems. In this chapter, we raise issues and propose strategies related to the software development of PIS using a model-driven development perspective.

Introduction

Through the years, organizational, technological, and social evolutions brought a shift from a usually monolithic organization's information systems, with well-defined and limited source inputs, into complex, distributed, and technologically heterogeneous information systems. Nowadays, a digital world emerges with prevalence over the real world; everything has or produces information in an increasingly real-time fashion. This world acquires computational and communication capabilities and is ever more ruled with digital information and processes, and produces more and faster information about everything and everyone. The future points to a world full of embedded or mobile computing devices, with an emerging robotics industry which is "developing in much the same way that the computer business did 30 years ago" (Gates, 2007). This reality and inherent potential has been the subject of study and research in the ubiquitous computing field (the term "pervasive computing" is commonly used with the same meaning).

The emerging innovative technological devices and its widespread availability called for organizations' attention for its potential on collecting, processing, and disseminating information. Organizations see this as an opportunity to improve their business's processes and, therefore, to better compete and respond to market pressures and challenges. Consequently, there is an increasing demand for software development to realize intended applications for these pervasive information systems, taking advantage of those technologies.

This chapter aims to show how model-driven development approaches can be used for software development of pervasive information systems in order to attain full benefits of these systems. It starts by presenting ubiquitous computing and pervasive information systems. Then it introduces MDD fundamental concepts, primary issues and thrusts on MDD research, and current practice on developing systems. It generically presents a project on ubiquitous field and the approach to development, and points out some issues and challenges that arise in the development of software for pervasive information systems. It concludes by presenting guidelines and suggestions to approach MDD development of pervasive information systems.

Ubiquitous Computing

Ubiquitous computing is a research field of computing technology that started at the '90s with Mark Weiser's seminal work entitled "The Computer for the 21st Century" (M. Weiser, 1991). In this work, he shared his vision of a new way of thinking about computers.

Ubiquitous computing represents a new direction on the thinking about the integration and use of computers in people's lives. It aims to achieve a new computing paradigm, one in which there is a high degree of pervasiveness and widespread availability of computers or other IT devices in the physical environment. Consequently, the physical world is enriched with the advantages of processing power, storage, and communications capabilities of computers.

This new computing paradigm is not simply restricted to enhancing the physical world with embedded computing devices, sensors, actuators or other elements to provide communications among these. It is also concerned with the way computing is made available for interaction with users in support of their activities. Ubiquitous computing proposes a philosophy that values the nuances of the real world and embodies the assumption that computers should fade into the physical environment in an "virtual or effective" invisible way to people (M. Weiser, 1993a). As stated by Weiser, "Ubiquitous computing takes place primarily in the background. (…) leaves you feeling as though you did by yourself" (M. Weiser, 1993a), ubiquitous computing is gracefully and seamlessly integrated in the environment in a way that people do not notice that it is there. In this way, people can fully focus on completion of their tasks, and benefit from a non-intrusive and non-distracting computing.

In its evolution, pervasive computing has been interpreted from several different perspectives, leading to different meanings and objectives by different people. In order to clarify what pervasive computing is about, Banavar (Banavar et al., 2000) defined pervasive computing with regard to three things. The first related the way people view and use mobile computing devices to perform tasks. The second related to the way applications are created and deployed in support of those tasks. The third related to how the environment is enhanced by the emergence and ubiquity of new information and functionality.

Banavar stated that in order to achieve the true benefit and science perspective of pervasive computing, it should be considered with different thinking about devices, applications and environment: (i) a device act as a portal to "an application data/space and not as a repository of custom software;" (ii) an application is for a user as a means to perform a task "not a piece of software that is written to exploit device's capabilities;" (iii) the computing environment is "the user's information enhanced physical surroundings, not a virtual space that exists to store and run software."

Considered a major evolutionary step in computing (Saha & Mukherjee 2003; Satyanarayanan, 2001) since the introduction the of the personal computer, ubiquitous computing is closely related to (and is an evolution step of) distributed computing and mobile computing, fields that already identified and studied several technical issues related to pervasive computing (Satyanarayanan, 2001). Several pervasive computing characteristics, issues and challenges have been identified (Abowd & Mynatt, 2000; Lyytinen & Yoo, 2002; Saha & Mukherjee, 2003; Satyanarayanan, 2001). Physical integration and spontaneous interoperation (Kindberg & Fox, 2002), quantity and heterogeneity of computing devices, services and applications that may be part at any moment of the system (Grimm et al., 2001), and the need of continuously available services (easily interrupted and resumed) (Abowd, Mynatt, & Rodden, 2002) are characteristics that must be taken into account when proceeding to the design of these systems. Context-awareness of applications and easy interoperability of devices and applications are also identified as requirements for system support of pervasive applications (Grimm, 2004).

It is common to find on literature undistinguished use of the terms pervasive and ubiquitous, and such current practice is generally accepted. Nonetheless, for the sake of clarification and contribution to the use of the terms ubiquitous and pervasive, it is convenient to say some words about the preferential use of those.

We think that computers and IT devices alike are, by themselves, not ubiquitous; they collectively provide support for pervasive systems and ubiquitous computing. Through embedment and mobility, we reach pervasive, and through pervasive, we achieve ubiquitous. Pervasiveness is related to the degree of penetration and dissemination of computing devices (or other IT like devices) or systems in our physical environment.

We think that ubiquitous computing comes as an emergent property of several interconnected computing (or other IT like) devices (embedded or mobile) or pervasive systems that are orchestrated in order to provide, in an invisible fashion, unobtrusive and helpful assistance to users' activities; that is how ubiquitous computing fits into place.

In short, conveniently orchestrated embedded and mobile devices allow us to compose pervasive systems that can provide users with ubiquitous services/applications, and as such, bring forward the ubiquitous computing conceived in Mark Weiser's vision.

Weiser stated that, "The real power of the concept comes not from any of these devices; it emerges from the interaction of all them" (Weiser, 1991). In fact, the individual device does not allow by itself the maximum exploration of its capabilities, or even allow for ubiquitous computing. Only by interaction with other devices can ubiquitous computing be sustained and the full exploration of device's capabilities achieved.

Weiser's statement, "Applications are of course the whole point of ubiquitous computing" (Weiser, 1993b) (and also cited by (Abowd et al., 2002)) reinforce that, among all the innovative and outstanding pervasive technologies, applications get the final focus on this novel computing vision. It is through these applications that the ultimate vision's objective is achieved—the invisibility of computing in the support and enhancement of everyday activity.

As expressed by Abowd (Abowd et al., 2002), it is not a single application or service that will realize such objective; rather "(…) it is a combination of services, available when needed and working as desired without extraordinary human intervention." It is not the technology, but applications and services that will influence our technological culture (Hansmann, Merck, Nicklous, & Stober, 2003). To realize Weiser's vision, Abowd (Abowd et al., 2002) believes that beyond the understanding of "everyday practices of people" and the augmentation of the world with heterogeneous inter-connected devices, it is necessary to orchestrate these devices in order to "provide for a holistic user experience."

Therefore, beyond technological innovations, attention needs to be given to the design of applications providing their supporting systems of coordinated devices. Research efforts so far have been mostly oriented towards physical and virtual integration, interaction models, deployment, communication technologies and connectivity, and software architectures. It is also important that new pervasive technologies and systems also become the subject of study and research from information systems and software engineering perspectives. The section that follows introduces the notion and importance of Pervasive Information Systems (PIS) and the need for an approach to software development for these kinds of systems.

Pervasive Information Systems

Pervasive systems and technologies have been increasingly employed either in business domains, trying to improve the way business is done or even to enable new and innovative ways of doing business, or in more personal or social domains, trying to improve the people's quality of life. Museums (Fleck et al., 2002), agriculture (Burrell, Brooke, & Beckwith, 2004), restaurants (Stanford, 2003), and health care (Varshney, 2003) are examples of domains that have been addressed by applications based on this kind of information technology.

Several areas have been addressed, including social concerns (Stone, 2003) and the economic implications of its deployment (Langheinrich, Coroama, Bohn, & Rohs, 2002). The advent of pervasive computing systems enabled information technology to gain further relevance in its role in human social lives (Dryer, Eisbach, & Ark, 1999), narrowing the relationship between humans and technology, and focusing on human to human communication. Assuming the spontaneous use of networking technologies for cooperation and access to information and Internet-based services, the potential for applications using smart objects is vast, given the limits "less of a technological nature than economic or even legal" (Mattern, 2001).

In order to be successful on a non-monopoly market environment, business competition among organizations demands that an organization meets market demand with the best suitable and competitive supply at minimal cost. Among others requirements, efficiency of business processes and effectiveness of processes' arrangement are central issues to the organization's ability to be competitive and successful. Beyond land and natural resources, human labour, and financial capital, information and knowledge are fundamental resources of an organization (Sage & Rouse, 1999). Information can be used not only as a resource for the production of goods or services, but also as an asset inherent in the organization structure, or even as a product to be commercialized (Gordon & Gordon, 2004). In this context, information, information technologies, information systems, and information management play a crucial role.

Organizations must possess the capability to be able to establish new or to change existing business requirements or processes in a short period of time. Such necessity, in conjunction with a reality of permanent technological innovations and developments, requires that an organization's supporting information systems and inherent subsystems be designed to deal with change and evolution with minimal business disturbance and reduced costs.

Widespread availability of affordable and innovative information technologies prompted the attention of individuals and organizations on the efficiency and effectiveness of information management – the way they acquire, process, store, retrieve, communicate, use (Gordon & Gordon, 2004) and share information . The adoption of these technologies, in fact, can contribute to more profitable and more advantageous business performance and ultimately, to maximize potential competitive advantages. To take full advantage of the opportunities offered by information technologies, these need to be "appropriately integrated within organizational frameworks" (Sage & Rouse, 1999). Hence, they will not only provide a solid basis to sustain the needed information and to achieve effectiveness at both the individual and organizational levels, but will also provide leverage of the investment on these information technologies.

Information systems (IS) known as systems that "collect, process, store, analyse, and disseminate information for a specific purpose" (Turban, McLean, & Wetherbe, 2001), are planned, designed and deployed in an organization with the purpose of supporting its business operations, to assist its management activities, or to produce business's valuable information assets or products. It is through the proper design of those information systems that it will be possible to satisfy the organizational or personal information needs in an efficient way. The correct definition and design of information systems are also important to greater satisfaction related to information security, privacy and other social concerns, thus, guaranteeing a higher degree of reliance on the system deployed.

Within an organization, and mainly from a management perspective, information systems can be classified in several ways. Gordon et al..(Gordon & Gordon, 2004) classify information systems according to two dimensions--their *purpose* and their sc*ope*. In the purpose dimension, several types of information systems are exemplified including the automation systems, transaction processing systems, management information systems (management reporting systems, decision supporting systems, groupware, executive information systems). In the scope dimension they are defined as (Gordon & Gordon, 2004) individual, departmental/functional, enterprise and inter-organizational systems.

Turban et al. (Turban et al., 2001) classify information systems by organizational levels (departmental IS, enterprise IS and inter-organizational IS), functional areas (accounting IS, finance IS, manufacturing IS, marketing IS, human resources management IS), support provided (transaction processing systems (TPS), Management IS (MIS), Knowledge management systems (KMS), Office automation systems (OAS), Enterprise IS (EIS), Group support system (GSS) and Intelligent support systems), and information system architecture.

In 1997, Birnbaum (Birnbaum, 1997), relating the concept "pervasive technology" to the notion of a technology "more noticeable for its absence than its presence," bring pervasive computing into relation with information systems and entitled his article "Pervasive Information Systems." Because of the advance of information appliances, the emergence of a digital infrastructure fostered by the Internet, and the increasing expectation on readily available information services (for which quality of service is would be a "crucial competitive differentiator"), Birnbaum presented the pervasiveness of computing and anticipated what he classified as a new paradigm shift, the client-utility computing. In this paradigm, clients connect to the utilities, computing's usage can be paid (in consequence, a new service industry could emerge), and the "standards-based open resources, located arbitrarily, are combined as needed for a particular job" (Birnbaum, 1997). Through the statement "I think it is only a matter of time before client-utility becomes the prevalent style in information systems (…) The consequence of pervasive information systems for business and society are enormous." (Birnbaum, 1997), Birnbaum reveals the association of the term "pervasive information systems" to the idea of widespread and common use of services, which are at the core of this perspective of the term. Other references on the relationship between the devices and information systems can also be found in literature, as "The Sensor-Net system using small wireless sensor nodes is a ubiquitous information system for monitoring real-time real-world phenomena.(…) "(Suzuki, 2004).

Services are supported and deployed over interconnected computing devices and other information augmented objects, enabling higher-level applications that come to the assistance of the user (either in a seamlessly or intensive interacting way). In this, "we become aware of the presence flow and processing of information, not only by the individual computing devices, but also, and with a more deep significance, by the overall system that emerges from the interactions of all the computing devices, linking them together in a coherent fashion" (J. E. Fernandes, Machado, & Carvalho, 2004). We can then recognize the presence of some sort of information system, which in this context of pervasive computing, we can refer to as a *pervasive information system (PIS)*. Indeed, all of these systems dealing with information constitute some form of information system; they gather, collect, process, store and produce information aimed at contributing to an organization or person in order to achieve a set of well-established objectives.

These pervasive information systems open the possibility of processing large quantity of information which, comprising an information system must be, in its essence, well designed, developed and deployed. In this way, it will be possible to satisfy requirements and explore the potential offered by pervasive computing, maximizing the revenue of these kinds of systems. Also, a good design will also provide for a better accommodation for the frequent technological evolutions and innovations on devices.

Consequently, software development for PIS needs to provide suitable accommodation and attention for issues at either the device or system level. At the device level, attention is needed on: the particular characteristics and capabilities of devices; the changes on software at level device due technological evolution of the device; the introduction of new software for new innovative technological device; changes on software at device due to business requirements changes. At the system level, attention is needed on: the development of software supporting the pervasive information system; the evolution of software for pervasive information system due to changes on new technology or on changes on business requirements; the evolution of software for pervasive information systems due to reconfigurations of the devices that compose the pervasive information systems.

Software development has been, for recent years, subject of research in a area denominated as Model-Driven Development (MDD). This research has been particularly fostered by the Model-Driven Architecture (MDA) initiative of the Object Group Management (OMG). Next section presents the fundamental concepts of MDD and of MDA initiative.

Model-Driven Development

Software engineering is a discipline whose objective is the "cost-effective development of software systems" (OMG, 2003; Sommerville, 2001). There have been several research efforts to reach greater performance and convenience in development of these systems, and to achieve better satisfaction on the accomplishment of its requirements and expectations. Improvements in programming and modelling languages, algorithms, techniques and paradigms (such as functional decomposition and object-orientation), processes and tools, patterns, and the "level of reuse in system construction" (Miller et al., 2004) (sub-routines, objects, components and frameworks) are among approaches undertaken in these research efforts.

Model-Driven Development (MDD) constitutes an approach to software design and development that strongly focuses and relies on models, through which "we build software-platform independent models" (Miller et al., 2004). MDD entails a rising of abstraction from higher-level programming languages to modelling languages.

Interest and focus on models arise today with further emphasis due to recent developments that resulted into the establishment of important and widely known and recognized standards, particularly those originated from the Object Management Group (OMG) such as (Unified Modelling Language (UML) standard and the Model-Driven Architecture (MDA) initiative).

These standards (and as well as others) represent, through common agreement and acceptance, what best we have reached in terms of practices, and set up the basis for further innovations or developments; they also enable re-use of knowledge and artefacts, tools' specialization and interoperation, thus providing a "significant impetus for further progress" (Selic, 2003b). Another key enabler of the movement into this new paradigm of software development is the availability of more powerful Computer-Aided Software Engineering (CASE) tools supporting the development and management of models and the generation of code.

For some, model-driven development is considered "the first true generational shift in programming technology since the introduction of compilers" (Selic, 2003b), and it can, in fact, profoundly change the way applications are developed (Atkinson & Kuhne, 2003). By automating many of the complex and routine programming tasks, MDD allows developers to be able to focus on the functionality that the system needs in order to deliver and on its general architecture, instead of worrying about every technical detail inherent in the use of a programming language (Atkinson & Kuhne, 2003).

In essence, MDA proposes a system development life cycle (SDLC), the development of a Platform Independent Model (PIM) of the system that, free from specific platform technological issues, details the structure and behaviour of the system. Given a chosen technological platform, this PIM is transformed into a Platform specific model (PSM) that incorporates all of the necessary technological details inherent in the chosen target technological platform on which the system is to be implemented.

From this PSM, system code foundations are generated for the target technological platform. This separation of concerns between PIM and PSM, allows that with no further modification to the PIM itself, other technological platforms can easily be targeted since the PIM still represents the desired system structure and functionality with no contamination of technological details.

Figure 1. MDA core concepts

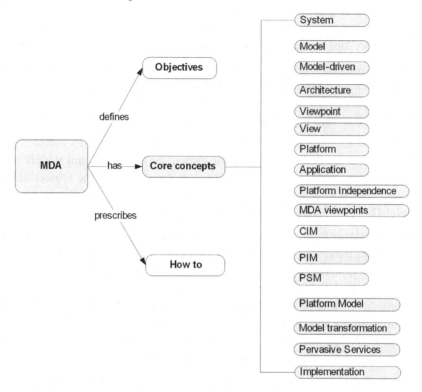

The model-driven architecture has a set of core concepts that must be understood in order to comprehend the essentials of this architecture. The MDA Guide (OMG, 2003) presents some basic concepts and terminology which are illustrated in Figure 1.

The MDA Guide (OMG, 2003) also describes how the model-driven architecture is to be used. Figure 2 presents a synthesis of the steps described and some inherent related concepts.

The following paragraphs detail some of the core concepts of MDA:

1. **Computational Independent Model (CIM):** The model driven approach establishes that requirements for the system are modelled in a Computational Independent Model (CIM). This is also referred as domain model or business model that is independent from how the system is to be implemented.

2. **Platform Independent Model (PIM):** The PIM, based on the previously elaborated CIM, whose requirements should be traceable into PIM constructs, describes the system; however, the PIM model does not reflect any decisions or details concerning platform issues. Nonetheless, the PIM may be "suited for a particular architectural style, or several" (OMG, 2003).

Figure 2. How MDA is to be used

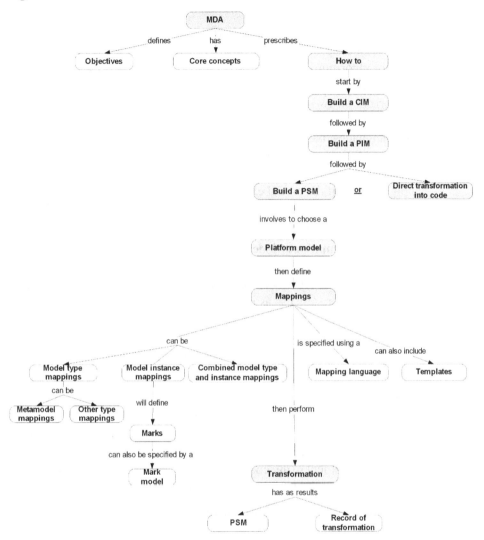

3.   **Platform Model (PM):** After the development of the PIM, a platform for its implementation is chosen. The chosen platform has a inherent model, the "platform model" - "often, at present, this model is in the form of software and hardware manuals or is even in the architect's head" (OMG, 2003), which the architect will use to the specify the mappings from the PIM to the target platform model, resulting in the PSM of the system.

4.   **Platform specific model (PSM):** The platform specific model reflects the platform independent model of the system, enriched with the concepts, services

and details of the chosen target deployment platform of which the system will make use.

5.   **Mappings:** The transformation from a PIM to a PSM model is done through a specification provided by a mapping. This specification is composed by rules (or algorithms) that determine how the transformation is prosecuted in order to obtain model elements of the PSM. Mappings can fundamentally be categorized on two types: (i) model type mappings and (ii) model instance mappings. Model type mappings are those based on model types of the PIM and PSM languages; being based on types, these kinds of mappings consequently specify transformations that apply to all respective instances. Model instance mappings are defined with the purpose of defining particular transformations to apply to some of the model elements of the PIM. In these kinds of mappings, marks are applied to model elements of the PIM with the primarily purpose of indicating how those model elements of the PIM should be transformed.

6.   **Model transformation:** Model transformation generally refers to the process of converting a PIM, or a marked PIM, into a PSM; this process can be done manually, with or without computer's tools support, or automatically. Typically, the model transformation process has as inputs the PIM/marked PIM and the mappings to be followed, and produces as output the PSM and a record of the transformation (showing the PIM elements and the associated resulting PSM elements produced in the transformation). This process is illustrated in Figure 3.

Today, when building large software systems, the main challenge for software developers is to "handle complexity and to adapt quickly to changes" (Schmoelzer et al., 2004). Model-driven approaches can be a response to this challenge. They have the objective of "increase productivity and reduce time-to-market," which is attained by a development using concepts closer to the problem domain than "those offered by programming languages" (Sendall & Kozaczynski, 2003).

Model-driven development approaches promote the idea that through the focus of development on models, one can obtain better software systems development and evolutions. For this, several aspects of MDD can be addressed:

1.   **Gains of productivity:** Atkinson et al. (Atkinson & Kuhne, 2003), stating that the productivity improvement from development efforts is the "underlying motivation for MDD," consider that such productivity is attained along two dimensions that MDD must strategically consider: (i) *short-term productivity*, which is obtained through the amount of functionality a software artefact can deliver; (ii) *long-term productivity*, which is obtained by augmenting the longevity of the software artefact. In order to increase productivity, Atkinson and Kuhne (Atkinson & Kuhne, 2003) understand that model-driven development approaches must take into account changes that effect longevity of software

Figure 3. Model transformation

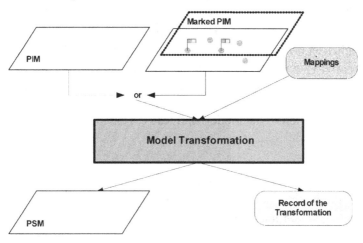

artefacts; these changes are considered in "four main fundamental forms:" (i) in personnel; (ii) in requirements; (iii) in development platforms; (iv) and in deployment platforms. These kinds of changes, which can occur concurrently, take to several needs that must be addressed by MDD infrastructures in order to decrease the sensitiveness to change of software artefacts. These needs include those of: software artefacts described with clear and concise concepts, and with an understandable notation accessible to a wide range of people; high interoperability of tools and artefact storage on well-established non-proprietary formats; user-defined mappings to shield models from specifics of technological platforms.

2. **Concepts close to domain and reduction of semantic gap:** Selic (Selic, 2003b) observes that development of software being made through models use concepts that are "much less bound to the underlying implementation technology and are much closer to the problem domain relative to most popular programming languages," which eventually enables non-computing specialists to "produce systems." MDD, though focus on models, allows for the reduction of or elimination of errors and semantic gaps in the passage from an abstract model at design into a final product for implementation, and an increased model accuracy since the "model is the system" (Selic, 2003a); furthermore, "there are no conceptual discontinuities that preclude backtracking" (Selic, 2003b).

3. **Automation and less sensitivity to technological changes:** Mellor et al. (Mellor, Clark, & Futagami, 2003) point out two potential benefits of MDD benefits: (i) automatic transformation of high-level design models to running systems allows for gain of productivity and inherent reduction of costs (beyond reduction of errors and elimination of semantic gaps); (ii) models are easier

to maintain, and are also "less sensitive to the chosen computing technology and to evolutionary changes to that technology."

4.   **Capture of expert knowledge and re-use:** Beyond the benefits of using higher-level concepts in a modelling language, MDD also enables the capture of expert knowledge. This is achieved through mapping functions that convey information to the transformation of one model to another, allowing for re-use when an application or its implementation changes. This enables an independent evolution of the models and leads to extended longevity models (Mellor et al., 2003).

For MDD to become a reality and succeed, automation and tools have a key role (beyond automation; other issues are considered pertinent to the success of MDD). Automation, which includes complete code generation and execution of models, is a key premise behind MDD (Selic, 2003b); tools must support the automation involved (in particular, any model transformations) in order to make model-driven development a reality (Sendall & Kozaczynski, 2003), allowing then for the collection of the full benefits of this approach to software development.

Automation represents "the most effective technological means for boosting productivity and reliability" (Selic, 2003b) and contributes to the enrichment of models' role on software development, taking those from a role of merely documentation support (and usually on divergence from reality). It "formalizes solutions and raises the level at which we can apply creativity" (Mellor et al., 2003), and contributes, beyond the support to vertical and horizontal model synchronization, to "significantly reduce the burden of other activities, such as reverse engineering, view generation, application of patterns, or refactoring" (Sendall & Kozaczynski, 2003).

Software modelling and automatic code generation have had few success in the past, these being limited to diagramming support and skeletal code generation, which were not enough to provide a relevant productivity return (Selic, 2003b). However, technology and knowledge have evolved, and today, beyond a better understanding of modelling, automation technologies have matured and world-wide accepted standards have emerged. Some of these are those provided by the Object Management Group – such as the Unified Modelling Language (UML) or the Meta-Object Facility (MOF), or de facto standards such as Extensible Markup Language (XML) and Simple Object Access Protocol (SOAP), contributing for a better MDD positioning to be successful in software development (Selic, 2003b).

Generating complete code from models is not a technically easy task, but neither was it when compilers were introduced in the past. Today, no questions are kept related to the efficiency of the code generated by compilers (technologically mature in current days) in transforming a high-level program code into machine-readable code; the same can become true for model compilers that transform models into code (Selic, 2003b).

Selic (Selic, 2003a) understands that the most benefits of model-driven development are reached when MDD methods offer the capabilities of: (1) automatic code generation of the implementation from the corresponding higher model level, meaning that "the model and implementation are one;" (2) execution of models, which allows for experimentation with models to acquire knowledge in a quick and inexpensive way, of a system's properties.

Atkinson and Kunhne (Atkinson & Kuhne, 2003) also refer to a goal of MDD the automation of "many complex (but routine) programming tasks –…– which have to be done manually today." For these capabilities, the modelling languages used "must have the same semantic precision as programming languages" (Selic, 2003a) (which doesn't necessarily mean having the same detail).

For MDD to succeed, Selic (Selic, 2003b) calls attention to the importance of also paying attention to issues, other than "defining suitable modelling languages and automatic code generation," namely, the need of tools that come in pragmatic support of model-driven development such as: (1) model-level reporting tools to assist on the reporting and the debugging of errors at model-level, in contrast to what happens with traditional programming language compilers and debuggers; (2) model-merging tools to enable the possibility of merging two or more models; (3) model difference tools to help to identify differences between two models; (4) the possibility of execution of models (eventually incomplete); executable models, in a simulation environment or in the target platform, allows for early experimentation of the system under development to analyse high-risk aspects or alternative solutions.

MDD for Pervasive Information Systems

This section begins by presenting a project developed in the field of ubiquitous and mobile computing that directed software development towards a model-driven software development basis, and exposes the approach taken on the development on software system. Following section presents a contributing framework and issues pertaining to software development for pervasive information systems.

uPAIN project

The uPAIN (Ubiquitous Solutions for Pain Monitoring and Control in Post-Surgery Patients) project is developed in the area of Information and Technology Systems and developed by its consortium's partners for a three years term (from 1st of October 2003 to end of September 2005). The scientific research and technological development entities forming the consortium responsible for the project prosecution were: (1) University of Minho, through its Information System Department

(UMinho-DSI); (2) MobiComp (MobiComp), a Portuguese mobile computing and wirelesses solution's provider; (3) and the Hospital "Senhora da Oliveira," localized on the city of Guimarães, Portugal (HSOG).

The uPAIN project is aimed at anaesthesiology services of healthcare centres and consists of an information system conceived to assist in monitoring and controlling pain of patients who underwent surgery, and who are in a relatively long period of recovery. During this period, analgesics are administered to them in order to minimize the pain that increases as the effect of the anaesthesia disappears. This administration of analgesics is controlled by means of specialized devices called PCAs (patient controlled analgesia) in order to take into account the personal characteristics of the patient and the kind of surgery which the patient has had. The PCA is "a medication- dispensing unit equipped with a pump attached to an intravenous line, which is inserted into a blood vessel in the patient's hand or arm. By means of a simple push-button mechanism, the patient is allowed to self administer doses of pain relieving medication (narcotic) on an "as need" basis" (Machado, Lassen, Oliveira, Couto, & Pinto, 2007).

The basis of uPAIN project is that different people feel and react to pain differently, and that the effective dose of narcotics varies greatly from patient to patient. Therefore, anaesthesiologists are interested in monitoring several variables in a continuous manner during patients' recovery in order to increase their knowledge of what other factors, besides those already known, are relevant to pain control, and in what measure they influence the whole process.

The main idea behind the uPAIN system is to replace the PCA push-button by an interface on a PDA (personal digital assistant), which still allows the patient to request doses from the PCA, and creates records in a database of all those requests along with other data considered relevant by the medical doctors. The uPAIN system is intended to provide a platform that supports the improvement of several relevant factors related to pain treatment services: (1) establish automatic regular assessment and registering of pain level, and enhanced and faster individual therapeutic prescription to pain symptoms; (2) support for written therapeutic protocols and storage of the therapeutics treatment given to patients; (3) and to facilitate, to the Director of the Anaesthesiology Services, the adjustment of the monitoring and controlling equipment to the particular capabilities of each different person comprising his/her staff and the establishment and supervision of all staff activities for evening or weekend periods.

The architectural solution for uPAIN project is illustrated in Figure 4, which reflects the devices and communications technology needed to provide support for the information system that accomplishes the function expected from the uPAIN system. The uPAIN project connects on a computer network system the monitoring equipment and the PCA (patient controlled analgesia), and support communication among staff and patients from the staff point of view, the ubiquity of the system's functionality. A central server receives information sent by the patient PDA (pPDA). This server (pSC) is responsible for the management of all services provided by UPAIN. Support is provided for data acquisition from all medical equipment (like patient monitors and PCAs), for accessing databases, for managing requests from all the pPDAs (patient PDAs) and sPDAs (staff PDAs), and so forth. The uPAIN system allows hospital staff, through wireless networks, to remotely control and monitor pain even outside the hospital network through mobile phone networks.

The uPAIN project emerged as an initiative in the ubiquity arena, guided by the requirements management based on effective necessity and the derivation system's executable artefacts from transformation of system's models. As such, an analysis of the project development under a perspective of model-driven development is henceforward done.

On assumption that clients and developers have different points of view towards requirements, two different categories for requirements were considered:

1. **User requirements** result from elicitation task focused in the problem domain (aiming to acquire and understand the needs of users and project sponsors with the ultimate purpose being the communication of these needs to the system developers); typically described in natural language and informal diagrams;

Figure 4. General architecture for the uPAIN system

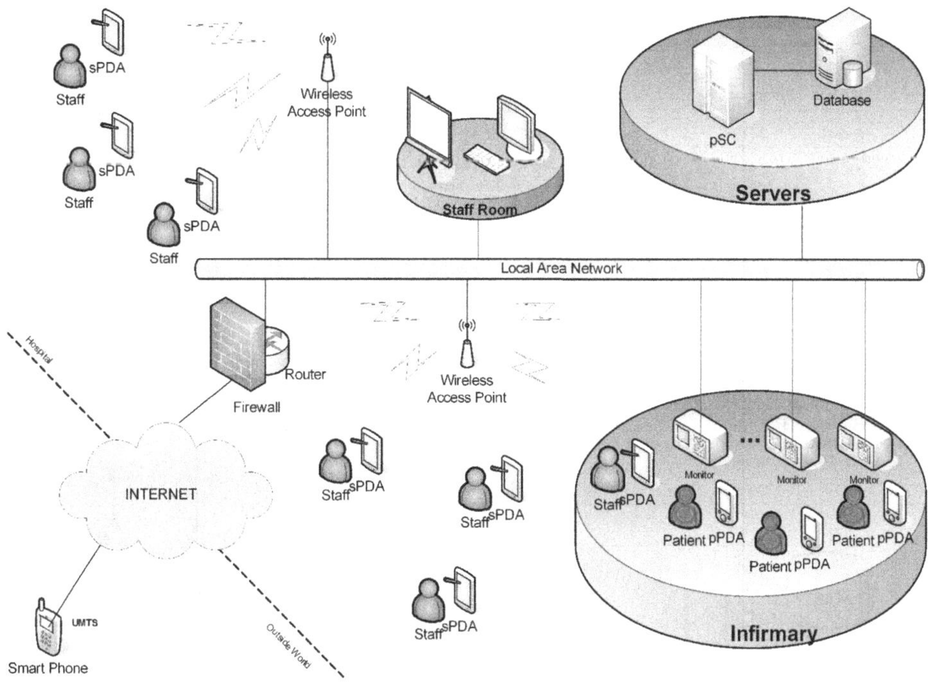

2. **System requirements** result from developer's effort to organize user requirements at the solution domain. High-level abstract models of systems are used to establish and structure these requirements and represent a first system representation for use in the design phase.

For worth of value in transforming user requirements models in systems requirements models, it was performed the *validation* of user requirements. The uPAIN methodological approach has done user's requirements validation, not only by the static requirements perspective, but also by bringing to user validation the top-level system behaviour. Such as been accomplished by documenting user requirements on system's functionality through *UML use case diagrams* (Figure 5 show the top-level use case diagram of the uPAIN use case model that expresses the user requirements), and by adoption of *stereotyped sequence diagrams*. These, involving only actors and use cases in the interactions, further illustrated the desired dynamic behaviour in what respect interaction with the environment. These sequence diagrams (see Figure 6) "allow a pure functional representation of behavioural interaction with the environment and are particularly appropriate to illustrate workflow user require-

Figure 5. A use case diagram of the use case model describing user requirements (from (Machado et al., 2007))

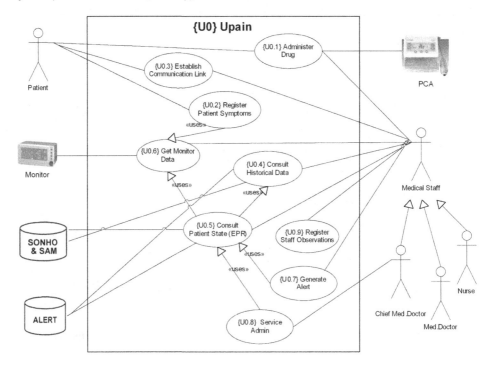

Figure 6. UML stereotyped sequence diagram for a uPAIN use case macro-scenario (from (Machado et al., 2007))

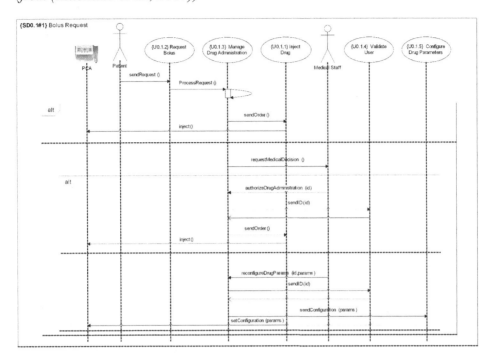

ments" (Machado et al., 2007). They do not model structural elements of the system and are understandable by the stakeholders.

The use of use case models and stereotyped sequence diagram is not enough to obtain requirements models that are capable of being fully understandable by common stakeholders. It is recognized that the difficulty for common stakeholders to comprehend dynamic properties of the system with its interaction with the environment, and as such, the static user requirements models (use case and stereotyped sequence diagrams) were used to derivate, through intermediating Coloured Petri-Nets (CPNs), animation prototypes.

These animation prototypes that presented user friendly visualizations of system behaviour, were automatically translated from formal system's models specifications, accepting user interaction for validation purposes." This approach to validation was "experimented with and proved to be very effective"(Machado et al., 2007), promoting a deeper stakeholder's involvement in the analysis phase, and a better clarification and elicitation of workflow requirements. Figure 7 shows an image of the animation prototype used for the uPAIN system user requirements validation, and Figure 8 presents a CPN responsible for the a animation prototype interaction related to an use case of the uPAIN project.

Figure 7. Interactive animation prototype for uPAIN system   (Machado et al., 2007)

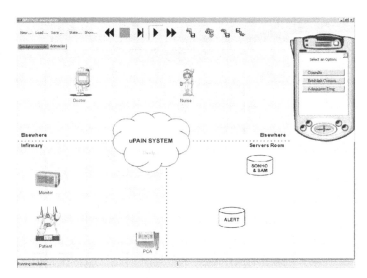

The behaviour of the animation prototypes used in this project resulted from a "rigorous translations of the sequence diagrams into Coloured Petri Nets (CPNs)" (Machado et al., 2007). The link between UML diagrams and CPNs are not obtained directly, but in two steps: the first is supported by the fact that the "sequence diagrams are directly derived from the use cases;" the second is ensured by a "direct transformation of sequence diagrams into CPNs." Two simple rules shown in Figure 9 and Figure 10 were used for that translation:

This methodological approach to user requirements reveals a special concern for validation of user requirements, recurring to an automatic *horizontal mapping* between models (UML sequence model and CPN model) in order to provide a formal behaviour to the animation prototype.

From validated user requirements, the design phase defines the models that comprise the structure and behaviour of the intended system, starting with the logical architecture of the system and followed by other models. Figure 11 shows the logical architecture of the system, composed of high-level objects/components of the system and the responsibilities and the relationships among them. Its construction is independent of implementation constraints.

The 4SRS (4 Step Rule Set) technique was applied to the transformation of user requirements to the logical system-level architecture (here represented by an object diagram) representing system requirements. Figure 12 presents the schematics of this technique; more information on the 4SRS technique can be found in (J. Fernandes & Machado, 2001). The 4SRS represents a vertical mapping based on a set of rules for transformation of a user requirements models into the logical structure model.

Figure 8. CPN responsible for prototype animation of a use case(Machado et al., 2007)

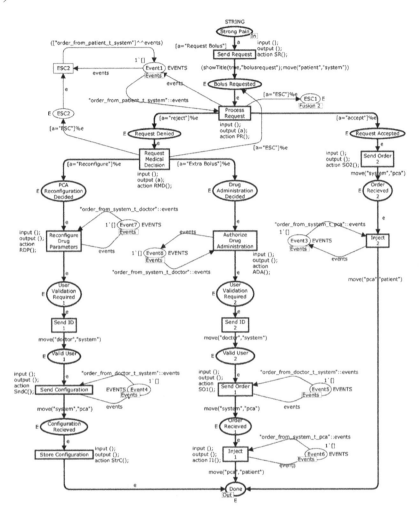

Figure 9. Transformation of messages (from (Machado et al., 2007)

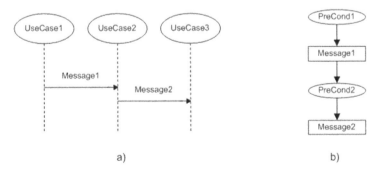

Figure 10. Transformation of an alternative block (from (Machado et al., 2007))

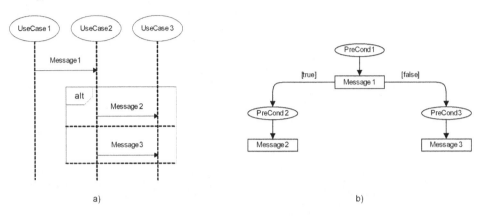

a)   b)

Figure 11. uPAIN logical architecture

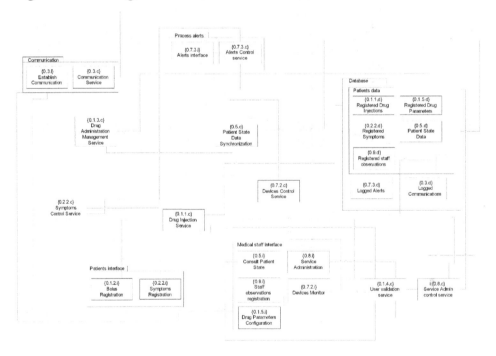

Figure 12. 4SRS Technique (adapted from (J. Fernandes & Machado, 2001)

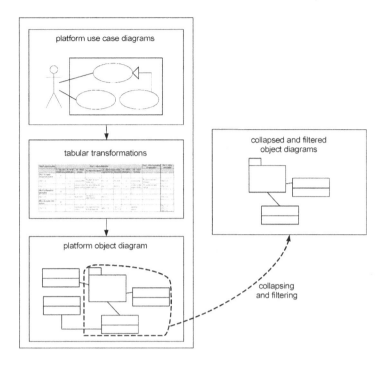

Several other artefacts (such as database models, sPDA and pPDAs models, pSC models, and other models of the uPAIN system) were developed along with the development of the uPAIN project. Figure 13 depicts a general schematic (not exhaustive) structure of the models, transformation models, code generation, and code resulting from an insight into artefacts produced on the project development.

Considering Figure 13, several methodological questions arise about some of the resulting artefacts, as well about the means of achieving those (such as some models transformations and the completeness of some models). For the sake of enforcement of a methodological model-development orientation, greater clarity and well-defined establishment is needed. Other questions may be raised, such as, how well the system will adapt for new PDA's platforms, or new kind of portable/embedded computing devices, or smart phones; how much effort will be needed in order to reflect change in requirements?

Research on model-driven development (MDD) approaches for pervasive information systems (PIS) tries to raise and to bring to light several issues (such as essential considerations, techniques, frameworks, tools, etc.) pertaining to the adoption of MDD in order to provide well-established foundations that allow for a smooth software development and maintenance of pervasive information systems.

Figure 13. Models, model mappings/transformations, and code generation in the development of the uPAIN system

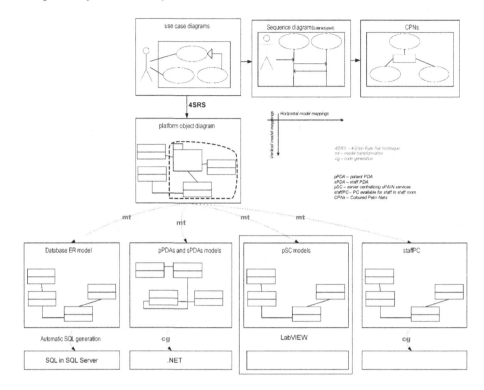

Approach to Software Development for PIS

Model-driven development (MDD) of software systems take an approach to development which is strongly based on models and transformations among models. It allows for the reduction of semantic gaps among the developed artefacts. It also enables higher independence and resilience of domain models from particular characteristics and changes on system's technological platforms.

Assuming a MDD approach to software development for PIS, it is important to consider what best MDD has to offer and which characteristics of pervasive information systems (PIS) become relevant to software development. This way, it will be possible to provide higher effectiveness in the development and evolution of PIS. On an MDD context, topics of interest for research and use reside in knowledge and techniques about models, modelling languages, development methods, model transformations, architectures/frameworks, patterns, automatic code generation, supporting tools, among others.

When intending to develop software for PIS, relevant characteristics of those are the elevated number of devices that can be involved, the pace of technological innovations, the heterogeneity of the devices, and potential complexity of interactions that may exist. Consequently, some thoughts and issues that may influence the strategy taken on the MDD approach for PIS arise. Among these, some relate to functionality management and others relate to the proper development of the PIS. The following paragraphs expose some of thoughts and issues:

1. **Functionality management.** (i) Objects may eventually participate in several systems, playing same functional roles in some of those and different roles with some others. Would it be of interest that, when "inserting" a device (a computationally enriched object) into a pervasive system, the interaction regarding setting up a specific role functionality on that device, be analogous to what we expect when we insert an USB devices into a computational system: just plug-in? When occurring a device plug-in, the pervasive system, attending to device's characteristics and with a minimal configuration (on the system and/or device), could assign the suitable functionality and set up the needed to enable and to integrate the device in the normal operation of the pervasive system. (ii) How to provide for functionality's reconfigurations when expanded capability is added to the device, allowing it to surpass functionalities' restrictions dictated by previous capabilities limitations? (iii) How to provide for replacement of a device by a new one that, fulfilling the role of the previous device, be, nonetheless, based on a new and completely different computational platform?

2. **Development.** (i) How to develop software for a PIS that, besides traditional coordination of system's functionality and information's flows, allows specific object-to-object interaction to obtain additional functionality (allowing for, among others, enhanced system's efficiency and robustness)? (ii) How to provide for coherent and consistent maintenance and evolution pervasive information systems that allows for proper accommodation of new or changed requirements, functionalities or technology? (iii) How low has to be the abstraction level at which software developers' work has to be done?

MDD approaches, centring development on models (thus raising the traditional level of abstraction for system's conception and design) and automating (as much as possible) the transformation of models and the generation of the final code, seem to offer key pathways that enable software developers to cope with complexity inherent do PIS. CASE tools, crucial to and effective MDD development, have continuously evolved: it can be expected enhanced support to creation, verification of PIMs and PSMs, models' transformations and code generations, changes' management and documentation for all artefacts and design decision.

The effort of using MDD concepts and techniques supported by suitable CASE tools is fundamental, but not sufficient. It is needed an approach, while adopting of modern and appropriate concepts, techniques, and tools, establishes a suitable development's strategy for the development of PIS framed on appropriate procedures and rigour. In the remainder of this section, we expose concepts, issues and strategy that such approach can assume.

The remainder of the section, while introducing some concepts, presents three development dimensions pertaining to and MDD approach to PIS development; they are classes dimension, functional dimension, and abstraction dimension. After this, the developmental framework associated with this approach will be presented.

Classes Dimension

It is suggested that, for a suitable MDD approach to software development for PIS, the devices be grouped into *classes of devices* (it can also be seen as categories) reflecting common basic resource and capabilities of the devices (see Figure 14). This perspective of looking for and grouping devices by common relevant properties constitutes the *classes dimension*. Eventually, where needed and justified, these classes of devices may be further classified through specialized relationships into subclasses of devices (in a reasoning context, this specialization process may also be applied to the subclasses).

Devices belonging to a class (or subclass) possess particular characteristics and capabilities that allow them to fulfil and support specific functionalities that can be demanded to those device types.

Functional Dimension

The classification of devices in classes is just one dimension (see Figure 15) concerning the global development of a pervasive information system. Considering that

Figure 14. Classes and subclasses of devices

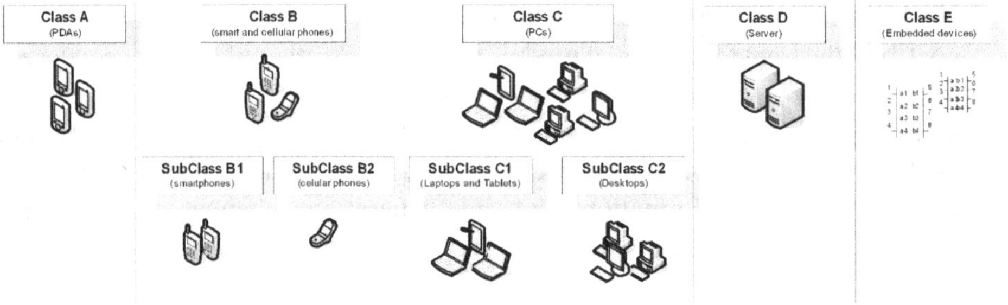

the same class of devices can be asked to fulfil different roles, or provide distinct sets of functionalities, it can be devised another dimension: the *functional dimension* that brings the perspective of looking and seeing sets of functionalities that classes can be responsible to provide support for. These sets of functionalities are herein called *functional profiles*. A functional profile comprises then a set of functionalities expected in the system and that is assigned to a specific class of devices. For example, in the uPAIN project, some PDAs were destined to act as a patient's PDA (pPDA) while others were destined to act as a staff's PDA (sPDA), providing services according to the functional profiles that they were assigned for. A class of devices can provide support for several functional profiles.

From a software development perspective, the assignment of a functional profile to a class of devices results on a specific *development structure* established for that functional profile. A development structure reflects a pathway of software development in order to satisfy a functional profile of a class. Figure 15 illustrates these development structures (represented as FPDS) for functional profiles for the several classes of devices, as well as a schematic representation for these two dimensions.

Classes may have an arbitrary number of assigned functional profiles representing sets of functionality of the systems assigned to those classes of devices. Eventually, some of these assigned functional profiles assigned to a class may represent redundant/secondary functionality as some other class may have the primary responsibility to service such functionality. It may happen as result of a design decision in order to, for example: (1) ensure enhanced fault tolerance of crucial functionality; (2) expand system flexibility on services provision; (3) or temporary accommodate function-

Figure 15. Development structures for functional profiles of classes

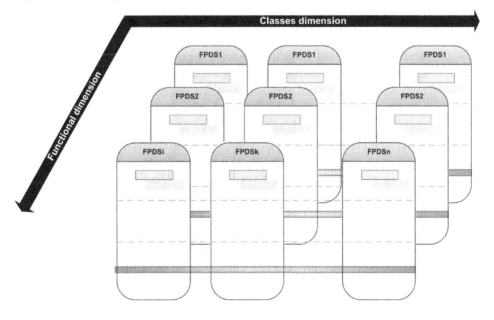

ality assigned to classes of devices that becoming obsolete or deactivated, are for replacement by new technological devices. These delimited units of development structures allow for comfortable incorporation and accommodation of changes and innovations, and consequently enhanced global elasticity of the system and control of changes' impact on the system.

Abstraction Dimension

Taking into account that, for each development structure there is a subjacent top-bottom abstraction course during its development, we can devise another dimension on PIS development--the *abstraction dimension*. At the abstraction dimension, developers focus interest on PIM, PSM (and other relative inner PIMs/PSMs), model transformations, and code generation (see Figure 17), in order to come to a realization of a piece of software that meets the functionality established on corresponding functional profile of that development structure.

For each of the development structures, and transversal to all of the development structures, development work is performed at a *modelling level* of abstraction at which development work is carried. The modelling levels that can be distinguished are the top, intermediate, and bottom modelling levels:

1. **Top modelling level:** At this level, the PIM for each of class of devices derivates from models resulting from initial development of the system as a whole (where all computing devices are integrated and orchestrated in order to provide functionality to the system).

2. **Intermediate modelling levels:** At these levels, there are relative PIM/PSM models, that can be either associated with subclasses of devices, or to design decisions reflecting particular choices regarding to platforms (architectural, technological, etc.) and that somehow introduce a certain degree of dependence. Depending on the point of view, an intermediate model can be seen as a PIM or a PSM; a model can be seen as a PSM when looking from a preceding higher abstraction model level, and can be seen as a PIM when looking from next lower abstraction model level. Note that for some development structures, these levels may eventually not exist, as it is possible to generate the bottom-level PSM or even the code itself (in Figure 16, DevStructure1, DevStructure4, and DevStructure5 do not have intermediate model levels do not have these intermediate levels). For illustration purposes, Figure 16 considers a simple case where one functional profile was assigned to (and corresponding development structure created) for each class. Nonetheless, a class may have several functional profiles, and consequently, several development structures.

Figure 16. Structure of PIMs and PSMs inherent to the previous device's classification

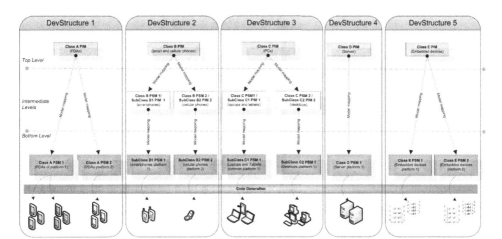

3.   **Bottom modelling level:** At this level, there are the ultimate PSMs from which the final code will be produced (either automatically generated or handcrafted). Note that from a PSM it may be possible to derive two or more different code artefacts due to slight platform differences where the code will be deployed. Such a task is usually delegated on the proper compiler or code generator, as for example, some particular differences on central processing units). Note also that a PIM may be directly transformed into code and, therefore, there is no need to have an ultimate PSM before code generation, as illustrated in reasoning through modelling levels.

The transformations between models are realized through model mappings. The two kinds of model mappings that exist in the development structures are:

1.   **Vertical model mappings:** Between modelling levels, there are vertical model mappings, which are based on well-established transformations that allow the transformation of a model to an equivalent model at a lower abstraction level. This is the mechanism that brings a more abstract system's model to a more concrete and refined system's model nearer to technological aspects and to its final realization (Figure 17 illustrates these kinds of mappings).

2.   **Horizontal model mappings:** Not expressed on Figure 16, are possible horizontal model mappings that, keeping the models at the same modelling level of abstraction, ,through specific transformations, other goals than the one of

Figure 17. Illustration of the abstraction process

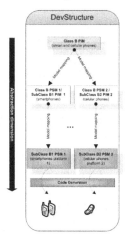

Figure 18. Direct code generation

decreasing the abstraction level. For example, these horizontal model mappings (see Figure 19) may exist in order to fulfil validation goals (uPAIN project presented before used horizontal mappings when creating the requirements' validation prototype through the CPN models).

Therefore, there are three dimensions pertaining to PIS software development--classes dimension, functional dimension, and abstraction dimension, as illustrated by Figure 20.

Figure 19. Horizontal mappings

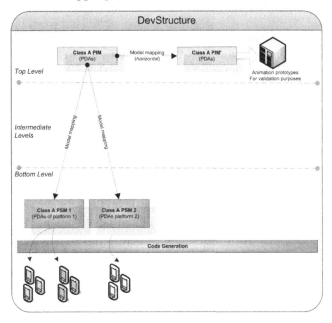

Figure 20. Dimensions on the development of pervasive information systems

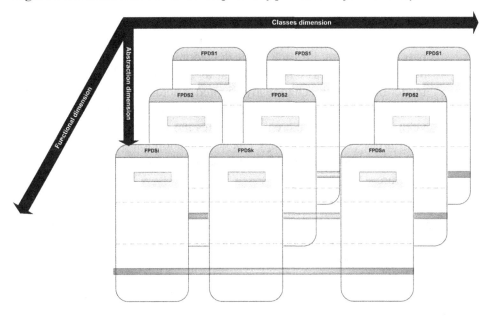

Development Framework

The development framework in which the concepts of these dimensions are integrated is illustrated in Figure 21, which presents a schema depicting a framework for a global system development for PIS. Essentially this framework proposes:

1. **Global development process.** A global development process is responsible for modelling requirements and for establishing high-level global system models (such as the logical architecture model of the whole system and the use case model of the system that expresses the functionality demand and expect from the system). From these, combinations of functional and device's type classes profiles are determined, and the high-level PIM for each combination needed on the system are specified. The global development process can establish milestones that each individual structure development has to accomplish. This framework also eases the assignment of those structure units to different collaborating teams, and eventually, to outsource the development. The global development process also is responsible for making all the necessary arrangements for integration of the several resulting artefacts from individual threads of development, and for final composition, testing, and deployment of the system.

2. **Individual development processes.** Development structures do not have to follow the same development process to carry out the development of that part of the system; for each of the development structures the *most adequate development process can be chosen*, as long as it respects the principles of model-driven approach globally adopted. Therefore, individual development structures for functional profiles may be subject of their own thread of development process; Figure 21 illustrates those as *individual FPDS development processes*. This strategy enables the adoption of development process and techniques most suitable to development of that individual development structure.

Besides the traditional documentation, a model-driven development approach should provide documentation for each development structure (which are units of development). Among this documentation, it should be found information about the platform independent models (PIMs) at the top model-level, PIMs/PSMs at the intermediate model-level, the PSM at the bottom model-level, the mappings (either vertical or horizontal) and inherent transformation rules used on the model's transformations, as well as information regarding to code generation.

It becomes clear that suitable CASE tools are needed to support global and individual development process developments as herein proposed. Use of well-established

Figure 21. Development framework for PIS

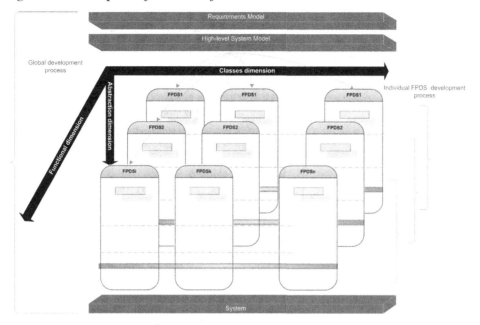

standards on languages and techniques for modelling (models and transformations models), support for code generation, change management, ad documentation of all artefacts, and design decisions are also expected from case tools.

Concluding the MDD approach for PIS presented, Table 1 presents a synthesis of the main concepts introduced.

Conclusion

This chapter focused on design methodologies for pervasive information systems, aiming to contribute to providing increased efficiency and effectiveness in the development of ubiquitous services/applications supported on pervasive systems composed of conveniently orchestrated embedded or mobile computing devices.

Considering the potential large number of computational devices, their high heterogeneity, and increasingly frequent changes needed on software at device and system levels, it turns out that attention is needed to design methodology in order to define and apply the best approaches and techniques to software development for pervasive information systems. In particular, model-driven development approaches

Table 1. Main concepts of the proposed approach to MDD for PIS

Concepts	Meaning
Class of devices	Heterogeneous devices are grouped into *classes of devices* (it can also be seen as categories) reflecting common basic resource and capabilities of the devices.
Development structure	Different *development structures* for the different functional profiles of the classes of devices reflect pathways of software development in order to satisfy major classes' functionality.
Modelling levels	For each of the development structures and transversal to all of the development structures, there are several *modelling levels*.
---Top level	*At the top level*, the platform-independent model (PIM) for each of class of devices is derived from models resulted from development of the system as a whole.
Intermediate levels	*At intermediate levels*, there are relative PSM/PIM models associated to subclasses.
---Bottom level	*At the bottom model level*, there are the ultimate (Platform-Specific Models) PSMs from which the final code is produced (either automatically generated or handcrafted).
Vertical model mappings	Between the model levels, there are *vertical model mappings*, which are based on well-established transformations, bring the abstract system's models to a more concrete and refined system model, nearer to technological aspects and to its final realization.
Horizontal model mapping	*Horizontal model mappings* are mappings that, keeping the models at the same modelling level, have the purpose to achieve, through specific transformations, other goals than the one of a decrease on the abstraction level. For example, these horizontal model mappings may exist in order to fulfil validation goals.
Dimensions	MDD for PIS have three dimensions concerning the software development.
---Classes dimension	Dimension that focus on classification of devices in classes according to common properties and capabilities of these devices
---Functional dimension	Dimension that focus on functional profiles specified for classes of devices
---Abstraction dimension	Dimension concerned with transformation of models from higher-levels to low-levels of models abstraction
Global development process	Main thrust of development effort responsible for modelling requirements and for the establishment of high-level global system's models. From these, combinations of functional and device's type classes profiles are determined, and the high-level PIM for each combination needed on the system are specified.
Individual FPDS development process	Individual development structures corresponding to the referred combinations are subject of their own thread of development process referred as *Individual FPDS development processes*.

(which essentially centre around the focus of development in models, and involves concepts such as Platform-Independent Models, Platform-Specific Models, model transformations, and use of established standards) currently in research at academic and industrial arenas to design of large systems, offer potential benefits that can be applied to the design and evolution of these pervasive information systems.

On a vision of model-driven development for pervasive information systems, other issues can be further explored, such as peer-to-peer device interaction, which can, for example, constitute an alternative way to provide partial functionality of the system on a contingency situation. Such peer-to-peer communication would allow the increase of system effectiveness due to an augment of system tolerance to sector faults. Another issue for further exploration is a "competencies delegation technique." Such a technique, applied to a given unit that is having continuous or extended faults, would do the necessary transformations in order to delegate the missing functionality to other unit(s) that could provide such functionality within and acceptable satisfaction. This poses challenging issues to modelling of strategies or mechanisms to deal with this situation.

The effort of analyzing real projects whose main purpose is the development of pervasive computing systems should be kept by the scientific community to allow a thorough understanding of the fundamental issues that model-driven methodologies should be capable of dealing with. Nowadays, pervasive computing systems are still considered a "special" kind of systems; however, in the near future, they will be so common that nobody will consider them to be "special" anymore. This will demand a completely transparent capability of designing computing solutions by means of model manipulations and technology abstraction.

References

Abowd, G. D., & Mynatt, E. D. (2000). Charting Past, Present, and Future Research in Ubiquitous Computing. *ACM Transactions on Computer-Human Interaction, 7*(1), 29-58.

Abowd, G. D., Mynatt, E. D., & Rodden, T. (2002). The human experience [of ubiquitous computing]. *Pervasive Computing, IEEE, 1,* 48-57.

Atkinson, C., & Kuhne, T. (2003). Model-driven development: a metamodeling foundation. *Software, IEEE, 20*(5), 36-41.

Banavar, G., Beck, J., Gluzberg, E., Munson, J., Sussman, J., & Zukowski, D. (2000). *Challenges: an application model for pervasive computing.* Paper presented at the 6th Annual International Conference on Mobile Computing and Networking, Boston, MA, USA.

Birnbaum, J. (1997). Pervasive Information Systems. *Communications of ACM, 40*(2), 40-41.

Burrell, J., Brooke, T., & Beckwith, R. (2004). Vineyard computing: sensor networks in agricultural production. *Pervasive Computing, IEEE, 3,* 38-45.

Dryer, D. C., Eisbach, C., & Ark, W. S. (1999). At what cost pervasive? A social computing view of mobile computing systems. *IBM Systems Journal, 38*(4), 652-676.

Fernandes, J., & Machado, R. J. (2001). *From use cases to objects: an industrial information systems case study analysis.* Paper presented at the 7th International Conference on Object-Oriented Information Systems (OOIS'01), Calgary, Canada.

Fernandes, J. E., Machado, R. J., & Carvalho, J. Á. (2004, May). *Model-driven methodologies for pervasive information systems development.* Paper presented at the MOMPES'04 - 1st International Workshop on Model-Based Methodologies for Pervasive and Embedded Software, Hamilton, Ontario, Canada.

Fleck, M., Frid, M., Kindberg, T., O'Brien-Strain, E., Rajani, R., & Spasojevic, M. (2002). From informing to remembering: ubiquitous systems in interactive museums. *Pervasive Computing, IEEE, 1,* 13-21.

Gates, B. (2007). A Robot in every home. *Scientific American, 296,* 58-65.

Gordon, S. R., & Gordon, J. R. (2004). *Information Systems—A Management Approach* (3rd ed.): Wiley.

Grimm, R. (2004). One.world: Experiences with a Pervasive Computing Architecture. *Pervasive Computing, IEEE, 03,* 22-30.

Grimm, R., Davis, J., Hendrickson, B., Lemar, E., MacBeth, A., Swanson, S., et al. (2001). *Systems directions for pervasive computing.* Paper presented at the Hot Topics in Operating Systems.

Hansmann, U., Merck, L., Nicklous, M. S., & Stober, T. (2003). *Pervasve Computing* (2nd ed.): Springer.

HSOG. Hospital da Senhora da Oliveira, Guimarães. Retrieved on October 2006, 11th, from http://www.hguimaraes.min-saude.pt/

Kindberg, T., & Fox, A. (2002). System software for ubiquitous computing. *Pervasive Computing, IEEE, 1,* 70-81.

Langheinrich, M., Coroama, V., Bohn, J., & Rohs, M. (2002). *As we may live – Real-world implications of ubiquitous computing*: Distributed Systems Group, Institute of Information Systems, Swiss Federal Institute of Technology, ETH Zurich, Switzerland.

Lyytinen, K., & Yoo, Y. (2002). Introduction [Issues and challenges in ubiquitous computing]. *Communications of ACM, 45*(12), 62-65.

Machado, R. J., Lassen, K. B., Oliveira, S., Couto, M., & Pinto, P. (2007). Requirements Validation: Execution of UML Models with CPN Tools. *International Journal on Software Tools for Technology Transfer (STTT), 9*(3-4), 353-369.

Mattern, F. (2001). The vision and techical foundations of ubiquitous computing. *UPGRADE, 2*(5), 3-5.

Mellor, S. J., Clark, A. N., & Futagami, T. (2003). Model-driven development - Guest editor's introduction. *Software, IEEE, 20*(5), 14-18.

Miller, G., Ambler, S., Cook, S., Mellor, S., Frank, K., & Kern, J. (2004). *Model driven architecture: the realities, a year later.* Paper presented at the Companion to the 19th annual ACM SIGPLAN conference on Object-oriented programming systems, languages, and applications.

MobiComp. MobiComp—Computação Móvel, Lda. from http://www.mobicomp.com/

OMG. (2003). OMG's MDA Guide Version 1.0.1. Retrieved on April 2007, from http://www.omg.org/docs/omg/03-06-01.pdf

Sage, A. P., & Rouse, W. B. (1999). Information Systems Frontiers in Knowledge Management. *Information Systems Frontiers, 1*(3), 205-219.

Saha, D., & Mukherjee, A. (2003). Pervasive computing: a paradigm for the 21st century. *Computer, 36*(3), 25-31.

Satyanarayanan, M. (2001). Pervasive computing: vision and challenges. *Personal Communications, IEEE [see also IEEE Wireless Communications], 8*(4), 10-17.

Schmoelzer, G., Teiniker, E., Mitterdorfer, S., Kreiner, C., Kovacs, Z., & Weiss, R. (2004). *Model-driven development of recursive CORBA component assemblies.* Paper presented at the 30th Euromicro Conference.

Selic, B. (2003a). *Model-driven development of real-time software using OMG standards.* Paper presented at the Sixth IEEE International Symposium on Object-Oriented Real-Time Distributed Computing, (ISORC'03).

Selic, B. (2003b). The pragmatics of model-driven development. *Software, IEEE, 20*(5), 19-25.

Sendall, S., & Kozaczynski, W. (2003). Model transformation: the heart and soul of model-driven software development. *Software, IEEE, 20*(5), 42-45.

Sommerville, I. (2001). *Software Engineering* (6th ed.): Addison-Wesley.

Stanford, V. (2003). Pervasive computing puts food on the table. *Pervasive Computing, IEEE, 2*, 9-14.

Stone, A. (2003). The dark side of pervasive computing. *Pervasive Computing, IEEE, 2*, 4-8.

Suzuki, K. (2004). *Ubiquitous services and networking: monitoring the real world.* Paper presented at the International Symposium on Applications and the Internet.

Turban, E., McLean, E., & Wetherbe, J. (2001). *Information Technology for Management: Transforming Business in the Digital Economy* (3rd ed.): John Wiley & Sons Inc.

UMinho-DSI. Minho University's Information System's Department (DSI) from http://www.dsi.uminho.pt/

Varshney, U. (2003). Pervasive healthcare. *Computer, 36*(12), 138-140.

Weiser, M. (1991). The Computer for the 21st Century. *Scientific American, 265*(3), 94-104.

Weiser, M. (1993a). Hot topics-ubiquitous computing. *Computer, 26*(10), 71-72.

Weiser, M. (1993b). Some computer science issues in ubiquitous computing. *Communications of ACM, 36*(7), 75-84.

Chapter IV

Device Localization in Ubiquitous Computing Environments

Rui Huang, The University of Texas at Arlington, USA

Gergely V. Záruba, The University of Texas at Arlington, USA

Sajal Das, The University of Texas at Arlington, USA

Abstract

In this chapter, we will study the localization problem in ubiquitous computing environments. In general, localization refers to the problem of obtaining (semi-) accurate physical location of the devices in a dynamic environment in which only a small subset of the devices know their exact location. Using localization techniques, other devices can indirectly derive their own location by means of some measurement data such as distance and angle to their neighbors. Localization is now regarded as an enabling technology for ubiquitous computing environments because it can substantially increase the performance of other fundamental tasks such as routing, energy conservation, and network security. Localization is also a difficult problem because it is computationally intractable. Furthermore, it has to be implemented in a highly dynamic and distributed environment in which measurement data is often subject to noise. In this chapter, we will give an overview of localization in terms of its common applications, its hardware capacities, its algorithms, and its computational complexity.

Introduction

In a ubiquitous computing environment, devices are often connected to one another on the fly to form an infrastructure-less network that is frequently referred to as a mobile ad hoc network (MANET). Since MANET serves as an abstract model that can be seen as a superset of diverse sub-areas such as sensor networks, mesh networks or an enabler for pervasive computing, it has attracted significant research interests in the past several years. A major advantage of MANETs over regular wired or wireless networks is their infrastructure-less nature, as MANETs can potentially be deployed more rapidly and less expensively than infrastructure-based networks. However, the lack of an underlying explicit infrastructure also becomes a major disadvantage in adapting MANETs to a wider array of applications, since existing network algorithms and protocols are often not "plug-in" solutions for such dynamic networks. New algorithms need to be designed for fundamental network tasks such as addressing, topology discovery, and routing.

Location discovery is emerging as one of the more important tasks as it has been observed that (semi-) accurate location information can greatly improve the performance of other MANET tasks such as routing, energy conservation, or maintaining network security. For instance, algorithms such as location aided routing (LAR) (Ko, 2000), GRID (Liao, 2001), and GOAFR+ (Kuhn, 2003) rely on location information to provide more stable routes during unicast route discovery. The availability of location information is also required for geocast (multicast based on geographic information (Jiang, 2002)) algorithms such as location-based multicast (LBM) (Ko, 1999), GeoGRID (Liao, 2000) and position-based multicast (PBM) (Mauve, 2003). To minimize power consumption, the geographical adaptive fidelity(GAF) algorithm (Xu, 2001) uses location information to effectively modify the network density by turning off certain nodes at particular instances. Furthermore, in (Hu, 2003), the authors have shown that wormhole attacks can be effectively prevented when location information is available. As more algorithms are being proposed to exploit location information of devices in ubiquitous networks, it is clear that obtaining such information efficiently and accurately becomes of great importance.

A direct way of obtaining location information is to install global positioning system (GPS) receivers on devices. However, this is currently impractical as GPS receivers are still relatively expensive, power-hungry, and require clear line of sight (i.e., making indoor usage impossible) to several earth-bound satellites. In ubiquitous environments (e.g., sensor networks), devices are imagined as small as possible and operating on a very restricted power source, thus, it may not be feasible to install GPS receivers onto all sensor nodes. *Localization* in MANET refers to the problem of finding the locations of those non-GPS enabled nodes based on limited information such as the locations of some known *beacons* (also referred to as *anchors*) and measurements such as *ranges* or *angles* among the neighbors. In this chapter, we will study why localization is important and how it can be accomplished within the ubiquitous computing environment.

Background

The localization problem is hard for a number of reasons:

1   **Geometric limitations:** To pinpoint its exact location in 2-D, a node needs to know the locations and its distances to at least three beacons. Alternatively, nodes could calculate their own location based on a distance and an (absolute) angle measurement from one beacon. However, even if obtaining such measurements were possible and the measurements were exact, guaranteeing that the right number of beacons surround each node is often impossible since MANETs may be randomly deployed and that in general only a small percentage of nodes are indeed beacons. Thus, localization algorithms often need to take advantage of multi-hop information, that is, estimating node locations based on other nodes' location estimates.

2   **Availability of measurements:** For localization algorithms that require distance or angle measurements, certain sensory devices will need to be available to provide such readings. However, it is likely that not all nodes have the same sensory capacity. In other words, there is a need for the localization algorithm to work in a heterogeneous environment, in which devices with different location sensory capacities coexist.

3   **Measurement error and error propagation:** Even when measurement devices are available, there is a general consensus that those measurements are prone to errors. For instance, a distance measurement can be derived based on a received signal strength indication (RSSI) reading, in which a receiving device measures the strength of the signal from a sending device and obtains the distance via an estimated signal propagation model. RSSI reading is prone to multi-path fading and far field scattering. The error can be especially high when there are a significant number of obstacles in between the sender and the receiver. Since most localization algorithms require measurements from nodes several hops away, the measurement error is likely to aggregate along the path and eventually completely throw off the location estimate.

Despite the difficulties listed above, there is an increasing amount research effort spent on the localization problem. The amount of effort is justified because localization is considered an enabling technology that needs to be resolved with the best possible outcome upon which other location-dependent technologies for MANETs can be successfully employed. Researchers have been working on problem in both hardware (i.e., improving measurement accuracy of devices) and software (i.e., improving the localization algorithm design). This chapter covers the latest advances in this field, including the following topics:

1. **Applications of localization:** In this section, we will establish the need for better localization techniques by surveying a number of proposed algorithms for MANETs that rely on localization.

2. **Measurement types for localization:** In this section, we will cover the latest advances in hardware design that enables localization on the smaller devices commonly seen in the ubiquitous computing environment, including the devices that measure distance ranging, angle of arrival (AoA), and interferometric ranging.

3. **Survey of localization algorithms:** We will survey some of the most popular localization algorithms, including those using connectivity information, ranging, and angle information. We will study the pros and cons of each algorithm, and suggest their appropriate applications in ubiquitous computing.

4. **Localization theory:** We will cover the theoretic basis of localization techniques. We will study the necessary and sufficient conditions for a network to be localized based on the latest results from graph theory. We will show that the localization problem in general is NP-Complete. We will also introduce the reader to the Cramer Rao Bound (CRB) that is often used to analyze the hardness of different localization scenarios.

5. **Future directions:** We will look into a number of promising future directions for the localization techniques.

Applications of Localization

There have been numerous algorithms proposed for MANETs that rely on localization data; in this section, we provide a brief survey of these algorithms. We will consider algorithms in four categories based on their functionalities: unicast routing; multicast routing; energy consideration; and network security.

Unicast Routing

Routing refers to the task of finding the correct route from a sending device (*source*) to a receiving device (*destination*). Routing is an especially challenging task for

MANETs because their frequent topology change implies the underlying instability of any established routes. As such, routes are needed to be frequently rediscovered, reestablished, and repaired. In general, routing (i.e., route discovery and repair) involves flooding the routing control packets throughout the network. Flooding can often be expensive in terms of delay and bandwidth usage it incurs, both of which can greatly affect the network performance. Thus, there is a strong incentive to design efficient routing algorithms that minimize the overhead caused by any unnecessary packet flooding. Unicast routing based on location information, often called *geometric routing* or *location based routing*, has shown to be one of the viable solutions to this problem.

Location-aided routing (LAR) (Ko, 2000) protocol is the first MANET routing algorithm proposed that uses location data. In LAR, every node is assumed to know its own location, and each individual location is then periodically broadcast throughout the network. Thus, at any time t, every node knows the locations of any other nodes at some previous time $<t$. Based on this location information and an estimated velocity, a node can derive an estimated location range, called "expected zone," of a target node at the current time. Instead of flooding the entire network, the routing request packets can be directed to search for the target node only at this expected zone. Global flooding is performed only after the location based routing request has failed. Limiting route discovery to a smaller expected zone with LAR reduces the number of routing requests compared to the standard flooding scheme.

GRID (Liao, 2001) protocol uses location information as a way to form geographical clusters within the network. Based on node locations and their residency within a pre-determined grid system, nodes within the same grid block are grouped into a cluster. A cluster head or "gateway" in (Liao, 2001) is then selected for each grid block. The cluster head is responsible for servicing the routing packets. Furthermore, the cluster head can monitor the status of existing routes and reroute packets as deemed necessary. Since the cluster formation effectively simplifies the network topology, the routing overhead is reduced. A critical requirement of forming such geographical-based clusters is the availability of node location information.

In (Kuhn, 2003), the authors provided a theoretical bound to the geometric routing problem and proposed an algorithm called GOAFR+. Assuming that node locations are known using some localization technique, GOAFR+ first tries to greedily route the packet by forwarding it to the neighbor located closest to the destination. However, such greedy selection does not guarantee message delivery since the intermediate node closest to the destination might not have a route to it. In such cases, GOAFR+ explores the boundaries of the faces of a planarized network graph by employing the local right hand rule (i.e., always turn right) to escape the local minimum. This method of escaping local minima is also called "parameter routing," which is used in a number of other location based routing protocols as well.

In terms of performance, simulations performed by (Ko, 2000) and (Liao, 2001) have shown up to 50% of reduction in routing packets when using geographic routing compared to standard flooding. Since the overhead of flooding is proportional to network density, it has been observed that the amount of performance gain becomes more significant when network density is increased. Furthermore, although the routing performance is impacted by the localization error, such impact is observed to be minimal. This indicates that in the case of routing, highly precise location data is not required. After all, location data is used by routing algorithms to give a direction that guides the routing packets; imprecise location data can still be used as long as the general direction is valid.

Multicast Routing

Similar to unicast routing, multicast routing can also benefit from location data. Multicast routing using geographic information is often referred to in the literature as *geocast routing*. The Location-Based Multicast (LBM) algorithm (Ko, 1999) is a multicast extension to the unicast Location-Aided Routing (LAR). Like LAR, which forwards the routing requests according to the location of the destination node, LBM forwards the requests according to the direction of the geocast region that contains all the multicast destinations. GeoGRID (Liao, 2000) is the multicast extension to GRID (Liao, 2001). Like in GRID, location information is used by GeoGRID to identify the grid block where nodes reside. Multicast is done through the gateway node selected at each grid block. Based on the location of the source node and the geocast region, LBM and GeoGRID define a "forwarding region" that contains the intermediate nodes responsible for forwarding packets. The size and shape of the forwarding region have a direct impact on the overall performance; shapes such as rectangles and cones have been proposed in (Ko, 1999).

While the standard shapes such as rectangles and cones work well in most cases, there are situations where viable routes exist only outside the forwarding region. For instance, a network can be partitioned into two sub-networks connected only through a narrow linkage due to some obstacles (e.g., two islands connected by a bridge). When the source and the destination are in separate partitions, a geometrically defined forwarding region is unlikely to cover the linkage. To prevent routing failure in such a case, a routing zone based on Voronoi diagrams was proposed in (Stojmenovic, 2006), which partitions the network graph based on the proximity of the nodes. Again, the proximity information relies on localization information.

The Position-Based Multicast (PBM) protocol proposed in (Mauve, 2003) attempts to optimize the multicast tree it generates by minimizing the overall path length and the overall bandwidth usage; two often contradictory objectives. To minimize the overall path length, PMB takes a greedy approach using location information. At each intermediate node, packets are forwarded to a set of neighbors based on their overall distances to the multicast destinations. In particular, a set of the neighbors with the minimum overall distance to every destination is selected as the next set of forwarding nodes. To take account of the bandwidth usage, the greedy selection also tries to minimize the size of the forwarding set. PBM also uses parameter routing to deal with local minima. Both greedy routing and parameter routing employed by PBM rely on the location information.

Power Management

MANET is often used as the model for sensor networks, an emerging technology for pervasive computing. One of the major challenges of sensor networks is power management. Since sensors are commonly small in size and are battery powered, conserving energy would prolong their service time and, thus, the lifespan of the entire network. The Geographical Adaptive Fidelity (GAF) algorithm (Xu, 2001) is a network topology management algorithm with reduced energy consumption as its primary objective. The idea behind GAF is that there are often a large number of nodes that are redundant during packet routing in MANETs. If the redundant nodes can be identified, they can then turn off their radio to save energy. For GAF, the identification of redundant nodes is accomplished by analyzing the relative location information among the neighboring nodes. More specifically, GAF divides the network into virtual grids such that all nodes in grid block *A* are the neighbors of all nodes in grid block *B*. This way, all nodes within the same virtual grid block can be considered equivalent. To conserve energy during packet routing, GAF only turns on the radio for one of the nodes in each grid block. The active node is periodically "round-robinned" to achieve load-balancing. Analysis and simulations performed in (Xu, 2001) show that GAF can reduce overall energy consumption by 40% to 60%.

Security

In (Hu, 2003) the authors proposed a technique called "packet leashes" to defend against wormhole attacks in MANETs. A wormhole attack is a type of security breach where an adversary intercepts incoming packets and tunnels them to another part of the network via a single long-range directional wireless link or through a direct wired link. From there, the adversary can retransmit the packets to the network. Note that this type of "capture-and-retransmit" attack can be immune to common packet encryption methods, since the adversary does not need to read the packet content. Wormhole attacks can severely disrupt ad hoc routing protocols such as Ad hoc On-Demand Distance Vector Routing (AODV) or Dynamic Source Routing (DSR), and cause a denial of service to the network. The core of "packet leashes" is based on two assumptions: i) all nodes know their own locations; and ii) all nodes are synchronized. To enable packet leashes, the sender node encloses its location and transmission time-stamp within the packet. At the receiver node, the packet leash is validated against the receiver's own location and clock. In particular, the sender location information gives the distance from the original sender to the receiver, and the time-stamp gives the transmission duration of the packet. Based on the transmission duration and signal propagation model, factored in some error tolerance, the receiver can validate the estimated distance the packet has traveled against the true distance to determine whether the packet is indeed coming from the original sender or an imposer at some other location. Thus, the location information and time-stamp provide a virtual leash to limit the effective range of the packet so that it cannot be exploited by wormhole attackers.

From the previous discussion on the location-dependent algorithms that encompass a wide range of problem domains, it is clear that providing location information (i.e., localization) to MANETs is becoming an increasingly important task. In fact, localization is now widely regarded as an "enabling technology" for MANETs that needs to be addressed before other location-dependent techniques can be realized in the real world (Patwari, 2003).

Measurement Types for Localization

In this section, we study a number of measurement types provided by onboard hardware devices that enable localization in MANETs for ubiquitous computing environments. A Global Positioning System (GPS) (Parkinson, 1996) receiver can provide the absolute location. However, its cost, size, and power requirement prevent it from being installed at every network node. How do nodes not equipped with GPS obtain their location information then? They have to rely on sensory measurements provided by alternative hardware devices. There are five general types of measurements: i) connectivity only; ii) RSSI (radio signal strength indicator) ranging; iii) ToA (time of arrival) ranging; iv) AoA (angle of arrival), and v) interferometric ranging. We will describe each of their capacity, usage and mathematical models when applied to the localization problem.

Connectivity Only Measurement

At a minimum, a node can detect connectivity to its immediate neighbors, that is, its one-hop neighborhood. The connectivity only measurement is a binary reading between two nodes of either "true" or "false" indicating whether they are neighbors. Based on this connectivity information, one can derive the general proximity of the nodes as a way to localize the network.

RSSI Ranging Measurement

A node can be localized using multilateration (Niculescu, 2001) if the distances (i.e., the ranges) to three or more known locations are obtained. The distances can be obtained, for example, by measuring RSSI (radio signal strength indicator) or ToA (time of arrival). In RSSI, the receiver measures the received signal strength and compares it with the transmitted signal strength. The difference (in dB) is then applied to the inverse of the signal propagation model to provide a distance estimate. Sensors that measure RSSI are widely available to mobile devices. Indeed, most off-the-shelf technologies implicitly provide such information (e.g., most WiFi, Bluetooth, and IEEE802.15.4 chipsets do). The drawback of RSSI-based measurements is that they can be very inaccurate because an exact model of the propagation environment is often unavailable. Experiments in (Savvides, 2001) have shown that when no obstacle exists between the sender and the receiver, RSSI can provide a distance estimate of accuracy within a few meters. However, in a less than ideal environment, the result is often unpredictable. Furthermore, low cost RSSI receivers are often variable in their transmission power due to the lack of calibration.

In the outdoor environment with a minimum of obstacles, signal propagation decay is proportional to d^{n_p}, where d is the distance the signal has traveled, and p is an environment-dependent path loss exponent. However, in the actual environment where obstacles exist, multipath signals and shadowing become two major sources of noise that impact the actual RSSI. In general, those noises are commonly modeled as a random process during localization. Let $P_{i,j}$ be the RSSI (in dB) obtained at the receiver node j from the sender node i. $P_{i,j}$ is commonly modeled as a Normal distribution (Patwari, 2003)

$$P_{i,j} = N(\overline{P}_{i,j}, \sigma_{dB}^2) \tag{1}$$

where $\overline{P}_{i,j}$ is the mean power in dB and σ_{dB}^2 is the variance caused by noise factor such as shadowing. $\overline{P}_{i,j}$ is further defined as the power reduction from a reference location:

$$\overline{P}_{i,j} = P_0 - 10n_p \log_{10}(d_{i,j} / d_0) \tag{2}$$

where P_0 is the power at a reference location at the distance d_0 (commonly $d_0 = 1m$). p is an environment-dependent path loss exponent that is assumed to be known from prior measurements (theoretically $p = 2$). $d_{i,j}$ is the Euclidean distance between nodes i and j.

ToA Ranging Measurement

Although ToA is used for radio signals in GPS, it is mostly used in the context of acoustic or ultrasonic signals in inexpensive ToA tracking (as propagation speeds are five orders of magnitude less). For instance, the Medusa node in (Savvides, 2001) is an implementation of ToA ranging using ultrasonic signals. ToA measures the time signals travel from the sender to the receiver. The distance between nodes is obtained by multiplying this time with the signal propagation speed. In spite of the additive noise and multipath, in general distance measures based on ToA are more accurate than RSSI-based measures. However, special acoustic transceivers have to be employed on each node and synchronization among the nodes needs to be established. Clock synchronization algorithms designed for sensor networks that are accurate to the order of $10\mu s$ have been reported (Sivrikaya, 2004). As mentioned earlier, ToA may also be used together with radio signals, but current technology is not mature enough to provide satisfactory precision over smaller distances inexpensively.

Let i be the sender node and j be the receiver node, ToA measurement $T_{i,j}$ is often modeled as a Normal distribution (Patwari, 2003):

$$T_{i,j} = N(d_{i,j}/c, \sigma_T^2)$$

where $d_{i,j}$ is the Euclidean distance between i and j, c is the signal propagation speed, and σ_T^2 is the variance caused by noise.

AoA Measurement

A node can be localized if the angles between it and two beacons are known. Thus, the angle information (i.e., bearing, or angle of arrival (AoA)) can be used to localize the network. Currently, there is no off-the-self device that offers AoA sensing capability. However, a number of prototype devices are available. For instance, Cricket Compass (Priyantha, 2001) is a small form device that uses ultrasonic measurements and fixed beacons to obtain acoustic signal orientations. In (Niculescu, 2004) a rotating directional antenna is attached to an 801.11b base station; by measuring the maximum received signal strength, a median error of can be obtained from the sensor. The challenge here is to design AoA sensing devices with small form factor and low energy consumption. In (Chintalapudi, 2004), the authors outline a solution with a ring of charge-coupled devices (CCDs) to measure AoA with relatively low energy consumption.

In general, AoA is also modeled as a Normal distribution. Let the true angle between the sender i and j be $\bar{A}_{i,j}$, the AoA measurement between i and j is therefore

$$A_{i,j} = N(\bar{A}_{i,j}, \sigma_A^2)$$

where σ_A^2 is the angle variance. Theoretical results for acoustic-based AoA estimation show standard deviation σ_A is between to, depending on range (Patwari, 2005). RSSI-based AoA method with σ_A on the order of has been reported in (Ash, 2004).

Interferometric Ranging Measurement

Interferometric ranging is a "widely used technique in both radio and optical astronomy to determine the precise angular position of celestial bodies as well as objects on the ground (Kusý, 2006)." Interferometric ranging exploits the property that the relative phase offset between two receivers determines their distances to two simultaneous senders. Due to the recent advancement in hardware, it is now possible to implement interferometric ranging sensors in much smaller form factor to be used for localization (Maróti, 2005). By synchronizing the transmission at the two senders, each of which sends a signal at a slightly different frequency, the receivers can derive the relative phase offset of the two signals by comparing the RSSI readings. The distance difference (also called the *q-range*) can then be calculated from the relative phase offset with high accuracy. A *q-range* obtained from interferometric ranging from two senders A and B, and two receivers C and D is the distance difference $d_{ABCD} = d_{AD} - d_{BD} + d_{BC} - d_{AC} + e$ where e is the measurement error (Figure 1).

Figure 1. The interferometric ranging measurement of the q-range $d_{ABCD} = d_{AD} - d_{BD} + d_{BC} - d_{AC} + e$. Here, node A and B are the senders, and node C and D are the receivers.

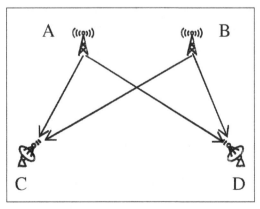

A major advantage of interferometric ranging is that the measurement could be extremely accurate compared to noise-prone RSSI readings. In a recent experiment (Maróti, 2005), in which 16 nodes are deployed in a 4x4 grid over a 18x18 meter flat grassy area with no obstruction, the maximum q-range error was shown to be around 0.1 meters while the medium error was less than 0.04 meters. However, interferometric ranging is more difficult to implement due to the following reasons.

1. The measurement can be impacted by various sources of noise such as frequency drift, ground multipath error, and time synchronization error (Maróti, 2005). Frequencies of the transmissions need to be precisely calibrated, as any carrier frequency drift and phase noise would directly impact the observed phase offset. Precise time synchronization is needed at the senders of a q-range. Thus, there will be overhead to maintain clock synchronization.

2. A significantly larger number of measurements are required for localization than using direct ranging techniques. While there are also a large number of measurements available ($O(n^4)$) even for a small network, only a small subset of them are independent of each other. The rest merely provide redundant information. It has been shown in (Kusý, 2006) that the number of independent measurement using interferometric measurements is $O(n^2)$, which is significantly higher than with RSSI and AoA ranging ($O(n)$). Considering the localization problem in relative coordinates, for a network of n nodes there are $2n-3$ unknowns in two dimensions and $3n-6$ unknowns in three dimensions. This is because the relative coordinates are invariant under translation, rotation, and reflection. Thus, in two dimensions, we have $2n-3$ degrees of freedom, where translation, rotation, and reflection each reduce one degree of freedom. Thus, the smallest network that can be localized using interferometric measurements is a fully-connected network with a population of $n=6$, where there are 9 independent measurements available to cover 9 unknowns. The large number of q-ranges available/required indicates a scalability issue for larger networks.

3. Since each measurement involves four nodes, more collaboration is required between nodes. Due to the requirement of synchronized transmission, the senders have to collaborate in scheduling their transmission. Also, the receivers have to collaborate to derive the relative phase offset. Such collaboration requires sophisticated protocols to be implemented in order to reduce the communication overhead.

Those difficulties rooted in the physical characteristics of interferometric ranging devices affect the algorithmic design of the localization algorithm. As we will see in the following section, the localization algorithms based on interferometric ranging measurements tend to be more difficult to design.

Table 1. Measurement types for localization

	Nodes	Accuracy	Cost	Measured Value	Math Model
Connectivity	2	N/A	Low	Proximity	1 – if two nodes are connected; 0 – otherwise
RSSI	2	Low	Low	Distance $d_{i,j}$ between node i and j, derived from power $P_{i,j}$	$P_{i,j} = N(\bar{P}_{i,j}, \sigma_{dB}^2)$ $\bar{P}_{i,j} = P_0 - 10n_p \log_{10}(d_{i,j}/d_0)$
ToA	2	High	High	Distance $d_{i,j}$ between node i and j, derived from time of arrival $T_{i,j}$	$T_{i,j} = N(d_{i,j}/c, \sigma_T^2)$
AoA	2	Low/ Medium	N/A	Angle $A_{i,j}$ between node i and j,	$A_{i,j} = N(\bar{A}_{i,j}, \sigma_A^2)$
Interfero metric Ranging	4	Very High	Medium/ High	q-range (distance difference between four nodes)	q-range $d_{ABCD} = d_{AD} - d_{BD} + d_{BC} - d_{AC} + e$ between node A, B, C and D. Noise to each q-range is modeled using a Normal distribution

Table 1 summarizes the five measurement types described in this section.

Localization Algorithms

The previous section introduced the primary types of measurement that can be used for localization. However, obtaining measurements such as distance ranging and angle of arrival is only the first step of localization. To calculate the actual node location, we will have to mathematically incorporate those measurement readings to derive localization algorithms. While there are various ways of classifying localization algorithms, we feel it is more logical to classify them according to the measurement assumptions as follows: i) connectivity-only; ii) range-based; iii) angle-based; iv) interferometric ranging based; v) hybrid, and vi) mobility-based.

Connectivity-Based Algorithms

A number of localization methods rely on connectivity information only. These types of methods are also referred to as "range-free" methods in the literature. For instance, the Centroid method (Bulusu, 2000) estimates the location of an unknown node as the average of its neighboring beacon locations. Clearly, in order for the location estimate to be reasonably accurate, a large number of beacons need to be heard. Thus, to provide sufficient localization coverage, the Centroid method requires more powerful beacons with a large transmission range.

The APIT (Approximated Point-In-Triangulation) method (He, 2003) estimates the node location by isolating the area using various triangles formed by beacons. For each triangle formed by three beacons, the node is either in or out of the triangle. For instance in Figure 2(a), if it can be determined the node G is inside ABC and DEF, G's location can be isolated to the shaded overlapping area of the two triangles. To determine whether a node is inside or outside the triangle, APIT compares the RSSI readings from the beacons at the node with those at its neighbors. Intuitively, smaller RSSI reading means a shorter distance (i.e., closer to the beacon) and vice versa. If there does not exist a neighbor that is further from (or closer to) all beacons simultaneously, then the node is inside triangle with high probability. For instance in Figure 2(b), a neighbor of D, E, can be measured to be further away from the beacon A, B and C because it has smaller RSSI readings comparing to D. Thus, D is considered as to be outside ABC. Conversely, if D is inside ABC (Figure 2(c)), then it is likely that its neighbors will be closer to (or further away from) *some* (but not *all*) of the triangle points. Clearly, this test does not guarantee correctness every time. However, since there are a large number of triangles available for the test ($(O(n^3)$ for n beacons), error can be effectively controlled. Indeed, simulations performed in (He, 2003) indicated that APIT gives more accurate localization than the Centroid method when the beacon density is higher. Note that although APIT makes use of RSSI, it is only used to derive the relative proximity, but not the absolute distance. Thus, we classify APIT as a connectivity-based algorithm.

Both the Centroid and APIT methods try to localize the node directly from the beacons 1 hop away. Thus, to provide better localization coverage, they require either a large number of beacons or an extended beacon transmission range. The DV-Hop method (Niculescu, 2001) relaxes such requirement by providing a way

Figure 2. APIT. (a) localization using overlapping triangles; (b) node outside a triangle; (c) node inside a triangle

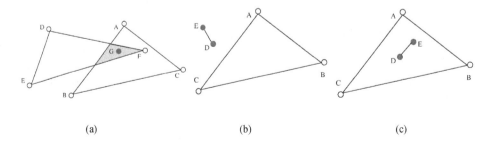

to localize from the beacons several hops away. In DV-Hop, each beacon floods its location to the entire network much like the distance vector (DV) routing protocol (Perkins, 1997). The algorithm contains two phases. In the first phase, a distance-per-hop estimate is obtained using DV. In the second phase, each node calculates its location estimate using the beacon locations and the distance-per-hop estimate. Each node maintains a DV table of the beacon locations it has heard along with the shortest hop count to them. A node will only forward the location broadcast if it has a shorter hop count than the current one in its table. In addition, when a beacon has heard the broadcast originated from another beacon, it can derive the distance-per-hop information based on the physical distance between the two beacons and the hop count accumulated along the path. The distance-per-hop information is then broadcast to other nodes. To localize, a node extracts the hop counts to the beacons from its DV table and converts them into distances using the average distance-per-hop information it has received. The node can then estimate its location using multilateration based on the distances to the beacons. For instance in Figure 3, the node D can triangulate based on the location broadcast from the beacons A, B, and C stored in its DV table. The distance-per-hop is calculated as the average of the distances per hop among all the beacons. Compared to Centroid and APIT, DV-Hop requires a much lower number of beacons. It does, however, have greater communication overhead since it requires multiple message flooding.

The above connectivity-based localization methods assume the nodes are stationary. The MCL (Monte Carlo localization) method (Hu, 2004) takes a novel approach by making use of node mobility. As a node moves, it becomes connected or disconnected to other nodes. Based on the connectivity observation, a unit-disk connectivity model, and a simple random movement model of the node, MCL updates the probability distribution of the possible node location. Simulation in (Hu, 2004) has reported as many as three times of localization accuracy when compared to the Centroid method.

Figure 3. DV-Hop

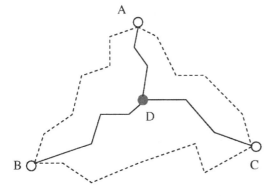

Node ID	Hop Count	Location	Distance
A	3	(100, 100)	distance-per-hop * 3
B	4	(0, 0)	distance-per-hop * 4
C	3	(200, 10)	distance-per-hop * 3

distance-per-hop = (|BC|/6 + |AB|/6 + |AC|/6)/3

In general, connectivity-based localization algorithms such as Centroid, APIT and DV-Hop tend to be simple to implement, and they depend less on special hardware. However, due to the lack of more precise measurement, the location estimates they provide tend to be less accurate. A large number of beacons need to be deployed in order to improve their accuracy. However, sparse networks by nature contain less connectivity information, and, thus, they are more difficult to localize accurately using connectivity-based localization methods.

RSSI and ToA Range-Based Algorithms

Many algorithms use the RSSI and ToA measurement to derive the distance to the senders. The DV-Distance method (Niculescu, 2001) behaves much like the connectivity-based DV-Hop method. But instead of incrementing the hop count, DV-Distance increments the distance between hop to hop as beacons broadcast their locations. Since the distance at each hop can be quite different, DV-Distance can obtain a more accurate range to the beacons compared to DV-Hop, which only considers the average case. However, its performance becomes dependent on the ranging measurement accuracy.

The Euclidean method (Niculescu, 2001) tries to derive the distance to a beacon that is several hops away by measuring RSSI or ToA to its neighbors. The distance is obtained by observing some simple Euclidean constraints. For instance in Figure 4, the node *D* is several hops away from the beacon *A*. To derive its distance to *A*, *D* obtains the distance using RSSI or ToA to two neighbors *B* and *C*, where the distance *AB*, *AC* and *BC* are known. The distance *AD* is the second diagonal of the quadrilateral *ABDC*. Depending on whether *ABDC* is convex or concave, two solutions of *AD* exist. This ambiguity can be resolved by examining multiple quadrilaterals like *ABDC*. Once the distances to at least three beacons have been

Figure 4. Multihop Distance Derivation in Euclidean

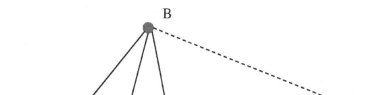

obtained, both DV-Distance and Euclidean method estimate the node location using multilateration.

The Collaborative Multilateration method (Savvides, 2001) is also based on multilateration from ranging. However, it allows nodes being triangulated from non-beacon nodes. Initially, all non-beacon nodes are assumed to be at some random locations. As a node receives its neighbors' estimated locations, it tries to triangulate its new location with the least mean square error. The newly estimated location is then sent back to the neighbors for their own multilateration. The process is iterated multiple times, and the idea is that eventually the location information from the beacons will propagate to remote nodes via collaborative multilateration. However, it is foreseeable that the nodes further away from the beacons would be slow to converge. The Hop-TERRAIN method (Savarese, 2002) makes an improvement in this regard by using the DV-Hop method to derive an initial coarse location. It then runs the collaborative multilateration to further refine the localization results from the distance and location information from the neighbors. The n-Hop Multilateration method proposed in (Savvides, 2003) uses a bounding box model instead of DV-Hop to provide initial location estimates. For instance in Figure 5, while node D is two hops away from the beacon B and one hop away from the beacon A, it is still bounded by distance constraints. The bound on the x coordinates is $[x_A - a, x_B + b + c]$, where $a=|AD|$, $b=|BC|$ and $c=|CD|$. Using this kind of geometric bounding through multiple hops, an initial location of the node can be derived.

The iterative multilateration provides a way to deal with the difficult question of how to effectively apply the beacon information several hops away. However, since it treats location estimates from non-beacons the same as beacons, the beacon information can be quickly watered down by the inaccuracy of non-beacons. The

Figure 5. Bounded Region in n-Hop Multilateration

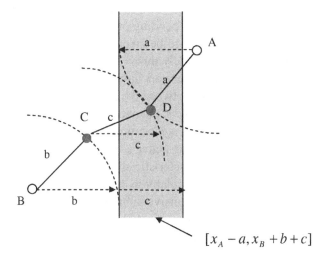

$$[x_A - a, x_B + b + c]$$

probabilistic localization method in (Huang, 2005) explicitly considers the location uncertainty of non-beacons by the means of probability distributions. In particular, each node location is not represented by a singular value, but a probability distribution in terms of particles. Initially, all non-beacons have a uniformly distributed particle distribution. To localize, nodes exchange their particle distributions among the neighbors and run Monte-Carlo filtering based on the RSSI or ToA measurement data to update the particles. Eventually, the particles will be refined to the true location of where the node resides. The particle filtering method allows collaborative localization as shown in Figure 6. Here, nodes 2, 3, and 4 are beacon nodes, while nodes 0 and 1 are non-beacons. Of the beacons, node 0 can receive signals only from nodes 1 and 4, and node 1 can receive signals from only nodes 0, 2, and 3. From the signal strength readings, non-beacons estimate their distances to their neighbors. The probability distribution of the estimated location is represented by the particles (dots) in the graph. In sub-figure (a), where node 1 is removed, node 0 can only receive signals from node 4; thus, as the particle distribution indicates, the probability distribution where node 0 is most likely located concentrates on a circle around node 4. In sub-figure (b), where node 0 is removed, node 1 can receive signals from nodes 2 and 3; thus the most likely locations for node 1 center around two areas where "transmission circles" around node 2 and 3 intersect. Intuitively, in order to localize itself, a node needs to receive location information from a minimum of three beacons either directly or indirectly. In both case (a) and case (b), the exact location of the nodes 0 and 1 cannot be deduced because they do not receive location information from all three beacons. In (c) and (d), where all nodes are available, nodes 0 and 1 are able to communicate to each other and exchange their particle distributions. Thus, their probability densities will represent their actual locations much closer even though neither node receives location information from all three beacons *directly*.

This section introduced range-based localization methods. Compared to range-free methods, range-based methods give more accurate location estimates when ranging data is reliable. However, depending on the deployment environment, ranging techniques based on RSSI tend to be error-prone and strong filtering is required. The ranging error could ultimately throw off the localization accuracy if it is allowed to propagate through the network unbounded. Furthermore, different methods generally exploit the trade-off between the estimation accuracy and the estimation coverage. For instance, given the same network scenario, the Euclidean method is capable of generating more accurate location estimates of a smaller subset of nodes, whereas the DV-Hop method has better coverage but worse accuracy. Regardless of the tradeoff, a common characteristic shared by many range-based localization algorithms is that they require a relatively high network density in order to achieve better results. Based on the extensive simulation of DV-Distance, Euclidean and multilateration methods performed in (Chintalapudi, 2004), it can be concluded that those range-based localization algorithms "require an average degree of 11-12 nodes within the ranging neighborhood in order to achieve 90% localization coverage with 5% accuracy (Chintalapudi, 2004)."

AoA-Based Algorithms

Even though the future of AoA sensing devices is still unclear, some works have been published on localization using angle information. Simulation studies in (Chintalapudi, 2004) also show that when AoA of the signals is used in addition to the distance measurement, the localization accuracy and coverage can be drastically improved. This should not come as a surprising conclusion, as nodes need to communicate with only one neighbor to perform localization if they can obtain both AoA and distance measurements. The work in (Chintalapudi, 2004) also presents three variations of a weighted mean square error algorithm that localizes the nodes, each of which is designed to work with one of the three measurement types: i) distance-only measure; ii) distance plus a more accurate AoA measure (up to of precision); and iii) distance plus a less accurate AoA measure (up to of precision). The less accurate AoA measurement method is sometimes referred to as *sectoring*. Simulations in (Chintalapudi, 2004) show that the localization accuracy and coverage can be greatly improved even with such coarse sectoring measurement as well.

In order to localize with *only* AoA measurement, the AoA triangulation method proposed in (Niculescu, 2003) can be used. The triangulation takes several AoA measurements from beacons and estimates the node location with least square error. To propagate the AoA measurement for more than one hop, the AoA triangulation method uses a method called *orientation forwarding* that is similar to the Euclidean method for distance ranging. For instance in Figure 7, let AoA measurement be the bearing against South. For node D to derive its bearing to the beacon A (i.e., D), it can contact two neighbors, B and C, with known AoA measurements from the beacon A (i.e., B and C are known). Furthermore, B, C and D can measure the AoA of each other to give the readings of B, B, C, C, D and D. From there, all angles in $\triangle ABC$ and $\triangle BCD$ can be determined. The bearing from A to D can be derived as DD, where D is known, and $\angle CDA$ can be determined from $\triangle ABC$ and $\triangle BCD$. Using the orientation forwarding method, the bearing to beacons can be propagated through mutlitops, which can then be used to triangulate from remote beacons. However, much like the case of distance propagation, measurement error becomes aggregated at each hop. Simulations in (Niculescu, 2003) have reported a near linear error increase to the hop count.

In summary, due to the limited availability of AoA sensing devices, relatively few algorithms have been proposed for AoA. However, it is conceivable that some localization algorithms originally proposed for RSSI or ToA ranging can be adapted to AoA. For instance, the probabilistic algorithm in (Huang, 2005) can be updated to

Figure 6. Collaborative Localization Using Particle Filters: (a) Particle distribution of node 0 when node 1 is not present; (b) Particle distribution of node 1 when node 0 is not present, (c) Particle distribution of node 0 when node 1 is present; (d) Particle distribution of node 1 when node 0 is present

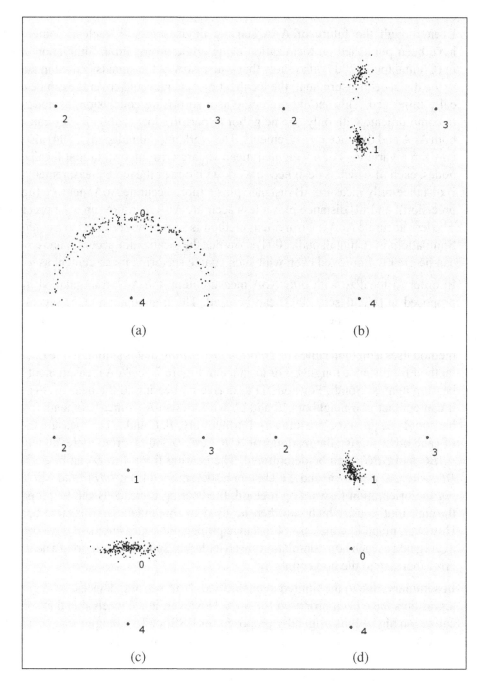

Figure 7. Multihop Distance Derivation in AoA Triangulation

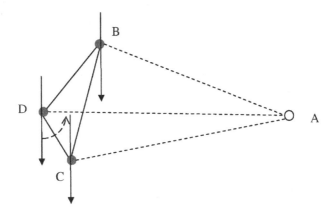

accept AoA measurements by simply providing an alternative measurement model for AoA during particle filtering.

Interferometric-Ranging Based Algorithms

Due to the fact that interferometric sensing devices for localization are relatively new, there have been only a limited number of localization algorithms proposed for this type of measurement. When compared to RSSI/ToA ranging and AoA, all of which involve two nodes for each measurement, interferometric ranging involves four nodes for each measurement and, thus, makes it more difficult to propagate location information through multihops. To eliminate the multihop propagation issue, a simple genetic optimization approach was taken in (Maróti, 2005), which propagates *all* interferometric readings within the network to a centralized location and runs a genetic algorithm to find the node locations that match the readings. Such an approach is of more theoretical (and prototyping) interest than practical use, since any centralized method is not scalable to large networks. A Pair-wise Distance method was proposed in (Patwari, 2006) that uses both interferometric and RSSI ranging. The method uses the interferometric ranging to derive pair-wise distances among the nodes. The node locations can then be optimized using the least square error method from the pair-wise distances. The algorithm then repetitively applies the RSSI ranging measurements to fine-tune the location estimates. Compared to the genetic algorithm, the Pair-wise Distance method is able to converge much faster. However, it is currently still a centralized algorithm, which presents the same scalability issue as the genetic algorithm.

Both of the above algorithms try to optimize for a global solution given an entire set of interferometric measurements. Intuitively, finding a global solution to the localization problem is often difficult because of the large search space and the large number of constraints given by the interferometric measurements. Thus, it is desirable to find solutions in some subspaces first and then incrementally build up to the global solution. For instance, an iterative approach has been proposed in (Huang, 2007) that localizes from a small set of seeding beacons. At each round, a set of nodes that can hear from the seeding beacons are localized. As additional nodes are localized at each round, they act as pseudo-beacons that allow other nodes to be localized at subsequent rounds. The iterative method is fully distributed. However, error propagation can be an issue since any localization error at pseudo-beacons would adversely affect the localization result at subsequent rounds. Simulation results in (Huang, 2007) have shown a linear increase of localization error at each round.

Hybrid Algorithms

A combination of the above techniques can be employed to form hybrid localization methods. For instance, a hybrid method is proposed in (Ahmed, 2005) that uses both DV-Distance (Niculescu, 2001) and Multi-Dimensional Scaling (MDS) (Shang, 2003). The algorithm contains three phases. In the first phase, a small subset of nodes is selected as reference nodes. In the subsequent phase, the reference nodes are then localized in relative coordinates using MDS. The final phase uses DV-Distance to localize the rest of the nodes in absolute coordinates. The rational behind such hybrid algorithms is to exploit the tradeoff between different localization algorithms. For example, MDS gives good localization accuracy, but as the network size is increased, MDS can be costly. Meanwhile, DV-Distance is less costly, but it only works well when beacon ratio is high. With the hybrid algorithm, the cost is minimized by only running MDS on the reference nodes, and then the reference nodes are used as beacons for DV-Distance.

Localization Using Mobility

While most previous methods assume stationary beacon locations, an alternative method is to localize devices using a mobile beacon. In this method, a mobile beacon travels through the deployment area while broadcasting its location along the way. Devices localize themselves by monitoring information coming from the beacon. A straight-forward technique using the above method is described in (Ssu, 2005), where devices are required to receive at least three communications with the same RSSI reading from the beacon. Given that the same RSSI reading implies similar distances to the beacon locations, the physical device location can be derived using simple geometric functions. This method is computationally simple, making it suitable for resource-limited sensors. However, it requires the beacon to directly pass by the ranging area of the device. In addition, in most cases, the beacon has to pass by the device twice because the sampling positions of the beacon when the three RSSI readings are taken should not be on the same line. This method also assumes that errors are insignificant in the RSSI to distance translation.

Instead of computing the location directly, a probabilistic approach may be taken; here device location is viewed as a probability distribution over the deployment area. In (Sichitiu, 2004), devices measure a series of RSSI readings from the mobile beacons and localize themselves by a sequential update process to the probability distributions of their locations. Each device starts with a uniform distribution covering the entire deployment area. As the beacon passes through, the distribution is updated to fit the received RSSI readings (using a signal propagation model). The method is further improved in (Peng, 2005) by adding the negative information (i.e., the information that the beacon is out of range), as well as RSSI readings from the neighbors. These probabilistic methods provide with much improved location estimates, but have the drawback of being complex. For a deployment grid of n by n units, the time and space complexity is $O(n^2)$. As the devices such as sensors at present time have very limited resources, it is difficult to directly implement these methods for large sensor deployment scenarios. Indeed, the experimental results shown in (Sichitiu, 2004) are performed on pocket PCs, which are much more powerful than cheap devices like sensors.

A similar method of localizing the networks using a mobile beacon is presented in (Galstyan, 2004). Instead of the actual probability distribution, the possible device locations are represented with a bounding box. As the beacon passes by, the area contained by the bounding box is progressively reduced as positive and negative information is processed. The bounding box method drastically simplifies the probability computation, making it possible to implement this method on sensor devices. However, such large simplification has its side-effects in that it sacrifices the preciseness of the distribution for its simplicity as the box cannot precisely describe multiple possible locations. There is also the problem of noise from ranging devices. This method may work well when ranging error is minimal; however, when noise is present (which is inevitable when using RSSI ranging), there might be situations where no bounding box exists to satisfy all readings.

Table 2 lists all the localization algorithms described in this section. In summary, different measurement types and their unique properties to a large degree dictate the design of localization algorithms. For instance, connectivity-based measurements can only provide coarse localization without a higher beacon ratio or nodal degrees. Range and AoA-based measurements can provide much finer localization results, but they are more prone to measurement error. A quantitative comparison between the more well-known algorithms such as DV-Hop, Euclidean and multilateralization can be obtained from (Langendoen, 2003), in which the comparison is done

Table 2. List of localization algorithms

Connectivity-based	Centroid (Bulusu, 2000), APIT (He, 2003), DV-Hop (Niculescu, 2001), MCL (Hu, 2004)
Range-based	DV-Distance (Niculescu, 2001), Euclidean (Niculescu, 2001), Collaborative Multilateration (Savvides, 2001), Hop-TERRAIN (Savarese, 2002), n-Hop Multilateration (Savvides, 2003), Probabilistic Localization (Huang, 2005)
Angle-based	Weighted Mean Square Error (Chintalapudi, 2004), AoA Triangulation (Niculescu, 2003)
Interferometric Ranging	Genetic Algorithm (Maróti, 2005), Pair-wise Distance (Patwari, 2006), Iterative (Huang, 2007)
Hybrid	DV-Distance + Multi-Dimensional Scaling (MDS) (Ahmed, 2005)
Mobility-based	Geometric Localization using Three RSSI Readings (Ssu, 2005), Sequential Update to Probability Distribution (Sichitiu, 2004).

in the context of specific constraints of sensor networks, such as error tolerance and energy efficiency. Their results indicate that there is no single algorithm that performs "best" and that there is room for further improvement.

Theoretical Results

While there have been many localization algorithms proposed for various scenarios, only recently have researchers started to address the theoretical aspects of the localization problem. In this section, we briefly cover the latest theoretical results with regard to the localization problem. Since ubiquitous computing environment is often modeled as a graph, it is not surprising that much of the theoretical work is based on graph theory. With regard to localization, we are particularly interested in the following three theoretic problems: i) localizability; ii) complexity of localization; and iii) localization error bounds.

First of all, we would like to know that given a network scenario (i.e., the nodes and their relative measurements such as ranging and angling) whether it is theoretically possible to uniquely localize the network. Such knowledge of *localizablity* is important to us because if we can easily identify the scenario that is impossible to localize uniquely, then it would be pointless to run any localization algorithm on it. Instead, we would have to request additional nodes or measurement data to be available (by possibly deploying more nodes or beacons) so that the localizablity requirement is satisfied. The following theorem gives the necessary and sufficient condition for distance-constrained network localizability in two dimensions.

Theorem 4.1 *The network is localizable in two dimensions if and only if the network graph is redundantly rigid and triconnected (Hendrickson, 1992; Berg, 2003).*

The above theorem makes use of some graph theory concepts. In graph theory, rigidity (or first-order rigidity) in general refers to the situation in a graph where there are no continuous motions of the vertices satisfying distance constraints on edges. A graph is redundantly rigid (or second-order rigid) if the induced graph remains rigid after removing any single edge.

Theorem 4.1 holds for two dimensions only. The sufficient condition for higher dimension is currently unknown. To test the localizability, there exists a polynomial time algorithm ($O(n^2)$ where n is the number of nodes) that tests for the first-order rigidity; see (Hendrickson, 2002) for one implementation. However, it is a known NP-Complete problem to test for the second-order rigidity of a graph (Saxe, 1979). A related but even more difficult problem is *node localizability*, which asks if a particular node (instead of the entire network) is localizable. No sufficient condition of node localizability is currently known even in the two dimensional case and, thus, no deterministic algorithm currently exists.

A second problem asks for the theoretic complexity of localization itself. In particular, we would like to know that given a network scenario that satisfies localizability whether there exists a deterministic polynomial time algorithm that would localize the network. This problem deals with the NP-Completeness of localization. Unfortunately, the hardness of graph realization has been shown as NP-Complete under the measurement of distance (Eren, 2004), angle (Bruck, 2005), connectivity (Breu, 1998; Kuhn, 2004), and interferometric ranging (Huang, 2007).

The above theoretical results indicate the general intractability of the localization problem even in the ideal case where measurements (such as edge distances) are 100% accurate. Unfortunately, measurements in the real world are a far-cry from being accurate, and any optimization method has to deal with not only different measurement types, but also noise. The localization inaccuracy attributed to the measurement types and noise can be statistically qualified using Cramer-Rao Bounds (CRB) (Patwari, 2005). The CRB is a lower bound on the covariance of any unbiased location estimator that uses measurements such as RSSI, ToA, or AoA. Thus, the CRB indicates a lower bound of the estimation accuracy of a given network scenario regardless of the localization algorithm. In other words, with CRB we have a way to tell the best *any* localization algorithm can do given a particular network, measurement type, and measurement noise scenario. CRB formulas of individual measurement types such as RSSI, ToA, and AoA under most common noise models (mostly Gaussian) are currently known.

The CRB of the localization error for a sample network is shown in Figure 8 as rings of radius being the standard deviation of the minimum localization error that can be possibly attained at the node. Here, the nodes represented by squares are beacons while circles represent nodes to be localized using RSSI ranging. The edges indicate the communication links available to measure RSSI readings. We assume the measurement model to be RSSI with the path loss exponent p and the standard

Figure 8. The CRB of the sample network is depicted as rings of the radius i. There are two exceptions: 1) beacons, depicted as squares, have 0 CRB, and 2) some regular nodes have infinite CRB (such as node 38, 48, 49 and 78 at the top left corner) indicating that they cannot be localized

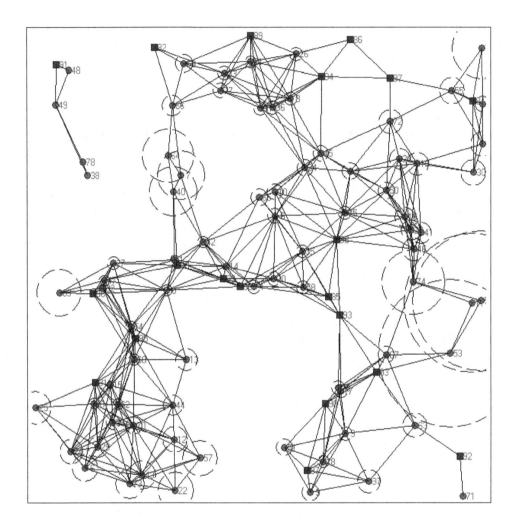

deviation of the noise *dB*. A ring with smaller radius (i.e., a smaller CRB) signals that more accurate localization result can be theoretically obtained. Conversely, a larger ring indicates a larger localization variance and, thus, a less accurate result. In the figure, two types of nodes do not have rings. First, all beacons have a CRB of 0. There are also regular nodes that have infinite CRB indicating that those nodes are theoretically impossible to localize. The latter case can be seen at nodes 38, 48, 49, and 78 in the top left corner. At a minimum, three beacons are needed to localize a connected network. However, those nodes in the top left corner are isolated to a different partition. Since they are connected to only one beacon (node 91), those nodes clearly cannot be localized. Other than those cases, the CRB rings at the main network partition clearly show the level of localization difficulty under various scenarios. In general, we observe that nodes closer to the beacons tend to have a smaller CRB than the ones that are several hops away. Even smaller CRB can be obtained when a node is closer to more than one beacon. All of the above observations are consistent with our common intuition about localization difficulty.

It is important to note that CRB is essentially a theoretic bound that depends on the measurement model. In the real world, its usefulness is limited by how accurate the measurement model reflects the reality. Nevertheless, CRB can be a useful tool in comparing various localization algorithms. It can be used to validate how close a particular algorithm can come to this theoretic lower bound and to see if there is any room for improvement in the algorithm design.

Conclusion

In this chapter, we studied the localization problem in ubiquitous computing environments. Localization in general refers to the problem of identifying the physical location of devices using a limited amount of available measurement data. The most common measurement types include device connectivity (i.e., whether two devices are neighbors), ranging using RSSI and ToA, angle of arrival (AoA), and interferometric ranging. Given a small number of nodes with accurate geometric location (e.g., using GPS receivers), localization algorithms try to derive the location of those devices that are not "GPS-enabled." The motivation of localization can be justified by the large number of algorithms proposed for ubiquitous computing that rely on (semi-)accurate location information and the fact that current technology prevents GPS from being installed on all network devices due to power constraints and form factors. It has been shown that localization in general, regardless of the measurement types used, is an NP-Hard problem. Thus, current effort in solving it relies on some sort of stochastic optimization. Meanwhile, as with other network-related problems in ubiquitous computing environments, the ideal solution calls for a distributed but efficient implementation, which leads to additional challenges.

Like other aspects of ubiquitous computing, the localization problem is relatively new. The problem is also conceptually straight-forward to characterize, and many results from other disciplines such as graph theory, optimization theory, online algorithms can be readily applied to this problem. Thus, researchers from other disciplines can provide valuable insight that could lead to better solutions to the problem. It is our hope that this brief introduction will provide the readers motivation and inspiration to perform research in this exciting field.

Future Directions

Device localization within ubiquitous computing environment has been an active research field in the past several years. Much work has been done in the area of hardware/sensor design (in particular, reducing the form factor and power consumption of sensory devices), algorithmic design and theoretical analysis. However, like many areas of ubiquitous computing, localization is still a relatively new front with much of the work yet to be done. In this section, we will briefly discuss a few directions which we feel could produce fruitful results in the near future. We hope our discussion will encourage the readers to actively participate and contribute their own ideas to this exciting and important field.

Implementation and Testing Environment

When reviewing the previous works on localization, one cannot help but notice a disturbing trend; a majority of works on localization have been based on either theoretical models or numerical simulations, while works based on the result of actual hardware implementation have been relatively few. It is not difficult to project that the primary reason for such trends is the hardware cost. To perform meaningful experiments for localization, especially for those collaborative localization methods such as DV-Distance and Euclidean, one would normally need a large number (100+) of devices. Although simple mobile ad hoc network devices (e.g., sensor motes) are becoming cheaper by the day, it is still quite costly to implement algorithms on physical devices on such a large scale. In addition, the sensing capacities of the current devices are usually limited to RSSI. Currently, there is no cheap hardware that implements AoA, ToA, or interferometric ranging and, thus, most works using those measurement types are all based on simulations. In a sense, the advances in algorithmic work on the localization problem are currently outpacing the advances in hardware. Future work needs to be done to significantly improve the hardware design to fill this gap.

Another issue related to the testing environment is that there is no common localization test bed. While large scale network simulators such as NS2 have modules for simulating mobile ad hoc networks, these modules do not contain localization. Smaller simulators for sensor networks such as SENSE (Chen, 2004) usually lack features on localization as well. Another simulator SENS (Sundresh, 2004) does explicitly implement localization, but it uses a rather primitive Centroid method and lacks more sophisticated methods. Since NS2 is the most widely-used network simulator, it would be very helpful for researchers to implement an interface to NS2 that allows a "plug-in" for future localization algorithms. This would give a common test bed for different localization schemes. More importantly, it would also allow those location-depended algorithms (such as location-aided routing methods) to be implemented and compared based on the result of localization. The localization module should also implement the Cramer Rao Bounds (CRB) so that the theoretic error bound can be calculated for different localization scenarios.

Interferometric Ranging

Since interferometric ranging is a relatively new type of measurement available to the localization problem, there are still many open problems in this area. Of the localization algorithms proposed for interferometric ranging, all but the iterative algorithm proposed in (Huang, 2007) is centralized. There is a definite need to design distributed localization algorithms for interferometric ranging so that it can be implemented with reasonable efficiency and scalability. To reduce the number of beacons, the distributed algorithms should make use of multi-hop location information, which unfortunately is much more difficult for interferometric ranging because each measurement involves four nodes. For instance, there is a scheduling issue, both at a high level and low level, of when a device should be scheduled to send or receive interferometric readings. At a high level, since not all q-ranges are independent, it is more desirable to schedule the senders and receivers in order to generate more independent q-ranges. At the low level, after the senders and receivers are selected, they have to be scheduled to coordinate the signal transmission because the transmission needs to be synchronized. The design of the scheduling algorithm can have a substantial impact on the overall performance of the localization algorithm in terms of the localization accuracy and communication overhead.

Furthermore, a simulation study in (Huang, 2007) has shown that the multi-hop error propagation has a big impact on interferometric ranging, which increases almost linearly as the localization results are propagated at each hop. Therefore, the control of the error propagation is another research issue. There is also a need for an algorithmic independent theoretic error bound (like CRB) for interferometric ranging. The bound would be more difficult to derive than those for distance ranging and angling because more than two nodes are involved in each measurement. Thus, the inter-dependence between the error and the relative locations of senders and receivers becomes more challenging to characterize mathematically. However, the payoff of obtaining such bound is that it would allow us to ultimately compare interferometric ranging with other measurement types and identify the scenarios that are preferable for each measurement type.

Collaborative Localization of Multiple Measurement Types

Previous localization algorithms often assume that the entire network has to be localized using the same type of measurement (such as connectivity-only, RSSI, ToA, AoA, or interferometric ranging). However, to be true to the spirit of ubiquitous computing, it is foreseeable that future networks will consist of devices of vastly different capacities in terms of i) different transmission coverage, ii) power requirement, and iii) measurement sensors. Thus, during localization it is often desirable to explicitly consider various devices capacities in such heterogeneous networks. For instance, in terms of power requirements, the localization algorithm should exploit the devices with more power capacity and try to minimize the calculation performed on less powerful devices. Furthermore, different measurement types have different error characteristics. It would be interesting to investigate how to collaborate multiple measurement types during localization, and in particular how the collaboration would impact the localization error. Intuitively, incorporating multiple measurement types in the same localization scenario should improve performance since such collaboration can potentially cover the drawbacks of individual measurement types for each other. Unfortunately, such collaboration could mean an increased complexity of the localization algorithms since heterogeneous networks would invalidate some assumptions often made by simple localization algorithms (such as uniform transmission range). While it is worthwhile to consider collaborative localization algorithms, it is equally imperative to keep the localization overhead under control.

References

Ahmed, A. A., Shi, H., & Shang, Y. (2005). SHARP: A new approach to relative localization in wireless sensor networks. In *Proceedings of the 25th IEEE International Conference on Distributed Computing Systems Workshops (ICDCS '05)* (pp. 892-898).

Ash, J. N., & Potter, L. C. (2004). Sensor network localization via received signal strength measurements with directional antennas. In *Proceedings of the 2004 Allerton Conference on Communication, Control, and Computing* (pp. 1861-1870).

Berg, A., & Jordan, T. (2003). A proof of Connelly's conjecture on 3-connected generic cycles. *Journal of Combinatorial Theory Series B, 88*(1), 77-97.

Breu, H., & Kirkpatrick, D. G. (1998). Unit disk graph recognition is NP-hard. *Computational Geometry. Theory and Applications, 9*(1-2), 3-24.

Bruck, J., Gao, J., & Jiang A. (2005). Localization and routing in sensor networks by local angle information. In *Proceeding of the 6th ACM International Symposium on Mobile Ad Hoc Networking and Computing* (pp. 181-192).

Bulusu, N., Heidemann, J., & Estrin, D. (2000). GPS-less low cost outdoor localization for very small devices. *IEEE Personal Communications Magazine, 7*(5), 28-34.

Chen, G., Branch, J., Pflug, M. J., Zhu, L., & Szymanski, B. (2004). SENSE: A sensor network simulator. *Advances in Pervasive Computing and Networking* (pp. 249-267). Springer.

Chintalapudi, K., Govindan, R., Sukhatme, G., & Dhariwal, A. (2004). Ad-hoc localization using ranging and sectoring. In *Proceedings of the IEEE (INFOCOM '04)* (pp. 2662-2672).

Eren, T., Goldenberg, D., Whiteley, W., Yang, Y. R., Morse, A. S., Anderson, B. D. O., & Belhumeur, P. N. (2004). Rigidity, computation, and randomization of network localization. In *Proceedings of the IEEE (INFOCOM'04)* (pp. 2673-2684).

Galstyan, A., Krishnamachari, B., Lerman, K., & Pattem, S. (2004). Distributed online localization in sensor networks using a moving target. In *Proceedings of the IPSN 2004,* (pp. 61-70).

He, T., Huang, C., Blum, B. M., Stankovic, J. A., & Abdelzaher, T. F. (2003). Range-free localization schemes in large scale sensor networks. In *Proceedings of the* ACM (*MOBICOM'03)* (pp. 81-95).

Hendrickson, B. (1992). Conditions for unique graph realizations. *SIAM Journal on Computing, 21*(1), 65-84.

Hu, L., & Evans, D. (2004). Localization for mobile sensor networks. In *Proceedings of the ACM (MOBICOM'04)* (pp. 45-57).

Hu, Y.-C., Perrig, A., & Johnson, D. (2003). Packet leashes: a defense against wormhole attacks in wireless ad hoc networks. In *Proceedings of the INFOCOM'03* (pp. 1976-1986).

Huang, R., Záruba, G. V., and Huber, M. (2007). Complexity and error propagation of localization using interferometric ranging. In *Proceedings of the* IEEE ICC.

Huang, R., & Záruba, G. V. (2005). Location tracking in mobile ad hoc networks using particle filters. In *Proceedings of the ADHOC-NOW'05* (pp. 85-98).

Jiang, X., & Camp, T. (2002). Review of geocasting protocols for a mobile ad hoc network. In Proceedings of the *Grace Hopper Celebration (GHC)*.

Ko, Y., & Vaidya, N. H. (2000). Location-aided routing (LAR) in mobile ad hoc networks. *Wireless Networks, 6*(4), 307-321.

Ko, Y. & Vaidya, N. H. (1999). Geocasting in mobile ad hoc networks: location-based multicast algorithms. In *Proceedings of the IEEE (WMCSA'99)* (pp. 101).

Kuhn, F., Moscibroda, T., & Wattenhofer, R. (2004). Unit disk graph approximation. In *Proceedings of the Workshop on Discrete Algorithms and Methods for Mobile Computing and Communications (DIAL-M)* (pp. 17-23).

Kuhn, F., Wattenhofer, R., Zhang, Y., & Zollinger, A. (2003). Geometric ad-hoc routing: of theory and practice. In *Proceedings of the ACM (PODC'03)* (pp. 63-72).

Kusý, B., Maróti, M., Balogh, G., V:olgyesi, P., Sallai, J., Nádas, A., Lédeczi, A., & Meertens, L. (2006). Node density independent localization. In *Proceedings of the 5th International Conference on Information Processing in Sensor Networks (IPSN 2006)* (pp. 441-448).

Langendoen, K., & Reijers, N. (2003). Distributed localization in wireless sensor networks: a quantitative comparison. *Computer Networks, 43*(4), 499-518.

Liao, W.-H., Tseng, Y.-C., & Sheu, J.-P. (2001). GRID: a fully location-aware routing protocol for mobile ad hoc networks. *Telecommunication Systems, 18*(1), 37-60.

Liao, W.-H., Tseng, Y.-C., Lo, K.-L., & Sheu, J.-P. (2000). Geogrid: a geocasting protocol for mobile ad hoc networks based on grid. *Journal of Internet Technology, 1*(2), 23-32.

Maróti, M., Kusý, B., Balogh, G., V:olgyesi, P., Nádas, A., Molnár, K., Dóra, S., & Lédeczi, A. (2005). Radio interferometric geolocation. In Proceedings of the *ACM 3rd Conference on Embedded Networked Sensor Systems (SenSys)* (pp. 1-12).

Mauve, M., Fuler, H., Widmer, J., & Lang, T. (2003). *Position-based multicast routing for mobile ad-hoc networks* (Technical Report TR-03-004). Department of Computer Science, University of Mannheim.

Niculescu, D., & Nath, B. (2001). Ad hoc positioning system (APS). In *Proceedings of the IEEE (GLOBECOM'01)* (pp. 2926-2931).

Niculescu, D., & Nath, B. (2003). Ad hoc positioning system (APS) using AoA. In Proc. of *IEEE INFOCOM'03* (pp. 1734-1743).

Niculescu, D., & Nath, B. (2004). VOR base stations for indoor 802.11 Positioning. In *Proceeding of the 10th Annual International Conference on Mobile Computing and Networking* (pp. 58-69).

Patwari, N., & Hero, A. O. (2006). Indirect radio interferometric localization via pairwise distances. In *Proceedings of the 3rd IEEE Workshop on Embedded Networked Sensors (EmNets 2006)* (pp. 26-30).

Patwari, N., Hero III, A. O., Perkins, M., Correal, N. S., & O'Dea, R. J. (2003). Relative location estimation in wireless sensor networks. *IEEE Transactions on Signal Processing, 51*(8), 2137-2148.

Patwari, N., Hero, A., Ash, J., Moses, R., Kyperountas, S., & Correal, N. (2005). Locating the nodes: cooperative geolocation of wireless sensors. *IEEE Signal Processing Magazine*, *22*(4), 54-69.

Parkinson, B. et al. (1996). Global positioning system: theory and application. *Volume I, Progress in Astronautics and Aeronautics*, (Vol. 163).

Peng, R., & Sichitiu, M. L. (2005). Robust, probabilistic, constraint-based localization for wireless sensor networks. In *Proceeding of the 2nd Annual IEEE Communications Society Conference on Sensor and Ad Hoc Communications and Networks (SECON 2005)* (pp. 541-550).

Perkins, C. E. (1997). Ad-hoc on-demand distance vector routing. In MILCOM '97 panel on Ad Hoc Networks.

Priyantha, N., Miu, A., Balakrishnan, H., & Teller, S. (2001). The Cricket compass for context-aware mobile applications. In Proceedings of the *6th ACM, (MOBICOM '01)* (pp. 1-14).

Savvides, A., Han, C.-C., & Srivastava, M. (2001). Dynamic finegrained localization in ad-hoc networks of sensors. In *Proceedings of the 7th ACM International Conerence. on Mobile Computing and Networking (MOBICOM)* (pp. 166-79).

Savvides, A., Park, H., & Srivastava, M. B. (2003). The n-hop multilateration primitive for node localization problems. *Mobile Networks and Applications*, 8, 443-451.

Savarese, C., Rabay, J., & Langendoen, K. (2002). Robust positioning algorithms for distributed ad-hoc wireless sensor networks. In *Proceeding of the USENIX Technical Annual Conference* (pp. 317-327).

Saxe, J. (1979). Embeddability of weighted graphs in k-space is strongly NP-hard. In *Proceedings of the 17th Allerton Conference in Communications, Control and Computing* (pp. 480-489).

Shang, Y., Ruml, W., Zhang, Y., & Fromherz, M. (2003). Localization from mere connectivity. In Proceedings of the *ACM (MobiHoc '03)* (pp. 201-212).

Sichitiu, M. L., & Ramadurai, V. (2004). Localization of wireless sensor networks with a mobile beacon. In *Proceedings of the 1st IEEE Conference on Mobile Ad-hoc and Sensor Systems (MASS 2004)* (pp. 174-183).

Sivrikaya, F., & Yener, B. (2004). Time synchronization in sensor networks: a survey. *IEEE Network*, *18*(4), 45-50.

Ssu, K.-F., Ou, C.-H., & Jiau, H.C. (2005). Localization with mobile anchor points in wireless sensor networks. In *Proceedings of the IEEE Vehicular Technology Conference (VTC 2005)* (pp. 1187-1197).

Stojmenovic, I., Ruhil, A. P., & Lobiyal, D. K. (2006). Voronoi diagram and convex hull based geocasting and routing in wireless networks. *Wireless Communications and Mobile Computing*, *6*(2), 247-258.

Sundresh, S., Kim, W., & Agha, G. (2004). SENS: A sensor, environment and network simulator. In *Proceedings of the 37th Annual Simulation Symposium (ANSS37)*.

Xu, Y., Heidemann, J., & Estrin, D. (2001). Geography-informed energy conservation for adhoc routing. In *Proceedings of the ACM/IEEE (MOBICOM'01)* (pp. 70-84).

Additional Reading

Bulusu, N., Heidemann, J., & Estrin, D. (2000). GPS-less low cost outdoor localization for very small devices. *IEEE Personal Communications Magazine, 7*(5), 28-34.

Eren, T., Goldenberg, D., Whiteley, W., Yang, Y. R., Morse, A. S., Anderson, B. D. O., & Belhumeur, P. N. (2004). Rigidity, computation, and randomization of network localization. In *Proceedings of the IEEE (INFOCOM'04)* (pp. 2673-2684).

Ko, Y., & Vaidya, N. H. (2000). Location-aided routing (LAR) in mobile ad hoc networks. *Wireless Networks, 6*(4), 307-321.

Langendoen, K., & Reijers, N. (2003). Distributed localization in wireless sensor networks: a quantitative comparison. *Computer Networks, 43*(4), 499-518.

Liao, W.-H., Tseng, Y.-C., & Sheu, J.-P. (2001). GRID: a fully location-aware routing protocol for mobile ad hoc networks. *Telecommunication Systems, 18*(1), 37-60.

Patwari, N., Hero III, A. O., Perkins, M., Correal, N. S., & O'Dea, R. J. (2003). Relative location estimation in wireless sensor networks. *IEEE Transactions on Signal Processing, 51*(8), 2137-2148.

Patwari, N., Hero, A., Ash, J., Moses, R., Kyperountas, S., & Correal, N. (2005). Locating the nodes: cooperative geolocation of wireless sensors. *IEEE Signal Processing Magazine, 22*(4), 54-69.

Savvides, A., Park, H., & Srivastava, M. B. (2003). The n-hop multilateration primitive for node localization problems. *Mobile Networks and Applications, 8*, 443-451.

Stojmenovic, I., Ruhil, A. P., & Lobiyal, D. K. (2006). Voronoi diagram and convex hull based geocasting and routing in wireless networks. *Wireless Communications and Mobile Computing, 6*(2), 247-258.

Chapter V

Enabling Programmable Ubiquitous Computing Environments:
A Middleware Perspective

Christine Julien, The University of Texas at Austin, USA

Sanem Kabadayi, The University of Texas at Austin, USA

Abstract

Emerging pervasive computing scenarios involve client applications that dynamically collect information directly from the local environment. The sophisticated distribution and dynamics involved in these applications place an increased burden on developers that create applications for these environments. The heightened desire for rapid deployment of a wide variety of pervasive computing applications demands a new approach to application development in which domain experts with minimal programming expertise are empowered to rapidly construct and deploy domain-specific applications. This chapter introduces the DAIS (Declarative Applications in Immersive Sensor networks) middleware that abstracts a heterogeneous and dynamic pervasive computing environment into intuitive and accessible programming constructs. At the programming interface level, this requires exposing some aspects of the physical world to the developer, and DAIS accomplishes this through a suite of novel programming abstractions that enable on-demand access to dynamic local data sources. A fundamental component of the model is a hierarchical view of pervasive computing middleware that allows devices with differing capabilities to support differing amounts of functionality. This chapter reports on our design of the DAIS middleware and highlights the abstractions, the programming interface, and the reification of the middleware on a heterogeneous combination of client devices and resource-constrained sensors.

Introduction

As networked computing capabilities become increasingly ubiquitous, we envision an instrumented environment that can provide varying amounts of information to applications supporting mobile users immersed within the network. While such a scenario relies on low-cost, low-power miniature sensors, it deviates from existing deployments of sensor networks, which are highly application-specific and generally funnel information to a central collection service for a single purpose. Instead, solutions for ubiquitous computing must target future scenarios in which multiple mobile applications leverage networked nodes opportunistically and unpredictably. To date, most application development for ubiquitous computing has been limited to academic circles. One significant barrier to the widespread development of ubiquitous computing applications lies in the increased complexity of the programming task when compared to existing distributed or even mobile situations. Sensor nodes, which provide computational platforms embedded in the environment, are severely resource-constrained, in terms of both computational capabilities and battery power, and therefore, application development must inherently consider low-level design concerns. This complexity, coupled with the increasing demand for ubiquitous applications, highlights the need for programming platforms (i.e., middleware) that simplify application development.

As will be described in more detail in later sections, much existing work in simplifying programming in sensor networks focuses on application-specific networks where the nodes are statically deployed for a particular task. Ubiquitous computing requires a more futuristic (but not unrealistic) scenario in which sensor networks become more general-purpose and reusable. While the networks may remain domain-specific, ubiquitous computing applications that will be deployed are not known *a priori* and may demand varying capabilities from the environment. Finally, existing applications commonly assume that sensor data is collected at a central location to be processed and used in the future and/or accessed via the Internet. Applications for ubiquitous computing, however, involve users immersed in a network environment who access locally sensed information on demand. This is exactly the vision of pervasive computing environments (Weiser, 1991), in which sensor networks must play an integral role (Estrin, Culler, Pister, & Sukhatme, 2002).

While this style of interaction is common in many application domains, we will refer to applications from the first responder domain, which provides a unique and heterogeneous mix of embedded and mobile devices. The former includes fixed sensors in buildings and environments that are present regardless of crises and ad hoc deployments of sensors that responders may distribute when they arrive. Mobile devices include those moving within vehicles, carried by responders, and even autonomous robots that may perform exploration and reconnaissance.

In this chapter, we will first demonstrate that immersive networks built of tiny sensing and actuating devices are an essential component of the vision of ubiquitous computing. We will carefully define what we mean by immersive networks and highlight how the definition differs from traditional uses of such technologies. Because these networks deviate so significantly from existing application environments, constructing tailored, adaptive applications necessary for ubiquitous computing is difficult. We will demonstrate this complexity through a handful of example applications and then provide a detailed survey of existing approaches to simplifying the development of ubiquitous computing applications that rely on immersive sensor networks. Following this survey of existing technologies, we will introduce a new paradigm for programming ubiquitous immersive networks that not only simplifies the programming task, but also improves the performance of the supportive network in terms of battery life, communication overhead, and latency.

The next section describes the operating environment of immersive sensor networks for supporting ubiquitous computing and provides a comparative analysis of existing approaches to simplifying programming for ubiquitous computing. We then introduce a new programming paradigm for immersive sensor networks that combines communication abstractions with high-level programming constructs.

Background

In ubiquitous computing applications that rely on immersive sensor networks, users with client devices need to interact directly with devices (or sensors) embedded in their environments. This allows the client applications to operate over information collected directly from the local area (as shown in Figure 1(b)). This is in contrast to existing sensor network deployments in which sensor networks are commonly accessed through a central collection point (as shown in Figure 1(a)). More directly, immersive sensor networks support ubiquitous computing applications, not remote distributed sensing. In this type of environment, we differentiate client devices (those on which ubiquitous computing applications run) from sensors (devices embedded

Figure 1. Comparison of (a) existing operational environments and (b) immersive sensor networks for ubiquitous computing

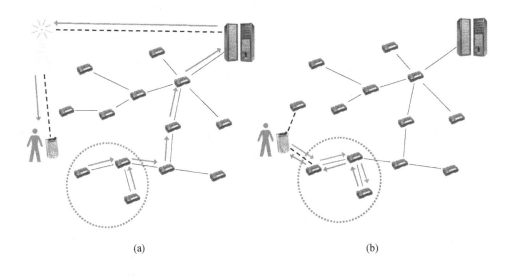

(a)   (b)

in the environment). The former commonly support users and have increased computational power, while the latter are heavily resource-constrained.

Supporting Ubiquitous Computing: An Operating Environment

The style of interaction apparent in ubiquitous computing and depicted in Figure 1(b) differs from common uses of sensor networks. First and foremost, applications require direct local interactions with embedded devices present in the immediately accessible environment. Second, the area from which an application desires to draw information is subject to the device user's movement. These mobility-induced dynamics demand a constant reevaluation of the sensors participating in ongoing interactions. Third, networks must support general classes of applications. Few *a priori* assumptions can be made about the needs or intentions of applications, requiring a middleware to handle unpredictable coordination. Finally, in immersive sensor networks, the programming complexity is drastically increased due to the above concerns coupled with traditional concerns associated with distributed, embedded computing. In addition, the desire to provide end-user applications (as opposed to more database-oriented data collection) increases the demand for applications and the number of programmers that will need to construct them.

Ubiquitous computing applications from domains such as intelligent construction sites (Hammer et al., 2006), aware homes (Kidd et al., 1999), and pervasive office environments (Voida, Maynatt, & MacIntyre, 2002) involve users immersed in the network who access locally sensed information on demand. Such application scenarios motivate a view of the ubiquitous computing environment that is device-agnostic. That is, applications, in general, do not care about devices embedded in the environment, but instead about information and resources available locally. Logically, the ubiquitous environment appears as a world of embedded information available for immersed applications. To support this view, it is essential to allow developers to distance themselves from explicit knowledge of devices and communication capabilities of the underlying pervasive computing network and instead focus on dynamically changing, locally available information.

Sensor networks for these environments will also need to provide reusability. Current efforts offer solutions that are specific to a particular application (e.g., once the sensor network has been tasked to do habitat monitoring, that is all it is expected to do), but the future will see multipurpose networks deployed to support numerous applications whose natures may not be known at the time the network is deployed. The cost of physically visiting each sensor to program it is prohibitive, and therefore, the ability to remotely and dynamically tailor sensor networks to particular applications will be essential.

The data collection schemes used in existing deployments of sensor networks commonly require sensors to relay raw data to sink nodes to perform further processing. For the sensing devices, communication is much more expensive than local computation; thus, the approaches used in existing deployments lead to short network lifetimes. Furthermore, the throughput at each node decreases as the network scales due to redundant broadcasts, leading to inefficient use of the network bandwidth. To support ubiquitous environments, sensor networks will need to perform complicated tasks and in-network processing to seamlessly transform raw data.

Related Work: Simplifying Programming for Ubiquitous Computing

It is largely recognized that constructing applications for ubiquitous computing environments is a significant undertaking. Several approaches have made strides in simplifying the kind of programming necessary for immersive networks. This section provides a thorough comparative investigation into these existing techniques, from middleware solutions to toolkits and programming languages.

Ubiquitous Computing Middleware

One strong example of a middleware for ubiquitous computing, Gaia (Roman et al., 2002), introduces *active spaces* as a programmable environment, by encapsulating the heterogeneity of devices that are located in them. It abstracts user data and applications into a *user virtual space* that has a dynamic mapping to the resources in the current environment. Users always have their virtual space available, even as they move across different active spaces. Furthermore, they can simultaneously interact with multiple devices, dynamically reconfigure applications, pause and resume applications, and use context attributes to program application behaviors (Roman et al., 2002). However, this model assumes a centralized system structure which is in direct opposition to the goal of deploying large numbers of applications over a widely dispersed immersive sensor as described in the previous section.

Blackbox Abstractions

In contrast, projects targeted directly for sensor networks more directly address the desire to reduce computational and power requirements and to operate in a more distributed fashion. Two demonstrative examples that have explored representing the sensor network as a database are TinyDB (Madden, Franklin, Hellerstein, & Hong, 2005) and Cougar (Yao & Gehrke, 2002). Generally, these approaches enable applications to generate data requests that flow out from a central point (i.e., a base station) and create routing trees that funnel replies back to this root (in a manner similar to that shown in Figure 1(a)). Much of the work in these approaches focuses on performing intelligent in-network aggregation and routing to reduce the overall energy cost while still keeping the semantic value of data high. Each node processes streams of sensor data much like the processing of streams in a database. In both approaches, data aggregation is specified using an SQL-like language over homogeneous data types. Ubiquitous computing applications often require the use of many nearby sensors, ultimately aggregating these disparate pieces of data into a cohesive piece of information for the application or user. Therefore, despite the fact that moving data across the network in approaches such as TinyDB and Cougar still requires centralized algorithms, they have much to offer in support of ubiquitous computing applications in immersive sensor networks. REED (Abadi, Madden, & Lindner, 2005) is an extension to TinyDB that supports joins between sensor data and static tables built outside the sensor network. Users can express queries with complex time- and location-varying predicates over multiple conditions using join predicates over these different attributes. REED organizes nodes into groups and stores a part of the predicate table at each group member, reducing storage costs at remote nodes. This in-network application of *join* can significantly reduce the communication overhead in the network. However, since the group members contain parts of an external table, they are all required to be in radio range of one another.

State-centric programming (Liu, Chu, Liu, Reich, & Zhao, 2003) mediates between an application developer's model of physical phenomena and the distributed execution of sensor network applications. It uses the notion of collaboration of groups to abstract common patterns in application-specific communication and resource allocation. Furthermore, it takes a signal processing and control theory approach, where dynamically created collaboration groups provide the input to applications written by application developers as algorithms for state update and retrieval. Consequently, the resulting software is more modular and can be ported to different platforms as these programs are less affected by system configuration changes. However, the state-centric programming implementation and evaluation relies on the software environment, PIECES (developed in Java and Matlab), which, unlike most other network simulators, does not simulate network behavior all the way down to the packet level (it only verifies the algorithms at the collaboration group level). While the implementation of collaboration groups needs to be distributed in real-world deployments, collaborations groups are implemented as centralized objects in PIECES. The Abstract Task Graph (ATaG) (Bakshi, Prasanna, Reich, & Larner, 2005) methodology provides system-level support for architecture-independent sensing application development. ATaG uses a combination of imperative and declarative programming styles and has a data-driven program flow. For example, in an environment monitoring application, it allows the periodic computation and logging of the maximum pressure in the system, and the periodic monitoring of temperature. However, it cannot combine these two different types of data to arrive at an abstracted measurement.

Virtual Machines and Code Generation

Other approaches have focused more specifically on the programmability of ubiquitous computing environments. VM* (Koshy & Pandey, 2005) is a virtual machine approach that can scale software components depending on the constraints of each device. This allows application developers to better manipulate unpredictable environments with a wide variety of devices, but has limitations in that the virtual machine must know about the applications in advance to be able to optimize resource usage. TinyGALS (Cheong, Liebman, Liu, & Zhao, 2003) allows programmers to represent applications in terms of relatively high-level components, which are subsequently synthesized into the low-level, lightweight, efficient programs that are deployed on the nodes. This eases the programming task but does not allow arbitrary applications to access the immersive sensor network and immediately start to use it. MiLAN (Heinzelman, Murphy, Carvallo, & Perillo, 2004) aims to enable applications to control the network's resource usage and allocation optimally to tune the performance of an entire sensor network through the definition of application policies that are enacted on the network. MiLAN tries to maximize network lifetime as well as meet the application's quality-of-service requirements. While such approaches are highly beneficial when the application is known and the networks are relatively application-specific, they do not map well to immersive sensor networks where the nodes must be able to service a variety of unpredictable applications.

Toolkits and Development Suites

More generalized approaches attempt to provide integrated suites of tools that enable simplified programming of sensor networks. For example, EmStar (Girod et al., 2004) provides a suite of libraries, development tools, and application services that focus on coordinating microservers (e.g., sensing devices with computational power equivalent to a PDA). However, EmStar functions only on Linux-based platforms such as the Stargate. The Sensor Network Application Construction Kit (SNACK) (Greenstein, Kohler, & Estrin, 2004) consists of a set of libraries and a compiler that makes it possible to write very simple application descriptions that specify sophisticated behavior using components written in nesC (the TinyOS programming language that runs on sensor motes). While EmStar and SNACK are programming environments for individual nodes, Agilla (Fok, Roman, & Lu, 2005) is an agent-based middleware that allows applications to inject agents into the sensor network that coordinate through local tuple spaces and migrate intelligently to carry out the applications' tasks. Multiple autonomous applications can run simultaneously over the sensor network. However, Agilla does not use any mechanisms for authenticating agent activities.

Coordination Approaches

One approach that does map well to the operational picture shown in Figure 1(b) is TinyLime (Curino et al., 2005), a tuple space based middleware that enables mobile computing devices to interact with sensor data in a manner decoupled in both space and time. Applications create tuple templates to subscribe for data that is of interest to them. The tuple spaces of a pair of devices are temporarily federated whenever the devices are within a single hop of one another. TinyLime allows client devices to connect to sensors available in the immediate environment, but does not enable multihop communication or aggregation. Another adaptation of the Lime model, TeenyLime (Costa, Mottola, Murphy, & Picco, 2006), uses the abstraction of a shared tuple space that contains the data of the local device and its one-hop neighbors. Since TinyLime targets sensor networks where users with mobile devices request data from sensors immediately around them, the applications are deployed on the client devices and the sensing devices are only data producers without any tuple spaces. On the other hand, TeenyLime applications are deployed directly on the sensing devices that have their own tuple spaces and play an active role in distributed coordination.

Location-Dependent Approaches

EnviroTrack (Abdelzaher et al., 2004) is an object-based and data-centric middleware designed specifically for embedded tracking applications. EnviroTrack associates a context-label with each entity. Upon initial detection of the entity, the context-label is dynamically created and logically follows the entity's movement through the sensor field. Application developers directly interact with the context label instead of a continuously changing collection of nodes that detect the entity, through the help of a directory service based on a geographic hash table. EnviroTrack relies on embedded sensors with precise knowledge of their locations to locate and track mobile objects.

Macroprogramming Approaches

Finally, Kairos (Gummadi, Gnawali, & Govindan, 2005) is a macroprogramming model that allows the specification of the network's global behavior through a centralized model. As such, it is not adaptive or general-purpose, requiring deployment-time knowledge of the intended application(s). Regiment (Newton & Welsh, 2004) also employs a macroprogramming approach to program sensor networks. A user writes a single program that is then distributed and run across the sensor network. Kairos provides abstractions to facilitate this task, while Regiment focuses on the suitability of functional programming to the sensor network domain.

In summary, while these systems for ubiquitous computing have addressed components of the problems associated with the operating environment described above, other components of the problem definition are not completely satisfied by these existing systems. Overall, the projects focus on specific facets of enabling application development in ubiquitous computing or sensor networks, but none take a holistic approach. We claim that any middleware for simplifying the creation of ubiquitous computing applications must provide constructs tailored to this unique and dynamic environment. These constructs must consider both communication and coordination aspects of tying together embedded devices as well as the application-level operations that are available to instruct these dynamic networks. In the next section, we introduce a new paradigm for immersive sensor networks targeted directly towards the application of such networks to the challenges posed by ubiquitous computing applications and their operating environments.

A New Middleware Paradigm for Immersive Networks

In this section, we introduce a new programming paradigm for immersive sensor networks that combines communication abstractions with high-level programming constructs. We argue that such knowledge about the communication environment by the programmer is essential to mediating performance and efficiency concerns, and our approach minimizes the complexity of knowing about communication using a pair of intuitive grouping abstractions, the *scene*, and the *virtual sensor*.

Scenes: Abstractions of Local Data

In an immersive sensor network, a user's operational context is highly dynamic. As the user moves through the environment, the set of embedded devices he interacts with should change accordingly. Furthermore, if the sensor network is well connected, the client device will be able to reach vast amounts of raw information that must be filtered to be usable. To enable efficient solutions, the application must be able to limit the scope of its interactions to include only the data that matches its needs. Therefore, an application developer must be conscious of the communication tasks required to satisfy his desired application behaviors.

In the middleware paradigm this chapter describes, such specification of the operating context is encapsulated in an abstraction called a scene (Kabadayi & Julien, 2007). Applications define scenes according to their needs, and each scene constrains which particular sensors may influence the application. The constraints may be on properties of hosts (e.g., battery life), of network links (e.g., bandwidth), and of data (e.g., type).

The declarative specification defining a scene allows an application programmer to flexibly describe the type of scene he wants to create. Multiple constraints can be used to define a single scene. The programmer only needs to specify three parameters to define a constraint:

Figure 2. Distributed scene computation

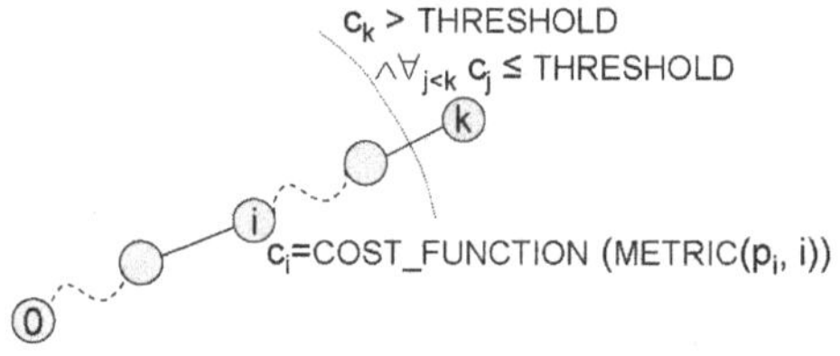

$$c_k > \text{THRESHOLD}$$
$$\wedge \forall_{j<k}\, c_j \leq \text{THRESHOLD}$$

$$c_i = \text{COST\_FUNCTION (METRIC}(p_i, i))$$

- **Metric:** A property of the network or environment that defines the cost of a connection (i.e., a property of hosts, links, or data)

- **Path cost function:** A function (such as sum, average, minimum, maximum) that operates on a network path to calculate the cost of the path

- **Threshold:** The value a path's cost must satisfy for that sensor to be a member of the scene.

Thus, a scene, S, is specified by one or more constraints, $C_1, C_2, ..., C_n$:

$$C_1 = \langle M_1, F_1, T_1 \rangle, C_2 = \langle M_2, F_2, T_2 \rangle, ..., C_n = \langle M_n, F_n, T_n \rangle$$

where M denotes a metric, F denotes a path cost function, and T denotes a threshold.

Figure 2 demonstrates the relationships between these components. This figure is a simplification that shows only a one-constraint scene and a single network path. The cost to a particular node in the path (e.g., node i) is calculated by applying the scene's path cost function to the metric. The metric can combine information about the path so far (p_i) and information about this node. Nodes along a path continue to be included in the scene until the path hits a node whose cost (e.g., c_k) is greater than the scene's threshold. This functionality is implemented in a dynamic distributed algorithm that can calculate (and dynamically recalculate) scene membership. The application's messages carry with them the metric, path cost function, and threshold, which are sufficient for each node to independently determine whether it is a member of the scene. Each node along a network path determines whether it lies within the scene, and if so, forwards the message. It is possible for a node to qualify to be within the scene based on multiple paths. These network paths correspond to branches of a routing tree that is set up as part of the distributed calculation of the scene. When a certain data source needs to relay a reply back to the user, the reverse of the path on the routing tree the message took to get to that node can be used. If a node receives a scene message that it has already processed, and the new metric value is not shorter, the new message is dropped. If the new message carries a shorter metric, then the node forwards the information again because it may enable new nodes to be included in the scene.

Scene construction can be formalized in the following way:

Given a client node α, a metric M, and a positive threshold T, find the set of all hosts S_α such that all hosts in S_α are reachable from α and, for all hosts β in S_α, the cost of applying the metric on some path from α to β is less than T. Specifically:

$$S_\alpha = \langle \text{set } \beta : M(\alpha, \beta) < T :: \beta \rangle$$

In the three-part notation: $= \langle$op *quantified_variables* : *range* :: *expression*$\rangle$, the variables from *quantified_variables* take on all possible values permitted by *range*. Each instantiation of the variables is substituted in *expression*, producing a multiset of values to which op is applied, yielding the value of the three-part expression. If no instantiation of the variables satisfies *range*, then the value of the three-part expression is the identity element for op, e.g., *true* if op is $\forall$, or $\varnothing$ if op is set.

The scene concept conveys a notion of locality, and each application decides how "local" its interactions need to be. A first responder team leader coordinating the team spread throughout the site may want to have an aggregate view of the smoke conditions over the entire site. On the other hand, a particular responder may want a scene that contains readings only from nearby sensors or sensors within his path of movement. The scene for the leader would be "all smoke sensors within the site boundaries," while the scene for the responder might be "all smoke sensors within 5m." As a responder moves through the site, the scene *specification* stays the same, but the data sources belonging to the scene may change.

In the ubiquitous computing scenarios we target, embedded nodes can come and go either because new devices are introduced to the environment, existing devices stopped functioning, or devices moved. Although existing systems treat such situations as exceptional conditions, they must be treated as commonplace. For this reason, the scene abstraction is specifically designed to handle such dynamics. Using the distributed computation detailed above, the scene implementation automatically recalculates and reconstructs an application's scene in response to such changes. This adjustment occurs automatically and seamlessly using the application's provided scene *specification* (which is now imprinted in the sensor network) and does not involve the application or user directly. Instead, the scene (or the set of devices with which the application interacts) automatically adjusts to reflect the application's changing operational environment.

To maintain the scene for continuous queries, each member sends periodic beacons advertising its current value for the metric. Each node also monitors beacons from its parent in the routing tree, whose identity is provided as previous hop information in the original scene message. If a node has not heard from its parent for three consecutive beacon intervals, it disqualifies itself from the scene. This corresponds to the node falling outside of the span of the scene due to client mobility or other dynamics. In addition, if the client's motion necessitates a new node to suddenly become a member of the scene, this new node becomes aware of this condition through the beacon it receives from a current scene member.

Table 1 shows examples of how scenes may be specified. These examples include restricting the scene by the maximum number of hops allowed, the minimum allowable battery power on each participating node, or the maximum physical distance. As one

Table 1. Example Scene Definitions

	Hop Count Scene
Metric	SCENE_HOP_COUNT
Cost Function	SCENE_SUM
Metric Value	number of hops traversed
Threshold	maximum number of hops
	Battery Power Scene
Metric	SCENE_BATTERY_POWER
Cost Function	SCENE_MIN
Metric Value	minimum battery power
Threshold	minimum allowable battery power
	Distance Scene
Metric	SCENE_DISTANCE
Cost Function	SCENE_DFORMULA
Metric Value	location of source
Threshold	maximum physical distance

example, SCENE_HOP_COUNT effectively assigns a value of one to each network link. Therefore, using the built-in SCENE_SUM path cost function, the application can build a hop count scene that sums the number of hops a message takes and only includes nodes that are within the number of hops as specified by the threshold. The scene can be further restricted using latency as a second constraint.

Intelligent Virtual Sensors

Our middleware paradigm also defines a virtual sensors model (Kabadayi, Pridgen, & Julien, 2006). Virtual sensors provide indirect measurements of abstract conditions (that, by themselves are not physically measurable) by combining sensed data from a group of heterogeneous physical sensors. As an example, the intelligent construction site domain that consists of users with mobile devices distributed over the site and sensors embedded in equipment presents substantial challenges to pervasive computing. For example, users may desire safe load indicators on cranes that determine if a crane is exceeding its capacity. Such a virtual sensor (as shown in Figure 3) would take measurements from physical sensors that monitor boom angle, load, telescoping length, two-block conditions, wind speed, etc. (Neitzel, Seixas, & Ren, 2001). Signals from these individual sensors are used in calculations within the virtual sensor to determine if the crane has exceeded its safe working load. With

Figure 3. An example of a virtual sensor for safe working load

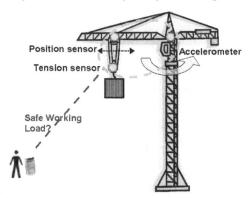

the virtual sensors model, an application interacts with a combination of physical and virtual devices embedded in the environment.

The physical sensors are the components of the model that provide the physical data types required to compute the desired abstract measurement. Creating a virtual sensor requires defining a group of physical sensors that have some locality relationship (i.e., belong to a local region, where "local" is defined by some property of the network or environment). The resulting virtual sensor has an interface similar to that of a physical sensor (from the application's perspective).

The virtual sensor hides the explicit data sources from the application, making them appear as one data source that provides the same type of interface as a physical sensor. Our approach to creating a virtual sensor's declarative specification assumes applications and sensors share knowledge of a naming scheme for the low-level data types the sensor nodes can provide (e.g., "location," "temperature," etc.). The types of sensors deployed in a network determine the available data types. The programmer, then, only needs to specify the following four parameters for the virtual sensor:

- **Input data types:** Physical (low-level) data types required to compute the desired abstract measurement. Each input data type also includes the number of different sensors (which could be *one*, *two*, *all*, etc.) the virtual sensor would like to obtain this data type from. For example, in deciding if a slab of concrete on a construction site is ready for use, a virtual sensor could combine measurements from concrete heat sensors and strain sensors. The specification of the number of different sensors of a certain type allows us to differentiate between requests for "all of the concrete heat sensors" and "one concrete heat sensor." The "all" count allows the virtual sensor's heterogeneous aggregation (over heat and strain sensors) to be combined with homogeneous aggregation (over heat sensors).

- **Aggregator:** A generic function defined to operate over the specific (possibly heterogeneous) input data to calculate the desired measurement

- **Resulting data type:** The abstract measurement type that is a result of the aggregation.

- **Aggregation frequency:** The frequency with which this aggregation should be made. This frequency determines how consistent the aggregated value is with actual conditions (i.e., more frequently updated aggregations reflect the environment more accurately but generate more communication overhead.). This is similar to the sample frequency of a physical sensor. At each aggregation frequency, the virtual sensor "samples" each physical sensor that it uses and aggregates these results.

By providing these virtual sensor specifications, an application delegates physical sensor discovery to the virtual sensor (and to the framework that supports the virtual sensor). Therefore, if the data sources that support the virtual sensor change over time, the virtual sensor adapts, but the application is not disrupted. This concept of data sources changing over time will be discussed in more detail in the following subsections.

In our model, the input data types carry simply the nature of the physical measure (e.g., "temperature") provided by a sensor. There could be a data type that is sometimes provided by a physical sensor and is sometimes provided by a virtual sensor (e.g., location provided by GPS (physical sensor) or by triangulation (virtual sensor)). From the application's perspective, this is only a single data type, and our model uses a data ontology (that may be application domain-specific) to describe these data types. The ontology is basically a simple listing of types. The application programmer can also insert new data types into the ontology to update or augment it over time. Before accessing sensors in the immersive network, the application checks the ontology to determine first if the type can be provided by a physical sensor and, if not, what virtual sensor needs to be deployed to provide the type.

As stated in the introduction, our goal is to support locality of interactions and access to local data. Thus, it is necessary to define the region from which it is allowable to select physical sensors to support a virtual sensor. This allows us to limit the reach of a virtual sensor to some small portion of the network in the immediate vicinity of the client device. When a virtual sensor construction is requested, the necessary scene is created first, and then the virtual sensor is constructed.

After specifying the constraints that build the scene (which consist of a metric definition and a maximum permissible cost for that metric), a client application would like to construct the virtual sensor using physical sensors from within the scene. That is:

Given the set of hosts S_α in the scene, the required physical data types D_1, D_2, ..., D_n, the aggregation function F, and the resulting data type, D_{res}, the virtual sensor can be formalized as:

$$D_{res} = F(D_1, D_2, ..., D_n) \text{ where}$$
$$\langle \forall D_i : 1 \le i \le n :: \langle \exists S : |S| = D_i.\text{count} \land \langle \forall s \in S : s \in S_\alpha \land D_i.\text{type} \rhd s \rangle \rangle \rangle$$

The "D_i.type $\rhd$ s" construct denotes the fact that "sensor s can provide the data type specified in D_i.type." In the above definition, the set S is the subset of S_α that defines which physical devices contribute to the virtual sensor. If the construct in the last line of the definition evaluates to false, it is not possible to construct the specified virtual sensor. As stated in the scene definition, the input data types (D_1, D_2, ..., D_n) are defined by the type of data they request and the number of independent readings of that type that are required. We assume the former is expressed as D_i.type and the latter is expressed as D_i.count. For example, the virtual sensor shown in Figure 3 requires two data types and one sensor of each type: a single crane base position and a single crane boom position. On the other hand, a virtual sensor that generates the average temperature of a curing pad of concrete requires temperature values from n temperature sensors. In this case, only one D is provided, and its count value reflects the number of sensors to be polled. As we described previously, the count value included in the declaration of the virtual sensor can be a number (e.g., one as in the case of the crane sensor above) or *all*, indicating that all matching sensors in the scene should be polled. In the latter case, the count value for the data type is set to be exactly the cardinality of the scene, $|S_\alpha|$.

To summarize, the virtual sensor aggregation function (F) operates on the input data that is of the specified type to yield the specified output data type. This function evaluation takes place at every interval specified by the aggregation frequency.

Dynamic sensor discovery, that is the discovery of the virtual sensor by the application, takes place on the basis of the virtual sensor specification. Virtual sensors provide the same interface to the user as physical sensors. The data type ontology that was mentioned above exists at this interface and defines the data types available to the application. A domain expert can create complex virtual sensors by hand and add their types to the ontology. Most importantly, the application does not have to know that it is discovering a virtual sensor instead of a physical sensor. The developer selects a data type listed in the ontology from a scene. If a physical sensor can provide that data type, no virtual sensor construction is necessary. Otherwise, the virtual sensor is activated and searches for supporting physical sensors in the scene. The ontology provides this mapping so that the application developer using virtual sensors must do nothing more than select the virtual sensor associated with the type in the ontology and request its deployment. This is handled automatically by the middleware at the time an application requests data of a particular type.

Figure 4. The dynamics associated with user movement

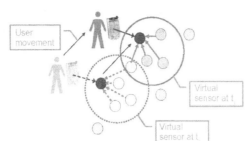

If a virtual sensor is being used to obtain periodic responses, it needs to be dynamically refreshed. At every refresh interval specified by the virtual sensor's aggregation frequency, the virtual sensor gets new measurements from each physical sensor contributing to it and recalculates the virtual measurement. During its lifetime, some sensors contributing to a virtual sensor may deplete their battery power and become nonfunctional. In this case, the virtual sensor attempts to discover a new sensor that can provide the data that sensor was providing; if another such sensor does not exist in the scene, the virtual sensor fails.

Furthermore, while the sensor nodes used in pervasive environments are embedded (hence stationary), the application interacting with them runs on a device carried by a mobile user. Therefore, the device's connections to particular sensors and the area from which the application desires to draw information (i.e., the scene) are subject to constant change. These changes need to be seamlessly handled without revealing the underlying dynamics to the user. The dynamics associated with user movement may cause the physical sensors that comprise the virtual sensor to change and are handled by the scene abstraction (see Figure 4). Since the physical data sources that can contribute to a virtual sensor are restricted by the scene, any data source that satisfies the data requirements from that scene is a valid data source for the virtual sensor.

To summarize, this dynamic maintenance allows the user to interact directly with a changing set of local information sources. The virtual sensor hides the underlying complexity from the user.

Figure 5 abstractly depicts *n* physical sensors, aggregated into a virtual sensor which can run (a) locally (on the client) or (b) remotely (in the network). The physical sensors are illustrated using circles, and the different shadings indicate their heterogeneous nature. The sensors inside the large dashed circle contribute to the virtual sensor, but only a few have been shown with arrows representing the data they send back, for ease of presentation. The virtual sensor code can either run locally on the client device or be deployed to a resource-constrained sensor within the network. When deployed remotely, this code will be dynamically received by a listener on the remote sensor and executed. If all of the physical sensors are in a cluster, and

Figure 5. Abstract depiction of a virtual sensor that uses n physical nodes; (a) n physical sensors, aggregated into a virtual sensor which runs locally, (b) n physical sensors, aggregated into a virtual sensor which runs remotely

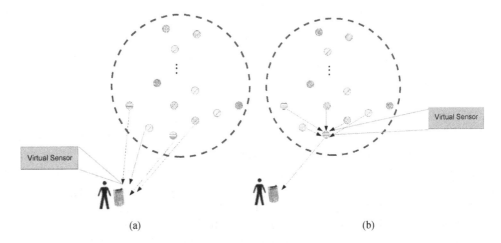

that cluster is several hops away from the user's device, then it may make sense to send the virtual sensor out to the cluster. On the other hand, if each of the sensors that make up the virtual sensor is within one hop of the user, then the virtual sensor should run on the user's device. With respect to the application interface, it does not matter if the virtual sensor is deployed on the client's device or remotely in the network, but it might improve performance to use a certain option depending on the application's situation.

Benefiting from Middleware in Ubiquitous Computing

In this section, we present a complete middleware solution, the DAIS middleware model, which incorporates the scene and virtual sensor abstractions, adheres to the requirements enumerated in the previous section, and provides a cohesive environment for ubiquitous computing application development. Figure 6 shows the DAIS architecture, which consists of a handheld component (running on, for example, a laptop or a PDA) and the immersive sensor environment (defined by a community of sensors). The figure shows DAIS's explicit hierarchical model which enables more powerful devices (i.e., client devices) to support more of the middleware's functionality than resource-constrained devices (e.g., physical sensors). As Figure 6 shows, a client application runs with the support of the two key abstractions introduced in the previous sections, namely *scenes* and *virtual sensors*. The types

Figure 6. The DAIS high-level architecture. The left-hand side shows the components comprising the model on the component carried by the user (e.g., PDA or laptop), and the right-hand side shows the DAIS components on the sensors.

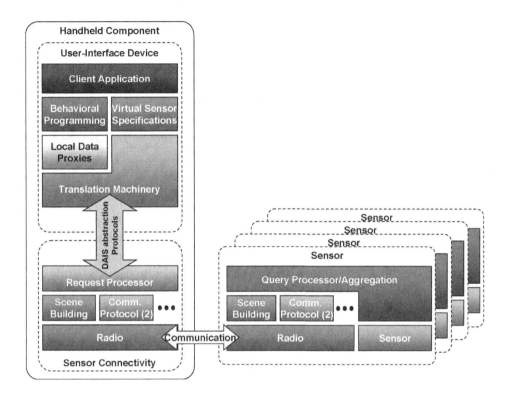

Figure 7. DAIS object diagram

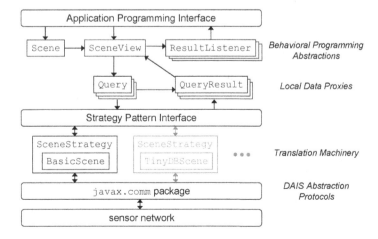

of queries possible in DAIS can be classified into *one-time queries* (which return a single result from each participating sensor) and *persistent queries* (which return periodic responses from participating sensors). To support these types, we provide two different methods for posing queries to the network. We also include versions of these two methods that request processing of the retrieved data before the result is handed back to the application.

In the remainder of this section, we describe the use of the strategy pattern to perform communication protocol encapsulation, how queries come from the application, and what happens as these queries travel through the middleware depicted in Figure 6. Figure 7 shows a simplified object diagram of the DAIS middleware layers. The names of the layers on the right of the figure correspond to the layers in Figure 6.

Strategy Pattern Interface

As shown in Figure 7, our middleware makes use of the *strategy pattern* (Gamma, Helm, Johnson, & Vlissides, 1995), a software design pattern in which algorithms (such as strategies for query dissemination) can be chosen at runtime depending on system conditions. The strategy pattern provides a means to define a family of algorithms, encapsulate each one as an object, and make them interchangeable. Such an approach allows the algorithms to vary independently from clients that use them.

In DAIS, the clients that employ the strategies are the queries, and the different strategies are the `SceneStrategy` algorithms. These algorithms determine how a `Query` is disseminated to the `Scene` and how the `QueryResult` is returned. If a particular dissemination algorithm other than the default is required for a specific application, an appropriate `SceneStrategy` algorithm is instantiated.

Two principle directives of object-oriented design are used in the strategy pattern: encapsulate the concept that varies, and program to an interface, not to an implementation. Using the strategy pattern, we decouple the `Query` from the code that runs it so we can vary the query dissemination algorithm without modifying the `Query` class. The loose coupling that the strategy pattern enables between the components makes the system easier to maintain, extend, and reuse.

For now, we provide only a single implementation of the strategy, the `Basic-Scene`. This is a simple, greedy scheme in which all data aggregation is performed locally. We have chosen this as a first step to provide a quick prototype of the entire middleware. Other communication approaches can be swapped in for the `Basic-Scene` (for example, one built around TinyDB (Madden et al., 2005) or directed diffusion (Intanagonwiwat, Govindan, Estrin, Heideman, & Silva, 2003), although the implementations of these approaches on the sensors may have to be modified slightly to accommodate scene construction). By defining the `SceneStrategy` interface, we enable developers who are experts in existing communication approaches to create simple plug-ins that use different query dissemination and/or aggregation protocols. Different communication paradigms can be used in different environments or to support different application domains depending on the resource constraints or domain-specific capabilities of the devices in a particular domain.

Each `SceneStrategy` interacts with the `javax.comm` package to provide the *DAIS abstraction protocols* that allow the portion of the middleware implemented in Java (described above) to interact with the sensor hardware. Each `SceneStrategy` requires not only a high-level portion implemented on the handheld device, but also a low-level portion that runs on the sensors. Next, we briefly discuss our `BasicScene` implementation that runs on the sensor nodes that respond to a client application's queries. Complete details of this implementation can be found in (Kabadayi & Julien, 2007). This serves as just one example of a particular implementation of the `SceneStrategy`.

In DAIS, we have developed the sensor components for the Crossbow MICA2 mote platform (Crossbow, 2007). Our initial implementation is written for TinyOS (Hill et al., 2000) in the nesC language (Gay et al., 2003) and helps the `BasicScene` strategy conform to the `SceneStrategy` interface.

Figure 8. Implementation of Scene functionality on sensors

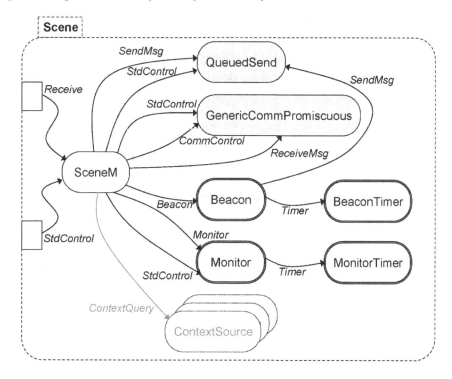

Building Scenes

In nesC, an application consists of *modules* wired together via shared interfaces to form *configurations*. We have created several components that form the fundamental functionality of the *Scene configuration*. Figure 8 abstractly depicts the necessary components and the interfaces they share.

This implementation functions as a routing component on each node, receiving each incoming message from the radio and processing it as our protocol dictates. In this picture, we show components as rounded rectangles and interfaces as arrows connecting components. A component *provides* an interface if the corresponding arrow points towards it and *uses* an interface if the arrow points away from it. If a component provides an interface, it must implement all of the *commands* in the interface, and if a component uses an interface, it can call any commands in the interface and must handle all *events* generated by the interface. In short, the SceneM component uses the messages sent as part of the scene construction protocol to determine whether the local node is contained within the specified scene. If so, the application-level message is propagated to the application layer on the sensor, and the scene construction message is propagated to the neighbors to allow includes of additional nodes.

Determining whether or not it is part of a scene may require the SceneM component to access local context information (through the *ContextSources* in Figure 8). For example, if a scene is defined based on physical locations, each node must access a location context sensor to determine the node's physical location.

When a node is part of a scene over which persistent queries have been issued, a Beacon message proactively maintains the connectivity among the scene members. If, in the exchange of these Beacon messages and monitoring the *ContextSources* that are in use, a node discovers that it no longer qualifies to be a member of the scene (e.g., the scene is based on physical location and the client device has moved), the node removes itself from the scene and ceases this proactive behavior.

Processing Dynamic Queries: A Step-By-Step Example

To describe the DAIS model and how it works, we follow a query from the application developer's hands all the way into the network to a participating sensor and back. To present the steps involved in the process, we use a single, specific application example taken from the intelligent construction site domain. In the example we have selected, the application's user would like to receive a notification if any crane load reading within 100m exceeds a safe threshold. The user would like this information to be updated every 10 seconds to ensure he has the most current information.

- **Step 1: Create a Virtual Sensor.** As depicted in Figure 3, whether or not a crane load is safe depends on several conditions and is not simply a factor of the weight of a load. In a simple scenario, we assume that the safety of a load depends on the position of the load on the crane arm (e.g., heavier loads should be kept closer to the center of the crane), the tension on the boom (e.g., heavier loads and windier conditions both imply greater tensions, which can increase danger), and the acceleration of the crane (e.g., moving heavier loads quickly is dangerous). An application domain expert (with knowledge about crane safety) can create a virtual sensor that collects these aspects of the crane environment and generates a crane safety value ("safe" or "unsafe"). The following code would define the virtual sensor:

```
VirtualSensor craneVS = new VirtualSensor({new CraneArmTension(),
                                           new CraneBoomPosition(),
                                           new CraneAcceleration()},
                                           new LoadAggregator(),
                                           new CraneSafety(),
                                           1);
```

Within this definition, the first argument to the constructor contains an array of the virtual sensor's input data types. We omit the count for each type for brevity; in this example, the virtual sensor requires only one data reading of each type. The second argument contains a function definition that dictates how these values should be combined to generate the crane safety type. The third argument specifies the return type of the virtual sensor; in this case, whether or not the crane is safe. The final argument, an integer, gives the desired aggregation frequency for this virtual sensor. In this example, the physical sensors supporting the virtual sensor should send updates of their values every second. The application domain expert must define the code for the `LoadAggregator` and the meaning of the `CraneSafety` type; the other types are assumed to be physical measures that can be provided within the deployed network. The definition of this virtual sensor must also be added to the data ontology so applications needing to query the network can locate its type and automatically deploy it when it is needed. This is accomplished through the following code, which associates the `CraneSafety` type with the `craneVS` virtual sensor definition.

```
ontology.add({new CraneSafety(), craneVS});
```

This allows applications searching the data ontology to locate the virtual sensor functionality when they request the `CraneSafety` type.

- **Step 2: Declare a Scene.** This is the first step is performed by an application developer when creating and interacting with an immersive sensor network through the programming interface. Nothing happens involving network communication until the application actually uses the scene, reducing communication overhead. For our application example, the developer uses the following code to invoke the constructor of a `Scene` object that defines a scene that includes every sensor (not just those measuring crane load safety) within 100m of the declaring device:

```
Scene s = new Scene(new Constraint(Scene.SCENE_DISTANCE,
                                   Scene.SCENE_DFORMULA,
                                   new IntegerThreshold(100)));
```

  When the application subsequently needs to query the constructed scene, it calls the `getSceneView()` method, which returns a handle to a `SceneView`. The application can then use this `SceneView` to send a `Query` over the scene.

- **Step 3: Issue a Query.** This step is performed by the application developer using the `SceneView` instance created and accessed in the previous step. In our example application, the developer must first create the query:

```
Query q = new Query({new Constraint("CraneSafety",
                Query.EQUALS_OPERATOR,
                "unsafe")});
```

  In this case, the `Query` is defined by a single `Constraint` that requires returns any crane safety value of "unsafe" within 100m to be returned to the developer. After creating the `Query` above and a `ResultListener` r to receive the results (omitted for brevity), the application developer dispatches it using the `SceneView`:

```
SceneView sv = s.getSceneView();
int receipt = sv.registerQuery(q, r, 10);
```

  where 10 refers to the fact that the application wishes to sense the safety of crane loads every 10 seconds. Upon receiving any query request, the `SceneView` object adjusts its state in several ways. First, for every query, a table within the `SceneView` is updated with a mapping from a unique query id generated for the query to the `ResultListener` handle provided with the query. In addition, for persistent queries, this unique id is returned as a receipt of registration that can be used in subsequent interactions to, for example, deregister the query.

- **Step 4: Initialize Necessary Virtual Sensors.** Before dispatching the query to the scene, the middleware checks the data ontology to determine if the request type (in this case `CraneSafety`) is a primitive type in this network (i.e., it can be provided by a physical sensor), or if it is a virtual type for which a virtual sensor must be deployed. In the latter case (and in the case of this example), it is at this instant that the middleware creates the virtual sensor in the network. It is possible that multiple virtual sensors could be supported within the scene (e.g., in our scenario, it is possible that there are multiple cranes within 100m). For now, our implementation assumes that only a single virtual sensor is constructed in the scene; the final section of this chapter discusses the potential research necessary in this area in more detail. In our current implementation, the virtual sensor is "deployed" locally (as in Figure 5(a)), and this step connects the remote physical sensors to the local virtual sensor. The virtual sensor is now present within the scene and can be discovered by subsequent queries (from this node or other nodes). It is available to the `QueryProcessor` as one of the `Sensors` shown in Figure 9 and described below.

- **Step 3: Create Local Data Proxy.** Control has passed from the application developer to the middleware, which is now responsible for ensuring that the application's `ResultListener` is called with the appropriate data at the appropriate times. DAIS creates a local proxy dedicated to handling return calls for this query. The local data proxy is especially important in facilitating the translation between the low-level language spoken by the sensors (nesC in our implementation) in the network and the high-level language the application uses (Java).

- **Step 4: Construct and Distribute Protocol Query.** The local data proxy with the DAIS middleware transforms the application's request into a protocol data unit for the scene implementation in use. As was shown in Figure 7, several different protocols can provide the communication functionality as long as they adhere to the specified strategy pattern interface. The scene implementations must handle both persistent and one-time queries, as dictated by the strategy pattern interface. In our current implementation of the scene protocol (Kabadayi & Julien, 2007), the scene protocol message carries the information about scene membership constraints *and* the data query at the same time. This reduces the communication overhead by constructing the scene on demand. The details of the communication protocol are omitted here (see the referenced paper); it suffices to say that, by its definition, the protocol ensures that the data query is delivered to exactly the set of sensor nodes that satisfy the scene's constraints. In our example application, this means that every sensor within 100m will receive the data query constructed above. *Every* sensor receiving this query

Figure 9. Implementation of the QueryProcessor functionality on sensors

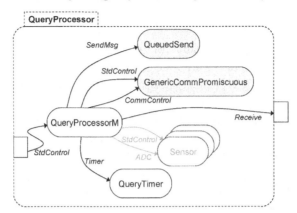

(i.e., all sensors within 100m) that supports the requested type (i.e., that have a CraneSafety sensor) periodically evaluates the query, but responds only if and when the sensor returns exactly the value unsafe.

- **Step 5: Process Scene Query on Remote Sensor.** We use TinyOS to implement functionality on the sensors; when the communication protocol receives and processes a scene message, if it determines that the node is within the scene, it passes the received message up to the application layer. In DAIS, the QueryProcessor, implemented in TinyOS, defines this application layer. This is essentially a slimmed down version of our middleware that is capable of running on the resource-constrained device. An abstract representation of the TinyOS implementation of the QueryProcessor is shown in Figure 9, which uses the same notational conventions used in Figure 8.

In our implementation, the QueryProcessor component provides the functionality shown at the top layer of the sensor portion of the architecture in Figure 6. The query arrives in the QueryProcessor through the receive event of the **Receive** interface. If the query is a one-time query (as indicated by a field in the TinyOS message), then the QueryProcessor simply connects to the onboard sensor that can provide the requested data type (depicted as Sensor in the figure). If the data request is for a sensor type that is not supported on this device (i.e., the sensor table stored in the QueryProcessor has no mapping to a sensor that can provide the specified data type), then the message is ignored. This sensor table includes both physical and virtual sensors available at this node. Even if the node ignores the application layer message because it cannot satisfy the data query, the node is still included in the scene because it may be a necessary routing node connecting the requester to another node that *does* have the required sensor.

If the query is persistent (as in our safe crane load example), then in addition to immediately returning the requested value if the query is satisfied, the `QueryProcessorM` module also initializes a `QueryTimer` using the request frequency specified in the `data` portion of the received message. When the timer fires, `QueryProcessorM` retrieves a value from the sensor and sends it back to the initial requester using the **SendMsg** interface of the `QueuedSend` module.

When a node is no longer in a scene (either because it moved, the client moved, or something happened in between to cause the scene membership requirement to no longer be satisfied), the scene communication implementation creates a null message that it sends to the `QueryProcessor` through the **Receive** interface. The `QueryProcessor` takes this message as a sign to cease streaming data back to the requester and stops the `QueryTimer`.

- **Step 6: Reply from Query Processor.** If the query processor possessed the correct sensor *and* the other components of the query are also satisfied (e.g., the constraints on the data value), the query processor replies (and continues to reply periodically to a persistent query). In our specific application scenario, every sensor node in the scene (i.e., within 100m) receives the `Query` for the `CraneSafety` type. In this case, only one of the sensors, the one supporting the virtual sensor, can actually provide the type. This `QueryProcessor` on this sensor monitors the values the virtual sensor generates over time (every 10 seconds) and returns a message to the application if the `CraneSafety` value is ever "unsafe." If the value is "safe," the node does not reply to the client application. Replies are sent through the **SendMsg** interface shown in Figure 9 and use basic multihop routing to return to the original requester.

- **Step 7: Distribute Result to Client Device.** After propagating through the underlying communication substrate, query replies will arrive at the client device's sensor network interface. At the client device, the result is demultiplexed by the *Request Processor* (shown in Figure 6) and handed off to the appropriate local proxy. Again, the local proxy is automatically generated and managed by the middleware. It translates the low-level query reply into a high-level `Result` and invokes the application's registered resultReceived() method. It is important to note that, as shown in Figure 7, multiple queries may be active over a single scene at any given time. For each scene, the `SceneView` controls all of these queries and connects them to the underlying implementation via the *strategy pattern interface*. When the result is passed off to the `ResultListener`, control transfers back to the application which handles the query's results (or queries' results if multiple matches existed). For persistent queries, as more results arrive, the same process occurs until the application deregisters the query.

This complete example demonstrates the few steps the application developer must accomplish to be able to leverage the automatic capabilities of the DAIS middleware. By simply interacting with the straightforward APIs the middleware provides, the application developer can define virtual sensors, create scenes over which to interact with a network, and dispatch queries. The persistent query capabilities of the DAIS middleware enable the application to monitor potentially dynamic situations as the user moves through an immersive sensor network. Both the scene and virtual sensor abstractions are capable of automatically adjusting to such changes and making the application's perspective on the world reflect the instantaneous operating conditions.

By coupling communication constructs (through the scene communication protocol) in addition to programming abstractions (through the virtual sensors and scene programming interfaces), the DAIS middleware exposes significant expressiveness to the application developer while accepting the burden of implementing the complex interactions in the ubiquitous computing network. From the application developer's perspective, the most complicated portions of interacting with the DAIS middleware lie in properly defining the virtual sensors and creating meaningful queries to issue over scenes. Both of these aspects require significant domain-specific knowledge, and the simple APIs we have designed allow domain experts to easily encode this knowledge which the DAIS middleware can subsequently translate to low-level code to run in the sensor network.

Conclusion

Given the extreme demands for simplified programming of ubiquitous computing applications, it is obvious that programming environments tailored to this domain are required. In this chapter, we have first argued that immersive sensor networks are essential to the future success of ubiquitous computing. We have then surveyed existing work in the area of providing simplified programming constructs for application developers working in both sensor networks and ubiquitous computing. Finally, the chapter has presented a new paradigm for *immersive sensor networks* that combines traditional sensor network technologies with the vision of ubiquitous computing.

Because any middleware for immersive environments must operate at least to some degree on resource-constrained devices, it is important to achieve reasonable performance with respect to battery lifetimes and communication overhead. Our work on the scene protocol (Kabadayi & Julien, 2007) has shown that, by localizing communication to a region surrounding the application in question (as depicted in Figure 1(b)), we greatly reduce the energy and communication impact on other devices in the network. In addition, this approach provides a localized view of the world, which is invaluable to ubiquitous computing applications. A similar performance characterization of the query processing capabilities on the sensor nodes themselves is underway; here we must ensure that responses (especially those indicating anomalous conditions) can be returned to client applications in a timely fashion.

Finally, the example application given in the previous section demonstrates the ease with which application developers can interact with the DAIS middleware constructs. By employing a few straightforward middleware interfaces, applications can easily define regions of interactions that expand and contract in response to context properties of the environment. Applications can also define expressive queries that the middleware dispatches to the network, allowing in-network query resolution, which can reduce communication overhead and latency.

Given the systems available as the current state of the art, we are lacking the ability to quickly and easily design, develop, and deploy expressive applications that allow localized interaction and coordination among users immersed in ubiquitous computing environments and the environments themselves. The DAIS middleware, presented in this chapter, takes a first step towards providing such an environment that focuses on localized interactions that are based on relative notions of locations between devices.

Future Directions

As our survey of existing research has indicated, there is a significant lack of availability of tools and development environments that enable application development in ubiquitous computing environments. Clearly, significant progress must be made in this area before applications can be rapidly and reliably created for ubiquitous computing environments. Such tools should be motivated directly by the characteristics specific to ubiquitous computing environments as detailed in this chapter, and they must provide support for coordination among users immersed in the environment. Such tools must allow applications to remain highly expressive while embedding much of the complexity within a middleware that eases the development burden.

Evaluation of the results of this research must also come to the forefront. Testing and evaluation of development constructs is inherently difficult; ubiquitous computing environments add extra concerns to the mix. New mechanisms for supporting easy and correct evaluation and testing must be developed that are tailored to the ubiquitous computing environment. Specifically, in addressing the above development environments, we must be able to evaluate the quality of the abstractions with respect to aiding application development.

Finally, in evaluating the coordination requirements for ubiquitous computing environments, an obvious central theme is the ability to group embedded nodes based on relative physical and logical properties. The scene abstraction is one example of this, and it is a natural approach to defining regions of coordination around an immersed application user. We have also used this scene approach to support the virtual sensor abstraction, but it is not as natural in this case. To enable abstractions such as the virtual sensor to accurately reflect an environment, new neighborhood abstractions must be developed that enable sensor nodes to self-organize in response to application queries.

In conclusion, while many positive steps have been made in enabling technologies for immersive sensor network support of ubiquitous computing applications, several research aspects remain open and must be addressed before we will see widespread adoption of ubiquitous computing networks and applications.

Acknowledgment

The authors would like to thank the Center for Excellence in Distributed Global Environments for providing research facilities and the collaborative environment. This research was funded, in part, by the National Science Foundation (NSF), Grants #CNS-0620245 and OCI-0636299. The conclusions herein are those of the authors and do not necessarily reflect the views of the sponsoring agencies.

References

Abadi, D. J., Madden, S., & Lindner, W. (2005). REED: Robust, efficient filtering and event detection in sensor networks. In K. Böhm, C. S. Jensen, L. M. Haas, M. L. Kersten, P.-A. Larson, & B. C. Ooi (Eds.), In *Proceedings of the 31st International Conference on Very Large Data Bases* (pp. 769-780). Saratoga: VLDB Endowment.

Abdelzaher, T., Blum, B., Cao, Q., Chen, Y., Evans, D., George, J., et al. (2004). EnviroTrack: Towards an environmental computing paradigm for distributed sensor networks. In D. Xuan, & A. Idoue (Eds.), In *Proceedings of the 24th International Conference on Distributed Computing Systems* (pp. 582-589). Los Alamitos: IEEE Computer Society.

Bakshi, A., Prasanna, V. K., Reich, J., & Larner, D. (2005). The abstract task graph: A methodology for architecture-independent programming of networked sensor systems. In R. Ambrosio, & C. Bisdikian (Eds.), In *Proceedings of the 2005 Workshop on End-to-End Sense-and-Respond Systems, Applications, and Services* (pp. 19-24). Berkeley: USENIX Association.

Cheong, E., Liebman, J., Liu, J., & Zhao, F. (2003). TinyGALS: A programming model for event-driven embedded systems. In B. Panda (Ed.), In *Proceedings of the 2003 ACM Symposium on Applied Computing* (pp. 698-704). New York: ACM Press.

Costa, P., Mottola, L., Murphy, A., & Picco, G. P. (2006). TeenyLIME: Transiently shared tuple space middleware for wireless sensor networks. In S. Michiels, & W. Joosen (Eds.), In *Proceedings of the International Workshop on Middleware for Sensor Networks* (pp. 43-48). New York: ACM Press.

Crossbow Technologies, Inc. (2007). *Wireless Sensor Networks: MICA2 868, 916 MHz.* Retrieved on May 15, 2007, from http://www.xbow.com/Products/productdetails.aspx?sid=174

Curino, C., Giani, M., Giorgetta, M., Giusti, A., Murphy, A. L., & Picco, G. P. (2005). TinyLIME: Bridging mobile and sensor networks through middleware. In *Proceedings of the 3rd International Conference on Pervasive Computing and Communications* (pp. 61-72). Los Alamitos: IEEE Computer Society.

Estrin, D., Culler, D., Pister, K., & Sukhatme, G. (2002). Connecting the physical world with pervasive networks. *IEEE Pervasive Computing, 1*(1), 59-69.

Fok, C.-L., Roman, G.-C., & Lu, C. (2005). Rapid development and flexible deployment of adaptive wireless sensor network applications. In D. Xuan, & W. Zhao (Eds.), In *Proceedings of the 25th International Conference on Distributed Computing Systems* (pp. 653-662). Washington: IEEE Computer Society.

Gamma, E., Helm, R., Johnson, R., & Vlissides, J. (1995). *Design Patterns.* Reading, MA: Addison-Wesley.

Gay, D., Levis, P., von Behren, R., Welsh, M., Brewer, E., & Culler, D. (2003). The nesC language: A holistic approach to networked embedded systems. In *Proceedings of the ACM SIGPLAN 2003 Conference on Programming Language Design and Implementation* (pp. 1-11). New York: ACM Press.

Girod, L., Elson, J., Cerpa, A., Stathopoulous, T., Ramanathan, N., & Estrin. D. (2004). EmStar: A software environment for developing and deploying wireless sensor networks. In *Proceedings of the 2004 USENIX Technical Conference* (pp. 283-296). Berkeley: USENIX Association.

Greenstein, B., Kohler, E., & Estrin, D. (2004). A sensor network application construction kit (SNACK). In A. Arora, & R. Govindan (Eds.), In *Proceedings of the 2nd International Conference on Embedded Networked Sensor Systems* (pp. 69-80). New York: ACM Press.

Gummadi, R., Gnawali, O., & Govindan, R. (2005). Macro-programming wireless sensor networks using Kairos. In P. Leone (Ed.), In *Proceedings of the*

International Conference on Distributed Computing in Sensor Systems (pp. 126-140). Berlin: Springer.

Hammer, J., Hassan, I., Julien, C., Kabadayi, S., O'Brien, W., & Trujillo, J. (2006). Dynamic decision support in direct-access sensor networks: a demonstration. In C. Westphal (Ed.), In *Proceedings of the 3rd International Conference on Mobile Ad-hoc and Sensor Systems* (pp. 578-581). Los Alamitos: IEEE Computer Society.

Heinzelman, W. B., Murphy, A. L., Carvallo, H. S., & Perillo, M. A. (2004). Middleware to support sensor network applications. *IEEE Network Magazine, 18*(1), 6-14.

Hill, J., Szewczyk, R., Woo, A., Hollar, S., Culler, D., & Pister, K. (2000). System architecture directions for networked sensors. In *Proceedings of the 9th International Conference on Architectural Support for Programming Languages and Operating Systems* (pp. 93-104). New York: ACM Press.

Intanagonwiwat, C., Govindan, R., Estrin, D., Heideman, J., & Silva, F. (2003). Directed diffusion for wireless sensor networking. *IEEE/ACM Transactions on Networking, 11*(1), 2-16.

Kabadayi, S., & Julien, C. (2007). A local data abstraction and communication paradigm for pervasive computing. In S. Ceballos (Ed.), In *Proceedings of the 5th Annual IEEE International Conference on Pervasive Computing and Communications* (pp. 57-68). Los Alamitos: IEEE Computer Society.

Kabadayi, S., Pridgen, A., & Julien, C. (2006). Virtual sensors: Abstracting data from physical sensors. In S. Ceballos (Ed.), In *Proceedings of the 2006 International Symposium on a World of Wireless, Mobile, and Multimedia Networks* (pp. 587-592). Los Alamitos: IEEE Computer Society.

Kidd, C. D., Orr, R., Abowd, G. D., Atkeson, C. G., Essa, I. A., MacIntyre, B., et al. (1999). The aware home: A living laboratory for ubiquitous computing research. In N. A. Streitz, J. Siegel, V. Hartkopf, & S. Konomi (Eds.), In *Proceedings of the 2nd International Workshop on Cooperative Buildings, Integrating Information, Organization, and Architecture* (pp. 191-198). London: Springer-Verlag.

Koshy, J., & Pandey, R. (2005). VM*: Synthesizing scalable runtime environments for sensor networks. In X. Koutsoukos (Ed.), In *Proceedings of the 3rd ACM International Conference on Embedded Networked Sensor Systems* (pp. 243-254). New York: ACM Press.

Liu, J., Chu, M., Liu, J., Reich, J., & Zhao, F. (2003). State-centric programming for sensor-actuator network systems. *IEEE Pervasive Computing, 2*(4), 50-62.

Madden, S. R., Franklin, M. J., Hellerstein, J. M., & Hong, W. (2005). TinyDB: An acquisitional query processing system for sensor networks. *ACM Transactions on Database Systems. 30*(1), 122-173.

Neitzel, R. L., Seixas, N. S., & Ren, K. K. (2001). A review of crane safety in the construction industry. *Applied Occupational and Environmental Hygiene*, *16*(12), 1106-1117.

Newton, R., & Welsh, M. (2004). Region streams: Functional macroprogramming for sensor networks. In A. Labrinidis, & S. Madden (Eds.), In *Proceedings of the 1ˢᵗ International Workshop on Data Management for Sensor Networks* (pp. 78-87). New York: ACM Press.

Roman, M., Hess, C., Cerqueira, A., Ranganathan, A., Campbell, R. H., & Narstedt, K. (2002). A middleware infrastructure for active spaces. *IEEE Pervasive Computing*, *1*(4), 74-83.

Voida, S., Mynatt, E. D., & MacIntyre, B. (2002). Supporting collaboration in a context-aware office computing environment. In P. Tandler, C. Magerkurth, S. Carpendale, & K. Inkpen (Eds.), In *Proceedings of the Workshop on Collaboration with Interactive Walls and Tables*. Berlin: Springer.

Weiser, M. (1991). The computer for the twenty-first century. *Scientific American*, *265*(3), 94-101.

Yao, Y., & Gehrke, J. (2002). The cougar approach to in-network query processing in sensor networks. *ACM SIGMOD Record*, *31*(3), 9-18.

Chapter VI

Determinants of User Acceptance for RFID Ticketing Systems

Dimitrios C. Karaiskos, Athens University of Business and Economics, Greece

Panayiotis E. Kourouthanassis, Athens University of Business and Economics, Greece

Abstract

RFID ticketing systems constitute a particular type of pervasive information systems providing spectators of sports events with a transparent mechanism to validate and renew tickets. This study seeks to investigate the factors that influence user acceptance of RFID ticketing systems. The theoretical background of the study was drawn from the technology acceptance model (TAM) and the innovation diffusion theory (IDT), and enhanced with factors related to privacy and switching cost features. The research model was tested with data gathered through a lab experiment (N=71). The participants perceived the system as useful and easy to use, and expressed the willingness to adopt it should it become commercially available. Moreover, the results of ANOVA tests suggest that the age and education of users influence their perception towards the usefulness of the system and its subsequent use.

Introduction

The advent of mobile and wireless technologies such as Wi-Fi, ZigBee (Geer, 2006), and RFID (Smith & Konsynski, 2003) have inspired new research fields that challenge our existing view of Information Systems (IS) and their use by envisioning new ways of interacting with them away from the boundaries imposed by the desktop computer. The gradual miniaturisation of electronic components, the massive reduction of their production and operation costs, and their ability to communicate wirelessly, contributed to the design and development of systems that are capable of being embedded in objects, places, and even people (Roussos, 2006). Information Systems scholars have named this new phenomenon using such terms as *nomadic computing* (Lyytinen & Yoo, 2002), *ubiquitous computing* (Weiser, 1993), and *pervasive computing* (Saha & Mukherjee, 2003). These terms share the common denominator that Information Technology pervades the physical space, operates in the periphery of humans' world, and supports a variety of applications and services in a context-aware and passive manner. Birnbaum (1997) identified these novel characteristics in the IS discipline by defining a new IS class entitled *pervasive information systems (pervasive IS)*.

Pervasive IS may support both personal and business activities. Kourouthanassis and Giaglis (2006) provide a taxonomy of pervasive IS and their features by identifying four pertinent application types--personal, domestic, corporate, and public. Personal pervasive IS rely on wearable hardware elements to provide a fully functional computing experience on the direct periphery of the user. Typical examples include biomedical monitoring systems (Jafari, Dabiri, Brisk, & Sarrafzadeh, 2005), human detection systems (Smith et al., 2005), and remote plant operation systems (Najjar, Thompson, & Ockerman, 1997). Domestic pervasive IS primarily automate tasks that otherwise require human supervision in the household (e.g., heating and lightning control, monitoring the home inventory, etc.). Typical examples include MIT's Home of the Future initiative (Intille, 2002) and the Aware Home (Kidd et al., 1999). Corporate pervasive IS may support enterprise-wide activities, such as supply chain management (e.g., warehouse management (Prater, Frazier, & Reyes, 2005)), workforce management (e.g., sales force automation (Walters, 2001)) and office support (Churchill, Nelson, & Denoue, 2003; Greenberg & Rounding, 2001), and customer relationship management (Kourouthanassis, 2004). Finally, public pervasive IS may provide interactive environments in public places. Examples include wireless museum guides (Hsin & Liu, 2006) and mobile information devices in hospitals (Xiao, Lasome, Moss, Mackenzie, & Faraj, 2001) to name a few popular applications.

RFID ticketing systems fall under the umbrella of public pervasive IS by providing spectators of sports events with a technology-augmented method for renewing and validating their tickets. The underlying technology is radio-frequency identification

(RFID) which is a generic term for technologies that use radio waves to automatically identify people or objects. The identification process involves the storage of a unique serial number to an RFID tag comprised of a microchip and an antenna. The antenna enables the chip to transmit the identification information to an *RFID Reader*. The reader converts the radio waves reflected back from the RFID tag into digital information that can then be passed on to computers that can make use of it. RFID technology already has been incorporated in sports tickets over the past few years with the most notable deployment being during the 2006 FIFA World Cup (Schmidt & Hanloser, 2006). The successful paradigm also has been followed by numerous football clubs in the U.K. such as Fulham, Coventry City, Manchester City, Reading, and Wigan.

The new ticketing scheme promises to bring the advantages of RFID technology to the sports events arena. Tickets incorporating the RFID technology have added value credited to the technical capabilities of RFID which are wireless connectivity, persistent memory, and computing power. In particular, a RFID-enabled ticket contains a microprocessor which allows encryption methods to be applied in order to be uniquely authenticated, thus, discouraging incidents of forgery, counterfeiting, and replication. Furthermore, the RFID-enabled ticket has the ability to store data regarding service details and owner's personal data, making possible the unique identification of the owner and the provision of added value services to him. Also, the wireless connectivity of the ticket allows its owner to pass control gates faster and to be more easily located for security reasons.

Although RFID tickets represent an excellent balance between cost, security, and access control, issues of reliability and durability have been received with scepticism due to their feature of uniquely identifying individuals and, indirectly, extrapolating their location; this raises privacy concerns for spectators.

Drawing from the aforementioned challenges, this chapter aims at identifying the factors that affect spectators' acceptance of RFID ticketing systems. To meet this objective, we have developed an *integrated user acceptance framework* that draws measurement variables from the disciplines of *psychology and information systems*. Although IS evaluation has been one of the most popular research topics with several models or frameworks attempting to explain the adoption and use of IT services (e.g., (Goodhue & Thompson, 1995; Taylor & Todd, 1995; Venkatesh, Morris, Davis, & Davis, 2003)), the properties of RFID ticketing systems in terms of wireless interaction modalities for users and prospective security and/ or privacy issues led us to enhance the existing user acceptance frameworks with factors addressing the aforementioned matters. The framework has been empirically validated through the design and implementation of a prototype RFID ticketing system and the execution of a lab experiment.

The chapter initially presents the architecture and design rationale of the RFID ticketing system in Section 2 (RFID Ticketing System). Section 3 (Research Model and

Method) presents the development of an appropriate measurement model to assess the acceptance of the system and the method used to acquire empirical data. Sections 4 (Results) and 5 (Discussion) address the results of the study, while section 6 provides a discussion and concluding remarks that identify the pertinent theoretical and practical implications of the proposed solution.

RFID Ticketing System

Overview of Technologies and Assessment

To select the appropriate underlying technology for the RFID ticketing system, we scrutinized the established practices followed by similar systems. Electronic ticketing is today a commodity in areas like entertainment (cinemas, theaters, and amusement parks to name a few popular application areas), sport events, public transportation, parking lots, automotive toll collections, and airline control. The technologies most commonly used are magnetic stripe tickets/cards, electronic tickets via internet, mobile ticketing systems, and smart cards. The advantages of these systems are cashless and queue-less transactions, flexible payments (e.g., by sending an SMS), reduction in operating and maintenance costs due to little or no manual intervention, accurate access control resulting in a reduced number of fare dodgers and in anti-counterfeiting, and efficient cost accounting with the potential of offering variable ticket pricing. Table 1, provides a summary of these approaches.

A comparative evaluation on the available technological solutions suggests that smart cards, and in particular contactless smart cards, are the prime candidates to support the interaction modalities of the proposed solution. Contactless smart cards can be used to automate the process of purchasing and validating tickets because of their inherent capabilities. They are typically credit card sized with an embedded microprocessor, memory, and an antenna providing them with the ability of wireless communication; thus, physical contact with a card reader is not required. Instead, the reader gains access to the card's data by emitting radio signals that are received by the card's built in antenna, thus facilitating two-way information exchange with the card's memory. This can include validation procedures, access controls, writing, and reading of the memory. Furthermore, such cards can be powered by induction using the reader, which extends the useful battery life of the card or does not require a battery at all (passive contactless smart cards). The most common technology that drives the ticketing solutions that are based in contactless smart cards is Radio Frequency Identification Technology (RFID).

Table 1. Technology-based ticketing systems

Technology	Functionality	Application Area	Advantages	Disadvantages
Magnetic Stripe Ticketing	access privileges and fare remaining are included and magnetically recoded after each use	commonly used to sports events and public transportation	technologically simple and inexpensive to produce	relatively small amount of information and may be easily read and copied
Electronic Ticketing	tickets are reserved or bought through a website (internet) or by telephone once a reservation is made an e-ticket exists only as a digital record in the computers customers usually print out a copy of their receipt which contains the record locator or reservation number and the e-ticket number	commonly used to airline flights and entertainment venues	cheap and efficient method, 24/7 accessibility	requires customers who know how to use computers and how to access the internet
Mobile Ticketing	mobile ticketing consider the mobile phone as the payment device the reservation and actual payment may occur through exchanging an SMS message or submitting a request through the mobile network	commonly used to parking lots, toll collection, and public transportation	cheap and efficient method	not a familiar method to the public
Contact Smart Cards	an embedded microprocessor and memory allows to save and manage access privileges and fare remaining	commonly used to sports events, public transportation and entertainment venues	programmable medium capable to offer advanced real time ticketing services (such as discounts, offers etc.)	expensive, requires sophisticated infrastructure and hinders security implications
Contactless Smart Cards	an embedded microprocessor and memory allows to save and manage access privileges and fare remaining, an embedded antenna gives the ability to communicate wirelessly with the infrastructure	commonly used to sports events, public transportation and entertainment venues	programmable medium capable to offer advanced real time ticketing services (such as discounts, offers etc.), time saving transactions	expensive, requires sophisticated infrastructure and hinders security implications

RFID Ticketing System: Rationale and Architecture

In our case, we propose a RFID-enabled ticketing system, henceforth referred to as SEAT that can be employed to manage ticketing procedures in any type of athletic event. The main innovation of the proposed approach is the incorporation of RFID technology to a traditional smart card. A prototype version of the system has been implemented and tested through a lab experiment.

The SEAT ticketing system manages all operations related to issuing and selling tickets, and also controlling access for athletic events hosted in stadiums. The system functionality is based on a RFID-enabled personal debit card (contactless smart card). The RFID card enables fans to buy tickets from properly equipped automated ticket kiosks and to enter the stadium through gates that provide automated access control. SEAT automates these processes resulting in decreased time and effort in buying tickets and passing through stadium gates while, at the same time, providing secure and effective access control. Furthermore, the system offers value-added services in the form of cashless transactions in the stadium, real time traffic information for the sport club, and personalized services to fans.

SEAT follows a 3-tier architecture based on distributed systems principles (Tanenbaum & Van Steen, 2003), supporting wide geographic dispersion of the system resources, independent modules providing the services, and central data storage and data access. The system consists of four distinct components:

1.   A **RFID contactless smart card** that stores important information regarding remaining price units and stadium access rights (operating at 13.56 MHz and supporting ICODE 1, 48 bytes read/write memory)

2.   A **RFID reader** (connected to the workstation) that reads/writes the RFID card and communicates all the information from and to the workstation (13.56 MHz frequency, supports ICODE 1, read/write capability, RS232 connectivity)

3.   **Workstations** (personal computers or laptops) that host a software module relative to the service provided (registration, kiosk, access control)

4.   A **server** that manages the database read/write access and the reader's (identification)

Figure 1 illustrates the system architecture.

In a typical usage scenario, a spectator of the athletic event issues a RFID contactless smart card from the registration kiosk (a one time registration) and charges it with a specific amount (see Figure 2).

The spectator can then go to a ticket kiosk and purchase a ticket for the event of his preference by swiping or placing the RFID card near the reader that is attached to

Figure 1. RFID ticketing system architecture

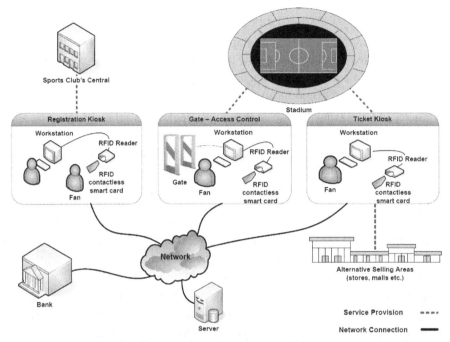

Figure 2. Registration kiosk: customer data form and registration's confirmation screen

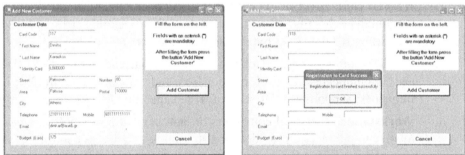

Figure 3. Ticket kiosk: welcome and PIN code authentication screen

Figure 4. Gate kiosk: welcome and PIN code authentication screen

the ticket kiosk. For security and authentication purposes a PIN number is requested (see Figure 3).

Finally, the spectator can enter the stadium by swiping or placing the RFID card near the reader that is attached to the gate's turnstile. One more PIN number is requested for security and authentication purposes (see Figure 4).

All system components have been developed following the .NET framework. Interfaces with the RFID reader have been developed using the corresponding SDK, and have been programmed in VB.NET. To measure the perceived acceptance of the proposed solution, we performed a lab experiment in which a representative set of spectators of athletic events where invited to use and assess the implemented prototype. Drawing from established theories that measure IS acceptance we developed an integrated research model and a set of corresponding hypotheses. The following section discusses the rationale and development of our research model.

Research Model and Method

Predicting an individual's intention to use an information system has been widely studied under the technology acceptance research stream in IS literature (e.g., Davis, 1989; Hartwick & Barki, 1994; Venkatesh, Morris, Davis, & Davis, 2003). Researchers in this area have adopted theories that predict human behavior and have tailored them to the IS domain to predict the usage of a particular Information Technology (IT) or System. Within the IS literature, these ideas have taken shape in the form of various models following the conceptual framework that individuals' reaction to using a particular technology may influence their intention of actually using that technology, as illustrated in Figure 5.

Figure 5. Basic concept underlying technology acceptance research stream (Venkatesh, Morris, Davis, & Davis, 2003)

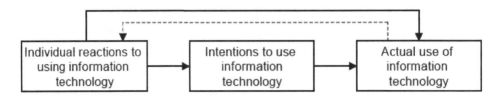

The dominant model in the IT domain is the technology acceptance model (TAM) (Davis, 1989), which contends that behavioral intention to use an IS is contingent on two salient beliefs, namely perceived usefulness and ease of use. Moreover, TAM posits that perceived usefulness and perceived ease of use determine an individual's intention to use a system, with intention to use serving as a mediator of actual system use. Perceived usefulness is also seen as being directly impacted by perceived ease of use. Thus, TAM uses questions in order to collect an individual's perceptions about the usefulness and the ease of use for a specific system, factors that affect the individual's intention to use the system, therefore, his acceptance to actually use it.

TAM has been widely used in technology acceptance studies and has provided rich empirical evidence of individuals' acceptance of technology. However, there is an ongoing debate as to whether the parsimonious TAM is explanatory enough, or whether additional factors should be included in the model to obtain a richer explanation of technology adoption and use (e.g., Mathieson, 1991; Plouffe, Hulland, & Vanderbosch, 2001; Taylor & Todd, 1995; Venkatesh, Morris, Davis, & Davis, 2003). Many researchers suggested that TAM needs to be enhanced with additional variables to provide an even stronger model (Kenneth, Kozar, & Larsen, 2003; Legris, Inghamb, & Collerette, 2003), especially when applied in contexts that are beyond the traditional workplace (Bruner & Kumar, 2005; Heijden, 2004; Weiser & Brown, 1996) as in the case of RFID ticketing systems.

For example, TAM has been modified to accommodate the new properties of wireless business environments, incorporating perceived playfulness and security as antecedents of intended system use, and task type as moderator to the aforementioned relationships (Fang, Chan, Brzezinski, & Xu, 2006). Similarly, Hung et al. (2003) extended TAM with factors from the Theory of Planned Behaviour (Ajzen, 1991) and Innovation Diffusion Theory (Rogers, 2003) to predict WAP services adoption. Finally, Cheong and Park (2005) suggested that perceived system quality, contents quality, and Internet experience may be used as predictors of the original salient beliefs of TAM, namely perceived ease of use and usefulness. They applied and validated the proposed model to assess mobile Internet acceptance in Korea.

Figure 6. Proposed research model

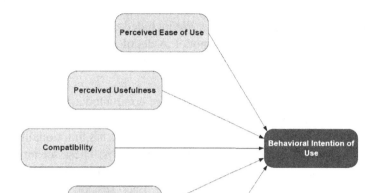

In our case, we chose to augment the technology acceptance model with issues related to innovation adoption, privacy and switching cost features, as shown in Figure 6, in order to predict behavioural intention to use the system.

The proposed system provides an alternative approach of purchasing tickets of sports events. Current practices suggest that a ticket to an athletic event may be purchased either physically or through electronic means (regardless of whether it is through the Internet or another medium--e.g., via phone reservation). Therefore, we considered it important to include in our model the *compatibility* factor from the diffusion of innovations theory (Rogers, 1995).

Moreover, since the proposed system employs automated monetary transactions via the RFID smart card, we needed to examine risk issues that might affect an individual's perception of the system's use. RFID technology has already raised many privacy fears as it is perceived that it would be used to track, identify, and acquire personal information in an intrusive way (Garfinkel, Juels, & Pappu, 2005; Ohkubo, Suzuki, & Kinoshita, 2005). To this end, people fear that commercial companies will use RFID to profile individuals and perform direct marketing activities based on that information. To predict the adoption of the RFID ticketing system, we need to take into consideration the *perceived risk* that might negatively affect an individual's decision to adopt and use the system.

Finally, because there are several competing approaches to RFID ticketing schemes ranging from season tickets, to phone reservations, and e-ticketing purchases, we can expect that their attractiveness may have a negative impact on a spectator's intention to accept the proposed service. We included the *attractiveness of alternatives* factor in our integrated research model. A detailed discussion on the formulation of the proposed research model and the resulting research hypotheses is available in Karaiskos et al. (2007).

To test and validate the research model, we conducted a lab experiment. The lab experiment lasted for one week and subjects were invited via e-mail. The experiment participants were given a demonstration of the system's functionality and were then prompted to use it following specific usage scenarios. These scenarios involved the issuing of the smart card, purchasing tickets for specific games, and entering the stadium (virtually) by using the RFID card. Each session lasted 30 minutes. After each session, participants were asked to complete a questionnaire, which included a set of items concerning the constructs of the proposed research model. The items

Table 2. Sample's descriptive statistics (N=71)

Gender	Men	70.4%		Elementary School	0.%
	Women	29.6%		Junior High/Middle School	19.7%
Age	<18	19.7%	Education	High School	33.9%
	18-24	39.4%		Bachelor's degree	22.5%
	25-34	28.2%		Master's degree (MSc, MA, MBA)	23.9%
	35-50	12.7%		Doctorate Degree (Ph.D)	0. %
	>50	0. %			

Table 3. First stage linear regression analysis (pu dependent variable)

Model	R^2	Adjusted R^2	Change in R^2	F	Sig. of F	Change in F	Sig. of change in F
Model Summary							
1	,619	,614	,619	112,195	,000	112,195	,000
Predictors: (Constant), PEOU Dependent Variable: PU							
Coefficients							
	Variable	**B**	**S.E. B**	**Beta**	**t**	**Sig.**	
1	(Constant)	,795	,299		2,661	,010	
	PEOU	,779	,074	,787	10,592	,000	
Dependent Variable: PU							

were drawn from relevant studies and were measured following a Likert scale from 1(totally disagree) to 5(totally agree).

The questionnaire was divided into two parts. The first part measured the perceived acceptance of the system while the second part collected the demographic details of the participants. The sequence of measurement items in the questionnaire was randomized to ensure internal consistency (Cook & Campbell, 1979) and construct validity (Karahanna, Straub, & Chervany, 1999).

Seventy eight (78) individuals participated in the lab experiment voluntarily, out of which 71 questionnaires where found to be consistent. The sample's descriptive statistics are presented in Table 2.

Results

The research model was found to satisfy content and construct validity as indicated by Straub et al. (1999) and appears in Karaiskos et al. (2007). Furthermore, in order to assess the measurement model, we performed linear regression analysis in two stages. The first stage considered *perceived usefulness* (PU) as the dependent variable with *perceived ease of use* (PEOU) being its predictor. The second stage measured *behavioral intention of use* (BI) as the dependent variable, with *perceived*

Table 4. Second Stage Linear Regression Analysis (BI dependent variable)

Model	R2	Adjusted R2	Change in R2	F	Sig. of F	Change in F	Sig. of change in F
Models Summary							
1	,636	,630	,636	120,411	,000	120,411	,000
Predictors: (Constant), PU, PR, AA, PEOU Dependent Variable: BI							
Coefficients							
	Variable	**B**	**S.E. B**	**Beta**	**t**	**Sig.**	
1	(Constant)	,414	,330		1,257	,213	
	PU	,909	,083	,797	10,973	,000	
Excluded Variables							
	PEOU			,207	1,789	,078	
	AA			,101	1,188	,239	
	PR			,016	,142	,887	
Dependent Variable: BI							

usefulness (PU), *perceived ease of use* (PEOU), *perceived risk* (PR), and *attractiveness of alternatives* (AA) being its predictors. Table 3 summarizes the results of the first stage that provide empirical evidence that *Perceived Ease of Use* significantly affects *Perceived Usefulness*.

Table 4 summarizes the results of the second stage that provide empirical evidence, which supports the prediction of *behavioral intention of use* from *perceived usefulness,* while the other independent variables where excluded because they were found to affect insignificantly the *behavioral intention of use*. The model explains 66.1% of the variance regarding spectators' intentions to use the system.

Profiling the Users of RFID Ticketing Systems

In order to identify the pertinent target groups for a potential commercial exploitation of the RFID ticketing system, we examined the effects of the demographics of the sample (age and education) to the dependent variable of the model (behavioral

Table 5. ANOVA statistics (factor AGE)

		Sum of Squares	df	Mean Square	F	Sig.
BI	**Between Groups**	10,619	3	3,540	4,315	,008
	Within Groups	54,959	67	,820		
	Total	65,577	70			
PU	**Between Groups**	7,156	3	2,385	3,690	,016
	Within Groups	43,311	67	,646		
	Total	50,467	70			

Figure 7. Mean plots of BI and PU (factor AGE)

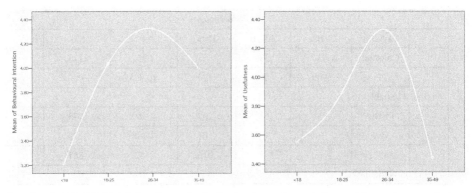

intention of use). Furthermore, we examined the effect of the demographic information of the sample to perceived usefulness because of the variable's strong predictive power to behavioral intention of use. We used One-Way ANOVA to measure the aforementioned effects.

Differences Based Upon Age

The results illustrated in Table 5 indicate that age plays an important role concerning *Behavioral Intention of Use* as differences between the age groups are significant at the level of 99,92% (sig=,008). This finding is graphically illustrated in Figure 7. Likewise, the usefulness of the systems is perceived differently across age groups, at significance level of 99,84% (sig=,014) especially between the age group of 26-34 and <18 as illustrated in Figure 7.

According to these results, the RFID ticketing system is considered useful by all age groups. Nevertheless, the age group of 26-34 should be considered prime candidates to use and adopt the system should it become commercially available. This is not surprising if we consider that older people (> 49 years old) are already accustomed to the traditional mechanisms of purchasing sports tickets, and might raise significant

Table 6. ANOVA Statistics (factor EDUCATION)

		Sum of Squares	df	Mean Square	F	Sig.
BI	**Between Groups**	13,836	2	6,918	9,092	,000
	Within Groups	51,741	68	,761		
	Total	65,577	70			
USE	**Between Groups**	8,909	2	4,454	7,289	,001
	Within Groups	41,558	68	,611		
	Total	50,467	70			

Figure 8.

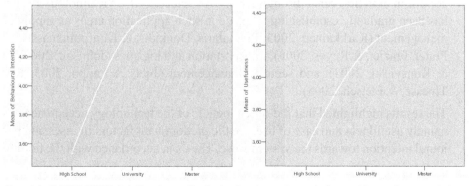

switching barriers to the proposed ticketing scheme. Therefore, the RFID ticketing system providers should develop the necessary awareness mechanisms that inform the public about the benefits of similar ticketing schemes or provide incentives (e.g., reduced season ticket prices) for early adopters.

Differences Based Upon Education

The results of Table 6 indicate that education also plays an important role concerning *Behavioral Intention of Use* as differences between the different levels of education are significant at the level of 100% (sig=,000), a finding showed in Figure 8. Likewise the usefulness of the systems is perceived differently across education groups, at significance level of 99,99% (sig=,001) especially between users of high school education level and users with a university diploma, as illustrated in Figure 8.

The results indicate that individuals with a higher education level perceive that the system is more useful, and express a stronger intention to use it. This result is confirmed by the innovation diffusion theory (Rogers, 1995), which poses that the education level positively affects the ability of an individual to comprehend and accept innovative technologies.

Discussion

Innovative technologies are used more and more in traditional everyday activities of our lives. These technologies formulate and support a new IS class which is commonly referred to as pervasive information systems. The present study aimed at investigating whether established factors from traditional IS user acceptance theories may be employed to predict user behaviour in the pervasive IS space. To this end, we developed an integrated model that incorporated factors stemming from heavily cited research models that measure IS acceptance and consequent use. To assess the model validity, we developed a pervasive IS that supports access control in athletic events through RFID. We selected RFID technology because it has been gradually establishing its place in such application areas as supply chain management (Karkkainen, 2003; Pramataris, Doukidis, & Kourouthanassis, 2004; Prater, Frazier, & Reyes, 2005), transportation and logistics (Johnson, 2000; Smith & Konsynski, 2003), and security management (Juels & Pappu, 2003; Staake, Thiesse, & Fleisch, 2005).

The results highlighted that the salient beliefs of the technology acceptance model, namely usefulness and ease of use, are the predominant factors in assessing behavioural intention towards the system's use. This is in accordance with the findings of several IS studies indicating the predominance of these factors in TAM (e.g., King & He, 2006; Legris, Inghamb, & Collerette, 2003; Ma & Liu, 2004; Mahmood, Hall, & Swanberg, 2001; Venkatesh, Morris, Davis, & Davis, 2003). At the same time, the remaining variables that stemmed from similar studies to TAM do not seem to be perceived as equally important by the study participants in terms of affecting their perceived acceptance and consequent use of the pervasive system.

We acknowledge that the application domain may have influenced the results of the proposed model. Indeed, the confirmation that ease of use remains the most significant variable provides a hint that, although over the past few years individuals have been familiar with smart card technologies (e.g., in the form of automatic teller machines), the task of issuing, purchasing, and using RFID tickets to grant access in athletic events, may not be as intuitive or free of effort. Poorly designed interfaces, bad physical placement of technical infrastructure, obscure usage guidelines, and complex payment and checkout procedures, all may contribute to increased consumer frustration when using RFID ticketing systems. Therefore, in order to attract and keep customers, it is imperative to design the system architecture in such a way that enhances overall usability.

One of the major inhibitors of online shopping has been the perception of poor security associated with payment methods. Indeed, it has been reported that online shoppers are still suspicious about transmitting credit card information over the Internet (Friedman, Kahn, & Howe, 2000; Grabner-Kraeuter, 2002; Miyazaki & Fernandez, 2001). However, in RFID ticketing systems, the perceived risk of the transaction does not seem to significantly concern users. One explanation is that the data contained in the RFID card are not critical because they do not lead to disclosure of personal information, and they cannot be abused for monetary purposes (the RFID card contains an encrypted identification number, which is crosschecked each time the card is used with a server's database). Moreover, users physically participate in all interactions with the system, thus further increasing their feeling of security. Finally, as a PIN code is expected from users by the system for each task they perform, security concerns are even further alleviated. Consequently, stakeholders aspiring to invest in such solutions need to develop the necessary security schemes and safeguards, and inform users about how their personal information will be manipulated.

The fact that factors stemming from the switching barrier theory and diffusion of innovation theory did not statistically affect the measurement model implies that users are still accustomed to the traditional means of purchasing tickets and did not perceive the benefits of the proposed system compared to existing practices. This might be attributed to the lab experimental setting, since participants were not exposed to a fully working prototype in real-life conditions. In effect, previous studies investigating user acceptance of emerging Information Technologies support our argument that such or similar factors should be included in the measurement model. For example, Lu et al. (2005) revealed that trust (similar to perceived risk in this study) is a predictor of intention of use in their study assessing perceived acceptance of wireless internet through mobile devices. Likewise, in the study of Wu et al. (2005), it was suggested that compatibility significantly affects the intention of using mobile health care services. Therefore, we suggest that future studies consider the proposed model in its entirety through field testing or longitudinal analyses to validate the conclusion reached in this study.

Acknowledgment

This research has been supported by the Reinforcement Programme of Human Research Manpower – "PENED" in the framework of Measure 8.3, Action 8.3.1, of the Operational Programme Competitiveness (Third Community Support Programme). The programme is co- funded by public expenditure from E.U. (European Social Fund, 75%), by public expenditure from Greek public sector (Ministry of Development, General Secretariat for Research and Technology, 25%), and from the private sector.

References

Ajzen, I. (1991). The theory of planned behavior. *Organizational Behavior and Human Decision Processes, 50*(2), 179-211.

Birnbaum, J. (1997). Pervasive Information Systems. *Communications of the ACM, 40*(2), 40-41.

Bruner, G. C., & Kumar, A. (2005). Explaining consumer acceptance of handheld Internet devices. *Journal of Business Research, 58*(5), 553-558.

Cheong, J. H., & Park, M. C. (2005). Mobile internet acceptance in Korea. *Internet Research, 15*(2), 125-140.

Churchill, E. F., Nelson, L., & Denoue, L. (2003, September 19-21). *Multimedia Fliers: Information Sharing With Digital Community Bulletin Boards.* Paper presented at the Communities and Technologies, Amsterdam, The Netherlands.

Cook, T. D., & Campbell, D. T. (1979). *Quasi Experimentation: Design and Analytical Issues for Field Settings.* Chicago: Rand McNally.

Davis, F. D. (1989). Perceived Usefulness, Perceived Ease of Use, and User Acceptance of Information Technology. *MIS Quarterly, 13*(3), 318-340.

Fang, X., Chan, S., Brzezinski, J., & Xu, S. (2006). Moderating Effects of Task Type on Wireless Technology Acceptance. *Journal of Management Information Systems, 22*(3), 123-157.

Friedman, B., Kahn Jr, P. H., & Howe, D. C. (2000). Trust online. *Communications of the ACM, 43*(12), 34-40.

Garfinkel, S. L., Juels, A., & Pappu, R. (2005). RFID Privacy: An Overview of Problems and Proposed Solutions. IEEE Security and Privacy, 34-43.

Geer, D. (2006). Pervasive Medical Devices: Less Invasive, More Productive. *IEEE Pervasive Computing, 5*(2), 85-88.

Goodhue, D., & Thompson, R. (1995). Task-Technology fit and individual performance. *MIS Quarterly, 19*(2), 213-236.

Grabner-Kraeuter, S. (2002). The Role of Consumers' Trust in Online-Shopping. *Journal of Business Ethics, 39*(1), 43-50.

Greenberg, S., & Rounding, M. (2001). The Notification Collage: Posting Information to Public and Personal Displays. *CHI Letters, 3*(1), 515-521.

Hartwick, J., & Barki, H. (1994). Explaining the Role of User Participation in Information System Use. *Management Science, 40*(4), 440-465.

Heijden, H. V. D. (2004). User Acceptance of Hedonic Information Systems. *MIS Quarterly, 28*(4), 695-704.

Hsin, C., & Liu, M. (2006). Self-monitoring of wireless sensor networks. *Computer Communications, 29*(4), 462-476.

Hung, S. Y., Ku, C. Y., & Chang, C. M. (2003). Critical factors of WAP services adoption: An empirical study. *Electronic Commerce Research and Applications, 2*(1), 42-60.

Intille, S. S. (2002). Designing a Home of the Future. IEEE Pervasive Computing, 1(2), 76-82.

Jafari, R., Dabiri, F., Brisk, P., & Sarrafzadeh, M. (2005). Adaptive and Fault Tolerant Medical Vest for Life-Critical Medical Monitoring. Paper presented at the ACM symposium on Applied Computing, Santa Fe, NM.

Johnson, J. R. (2000). RFID Gets the Green Light. *Warehousing Management, 7*(4), 28-29.

Juels, A., & Pappu, R. (2003). Squealing Euros: Privacy Protection in RFID-Enabled Banknotes. In R. Wright (Ed.), Financial Cryptography (Vol. LNCS 2742, pp. 103-121). London: Springer-Verlag.

Karahanna, E., Straub, D. W., & Chervany, N. L. (1999). Information Technology Adoption Across Time: A Cross-Sectional Comparison of Pre-Adoption and Post-Adoption Beliefs. *MIS Quarterly, 23*(2), 183-213.

Karaiskos, D. C., Kourouthanassis, P. E., & Giaglis, G. M. (2007). User Acceptance of Pervasive Information Systems: Evaluating an RFID Ticketing System. Paper presented at the 15th European Conference on Information Systems, St. Gallen, Switzerland.

Karkkainen, M. (2003). Increasing Efficiency in the Supply Chain for Short Life Goods using RFID Tagging. *International Journal of Retail & Distribution Management, 31*(10), 529-536.

Kenneth, Y. L., Kozar, A., & Larsen, K. R. T. (2003). The Technology Acceptance Model: Past, Present, and Future. *Communications of the Association for Information Systems, 12*(50), 752-780.

Kidd, C. D., Orr, R., Abowd, G. D., Atkeson, C., Essa, I., MacIntyre, B., et al. (1999). The Aware Home: A Living Laboratory for Ubiquitous Computing Research. Paper presented at the Second International Workshop on Cooperative Buildings, Berlin.

King, W. R., & He, J. (2006). A meta-analysis of the technology acceptance model. *Information & Management, 43*(6), 740-755.

Kourouthanassis, P. (2004). Can technology make shopping fun? *ECR Journal, 3*(2), 37-44.

Kourouthanassis, P., & Giaglis, G. M. (2006). The Design Challenge of Pervasive Information Systems. In P. Kourouthanassis & G. M. Giaglis (Eds.), Pervasive Information Systems (pp. forthcoming): M.E. Sharpe.

Legris, P., Inghamb, J., & Collerette, P. (2003). Why do people use information technology? A critical review of the technology acceptance model. *Information & Management, 40*(3), 191–204.

Lyytinen, K., & Yoo, Y. (2002). The Next Wave of Nomadic Computing: A Research Agenda for Information Systems Research. *Information Systems Research, 13*(4), 377-388.

Ma, Q., & Liu, L. (2004). The Technology Acceptance Model: A Meta-Analysis of Empirical Findings. *Journal of Organizational and End User Computing, 16*(1), 59-72.

Mahmood, M. A., Hall, L., & Swanberg, D. L. (2001). Factors Affecting Information Technology Usage: A Meta-Analysis of the Empirical Literature. *Journal of Organizational Computing and Electronic Commerce, 11*(2), 107-130.

Mathieson, K. (1991). Predicting User Intentions: Comparing the Technology Acceptance Model with the Theory of Planned Behavior. *Information Systems Research, 2*(3), 173-191.

Miyazaki, A. D., & Fernandez, A. (2001). Consumer Perceptions of Privacy and Security Risks for Online Shopping. *Journal of Consumer Affairs, 35*(1), 27-44.

Najjar, L., Thompson, J. C., & Ockerman, J. J. (1997). A Wearable Computer for Quality Assurance in a Food-Processing Plant. Paper presented at the 1st International Symposium on Wearable Computers, Los Alamitos, CA.

Ohkubo, M., Suzuki, K., & Kinoshita, S. (2005). RFID Privacy Issues and Technical Challenges. *Communications of the ACM, 48*(3), 66-71.

Plouffe, C. R., Hulland, J. S., & Vanderbosch, M. (2001). Research Report: Richness Versus Parsimony in Modeling Technology Adoption Decisions –Understanding Merchant Adoption of a Smart Card-based Payment System. *Information Systems Research, 13*(2), 208-222.

Pramataris, K., Doukidis, G. J., & Kourouthanassis, P. E. (2004). Towards Smarter Supply and Demand Chain Collaboration Practices Enabled by RFID Technology. In P. Vervest, E. Van Heck, K. Preiss & L. F. Pau (Eds.), Smart Business Networks (pp. 197-208). London: Springer-Verlag.

Prater, E., Frazier, G. V., & Reyes, P. M. (2005). Future Impacts of RFID on E-Supply Chains in Grocery Retailing. Supply Chain Management: *An International Journal, 10*(2), 134-142.

Rogers, E. M. (1995). *Diffusion of Innovations* (4th ed.). New York: Free Press.

Rogers, E. M. (2003). *The Diffusion of Innovation* (5th ed.). New York: Free Press.

Roussos, G. (2006). Ubiquitous Computing for Electronic Business. In G. Roussos (Ed.), *Ubiquitous and Pervasive Commerce: New Frontiers for Electronic Business* (pp. 1-12). London: Springer-Verlag.

Saha, D., & Mukherjee, A. (2003). Pervasive Computing: A Paradigm for the 21st Century. *IEEE Computer*, (3) 25-31.

Schmidt, S., & Hanloser, S. (2006). RFID-Ticketing bei der FIFA-Fussball-Weltmeisterschaft Deutschland. *Computer und Recht, 22*(1), 75-76.

Smith, H., & Konsynski, B. (2003). Developments In Practice X: Radio Frequency Identification (RFID) - An Internet For Physical Objects. *Communications of the Association for Information Systems, 12*, 301-311.

Smith, J. R., Fishkin, K., Jiang, B., Mamishev, A., Philipose, M., Rea, A. D., et al. (2005). RFID-based Techniques for Human-Activity Detection. *Communications of the ACM, 48*(9), 39-44.

Staake, T., Thiesse, F., & Fleisch, E. (2005). Extending the EPC Network: The Potential of RFID in Anti-Counterfeiting. Paper presented at the ACM Symposium on Applied Computing, Santa Fe, NM.

Tanenbaum, A. S., & Van Steen, M. (2003). *Distributed Systems: Principles and Paradigms*: Prentice Hall.

Taylor, S., & Todd, P. A. (1995). Understanding Information Technology Usage: A Test of Competing Models. *Information Systems Research, 6*(2), 144-176.

Tschudin, C., Gunningberg, P., Lundgren, H., & Nordstrom, E. (2005). Lessons from experimental MANET research. *Ad-Hoc Networks, 3*(2), 221-233.

Venkatesh, V., Morris, M. G., Davis, G. B., & Davis, F. D. (2003). User Acceptance of Information Technology: Toward a Unified View. *MIS Quarterly, 27*(3), 425-478.

Walters, G. J. (2001). Privacy and Security: An Ethical Analysis. *Computers and Society, 31*(2), 8-23.

Weiser, M. (1993). Some Computer Science Issues in Ubiquitous Computing. *Communications of the ACM, 36*(7), 75-84.

Weiser, M., & Brown, J. S. (1996). The Coming Age Of Calm Technology. from http://www.webcitation.org/5LlPcmfyn

Wu, J. H., & Wang, S. C. (2005). What drives mobile commerce?An empirical evaluation of the revised technology acceptance model. *Information & Management, 42*(5), 719–729.

Xiao, Y., Lasome, C., Moss, J., Mackenzie, C., & Faraj, S. (2001, September 16-20). Cognitive Properties of a Whiteboard: A Case Study in a Trauma Centre. Paper presented at the 7th European Conference on Computer Supported Cooperative Work, Bonn, Germany.

Chapter VII

Designing for Tasks in Ubiquitous Computing:
Challenges and Considerations

Stephen Kimani, Jomo Kenyatta University of Agriculture and Technology,
Kenya

Silvia Gabrielli, University of Rome "La Sapienza," Italy

Tiziana Catarci, University of Rome "La Sapienza," Italy

Alan Dix, Lancaster University, UK

Abstract

The traditional desktop computing paradigm has had major successes. It also should be noted that we are in a day and age where many good computer and device users are increasingly finding themselves being required to perform their activities not in offices/desktops but in real-world settings. Ubiquitous computing can make possible in the real-world setting what would have otherwise been impossible through desktop computing. However, there is a world of difference between the real-world and the desktop settings. The move from the desktop to the real-world settings raises various issues when we consider the nature of tasks that the ubiquitous devices/applications would be expected to support and the real-world context in which they will be used. A careful study of the nature of tasks in ubiquitous computing can make some design requirements in the development of ubiquitous applications more evident. This chapter proposes ubiquitous application design and evaluation considerations emerging from a deeper understanding of the nature of tasks in ubiquitous computing.

Introduction

It is worth acknowledging that the traditional desktop computing paradigm has had major successes. On the same note, it should be observed that we are in a day and age where many people have become good computer and device users. However, these users are increasingly finding themselves performing or being required to (or having to) perform their activities not in offices and desktops but in the real world settings. In describing the situation, Kristoffersen and Ljungberg indicate that the hands of such users "are often used to manipulate physical objects, as opposed to users in the traditional office setting, whose hands are safely and ergonomically placed on the keyboard." (Kristoffersen & Ljungberg, 1999). It is interesting to observe how ubiquitous computing can come in handy toward making possible in the natural setting what would have otherwise been impossible through the desktop computing paradigm. It is therefore not uncommon to encounter a user who "carries out one or many parallel activities from virtually anywhere at anytime while at the same time interacting with other user(s) and/or device(s)." (Bertini et al., 2003).

However, it is worth noting that there is a world of difference between the real world setting and the desktop setting. As we consider the move from desktop computing (fixed user interfaces) to the real world settings, various issues and demands arise when we consider the nature of tasks the ubiquitous devices/applications (and thus ubiquitous user interfaces) would be expected to support and the real world context in which they will be used.

Consequently, it does turn out that a careful study of the nature of tasks in ubiquitous computing can make some requirements in the design and evaluation of ubiquitous applications become more evident, which forms the basis of this chapter. In particular, we will describe the nature of tasks in ubiquitous computing, and then propose and describe ubiquitous application user interface design and evaluation considerations emerging from a deeper understanding of the nature of tasks in ubiquitous computing.

The rest of the chapter is organized as follows; it first provides some background knowledge. It then gives an overview of the nature of tasks in ubiquitous computing. After that we propose and describe ubiquitous application design and evaluation considerations respectively based on the foregoing. We then highlight some open issues and conclude the chapter.

Background Knowledge

In this section, we describe some of the key concepts relevant to the chapter. In particular, we describe ubiquitous computing. It should be noted that in the history of computing, the requirement to take into consideration the real world context has arguably never been more critical and pressing than in this day and age of ubiquitous computing. After describing ubiquitous computing, we then focus the description on the concept of context.

Ubiquitous Computing

Weiser coined the term ubiquitous computing (ubicomp) and gave a vision of people and environments augmented with computational resources that provide information and services when and where desired (Weiser, 1991). Dix et al. define ubicomp as: "Any computing activity that permits human interaction away from a single workstation" (Dix et al., 2004). Since then, there have been tremendous advances in mobile and wireless technologies toward supporting the envisioned ubiquitous and continuous computation and, consequently, ubiquitous applications that are intended to exploit the foregoing technologies have emerged and are constantly pervading our life. Abowd et al. in (Abowd et al., 2000) observe that ubicomp applications are characterized by the following:

- **Natural interfaces:** Supporting interaction techniques that permit humans to interact with computing machines through the use of more natural interaction paradigms (e.g., speech, gesture, pen writing).
- **Context-awareness:** Ubicomp applications are expected to exploit the whole set of computing and telecommunication technologies that operate taking into account the context.
- **Automatic capture of live experiences:** Ubicomp applications often adopt or provide techniques that enable the user to record elements of their live experiences (e.g., photos, video, audio) and the management of the same.

Context

Context has been defined as "any information that can be used to characterize the situation of an entity." (Dey, 2000), where an entity refers to "a person, place, or object that is considered relevant to the interaction between a user and an application, including the user and applications themselves." (Dey, 2000). Context entails aspects such as location, infrastructure, user, environment, entities, and time. The infrastructure could include technical resources such as server and network capabilities and connections, applications, and so forth. User includes user data/profile, usage patterns, and so forth. The environment refers to the physical condition of the setting an could include light, temperature, and so on. Entities refer to people, devices and objects. Time could include date, time of the day, season, and so on. Abowd et al. provide in (Abowd et al., 2000) a review of ubicomp research and summarize context in the form of "five W 's":

- **Who:** As human beings, we tailor our activities and recall events from the past based on the presence of other people.

- **What:** Perceiving and interpreting human activity is a difficult problem. Nevertheless, interaction with continuously worn, context-driven devices will likely need to incorporate interpretations of human activity to be able to provide useful information.

- **Where:** In many ways, the "where" component of context has been explored more than the others. Of particular interest is coupling notions of "where" with other contextual information, such as "when."

- **When:** With the exception of using time as an index into a captured record or summarizing how long a person has been at a particular location, most context-driven applications are unaware of the passage of time. Of particular interest is the understanding of relative changes in time as an aid for interpreting human activity. Additionally, when a baseline of behavior can be established, action that violates a perceived pattern would be of particular interest.

- **Why:** Even more challenging than perceiving "what" a person is doing is understanding "why" that person is doing it.

Nature of Tasks

The interaction of the user with the ubiquitous device/application can be viewed in at least two dimensions:

- user-ubiquitous *application interaction* dimension and
- user-ubiquitous *device* dimension.

User-ubiquitous application interaction dimension entails tasks in which the user is primarily interacting with the ubiquitous application and the device I/O modalities in order to access services such as support services (e.g., emergencies, help/service), information services (e.g., gathering/recording information, accessing/retrieving information, sharing information, communicating) and entertainment services (e.g., games, music, videos). User-ubiquitous device dimension categorizes tasks that entail the actual handling of the device (such as holding the device, wearing the device, attending to the device).

There are situations whereby interaction with the ubiquitous application, though important, is not the primary task but rather a secondary/supplementary task. In such a case, such ubiquitous devices/applications would be used to provide support/assistance and gather/make available some resources (such as information) on behalf of a user who is engaged in another primary task in the real environment/setting. In fact, the tension between the primary tasks of a ubiquitous user and the user's interaction with the ubiquitous device/application can be seen in the literature (e.g., Pascoe et al., 2000). Notwithstanding the foregoing, there also are situations in which interaction with the ubiquitous application is the primary contributor to the user's accomplishment of the primary task; interacting with the ubiquitous device/application can be viewed as directly carrying out the primary task. In this case, the use of the ubiquitous device/application tends to be more intimately connected with what the user is really doing (or intends to achieve) in his/her embodied/physical self. For instance, where the user is using the ubiquitous application to inform him/her about the location he/she is in. However, it is also worth pointing out that at different time granularities, the primary task and secondary task may swap in ubiquitous computing. The foregoing situations raise challenges and that would need to be taken into consideration when designing and evaluating (developing) ubiquitous application user interfaces.

Some ubiquitous interactions are *low-intention* or *incidental interactions*--that is one where the user is not focused on the interaction being supported by the ubiquitous system and may not even be directly aware of the support (Dix et al., 2004, Dix, 2002). In such cases, the primary task or purposeful task needs to be understood in order to interpret sensor data. However, the supported task also needs to be understood in order to be able to administer appropriate support. This distinction is likely to be useful in other context sensitive situations. For example, if a user has recently consulted an online diary related to a coming birthday and a short while later starts to initiate a phone call, then it may be appropriate for the number of the person whose birthday is coming to be at the top of the list of suggested numbers. The former task, looking up the diary entry, is the initial purposeful task and needs to be interpreted in order to determine which people are important or relevant. The latter task, phoning, is the supported task and the knowledge of which people are currently significant is used to support this task.

While simpler task models assume a level of pre-planning or training, it is expected that most ubiquitous interactions are worked out at the moment (see situated action below) or maybe triggered from things in the environment (Dix et al., 2004b). Furthermore, being in a particular place or meeting a particular person may prompt tasks or activities that were not particularly waiting to be done, but were either very low priority but suggested by having the right resources available. Whilst more goal-oriented models of tasks assume one gathers resources to perform a task, in many real-world situations this gathering of resources is the hard or expensive thing, and it is worth doing activities using the resources and location available, even preparatory 'just in case' activities.

Design Considerations

It is worth noting that the user of a ubiquitous device often has to focus on more than one task because s/he might have to interact with the device itself (which is itself a task) while probably performing another task in the real world setting (where this could be the primary task or the secondary task). On one hand, interaction with the ubiquitous device/application to some extent requires user's innate resources (such as attention). On the other hand, the latter task often too does require the user's physical, visual, and cognitive involvement/resources (such as hands, visual attention, mental focus). The user's physical, visual, and cognitive involvement/resources are therefore likely to get constrained. Ideally, the ubiquitous application (including interactions with the device) should support the user in carrying out that which is the primary task without 'supporting' the user in tampering with the primary task. We should minimize distracting the user from the primary task or disrupting the user's primary task, unless the disruption/distraction is of genuine (and great) value or of critical importance. In the words of Holland and Morse: "It is important that the critical focus of the user's attention be directed towards the primary task at hand" (Holland & Morse, 2001). In adopting ways to meet the requirement, it is also critical to consider the status of a user's attention in the timing of the tasks on the ubiquitous device. Borrowing from a research effort on guidelines for using agents and direct manipulation (Horvitz, 1999), it is important to "consider the costs and benefits of deferring action to a time when action will be less distracting." Where necessary, the ubiquitous application should enable/allow the user to temporarily halt a task on the device and to resume the interrupted task.

One of the challenges with a new or innovative technology/application is that its users may try to use it in situations or ways the designers and developers had never thought of. This is true in mobile computing (Gorlenko & Merrick, 2003). There is therefore a sense in which the user may perform tasks on the device (and otherwise) in unpredictable and opportunistic ways. Taking into account all possible scenarios of use for a product is a non-trivial challenge to the ubiquitous application analysts and designers. It is also worth observing that the variability of the environment/natural setting may affect the course of a task. Therefore, analysts and designers may also need to account for such variability in the task analysis (Gorlenko et al., 2003).

The model human processor model (Card et al., 1983) has been a benchmark for a lot of work in HCI. The model is a simplified view of the human processing while interacting with computers. It focuses on the internal cognition driven by the co-operation of the perceptual system, the motor system, and the cognitive system. Each of the systems maintains its own processing and memory. However, as the role and domain of the computers (and devices) have widened, researchers and designers have been considering theories and approaches that take into account the relationship between the internal cognition and the outside world (Dix et al., 2004). Among these, researchers are exploring the following three main understandings of cognition for possible application in ubiquitous computing; they are activity theory model, situated action model, distributed cognition model (Abowd et al., 2002), and even their variants.

Activity Theory

The activity theory model provides a broad conceptual framework for describing the structure, development, and context of computer-supported activities. It was developed by the Russian psychologists Vygotsky, Rubinshtein, Leont'ev and others (Kaptelinin et al., 1995; Leont'ev, 1978). Activity theory is comprised of a set of basic principles that constitute a general conceptual system, rather than a highly predictive theory. The principles include the hierarchical structure of activity, object-orientedness, internalization/externalization, tool mediation, and development. It should be noted that the principles should be considered as an integrated system, because they are associated with various aspects of the whole activity. In activity theory, the unit of analysis is an activity. The activity is directed at an object which motivates the activity, giving it a specific direction. An activity is made up of goal-directed actions that must be undertaken to fulfill the object. Different actions may be undertaken to meet the same goal. Actions are conscious and they are implemented through automatic operations. Operations do not have their own goals, but rather they provide an adjustment of actions to suit current situations. Therefore, the constituents of activity are not fixed, but can dynamically change (or adjust) as situations/conditions change. This principle is of great interest in ubiquitous computing, since it is desired that the ubiquitous application appropriately adapt to the changing conditions/context. In the context of activity theory, the principle of object-orientedness states that human beings live in a reality that is objective in a broad sense; the things that constitute this reality have not only the properties that are considered objective according to natural sciences, but also socially/culturally defined properties as well. The principle of object-orientedness is very relevant to ubiquitous computing since the ubicomp to a great extent leads to situations where the user directly interacts with other people while (at the same time) using the ubicomp device or application. Therefore the social and cultural issues become even more crucial. An example is society's perspective regarding a person's speaking on a cellphone while directly interacting with another person. Internalization is the transformation of external activities into internal ones. Externalization transforms internal activities into external ones. Activity theory emphasizes that internal activities cannot be understood if they are analyzed separately from external activities, because they transform into each other. The external activities in this case can be closely associated with the contextual aspects in ubiquitous computing. For instance, the way the activity of speaking on the cellphone is designed could be better informed by considering the contextual aspects such as the simultaneous but direct interaction with another person, the noise level in the locality, and so forth. Activity theory emphasizes that human activity is generally mediated by tools. Tools are created and transformed during the development of the activity itself. Tools carry with them a particular culture, and therefore the use of tools is an accumulation and transmission of social knowledge. In ubiquitous computing, such tools could in a way be viewed as the ubicomp devices and applications. As far as activity theory is concerned, development is not only an object of study, but also a general research methodology. Gay and Hembrooke have noted a weakness in the original formulation of the activity theory model by pointing out that the model "has traditionally been understood as asynchronic, point-in-time depiction of an activity" (Gay & Hembrooke, 2003).

They go on to note that the model "does not depict the transformational and developmental processes that provide the focus of much recent activity theory research" (Gay & Hembrooke, 2003). In (Boer et al., 2002), Boer et al. do propose an extension of activity theory across time and the levels of an organization to explain connections between different activities as well as the influence that an activity may have on itself. Moreover, Boer et al. also consider the role that an activity may play in other activities at different levels of analysis. Those extensions to the activity theory can serve at least two purposes; they can help to explain tensions present in real-world systems and yield a model with a greater degree of agility in representing complex, distributed cognition. Other work (Uden, 2007) describes how activity theory was used to develop a framework for the design of a context-aware mobile learning application. Pinto and Jose (2006) propose ActivitySpot, a ubicomp framework for localized activities such as activities that are strongly related to a specific physical environment and that only can be achieved there. The framework defines a conceptual model that has been inspired by activity theory model. In their attempt to develop a context model for ubiquitous computing, Kaenampornpan and O'Neill in (2004) have relied extensively on activity theory. They give the following three reasons for using activity theory:

- Activity theory provides a simple standard form for describing human activity. It acknowledges that although, as fellow humans, we cannot fully understand the full moment-to-moment richness of other humans' activities, states, goals, and intentions, we do manage to interact and to interpret others' actions with an enormously higher degree of success than any existing context-aware computer based system. Therefore, in attempting to produce better context-aware systems, it is neither possible nor necessary to model all the richness of human activity.

- Activity theory takes into account the concepts of tool mediation and social environment, which are important in the ubiquitous computing world. This is because in ubicomp, users are allowed to use different computing devices, both physical and virtual. Moreover, the users can use computing services anywhere and anytime which means that they use the services in different social environments. The social environments and tools are important elements that have an influence on users' intentions in doing activities.

- Activity theory models the relationships amongst the elements. Therefore, it can be a useful way to model the relationship between each element in a context model. Activity theory has also been used in the arena of peripheral displays.

In (Matthews et al., 2007), activity theory was used to perform an analysis of peripheral displays. In the same effort, the authors also used activity theory to develop an approach for designing and evaluating peripheral displays.

Situated Action

The situated action model emphasizes the emergent, contingent nature of human activity, that is, the way activity grows directly out of the particularities of a given situation. The focus is situated activity or practice. The situated action model does not underestimate the importance of artifacts or social relations or knowledge or values, but rather its true locus of inquiry is the "everyday activity of persons acting in [a] setting" (Lave, 1988). The world of computing has always faced contextual issues. However, the current wide adoption and usage of ubiquitous computing (e.g., cellphones, personal digital assistants, etc.) have made contextual issues arguably more prominent than during any other time in history of computing. The main reason is that the ubiquitous devices and applications primarily are used in real settings and therefore, there is a need for the ubiquitous devices and applications to support situated activities. The basic unit of analysis in situated action models is "the activity of persons-acting in setting." (Lave, 1988). The unit of analysis is thus neither the individual, nor the environment, but rather a relation between the two. The situated action model stresses responsiveness to the environment and the improvisatory nature of human activity. Users under the influence of the environment, may use or attempt to use ubiquitous technologies/applications in "new" ways that even the designers had not anticipated. The situated action model, therefore, can be suitable for capturing and accommodating such user improvisations. On the same note, the situated action model deemphasizes the study of more durable, stable phenomena that persist across situations (Nardi, 1996). A central tenet of the situated action approach is that the structuring of activity is not something that precedes it, but can only grow directly out of the immediacy of the situation (Nardi, 1996; Lave, 1988). The authors of the effort (Fithian et al., 2003) report that they mainly used the situated action model during the design and evaluation of an integrated location-aware event and meeting planner built to work in a PDA form factor. Their justification for adopting the situated action model was that they "wished to examine the behavior and performance of users in real-world situations, where environmental and social factors are a source of both distraction and motivation" (Fithian et al., 2003; Taylor & Harper, 2002). Fithian et al. actually attribute their meaningful evaluation results to their choice of the situated action model.

Distributed Cognition

Flor et al. in (Flor et al., 1991) describe distributed cognition as "a new branch of cognitive science devoted to the study of: the representation of knowledge both inside the heads of individuals and in the world ...; the propagation of knowledge between different individuals and artifacts ...; and the transformations which external structures undergo when operated on by individuals and artifacts.... By studying cognitive phenomena in this fashion it is hoped that an understanding of how intelligence is manifested at the systems level, as opposed to the individual cognitive level, will be obtained." It should be observed that ubiquitous devices and applications are primarily used within real settings/context (the world). Therefore, it is important that knowledge pertaining to the real settings be modeled. As has been the case with the desktop computing applications, knowledge about the target user too is important in the arena of ubiquitous computing. On the same note, it is worth noting that the users of ubiquitous technologies tend to operate in real settings and, therefore, often have to simultaneously interact with other people/individuals and artifacts. Knowledge pertaining to such artifacts and such other individuals is, therefore, important to the design and development of the ubiquitous applications and devices being used. In distributed cognition, the unit of analysis is a cognitive system composed of individuals and the artifacts they use (Flor et al., 1991). Distributed cognition moves the unit of analysis to the system and finds its center of gravity in the functioning of the system (Nardi, 1996). In a manner similar to traditional cognitive science (Newell et al., 1972), distributed cognition is concerned with structure (representations inside and outside the head) and the transformations these structures undergo. However, the difference is that cooperating people and artifacts are the focus of interest, not just individual cognition "in the head" (Nardi,

1996). Another aspect that distributed cognition emphasizes is the understanding of the coordination among individuals and artifacts. The work reported in (Spinelli et al., 2002) is an investigation of users involved in carrying out collaborative activities, locally distributed and mobile. The investigation utilizes the distributed cognition framework and contextual design for representing and analyzing the work observed. By using distributed cognition to model cognition across users and artifacts, the study could look at collaboration from an innovative point of view that highlights how context and external resources impact collaboration. In (Laru & Järvelä, 2003), the authors address an effort that has used distributed cognition and collaborative learning in order to develop a pedagogical model of mobile learning. UbiLearn is a ubiquitous and mobile learning project (Laroussi, 2004). Its work is based on two mobile learning viewpoints; the first is the technical oriented perspective which focuses on a traditional behaviouristic educational paradigm as given and tries to represent or to support it with mobile technologies. The second is the pedagogical socio-cognitive and distributed cognition paradigms, where we face traditional designs of teaching and learning to push community oriented learning (e.g., collaborative learning, problem based learning; informal and ad-hoc learning, etc.). The work (Fischer et al., 2004) explores the concept of distributed cognition in ubiquitous computing from two directions. On the one hand, it explores the unique possibilities that computational media can have on distributed cognition (how ubicomp technologies can be used to support the users' distributed cognition). On the other hand, it describes a set of interrelated socio-technical developments that support distributed cognition among communities in ubicomp environments, such as a mobile architecture that links mobile travelers with caregiver communities and transportation systems. The architecture embodies "a distributed cognition framework that avoids common cognitive barriers found in current transportation systems (i.e., generic maps, schedules, labels, landmarks and signs) while synthesizing personalized multi-modal attention and memory prompts from the transportation environment to provide travelers with the right information, at the right time, and in a form best suited for the individual traveler" (Fischer et al., 2004).

Situated Interaction

It may be resourceful to highlight an interaction paradigm, namely situated interaction that has been defined based on and motivated by some of the above models. Situated interaction refers to the integration of human-computer interaction and the user's situation in a particular working context in a mobile environment (Hewagamage & Hirakawa, 2000). This combination perceives that the interaction is not only a function of device, but also strongly dependent on the user's activities and context in which the device is used. The concept of situated interaction can be discerned in, and may be said to have been inspired by, both the situation action model and the activity theory model. Situated interaction actually introduces a new paradigm of computing by extending the conventional applications and also by creating a new set of applications. It is worth noting that mobile computing has become popular in enhancing the shopping experience as discussed in (Newcomb et al., 2003) where they utilized ideas from situated computing. They go on to say that understanding situated interactions, where the customer utilizes the user interface while shopping, became the greatest challenge for designing the ubiquitous user interface.

It is worth noting that the acknowledgement of such challenges could also be supported by the adoption of design approaches and methodologies inspired by participatory design, which is based on the observation of users' activities in authentic everyday settings where mobile computing takes place (Rogers et al., 2002; Strömberg et al., 2004); as an example, micro-learning is an emergent area of investigation that could find useful resources in these methods while addressing its objective of designing and distributing series of very small units of knowledge to be experienced by learners (for lifelong learning purposes) as intertwined in their everyday working practices and ubiquitous computing activities (Gabrielli et al., 2005).

Evaluation Considerations

Conventional user-centered methods could be appropriately exploited in the development process of ubiquitous applications. On the same note, some of the traditional usability evaluation techniques might become useful when adapted for ubiquitous computing. For instance, there are several efforts toward realizing usability principles and heuristics for the design and evaluation of ubiquitous environments/systems, such as ambient heuristics (Mankoff et al., 2003) and groupware heuristics (Baker et al., 2001). On the same note, we actually already have proposed a review of usability principles for mobile computing (Bertini et al., 2005). We have also developed usability heuristics that are appropriate for evaluation in mobile computing (Bertini et al., 2006).

Much traditional understanding of work organizations has its roots in Fordist and Taylorist models of human activity, which assume that human behavior can be reduced into structured tasks. HCI has not been spared from this either. In particular, evaluation methods in HCI have often relied on measures of task performance and task efficiency as a means of evaluating the underlying application. However, it is not clear whether such measures can be universally applicable when we consider the current move from rather structured tasks (such as desktop activities) and relatively stable settings to the often unpredictable ubiquitous settings. Such primarily task-centric evaluation may, therefore, not be directly applicable to the ubiquitous computing domain. It would be interesting to consider investigating methods that go beyond the traditional task-centric approaches (Abowd & Mynatt, 2000). It is also worth keeping in mind that tasks on the ubiquitous device (and elsewhere) tend to be unpredictable and opportunistic.

In this era of ubiquitous computing, the real need to take into account the real-world context has become more crucial than at any other time in the history of computing. Although the concept of context is not new to the field of usability (e.g., ISO 9241 guidelines propose a "model" consideration of context), evaluation methods have, however, found it challenging, in practice to adequately/completely integrate the entire context during the evaluation process. There are various ways to address this challenge.

One option is the employment of observational techniques (originally developed by different disciplines) to gain a richer understanding of context (Abowd et al., 2002; Dix et al., 2004). Main candidates are ethnography, cultural probes, and contextual design. Another option is to use the "Wizard-of-Oz" technique, other simulation techniques, or even techniques that support the participant's imagination. Prototyping too presents an avenue for evaluating ubiquitous computing applications.

Ethnography

Ethnography is an observational technique that uses a naturalistic perspective; that is, it seeks to understand settings as they naturally occur, rather than in artificial or experimental conditions, from the point of view of the people who inhabit those settings, and usually involves quite lengthy periods of time at the study site (Hughes et al., 1995). Ethnography involves immersing an individual researcher or research team in the everyday activities of an organization or society, usually for a prolonged period of time. Ethnography is a well established technique in sociology and anthropology. The principle virtue of ethnography is its ability to make visible the 'real world' aspects of a social setting. It is a naturalistic method relying upon material drawn from the first-hand experience of a fieldworker in some setting. Since ubiquitous devices and applications are mainly used in 'real world' settings, then ethnography has some relevance to ubiquitous computing. The aim of ethnography is to see activities as social actions embedded within a socially organized domain and accomplished in and through the day-to-day activities of participants (Hughes et al., 1995). Data collected/gathered from an ethnographic study allows developers to design systems that take into account the sociality of interactions that occur in the "real world." The work by Crabtree et al. (Crabtree et al., 2006), shows how ethnography is relevant to and can be applied in the design of ubiquitous computing applications. The ultimate aim of the effort is to "foster a program of research and development that incorporates ethnography into ubiquitous computing *by design*, exploiting the inherent features of ubiquitous computing applications to complement existing techniques of observation, data production, and analysis." While describing how mobile computing has been used in the fashion retail industry, Supawanich et al. highlight challenges such as those pertaining to usability, system tailoring, and the manager-client user experience (Supawanich et al., 2005). It is worth noting that they applied ethnography toward addressing the foregoing challenges. In the work (Newcomb et al., 2003), which we have mentioned before, the authors also have applied ethnography in their effort to examine how grocery shopping could be aided by a mobile shopping application for the consumers. In particular, the authors shopped with customers and followed them throughout the task of shopping, observing their shopping habits. In (Berry & Hamilton, 2006), the authors report that they used ethnography in order to understand multimedia students and how they use Tablet PCs in their everyday design studies.

Cultural Probes

Cultural probes (Gaver et al., 1999a) represent a design-led approach to understanding users that stresses empathy and engagement. They were initially deployed in the Presence Project (Gaver et al., 1999b), which was dedicated to exploring the design space for the elderly. Gaver has subsequently argued that in moving out into everyday life more generally, design needs to move away from such concepts as production and efficiency and instead focus and develop support for "ludic pursuits." This concept is intended to draw attention to the "playful" character of human life, which might best be understood in a post-modern sense. Accordingly, the notion of "playfulness" is not restricted to whatever passes as entertainment, but is far more subtle and comprehensive, directing attention to the highly personal and diverse ways in which people "explore, wonder, love, worship, and waste time" together and in other ways engage in activities that are "meaningful and valuable" to them (Gaver, 2001). This emphasis on the ludic derives from the conceptual arts, particularly the influence of Situationist and Surrealist schools of thought (Gaver et al., 1999a). Cultural probes draw on the conceptual arts to provoke or call forth the ludic and so illuminate the "local culture" in which people are located and play out their lives. During their course of use, ubiquitous devices and applications typically get embedded in the users' lives and cultures. For instance, people often get personally attached to their cellphones. Cultural probes offer fragmentary glimpses into the rich texture of people's lives (Gaver, 2002). Cultural probes are not analytic devices but "reflect" the local culture of participants and are drawn upon to inspire design. In the Presence Project, cultural probes inspire design by providing a rich and varied set of materials that help to ground designs in the detailed textures of the local cultures (Gaver et al., 1999a). These materials are products of the probe packs, each consisting of a variety of artifacts relevant to the study. Such artifacts provide a range of materials reflecting important aspects of the participant's local cultures and, on being returned to the investigators, these reflections inspire design.

For instance, in the Presence Project, the artifacts include: postcards with questions concerning participants' attitudes to their lives, cultural environment, and technology; maps asking participants to highlight important areas in their cultural environment; cameras with instructions asking participants to photograph things of interest to them and things that bored them; photo albums asking participants to assemble a small montage telling a story about participant's lives; and media diaries asking participants to record the various media they use, when, where, and in whose company. The original idea of culture probes has been extended to include technology and thus the concept, *technology probes* (Hutchinson et al., 2003; Paulos &Goodman, 2004; Paulos & Jenkins, 2005). According to (Hutchinson et al., 2003), technology probes can assist in achieving "three interdisciplinary goals: the social science goal of understanding the needs and desires of users in a real-world setting; the engineering goal of field testing the technology; and the design goal of inspiring users and researchers to think about new technologies." It is also possible to consider a probe that is entirely simulated, such as with *paratypes* (Abowd et al., 2005). In a research effort aimed at exploring issues of dependability in ubiquitous computing in domestic settings (Crabtree et al., 2002), cultural probes are one of the qualitative methods that was used. In this case, some participants agreed to keep personal diaries of their daily activities. However, all participants were supplied with polaroid cameras, voice activated dictaphones, disposable cameras, photo albums, visitors books, scrapbooks, post-it notes, pens, pencils and crayons, postcards, and maps. In an attempt to elicit the methods and guidelines for designing and developing applications for domestic ubiquitous computing, Schmidt and Terrenghi in (Schmidt & Terrenghi, 2007) adopted various methods including cultural probes. In a study of the possible applications of mobile technology for industrial designers and architects for their daily work, Muñoz Bravo et al. in (Muñoz Bravo et al., 2007) conducted user studies in which one of the studies consisted of using cultural probes.

Contextual Inquiry

Contextual inquiry (Holtzblatt et al., 1993) is a method that aims at grounding design in the context of the work being performed. Contextual inquiry recommends the observation of work as it occurs in its authentic setting, and the usage of a graphical modeling language to describe the work process and to discover places where technology could overcome an observed difficulty. It is worth noting that in its application, contextual inquiry does combine various methods such as field research and participatory design methods (Muller et al., 1993) in order to provide designers with grounded and rich/detailed knowledge of user work. Contextual inquiry is one of the parts of what is referred to as contextual design. Contextual design is a design approach that was developed by Holtzblatt and Beyer (Beyer et al., 1998). It is an approach for designing customer-centered products based on an understanding of the existing work contexts and practices. It is worth noting that ubiquitous devices and applications are often intended to be used and get used in the real world where real work (or primary tasks) take(s) place. Therefore, the design of such devices and applications should be informed by an understanding of the way customers work (or would like to work) in the real world. Contextual design starts with the premise that any product embodies a way of working. The product's function and structure introduce particular strategies, language, and work flow on its users. A successful design should therefore offer a way of working that customers would like to adopt. Contextual design has seven parts: contextual inquiry; work modeling; consolidation; work redesign; user environment design; testing with customers; and putting it into practice. One of the proponents of contextual design, Holtzblatt, has actually reported on how contextual design can be appropriated to produce a mobile application (Holtzblatt, 2005). It is interesting to observe that the work by Newcomb et al. (Newcomb et al., 2003), did come up with a contextual design which was meant to serve two purposes; these are in the shopper's home to aid him/her in creating a shopping list, and in the store for the actual shopping. In the effort by Schmidt and Terrenghi (Schmidt & Terrenghi, 2007), which we came across before, contextual inquiry too was used for understanding and proposing methods and guidelines for designing and developing domestic ubiquitous computing applications. The previously mentioned work by Spinelli et al. (2002) on locally distributed and mobile collaborative activities, which we came across before, did use contextual design. The authors defend their choice of contextual design by stating that "the representation of work activities, utilising the methods of contextual design, aid researchers in conceptualising technologies that truly meet the informational and communicative needs of dynamic and fragmented users and their communities. ... This has allowed us to develop an understanding of, and to design for, users and their communities-in-context, by applying techniques such as affinity diagramming (for theme building) and work models to capture such essential elements as cultural and social models of technology use; 'breakdowns' ... in working practices and artefact models ... that allows us to represent users resources and their relationship with these resources. In the process, it also promotes an effective coupling of well-designed technologies with the fast changing physical environments that their users may inhabit" (Spinelli et al., 2002).

'Wizard-of-Oz' Simulation and Supporting Immersion

Another possibility is to use the "Wizard-of-Oz" technique or even other simulation techniques such as virtual reality. The "Wizard-of-Oz " technique is an evaluation method where the user of the system is made to believe or perceive that he or she is interacting with a fully implemented system though the whole or a part of the interaction of the system is controlled by a human being, the "wizard ," or several of them. Such techniques are especially appropriate where the ubiquitous application is not fully complete. However, the simulation should closely reflect the real context as much as possible (realistic simulation). There exist various ubiquitous computing applications that have at some point been evaluated using the "Wizard-of-Oz" technique, for example, (Carter et al., 2007; Mäkelä et al., 2001; Rudström et al., 2003), and so on. Another alternative is to adapt more traditional inspection methods to the analysis of ubicom settings by enriching the range and quality of discovery resources provided to usability experts to support their imagination and immersion about the real world usage settings. We have recently conducted a study in this direction where video data about user interaction with an e-learning course delivered on PDAs were used as additional resources supporting a more effective performance of cognitive walkthrough evaluation by usability experts involved in the study (Gabrielli et al., 2005).

Prototypes

In the formative stages of the design process, low fidelity prototypes can be used. However, as the design progresses, user tests need to be introduced. In the context of ubiquitous computing, user tests will not only require the inclusion of real users, real settings, and device interaction tasks, but also real or primary tasks (or realistic simulations of the real tasks and of the real settings). As mentioned previously, realistic simulations of the real tasks and of the real settings could be adopted as an alternative. Therefore, there would be the need to provide a prototype that supports the real tasks and real settings or their simulations. This does imply some cost in the design process because the prototype at this level would need to be robust and reliable enough in order to support primary tasks in real settings or the simulations. In fact, the technology required to develop ubiquitous computing systems is often on the cutting edge. Finding people with corresponding skills is difficult. As a result, developing a reliable and robust ubiquitous computing prototype or application is not easy (Abowd & Mynatt, 2000; Abowd et al., 2002).

Open Issues and Conclusion

We have attempted to describe the nature of tasks in ubiquitous computing. We have then proposed and discussed various models and methods appropriate for supporting the development process of ubiquitous computing applications based on the deeper understanding of the nature of tasks. However, still there are many other pertinent aspects which too would need to be addressed and which we consider worthy of our further investigation. These include: the choice of the methods; the choice of the models; the classification/categorization and characterization of tasks for mobile and ubiquitous computing; formal specification of social and collaborative aspects; and so forth.

Choice of methods

We have described several methods appropriate for evaluating in ubiquitous computing. One of the major issues is deciding which of the methods to choose. Of such evaluation methods, one may want to know which one(s) will be most suitable for a certain ubicomp application. Considering evaluation methods in general (not just evaluation methods for ubicomp), Dix et al. indicate that: "there are no hard and fast rules in this – each method has its particular strengths and weakness and each is useful if applied appropriately." (Dix et al., 2004). They, however, point out that there are various factors worth taking into consideration when choosing evaluation method(s), namely:

- the stage in the lifecycle at which the evaluation is carried out;
- the style of evaluation (field or laboratory);
- the level of subjectivity or objectivity of the method;
- the type of measures provided by the method;
- the level of information provided by the method;
- the immediacy of the response provided by the method;
- the level of interference or intrusiveness of the method;
- the resources required by the method.

The foregoing factors may be appropriately borrowed from when we consider the evaluation of ubicomp applications. According to Carter et al. (Carter et al., 2007), in determining which methods for ubiquitous computing to use, (among paper prototypes, interactive prototypes, "Wizard-of-Oz," and probes,) the designer must make trade-offs between realism , unobtrusiveness, data sparsity, ambiguity, and cost/time. They go on to say that paper prototypes and "Wizard-of-Oz" can be used to explore ambiguity. Probes that can be employed in real-world situations over a period of time can support both realism and sparsity. Moreover, paper and interactive prototypes may be the least costly methods, but they may also be the least flexible methods. It therefore comes as no surprise that some researchers have begun carrying out corresponding comparative studies (Liu & Khooshabeh, 2003; Mankoff & Schilit, 1997).

Many of the methods considered in this chapter are very "open" compared to more traditional task analysis techniques. This reflects the often spontaneously planned and re-planned nature of many tasks "in the wild" compared to (relatively) more constrained office tasks. Methods that embody a fixed or pre-understood idea of human behaviour are likely to miss some of the nuanced activity that is the focus of more open observational techniques such as ethnography. However, without models it is hard to move from what is observed to potential, especially as this potential often involves users appropriating technology for themselves. For this prompting to see what could happen, as well as what does happen, more interventionist methods in particular forms of technology probes or at least rich prototypes seem more appropriate. That is, the more open methods seem best suited for early and late stages in design for understanding the initial situation and later for assessing the impact of a deployment. However in mid-stages, when establishing potential is more important, more structured models and more interventionist methods seem more appropriate.

Choice of Models

Fithian et al. in (Fithian et al., 2003) observe that mobile and ubiquitous computing applications lend themselves well to the models: situated action; activity theory; and distributed cognition. As for which of these models are most suitable for a certain mobile or ubiquitous application, the foregoing authors say that the choice depends largely on the kind of application and of which aspects of design are in the limelight. They recommend that the choice be based on a critical analysis of the users and their knowledge, the tasks, and the application domain.

In (Fithian et al., 2003), Fithian et al. also note that basing entire evaluation on just time measurements can be very limiting, especially if the tasks are benchmarked in a situated action setting. Although time measurements are important, other performance measures that may be much more useful for evaluating such ubicomp applications include interruption resiliency, interaction suspensions, interaction resumptions, and so forth.

Interestingly, these richer metrics require a far richer model of what is going on than simpler end-to-end timing. This reinforces the message on other areas of evaluation that understanding mechanism is critical for appropriate and reliable generalization (Ellis & Dix, 2006).

Classification of Tasks

In a study found in (Carter et al., 2007), Carter et al. report that respondents felt that the current mobile tools are poorly matched to the user tasks of meeting and "keeping up with" friends and acquaintances. The study observed that location-based technology might assist users in such tasks. Moreover, the study found that users would prefer to have cumbersome and repetitive tasks carried out by their mobile technology artifacts (e.g., the device, the application, etc.). Carter et al. also found that planning tasks vary in nature and detail depending on the formal or informal nature of the event. It might be interesting to consider how level of formality could be used as one of the means of classifying tasks in mobile and ubiquitous computing. Carter et al. observe that events with differing levels of formality require different tasks and, therefore, different support. They note that users showed most interest in the systems that supported informal gathering, rather than formal gatherings. Another possible criterion for classifying or categorizing user tasks could be by borrowing from the activity theory's framework for describing human behavior (e.g., activities, operations, actions, etc.) or more specialized frameworks such as (Bardram, 2005; Bardram & Christensen, 2004). The work (Matthews et al., 2007), proposes the following classification for the types of activities peripheral displays are likely to support: dormant, primary, secondary, and pending.

Characterization of Tasks

In a work which primarily describes the challenges for representing and supporting user's activity in the desktop and ubiquitous interactions, Voida et al. in (Voida et al., to appear) characterize activities as follows:

- activities are dynamic, emphasizing the continuation and evolution of work artifacts in contrast to closure and archiving;

- activities are collaborative, in the creation, communication, and dissemination of work artifacts;

- activities exist at different levels of granularity, due to varying durations, complexity and ownership; and

- activities exist across places, including physical boundaries, virtual boundaries of information security and access, and fixed and mobile settings.

In (Abowd & Mynatt, 2000), Abowd and Mynatt describe everyday computing as an area of interaction research which results from considering the consequences of scaling ubiquitous computing with respect to time. They indicate that designing for everyday computing requires focus on the following features of informal, daily activities:

- they rarely have a clear beginning or end;
- interruption is expected;
- multiple activities operate concurrently;
- time is an important discriminator;
- associative models of information are needed.

Like Fithian et al.'s metrics described above (Fithian et al., 2003), these properties all emphasize the fact that activities in a ubiquitous interaction are more fragmented and require more divided attention than "architypal" office applications, although arguably these were never as simple as the more simplisitic models suggested. However, the first point also suggests that at a high-level there may be more continuity, and this certainly echoes Carter et al.'s study (Carter et al., 2007) with the importance of informal gathering and communication a life-long goal.

Formal Specification of Social and Collaborative Aspects

With a formal specification, it is possible to "analyze" a system long before it gets designed or implemented. Although this benefit applies to virtually all types of systems, it is interesting to the world of ubiquitous computing where, as we have noted, at the end of the previous section, developing a reliable and robust prototype or application is not an easy undertaking. Formal specifications, therefore, can be useful in supporting the development of ubiquitous applications. On the same note, in ubiquitous computing users perform their activities in the real world settings, where there are other people. In other words, ubiquitous computing involves context, which includes other people besides the user. Therefore, collaborative and social aspects have a lot of weight in ubiquitous computing. It has been rightly noted in (Abowd & Mynatt, 2000) that human beings tailor their activities and recall events from the past based on the presence (or even the help) of other people. Therefore, it is important to consider how we can realize formal specifications that can represent collaborative and social aspects for ubiquitous applications. It is worth observing that much of the research in ubiquitous computing has focused on mobility (and other contextual aspects) with regard to an individual user, with little being done regarding social and collaborative aspects.

One of the possible approaches to the formal modeling of social aspects is through the use of agents. It might be worth investigating to what degree such agent-based models can be applied in ubiquitous computing. One such model is OperA (Dignum et al., 2002a; Dignum et al., 2002b; Dignum, 2004). The authors indicate that the concept of agents is useful for representing organizational interaction for two main reasons. The first is that it enables the reference to any autonomous entity participating in an interaction, including people. The second is that it provides theoretical models for entities and interaction. OperA "abstracts from the specific internal representations of the individual agents, and separates the modeling of organizational requirements and aims. Contracts are used to link the different models and create specific instances that reflect the needs and structure of the current environment and participants" (Dignum, 2004).

It might also be appropriate to borrow a leaf from Grid Computing where the need for models for addressing collaborative and social aspects has been identified (Liu & Harrison, 2002). According to Liu (Liu, 2003), in Grid Computing the development of such models has been based on the early work on information systems (Liu, 2000; Stamper, 1973; Stamper, 1996) and computer-supported collaborative work (CSCW), (Liu et al., 2001). One particular model that has been proposed is the SPS model, which entails the integrated modeling of semantic, pragmatic and social aspects (Liu, 2003). Regarding formal specifications for CSCW in general (and not just under Grid Computing), one interesting effort is the work by Johnson (Johnson, 1999), which describes how formal methods can be used creatively to solve a vast range of design problems within CSCW interfaces. It is worth noting that the work does show how mathematical specification techniques can be enhanced to capture physical properties of working environments, thereby providing a link between the physiological studies from ergonomics and the HCI user interface design techniques.

A related and interesting work is found in (Musolesi et al., 2004), in which there is a proposal of a two-level mobility model that is based on artificially generated social relationships among individuals carrying mobile devices. The generation process respects the mathematical basis of social networks theory and, thus, is grounded in empirical experience of actual social relationships. The second level/stage maps the social organization onto topographical space such that the actual generated topography is biased by the strength of social ties.

At a very low level, more traditional formal models become applicable as we are "below" the level of the more complex considerations of ubiquitous computing. In particular, variations of Fitts' law have been used extensively to understand and to design interfaces for pointing tasks on tiny devices (Guiard & Beaudouin-Lafon, 2004).

Summary

As a way of emphasizing the relevance of the theme of this chapter, it is worth observing that there is a growing interest within the research community regarding tasks in ubiquitous computing. Therefore, it comes as no surprise that we are now seeing the emergence of fields such as activity-centered design (Gay & Hembrooke, 2003), activity-based computing (Bardram, 2005; Bardram & Christensen, 2004), and activity-based ubiquitous computing (Li & Landay, 2006).

As we consider the move from the conventional desktop setting to the real world setting, various design issues and demands arise when we consider the nature of tasks the ubiquitous devices/applications would be expected to support and the real world context in which they will be used. A close study of the nature of tasks in ubiquitous computing has the potential to bring to light some of the requirements in the development of ubiquitous applications.

In particular, we have seen how tasks in ubiquitous environments tend to be more dynamic, less pre-planned, and more situated than those commonly assumed to be the case for more traditional desktop applications. In addition, users are likely to be involved in multiple activities, and the task involving a ubiquitous device may not be the primary task for the user either because there is a real world task(s) such as driving that takes precedence, or because the device interaction is merely supporting an ongoing activity such as social coordination. Interruptions and resumptions of activity become the norm (although there is plenty of evidence that this is also the case in the office) and so the need, as advocated in distributed cognition, to offload memory into the device becomes important.

Because of the dynamic nature of tasks we have discussed, various methods and theories that emphasise the richer nature of human activity, and any methods used to study tasks for ubiquitous interaction have to be open to seeing unexpected patterns of activity. However, there are clearly also generic meta-tasks and common issues found in many ubiquitous interactions including offloading of memory, interruption management, location sensitivity, and so forth. It is essential to understand the former, situation specific issues, in order to avoid designs that are not fit for that purpose; however, the latter, generic issues, offer the potential for lessons to be learnt across systems and for ongoing fruitful research directions.

References

Abowd, G. D., & Mynatt, E. D. (2000). Charting Past, Present, and Future Research in Ubiquitous Computing. *ACM Transactions on Computer-Human Interaction, 7*(1), 29-58.

Abowd, G. D., Mynatt, E. D., & Rodden, T. (2002). The Human Experience. *IEEE Pervasive Computing, 1*(1), 48-57.

Abowd, G. D., Hayes, G. R., Iachello, G., Kientz, J. A., Patel, S. N., & Stevens, M. M. (2005). Prototypes and paratypes: Designing mobile and ubiquitous computing applications. *IEEE Pervasive Computing, 4*(4), 67–73.

Baker, K., Greenberg, S., & Gutwin, C. (2001). Heuristic Evaluation of Groupware Based on the Mechanics of Collaboration. In *Proceedings of the 8th IFIP International Conference on Engineering for Human-Computer Interaction* (pp. 123-140).

Bardram, J. E. (2005). Activity-Based Computing: Support for Mobility and Collaboration in Ubiquitous Computing. *Personal and Ubiquitous Computing, 9*(5), 312-322.

Bardram, J. E., & Christensen, H. B. (2004). *Open Issues in Activity-Based and Task-Level Computing*. Paper presented at the Pervasive'04 Workshop on Computer Support for Human Tasks and Activities (pp. 55-61), Vienna, Austria.

Berry, M., & Hamilton, M. (2006). Mobile Computing, Visual Diaries, Learning and Communication: Changes to the Communicative Ecology of Design Students Through Mobile Computing. In *Proceedings of the eighth Australasian Computing Education Conference (ACE2006)—Conferences in Research in Practice in Information Technology* (pp. 35-44). Hobart, Tasmania, Australia. Australian Computer Society, Inc.

Bertini, E., & Kimani, S. (2003). Mobile Devices: Opportunities for Users with Special Needs. In *Proceedings of Mobile HCI Conference 2003* (pp. 486-491).

Bertini, E., Catarci, T., Kimani, S., & Dix, A. (2005). A Review of Standard Usability Principles in the Context of Mobile Computing. *International Journal of Studies in Communication Sciences, 5*(1), 111-126.

Bertini, E., Gabrielli, S., Kimani, S., Catarci, T., & Santucci, G. (2006). *Appropriating and Assessing Heuristics for Mobile Computing*. Paper presented at the International Conference in Advanced Visual Interfaces (AVI) (pp. 119-126).

Beyer, H., & Holtzblatt, K. (1998). *Contextual Design: Defining Customer-Centered Systems*. Academic Press: Kaufmann Publishers.

Boer, N., van Baalen, P.J., & Kumar, K. (2002). An activity theory approach for studying the situatedness of knowledge sharing. In *Proceedings of the 35th Annual Hawaii International Conference on System Sciences (HICSS-35'02)* (pp. 1483-1492).

Card, S. K., Moran, T. P., & Newell, A. (1983). *The Psychology of Human-Computer Interaction*. Lawrence Erlbaum Associates.

Carter, S., Mankoff, J., Klemmer, S. R., & Matthews, T. (2007). Exiting the cleanroom: on ecological validity and ubiquitous computing. *Journal of Human-Computer Interaction, 22*(1/2).

Crabtree, A., Hemmings, T., Rodden, T., Clarke, K., Dewsbury, G., Hughes, J., Rouncefield, M., & Sommerville, I. (2002). Sore Legs and Naked Bottoms: Using Cultural Probes in Dependability Research. *DIRC Conference on Dependable Computing Systems*. London: The Royal Statistical Society.

Crabtree, A., Benford, S., Greenhalgh, C., Tennent, P., Chalmers, M., & Brown, B. (2006). Supporting Ethnographic Studies of Ubiquitous Computing in the Wild. In *Proceedings of the sixth ACM conference on Designing Interactive Systems* (pp.60-69). ACM Press.

Dignum, V., Meyer, J-J., Weigand, H., & Dignum, F. (2002a). An Organizational-oriented Model for Agent Societies. In *Proceedings of the International Workshop on Regulated Agent-Based Social Systems: Theories and Applications (RASTA'02)*, at AAMAS, Bologna, Italy.

Dignum, V., Meyer, J-J., Dignum, F., & Weigand, H. (2002b). Formal Specification of Interaction in Agent Societies. Paper presented at the *Second Goddard Workshop on Formal Approaches to Agent-Based Systems (FAABS)*, Maryland.

Dignum, V. (2004). *A model for organizational interaction: based on agents, founded in logic*. Unpublished doctoral dissertation, Utrecht University.

Dix, A. (2002). Beyond intention - pushing boundaries with incidental interaction. In *Proceedings of Building Bridges: Interdisciplinary Context-Sensitive Computing*, Glasgow University, Sept 2002. http://www.hcibook.com/alan/topics/incidental/

Dix, A., Finlay, J., Abowd, G., & Beale, R. (2004). *Human-Computer Interaction*. Prentice Hall (Third Edition).

Dix, A., Ramduny-Ellis, D., & Wilkinson, J. (2004b). Trigger Analysis - understanding broken tasks. Chapter 19 in *The Handbook of Task Analysis for Human-Computer Interaction*. D. Diaper & N. Stanton (Eds.) (pp.381-400). Lawrence Erlbaum Associates.

Ellis, G., & Dix, A. (2006). An explorative analysis of user evaluation studies in information visualisation. *Proceedings of the 2006 Conference on Beyond Time and Errors: Novel Evaluation Methods For information Visualization (BELIV '06)* (pp. 1-7), Venice, Italy. ACM Press, New York, NY.

Fischer, G., Arias, E., Carmien, S., Eden, H., Gorman, A., Konomi, S., & Sullivan, J. (2004). Supporting Collaboration and Distributed Cognition in Context-Aware Pervasive Computing Environments. *Meeting of the Human Computer Interaction Consortium "Computing Off The Desktop"*.

Fithian, R., Iachello, G., Moghazy, J., Pousman, Z., & Stasko, J. (2003). The design and evaluation of a mobile location-aware handheld event planner. In *Proceedings of Mobile HCI Conference 2003* (pp. 145-160).

Flor, N., & Hutchins, E. (1991). Analyzing distributed cognition in software teams: A case study of team programming during perfective software maintenance. In J. Koenemann-Belliveau et al. (Eds.), In *Proceedings of the Fourth Annual Workshop on Empirical Studies of Programmers* (pp. 36–59). Norwood, N.J.: Ablex Publishing.

Gabrielli, S., Mirabella, V., Kimani, S., & Catarci, T. (2005). Supporting Cognitive Walkthrough with Video Data: Results from a Mobile Learning Evaluation Study. In *Proceedings of Mobile HCI Conference 2005 Conference* (pp. 77-82).

Gabrielli, S., Kimani, S., & Catarci, T. (2005). *The Design of MicroLearning Experiences: A Research Agenda*, Paper presented at the Microlearning Conference 2005.

Gaver, W.H., Dunne, A., & Pacenti, E. (1999a). Cultural probes. *ACM Interactions, 6*(1), 21-29.

Gaver, W.H., Hooker, B., & Dunne, A. (1999b). *The Presence Project*. London: Department of Interaction Design.

Gaver, W. (2001). Designing for ludic aspects of everyday life, *ERCIM News, 47*. www.ercim.org/publication/Ercim_News/enw47/gaver.html.

Gaver, W. (2002). *Domestic Probes*. www.crd.rca.ac.uk/equator/PROBE.htm.

Gay, G., & Hembrooke, H. (2003). *Activity-Centered Design: An Ecological Approach to Designing Smart Tools and Usable Systems*. Cambridge, MA. MIT Press.

Gorlenko, L., & Merrick, R. (2003). No Wires Attached: Usability Challenges in the Connected Mobile World. *IBM Systems Journal, 42*, 639-651.

Guiard, Y., & Beaudouin-Lafon, M. (2004) Target Acquisition in Multiscale Electronic Worlds. *International Journal of Human-Computer Studies, 61*(6), 875-905.

Hewagamage, K. P., & Hirakawa, M. (2000). Situated Computing: A Paradigm to Enhance the Mobile User's Interaction. *Handbook of Software Engineering and Knowledge Engineering, 0*(0). World Scientific Publishing Company.

Holland, S., & Morse, D. R. (2001). Audio GPS: Spatial Audio in a Minimal Attention Interface. In *Proceedings of Mobile HCI Conference 2001* (pp. 28-33).

Holtzblatt, K. (2005). Customer-Centered Design for Mobile Applications. *Personal and Ubiquitous Computing, 9*(4), 227-237.

Holtzblatt, K., & Jones, S. (1993). Contextual Inqury: Principles and Practice. *Participatory Design: Principles and Practices*. Lawrence Earlbaum, New York.

Horvitz, E. (1999). Principles of Mixed-Initiative User Interfaces. In *Proceedings of the ACM SIGCHI Conference on Human Factors in Computing Systems* (pp. 159-166).

Hughes, J., Rodden, T., King, V., & Anderson, K. (1995). The Role of Ethnography in Interactive Systems Design. *ACM Interactions*, (4), 56-65.

Hutchinson, H., Mackay, W., Westerlund, B., Bederson, B. B., Druin, A., Plaisant, C., Beaudouin-Lafon, M., Conversy, S., Evans, H., Hansen, H., Roussel, N., & Eiderback, B. (2003). Technology probes: Inspiring design for and with families. In *Proceedings of the ACM SIGCHI Conference on Human Factors in Computing Systems* (pp. 17–24). New York: ACM Press.

Johnson, C. (1999). Expanding the role of formal methods in CSCW. In M. Beaudouin-Lafon (Ed.), *Computer Supported Co-operative Work, Volume 7 of Trends in Software*, 221-255. John Wiley & Sons.

Kaenampornpan, M., & O'Neill, E. (2004). An Integrated Context Model: Bringing Activity to Context. In *Proceedings of the Workshop on Advanced Context Modelling, Reasoning and Management at UbiComp 2004.*

Kaptelinin, V., Kuutti, K., & Bannon, L. (1995). Activity Theory: Basic Concepts and Applications. In Blumenthal et al. (Eds.), *Human-Computer Interaction.* (LNCS, pp. 189-201). Springer.

Kristoffersen, S., & Ljungberg, F. (1999). "Making Place" to Make IT Work: Empirical Explorations of HCI for Mobile CSCW. In *Proceedings of the International ACM SIGGROUP Conference on Supporting Group Work,* (pp. 276-285).

Laroussi, M. (2004). *New E-Learning Services Based on Mobile and Ubiquitous Computing: Ubi-Learn Project.* Paper presented at the Computer Aided Learning in Engineering Education *(CALIE'04).* Grenoble, France.

Laru, J., & Järvelä, S. (2003). Applying wireless technology for co-ordinating collaboration in distributed university teacher's team. *Poster at Computer Supported Collaborative Learning (CSCL2003).*

Lave, J. (1988). *Cognition in Practice.* Cambridge: Cambridge University Press.

Leont'ev, A. N. (1978). *Activity, Consciousness, Personality.* Englewood Cliffs, NJ, Prentice Hall.

Li, Y., & Landay, J. A. (2006). Exploring Activity-Based Ubiquitous Computing Interaction Styles, Models and Tool Support. In *Proceedings of the Workshop What is the Next Generation of Human-Computer Interaction? at the ACM SIGCHI Conference on Human Factors in Computing Systems.*

Liu, K. (2000). *Semiotics in Information Systems Engineering.* Cambridge University Press.

Liu, K., Clarke, R., Stamper, R., & Anderson, P. (2001). *Information, Organisation and Technology: Studies in Organisational Semiotics – 1.* Kluwer, Boston.

Liu, K., & Harrison, R. (2002). Embedding "Softer" Aspects into the Grid. *Poster at EUROWEB 2002 - The Web and the GRID: from e-science to e-business* (pp. 179-182). The British Computer Society.

Liu, K. (2003). *Incorporating Human Aspects into Grid Computing for Collaborative Work.* Paper presented at the ACM International Workshop on Grid Computing and e-Science. San Francisco, CA.

Liu, L., & Khooshabeh, P. (2003). Paper or interactive? A study of prototyping techniques for ubiquitous computing environments. In *Proceedings of the*

ACM SIGCHI Conference on Human Factors in Computing Systems, extended abstracts, (pp. 130–131). New York: ACM Press.

Mäkelä, K., Salonen, E-P., Turunen, M., Hakulinen, J., & Raisamo, R. (2001). Conducting a Wizard of Oz Experiment on a Ubiquitous Computing System Doorman. In *Proceedings of the International Workshop on Information Presentation and Natural Multimodal Dialogue* (pp. 115-119). Verona.

Mankoff, J., & Schilit, B. (1997). Supporting knowledge workers beyond the desktop with PALPlates. In *Proceedings of the ACM SIGCHI Conference on Human Factors in Computing Systems*, extended abstracts, (pp. 550–551). New York: ACM Press.

Mankoff J., Dey A. K., Hsieh G., Kientz J., Lederer S. & Ames M. (2003). Heuristic Evaluation of Ambient Displays. *Proceedings of the ACM SIGCHI Conference on Human Factors in Computing Systems* (pp. 169-176).

Matthews, T., Rattenbury, T., & Carter, S. (2007). Defining, Designing, and Evaluating Peripheral Displays: An Analysis Using Activity Theory. *Journal of Human-Computer Interaction*, 22(1/2).

Muller, M.J., Wildman, D.M., & White, E.A. (1993). A Taxonomy of PD Practices: A Brief Practitioner's Guide. *Communications of the ACM, 36*(4), 26-28.

Muñoz Bravo, J., Lucero, A., & Aliakseyeu, D. (2007). Probing the Need for Mobile Technologies for Designers. In *Proceedings of the Second IASTED International Conference on Human-Computer Interaction*. Chamonix, France. ACTA Press.

Musolesi, M., Hailes, S., & Mascolo, C. (2004). An Ad Hoc Mobility Model Founded on Social Network Theory. In *Proceedings of the Seventh ACM/IEEE International Symposium on Modeling, Analysis and Simulation of Wireless and Mobile Systems (MSWiM 2004)* (pp. 20-24). Venezia, Italy.

Nardi, B. (1996). Studying context: a comparison of activity theory, situated action models, and distributed cognition. In: B. Nardi (Ed.), *Context and Consciousness: Activity Theory and Human-Computer Interaction* (pp. 69-102). MIT Press, Cambridge, MA.

Newcomb, E., Pashley, T., & Stasko, J. (2003). Mobile Computing in the Retail Arena. In *Proceedings of the ACM SIGCHI Conference on Human Factors in Computing Systems* (pp. 337-344).

Newell, A., & Simon, H. (1972). *Human Problem Solving*. Englewood Cliffs, NJ: Prentice-Hall.

Pascoe, J., Ryan, N., & Morse, D. (2000). Using While Moving: HCI Issues in Fieldwork Environments. *ACM Transactions on Human-Computer Interaction*, 7(3), 417-437.

Paulos, E., & Goodman, E. (2004). The familiar stranger: Anxiety, comfort, and play in public places. *Proceedings of the ACM SIGCHI Conference on Human Factors in Computing Systems* (pp. 223–230). New York: ACM Press.

Paulos, E., & Jenkins, T. (2005). Urban probes: Encountering our emerging urban atmospheres. In *Proceedings of the ACM SIGCHI Conference on Human Factors in Computing Systems* (pp. 341–350). New York: ACM Press.

Pinto, H., & Jose, R. (2006). Activity-centered ubiquitous computing support to localized activities. In *Proceedings of the Conference on Mobile and Ubiquitous Systems (CMUS)* (pp. 119-128). Guimarães.

Rogers, Y., Scaife, M., Muller, H., Randell, C., Moss, A., Taylor, I., Harris, E., Smith, H., Price, S., Phelps, T., Corke, G., Gabrielli, S., Stanton, D., & O'Malley, C. (2002). Things Aren't What They Seem to be: Innovation Through Technology Inspiration. In *Proceedings of ACM-SIGCHI DIS02* (pp. 373-378).

Rudström, Ä., Cöster, R., Höök, K., & Svensson, M. (2003). Paper prototyping a social mobile service. In *Proceedings of the MUM Workshop on Designing for Ubicomp in the Wild: Methods for Exploring the Design of Mobile and Ubiquitous Services.*

Schmidt, A., & Terrenghi, L. (2007). Methods and Guidelines for the Design and Development of Domestic Ubiquitous Computing Applications. In *Proceedings of PerCom2007* (pp. 97-107). New York, USA.

Spinelli, G., Brodie, J., & Perry, M. (2002). Using Distributed Cognition and Contextual Design to Analyse and Represent Collaborative Activities. In *Proceedings of CSCSW2002 Conference workshop Analyzing Collaborative Activity.* New Orleans, Louisiana, USA.

Stamper, R. K. (1973). *Information in Business and Administrative Systems.* Wiley.

Stamper, R. K. (1996). Signs, Information, Norms and Systems. In P. Holmqvist, P. B. Andersen, H. Klein, & R. Posner (Eds.), *Signs of Work* (pp. 349-397). Walter de Gruyter.

Strömberg, H., Pirttilä, V., & Ikonen, V. (2004). Interactive Scenarios-building Ubiquitous Computing Concepts in the Spirit of Participatory Design. *Personal and Ubiquitous Computing, 8,* 200-207.

Supawanich, A., Rangos, J., Harriman, J., & Schmitt, G. (2005). Mobile Computing in High-End Retail. In *Proceedings of the conference on Designing for User eXperience.* American Institute of Graphic Arts. New York, USA.

Taylor, A., & Harper, R. (2002). Age-old Practices in the 'New World': A study of gift-giving between teenage mobile phone users. In *Proceedings of the ACM SIGCHI Conference on Human Factors in Computing Systems* (pp. 439–446). ACM Press.

Uden, L. (2007). Activity theory for designing mobile learning. *International Journal of Mobile Learning and Organisation, 1*(1), 81-102.

Voida, S., Mynatt, E. D., & MacIntyre, B. (2007). Supporting Activity in Desktop and Ubiquitous Computing. In V. Kaptelinin, & M. Czerwinski (Eds.), *Designing integrated digital work environments: Beyond the desktop metaphor* (pp. 195-222). Cambridge, MA: MIT Press.

Weiser, M. (1991). The Computer for the 21st Century. *Scientific American, 265*(3), 91-104.

Chapter VIII

Kinetic User Interfaces:
Physical Embodied Interaction with Mobile Ubiquitous Computing Systems

Vincenzo Pallotta, University of Fribourg, Switzerland

Pascal Bruegger, University of Fribourg, Switzerland

Béat Hirsbrunner, University of Fribourg, Switzerland

Abstract

This chapter presents a conceptual framework for an emerging type of user interfaces for mobile ubiquitous computing systems, and focuses in particular on the interaction through motion of people and objects in physical space. We introduce the notion of Kinetic User Interface as a unifying framework and a middleware for the design of pervasive interfaces, in which motion is considered as the primary input modality.

Introduction

Internet and mobile computing technology is changing the way users access information and interact with computers and media. *Personal Computing* in its original form is fading and shifting towards the ubiquitous (or pervasive) computing paradigm (Want et al., 2002). Ubiquitous Computing systems are made up of several interconnected heterogeneous computational devices with different degrees of mobility and computing power. All of these devices and appliances are embedded in everyday objects, scattered in space, capable of sensing the environment and of communicating with each other, and carried or exchanged by people. Therefore, we are facing a new ecology of computing systems that poses new issues in their integration and usability. Human-computer interfaces that were designed for desktop personal computers must be re-conceived for this new scenario. Due to the different capabilities of mobile and embedded devices, the pervasive computing infrastructure, and the nature of their expected usage, it is apparent that new types of user interfaces are needed in order to unleash the usability of new generation distributed computing applications (see (Rukzio, 2006) for a classification of mobile devices interfaces). Additionally, the concept of user interface itself seems to be no longer adequate to cope with ubiquitous computing systems. Rather, it is the concept of interaction and user experience that will take over (Beaudouin-Lafon, 2004).

Ubiquitous Computing

Ubiquitous Computing (henceforth Ubicomp) is an emerging research sub-area of Distributed Systems whose main focus is studying how heterogeneous, networked computing devices can be embedded in objects of daily use in order to enable new applicative scenarios and user experiences. Mark Weiser (1991; 1993; 1994) introduced the term Ubiquitous Computing in the '90s as a new way to understand computer technology and to lay the foundations of an expected and necessary computing paradigm revolution. Weiser's vision has been adopted and interpreted by a great number of researchers, among whom we consider relevant for our goals the works of (Abowd & Mynatt, 2000; Abowd et al., 2002; Banavar & Bernstein, 2004; Bellotti et al., 2002; Greenfield, 2006; Norman, 1999; Want et al., 2002). We summarize the Ubicomp vision in four fundamental points that motivate our effort of providing a new conceptual framework for Ubicomp user interfaces:

1.   Today's computer (e.g., the personal computer) will disappear, and the computing power will fade inside the network infrastructure, as it is already the case to some extent with existing web-services.

2. Computing will be extremely distributed and heterogeneous. This will result from the interconnection of several computing devices, each specialized in specific tasks and scattered in the physical environment (ranging from embedded devices to high-performance servers).

3. Computer interfaces will no longer capture the full attention of users. Rather, computer applications will run in "background" most of the time, accomplishing "routinized" operations, and they will try to gain user's attention only when strictly required.

4. Computer interfaces will be unobtrusive and based on new emerging interaction models obtained by direct interaction with physical objects and with the whole environment.

Ubiquitous Computing is often equated to (or better, confused with) nomadic computing (Kleinrock, 1997). Nomadic computing is a form of computing environment that offers its users access to data or information from any device and network while they are in state of motion. In nomadic computing, the use of portable devices (such as laptops and handheld computers) in conjunction with mobile communications technologies enables users to access the Internet and data on their home or work computers from anywhere in the world. Mobile connectivity certainly does play an important role in Ubicomp, but it is not the only one. We consider of central importance the *user's mobility* intended as the user's *ability of moving objects and themselves in the physical space*. In fact, in using Ubicomp systems, users are no longer forced to sit in front of a desktop computer and to operate it with mice, keyboards and local input/output devices. Users will interact through actions performed on everyday objects that surround them. As pointed again by Weiser[1]:

[ubiquitous computing] *is different from PDAs, dynabooks, or information at your fingertips. It is invisible, everywhere computing that does not live on a personal device of any sort, but is in the woodwork everywhere.*

User Interfaces for Ubicomp Systems

Human-computer interaction (HCI) is a very large domain of research, which includes all related aspects of interaction with digital appliances. Although HCI has been mostly focused on graphical user interfaces (GUIs), we consider here those aspects that pertain to how users will interact with computers in the 21st century (Winograd, 2000), that is, by direct manipulation of objects in their physical environment. Paul Dourish (2001) defined this paradigm as *embodied interaction*. According to his definition, meaningful embodied interaction with a digital system can be obtained only if an alignment is maintained between the physical and the digital world. In other terms, "bits" and "atoms" must live together in peace (Negroponte, 1995). As recently pointed out in (Sparacino, 2005, p. 2):

[...] *computation and sensing are moving from computers and devices into the environment itself. The space around us is instrumented with sensors and displays, and this tends to reflect a widespread need to blend together the information space with our physical space.*

Embodied interaction is thus aimed at exploring new *interaction patterns* where people are exploring how to move the interface "off the screen" and into the real world (Shafer et al., 2001). For instance, in Tangible User Interfaces (TUIs) (Ulmer and Iishi, 2000; Holmquist et al., 2004), tangible interaction is intended to replace desktop GUI's interaction and elements with operations on physical objects. The motion of objects in the physical space determines the execution of actions, such as item selection (by means of what in TUI are called "phicons" i.e., *physical icons*), service requests, database updates, and so forth. Rekimoto (1997) proposed the Pick&Drop pattern, an extension of the Drag&Drop pattern, to move items across computers. In his work on graspable user interfaces, Fitzmaurice (2000) proposed to extend the interaction with classical GUI by means of physical objects (such as LEGO bricks) over an augmented desktop surface. Tangible and graspable user interfaces are undoubtedly a great achievement in HCI. However, they are strongly biased by GUIs interfaces; nearly no new types of interaction induced by the nature of the physical space and objects have been proposed other than replications of those available on ordinary desktop GUIs.

The development of the ideas introduced by TUIs, combined with the ubiquity of information over the Internet, has led to a new concept of what counts as an Ubicomp system. Moving from the assumption that only information appliances could constitute a ubiquitous system, the whole material world of things and people now can be made computational and connected. The movement of the "Internet of Things" (ITU, 2005; Bleeker, 2006) is aimed at promoting the idea that any object can have a *virtual identity* in the Internet realm, as long as the object can embed a unique identifier, which corresponds to an IP address. This is now possible because of the larger 128 bits IP address space offered by the new IPv6 protocol (i.e., 3.4×10^{38} addresses). According to (Greenfield, 2006), the type of infrastructure that enables Ubiquitous Computing is already technically feasible and it will soon scale up to a level that will make it possible to safely connect a huge number of small heterogeneous devices, possibly embedded in everyday objects.

Augmented Reality (AR) (Mackay, 1998) and Wearable Interfaces (Barfield & Caudell, 2001) are emerging technologies that support embodied interaction for Ubicomp systems. We believe that Augmented Reality focuses more on how feedback is provided, whereas Wearable Interfaces focuses on the types of devices that can support embodied interaction.

Unobtrusive Interfaces

When HCI intersects Ubicomp, many assumptions that were made when designing interaction for ordinary computing devices are no longer valid. In Ubicomp, computers exist in different forms and only in a minimal portion as ordinary desktop computers (i.e., where interaction is performed through screens, keyboards, mice). As pointed out by Weiser and other promoters of Ubicomp, interacting with a ubiquitous system should be realized through an *unobtrusive interface*, more precisely, an interface that does not capture the full attention of the user, who can still use the system to perform the foreground tasks (Nardi, 1996). In contrast, an obtrusive interface is one that requires an unjustified cognitive effort to be operated, thus interfering with the normal usage of the system. Weiser & Seely Brown (1996) call this setting "Calm Technology" in order to stress the importance of adapting the computers and their interfaces to human pace, rather that the other way around. In this vision, computers should follow users in their daily activity and be ready to provide information or assistance on demand. Moreover, they should not require much attention from the user by asking information that can be autonomously obtained from the actual usage context. They must be "aware" of the context and be able to adapt their behaviour and interfaces to different usage situations. In other words, ubiquitous computers must be *smart* and *adaptive*.

Kinetic-Awareness

Context awareness is considered as the most important issue in Ubicomp (Baldauf et al., 2006; Dourish, 2004; Hong et al., 2005). Specifically, location-awareness is considered a key component of context in designing user interfaces for mobile systems. Location-awareness has been always treated as a sub-case of context-awareness, and motion as a form of context change. Location change is taken as a context change for adapting the application's behaviour, rather than as an explicit intentional act within the application's interface.

We believe that location changes occurring over time can represent more than just context-change. It can be considered as input modality. This does not mean that location or motion context has to be neglected. Motion input and location context can be used together in the same way as in handheld GUIs, where interaction with the mobile devices can be contextualized through location or motion. For instance, it does make sense to consider a different interpretation for an object's motion that occurs in a different location, or to interpret the GUI input differently when the mobile device is moving with different kinetic properties. To clarify this aspect let us consider two examples.

The first example is about two possible situations where a paraglide is flying i) over a lake, or ii) over the ground. Motion input is treated accordingly to the actual situation; when flying over the lake some manoeuvres are considered risky, while they are considered safe if flying over the ground (landing is possible everywhere).

The second example is a situation where implicit interaction with GUI is enabled if the handheld device is detected moving with a certain speed. For instance, suppose that a dialogue box asking for a confirmation pops up on the handheld's GUI. If the user is moving, at a speed of more than 5 Km/h, then after a timeout, the interface assumes that the default choice has been (implicitly) selected. If the user is moving at lower speed or is still, the interface will wait for input without the timeout.

According to Dix et al. (2000), *space* and *location* define a new design space for interactive mobile systems. Mobile devices have increasing capacity in providing location and motion information as part of their usage context. They also acknowledged that accounting for motion as an input modality for location-aware mobile Ubicomp systems opens potential research opportunities. In fact, they propose and instantiate a taxonomy of the degrees of mobility with available technologies and applications. They categorize degrees of mobility along three dimensions *level of mobility* (i.e., the physical bound of the device to the environment), *level of independence* (i.e., the relation of the used location-aware device with other devices or to the environment), *level of cooperativeness* (i.e., the extent to which the device is bound to a particular individual or group). Some existing mobile devices and applications are then categorized according to this three-dimensional taxonomy. Some difficult or even impossible cases, such as a *fixed-pervasive-personal*, that might be instantiated by a fully isolated active cell (e.g., a prison cell with motion sensors). The combination that is relevant for us is that of *pervasive-mobile-personal/group* devices. Such devices might be location/motion-aware objects that can be used to interact with Ubicomp systems.

Systems combining location and motion awareness, henceforth, will be referred to as *kinetic-aware systems*. Our analysis of how kinetic information is taken into account in existing Ubicomp systems revealed that there are two main views on the role of kinetic information in user interfaces:

1. In the first view, location and motion are used as a component of the usage context that is exploited by applications running on the mobile information computing devices for adapting their behaviour. In this view, there is no physical interaction with the place (and its contained artefacts) where the users are using their own devices. The environment is not "sensing" the presence and the physical action of the user. Moreover, neither the system nor the environment is supposed to handle spatio-temporally located events.

2. In the second view, location change and motion are considered as *primary input modalities* reflecting the user's goals and intentions while using Ubicomp applications. That is, users can intentionally perform explicit and implicit actions through physical motion. These actions are recognized and contextualized in the place where they occur, by possibly affecting the state of co-located devices and remote systems. Interaction through motion with physical space becomes the main focus, rather than simply contextualizing applications based on ordinary user interfaces running on mobile devices.

While the majority of research on location-aware Ubicomp systems focuses on the first view on kinetic awareness, we focus instead on the second view, which can be achieved by recognizing users' goals and intentions from various properties of motion of objects in the physical space through what we call the *Kinetic User Interface* (KUI).

Kinetic awareness can be seen as part of a more general paradigm, defined in (Dix et al., 2004) as *context-aware computing*. This emerging paradigm poses several challenges. One of the biggest recognized difficulties for this type of system is *interpreting human activity*. We do not propose algorithms for automatic recognition of human activities (which is a machine learning task). Instead, we propose a framework in which activities can be decomposed into smaller and easier-to-detect patterns. These patterns are instantiated by acquiring input from sensors that are linked to software components representing physical objects. We believe that providing a level of abstraction for activities will make easier the design and the implementation of Kinetic User Interfaces for Ubicomp systems.

Related Works and Technologies

Location-aware services are nowadays available to mobile Internet users. With the advent of Web2.0[2], a great deal of applied research and development recently has been devoted to embedding Internet technology into everyday life mobile devices, ranging from pure entertainment to critical applications such as healthcare, national security, military (Cáceres et al., 2006). The rationale behind these efforts is to provide the mobile Internet users with great flexibility in authoring, publishing, and retrieving information, as well as in accessing services that are relevant in a given situation and place. A remarkable example of Web2.0 mobile application for multimedia information retrieval is SocialLight[3], which allows the tagging of geographical location with multimedia tags (e.g., shadow-tags). The roaming users can "geo-tag" a place either by using a mobile phone when they are physically present there, or by attaching the tag on the SocialLight Web page with a GoogleMap mashup. Information can further be retrieved from the Web site through the mashed-up map or by querying the system by using a mobile, GPS-enabled Internet device.

Geo-tagging is also the focus of the Mobile Multimedia Metadata project of the Garage Cinema Lab (Davis et al., 2004), whose main purpose is to cooperatively annotate geo-located pictures. (Ashbrook et al., 2006) push this concept further and propose a roadmap for future research with a new type of scenario based on location-awareness and motion tracking, in which users can capture media while moving, and share their experience by making the captured media stream available to Internet users in real-time.

Location-awareness in Ubicomp has been the main focus of several projects since 1990. Among the projects that heavily rely on location context are the Aware Home (Kidd et al., 1999) at GeorgiaTech, the GUIDE project at Lancaster University (Chervest et al., 2000), the AURA project at Carnegie Mellon University (Sousa & Garlan, 2002), the GAIA's Active Space project at University of Illinois Urbana Champaign (Román et al., 2002), the Interactive Maps at ETHZ (Norrie, 2005), and the Global Smart Places project (Meyer et al., 2006). It might seem that this is a widely explored research area, but a closer analysis reveals that all of these projects deal with a very basic form of motion-awareness. Location change is taken as a user's context change, which is used for dynamically adapting the application's behaviour. They all consider a user's location as an additional parameter of an explicit service request. Then, the service's output is delivered on the handheld device carried by the user or on a nearby display.

The Cyberguide project (Abowd et al., 1996) is one among the first attempts in taking a user's motion into account (see also (Schilit, 1995)). A tourist equipped with indoor (IR beacons) and outdoor (GPS) localization devices can automatically receive contextual relevant information on a PDA while moving, and feed a trip journal.

In the EasyLiving project at Microsoft (Brumitt et al., 2000), a geometric model of the physical space is used in order to enable physical embodied interaction by representing the physical relationships between entities in the world. Unfortunately, this model has a limited scope since it is adapted to room scale, and it only considers current spatial relationships between objects, while ignoring their motion within the tracked space.

The Intelligent Workspace project at MIT (Koile et al., 2003) is a system that records the user's location history and learns the so-called *activity zones*. Activity zones are portions of the physical space where the user is doing specific activities and which are repeatedly observed by the system. Once an activity zone is learned, the settlement of user in it will automatically trigger a number of pre-defined services that support the observed activity. In other words, the system reacts to context change and, in particular, to the user's location change.

However, none of the above-mentioned systems explicitly recognize motion as the primary input modality and as a mean of performing a purposeful (explicit or implicit) action within the application's interaction space. The following systems make a further step towards a more explicit notion of kinetic-awareness.

In the Sentient Computing project at AT&T Cambridge Research labs (Addlesee et al., 2001), motion tracking is an essential feature for interacting with the system. The system is built around the ActiveBat infrastructure for tracking location and motion using ultrawide-band sensors (now commercialized by Ubisense[4]). A few applications for the ActiveBat have been proposed, such as "FollowMe" that allows users to move their input-output environments over several devices scattered in the environment (e.g., phone call forwarding, virtual desktop displacement), or the "Virtual Mouse" that allows users carrying the ActiveBat device to use it as a mouse over a wall display. A relevant aspect of this project for us is the adopted context modelling techniques. The application-level and the user-level (mental) model of the environment are kept aligned by the system (Harter et al., 2002). In other words, when users perform actions, they update their mental representation of the resulting state of the environment by directly observing it. This representation might not be consistent with the information that applications have gathered through sensors. The system must take care of checking and possibly restabilising the lost alignment.

The Sonic City project (Gaye et al., 2003) exploits motion in the urban landscape as a way for interactively creating a musical experience. The user motion is tracked, as well as the current position over the city map. Motion and location contexts are combined with other contexts obtained through wearable sensors in order to influence the composition of music content in real-time. Users of the Sonic City interface can hear the result of musical composition during their walking activity.

Other applications of the motion context are pervasive games and races. Games that involve location tracking (like trails in (Spence et al., 2005)) are suited for exploiting the motion context. For instance, in CatchBob (Nova et al., 2006), a multi-player game developed at EPFL, the players' motion is tracked and their paths are made visible to other team members on a digital map. The goal of the game is to cooperatively perform a task by looking at the motion of the other team members on a handheld display and by communicating direction suggestions in real-time.

Overview of the Chapter

In this chapter, we propose a unifying framework for the design and implementation of Kinetic User Interfaces for Ubicomp systems by (i) defining a set of fundamental concepts and (ii) by presenting a middleware that enables the use of motion in physical spaces as the primary interaction modality.

The remainder of this chapter is structured as follows. In Section 2, we provide some backgrounds and intuitions about the distinguishing features of KUIs compared to other types of user interfaces. We also present a few motivating applicative KUI-based scenarios. In Section 3, we detail the main concepts of KUI and we present the structure of its middleware architecture. Conclusions are finally discussed in Section 4.

Kinetic User Interfaces

The term "Kinetic" is derived from the Greek *kinetikos*, which means "moving of, relating to or resulting from motion (the action or process of moving)." In physics, kinetic theory explains the physical properties of matter in terms of the movement of its constituent parts; kinetic energy refers to energy, which a body possesses by virtue of being in motion. Kinetic abilities of humans are of no question. People move and change their current spatial location all the time and in a mostly unconscious way. Humans are also capable of "modulating" motion in several ways, by keeping or varying their speed, by following different trajectories or patterns (e.g., dancing), or by executing various types of motion in parallel (e.g., gesturing while walking).

At different scales and contexts, motion (or absence of motion) can be recognized as a purposeful action. For instance, if a tourist stops long enough in front of a statue, it might be reasonable to assume that he or she is observing the monument. What if the statue (or the environment) would be smart enough to provide the tourist with relevant information about its author or style, or, even smarter, to figure out that the tourist has already stopped at the statue, to avoid repeating the old information unless the tourist explicitly requests it?

A familiar everyday situation occurs when items are passed through a bar code reader in a grocery store counter. Their motion (the passage in a given place) is recognized as a purchase transaction. Another typical KUI situation takes place when somebody, possibly unconsciously, performs dangerous actions such as moving into dangerous areas. In these cases, a monitoring system could alert the user by signalling the potential danger.

KUI vs. GUI

Motion in the physical space is such a common and pervasive phenomenon that we hardly recognize its status of an interaction modality with a computer. While it is apparent that motion plays an essential role in WIMP[5] Graphical User Interfaces (GUI), the virtual and limited nature of GUI's space, the "desktop," seems not to afford the full bodily motion interaction (Beaudoin-Lafon, 2000). For instance, it does make little or no sense to talk about speed or acceleration of the pointer. Sometimes, however, these properties are taken into account by specific types of PC applications like games or flight simulators.

We introduce the concept of *Kinetic User Interface* (KUI) as a way of endorsing Weiser's Ubiquitous Computing vision (Weiser, 1993) and the Dourish's Embodied Interaction vision (Dourish, 2001) discussed in the previous section. Accordingly, KUIs are intended to enable a new interaction model for pervasive computing systems in which the motion of objects and users in the physical space are recognized as events and processes to which the system reacts. To make a parallel with ordinary, pointer-controlled Graphical User Interfaces (GUIs), moving the pointer on the display and clicking on a graphical item is recognized by the system as an intentional act, which usually triggers a system's reaction on the software representation of the domain object associated to the selected graphical item and, possibly, the execution of an action on the domain object specified in the application currently running on the computer. Similar to "hovering" the pointer over a desktop in GUIs, in KUIs users can trigger input events for the computing environment by moving themselves and by displacing tracked objects. Users can exploit the physical space by executing actions/operations on physical objects, such as moving, grabbing, touching, juxtaposing, whose effects are reflected in the application objects. For instance, following a path or executing a pre-defined motion pattern can be viewed as similar to "mouse gestures" in ordinary desktop GUIs and can consequently trigger reactions by the gesture-enabled application.

KUIs are not limited to single-user interfaces and do not impose a unique locus of interaction. Hence, it enables richer interactions than GUIs and it is better suited to ubiquitous and mobile computing environments. Motion as an input modality can be used alone or in combination with other input modalities available to the user for interaction with the system, which are directly afforded by other mobile devices carried by the users and by fixed input devices located in the interaction space (e.g., ordinary point and click, or speech recognition).

Feedback Management

As in GUIs, an important issue in KUIs is *feedback management*. Due to the different nature of physical space with respect to GUI's synthetic space, feedback cannot be provided in the same way as for GUIs. Since one of the goals of KUI is to help build unobtrusive interfaces, we give back to users only the minimal amount of information required to inform them that their interaction with the physical space has been successfully recognized. In turn, the system should avoid interfering with the user's current activity if the effects of the recognized action have only a peripheral importance to the current foreground task (i.e., if the effects impact only objects that are not in the current focus of attention of the user). Moreover, since the physical space already allows for the direct manipulation of real objects, feedback should only inform users about those effects produced in the computing space to (virtual) domain objects.

Although users might not always be aware of what effects are caused by their motion and the motion of tracked objects, they will be unobtrusively notified when their motion has been detected and interpreted by the system. Different than GUIs or even in Augmented Reality systems, there will be no need to display a synthetic image of the moving object. The only graphical components of the interface will be those corresponding to additional modalities. For example, we can imagine a scenario where a dialog box is prompted on a mobile device or on an embedded display when the user is detected[6] to walk by or stop at a specific point of interest.

A feedback mechanism of control is also necessary for other reasons, such as privacy; to grant a certain level of protection, users must be somehow aware when their presence and motion is being currently tracked. Consequently, they must always be given the possibility to stop the tracking of the mobile device and to be allowed to use an alternative interaction modality.

KUI Interaction Patterns

Although KUI interaction patterns can be radically different from GUI patterns, some of the most effective GUI patterns, such as Drag&Drop, can be transferred and adapted to KUI interaction with physical space. For instance, in a KUI-enabled SmartHome, the user can "drag" the media being currently played in the living room and "drop" it to the bedroom just by moving a representative localizable object such as the remote controller. It is worth noting that the "Drag&Drop" pattern is provided as an interaction pattern by the KUI middleware and can be activated (and recognized) for specific applications such as the SmartHome control system[7].

Another useful pattern we include in KUI is *continuous tracking*. Continuous physical motion is comparable to mouse-gestures in GUIs. KUI-enabled applications are supposed to recognize certain *kinetic patterns* that might be naturally performed by users during other activities or specific situations.

As an example of the continuous tracking pattern, consider the scenario where the user is driving a car and some of the car's motion parameters are obtained by embedded sensors such as a GPS tracking system and an accelerometer. The sensors reveal that the car is decelerating in the proximity of a gas station (i.e., a geo-located point of interest already known by the application). This kinetic pattern (deceleration) is detected by the KUI and interpreted by the application as the user's intention of refuelling at the gas station. This hypothesis might be corroborated by other contextual information from the current car's sensors (e.g., the fuel level being almost zero). As a result of this behaviour, the system will pro-actively prompt the driver with the current gas prices at the approaching gas station. The application might also perform further contextual inferences and inform the user that keeping the current speed and considering the current fuel level he/she can reach the next gas station that has better gas prices. However, if the system detects that the fuel level is high or the fuel tank is even full, it will not react because it can infer that the driver stops for other (unknown) reasons (e.g., to take a pause).

This is a clear example of how KUI interaction differs from ordinary location-aware user interfaces. In this scenario, the driver passing by a gas station does not need to explicitly inquire about the gas prices. Current location information is only used to contextualize the query that is triggered as a result of the speed change occurring in the proximity of a given point of interest.

With regard to enabling technologies, continuous motion tracking is already available with current GPS-based car navigation systems, and easily can be integrated with personal mobile devices (e.g., SmartPhones, PDAs) connected to mobile Internet infrastructures (such as UMTS, GPRS, WiMax). With ordinary GPS navigation systems, the user can always check the current location on a graphical map and the proximity to point of interests. With KUI, we extend the possibilities of these systems with an additional level of interactivity and integration with networked services (Pallotta et al., 2006).

KUI-Enabled Scenarios

KUI-enabled applications have a different purpose compared to ordinary location-aware ones. Since motion is used as an input modality, KUI-based applications are expected to provide a higher level of fluidity in interaction and user experience. In those situations in which the interface should not interfere with the foreground user's activity (which in turn might or might not be a computer-based one), KUI will allow unobtrusive interaction with a computer. We consider here three case studies that have been developed so far and that exemplify the benefits of KUI interaction patterns.

Safety in Air Sports

Jane is flying with her paraglide over the Alps and is trying to reach the other side of a lake she is currently over. Can she do it without any risks? The UbiGlide flight navigator detects the motion of the paraglide. By interpreting her current activity UbiGlide infers Jane's intention to cross the lake. UbiGlide then senses the environment, namely, the wind's force and direction, the lake altitude, the distance between the paraglide and the opposite shore, and finally concludes that the crossing is not possible. Jane is informed immediately about the risk of danger. Later, she is so focused on the flight that she finds herself approaching a no-fly zone (e.g., an airplane landing strip). UbiGlide detects this possibility and alerts her about the danger.

In this scenario the current paraglide motion is not only tracked but also interpreted. An activity report is obtained by composing a number of basic flight movements in order to recognize more complex behaviour patterns. For instance, *spiral ascension* is made of several *turns* and *altitude changes*. Moreover, activities are filtered by other contextual information such as wind speed and direction, air humidity, and so forth.

SmartHome and SmartCity

Julia, Steve, and their daughter Monica live in Geneva. Julia is a busy businesswoman and Steve is a researcher at the university. Monica is in her last year of college. They live in a flat equipped with latest IT technology. They own a networked SmartFridge, which detects when food items go in and out, and automatically generates a list of missing items. The UbiShop system looks at the list generated by the SmartFridge and sends requests to buy the missing items to any family members who pass by a grocery store. Monica is on her way back home after school and passes by a grocery store. A reminder to buy milk is sent on her mobile phone by the UbiShop system. She decides to ignore the reminder since she knows that another grocery store is on her way home. Meanwhile, Steve is also on his way home and near a grocery store. He also receives the reminder and decides to buy the milk. This purchase causes the deletion of the milk from the shopping list, so that Monica will no longer be bothered. When back home, Steve does not put the milk in the fridge. After a while, the SmartFridge "wonders" why the milk has not yet been put inside, so a request about this item is sent to Steve who had simply forgot the milk in the car.

This illustrates how KUI can contribute to context-aware collaboration[8] in a mixed urban/home environment. Family members' activities are coordinated according to actual members' mobility. The system decides to adapt a workflow by interpreting team members' behaviors in context. Here, the role of the KUI interface is twofold. First, it allows triggering the task assignment when the user is moving into a zone where the task could be accomplished. Second, it detects from the user's speed whether he/she is likely to be willing to perform the assigned task. For instance, if the user is running, the application could interpret this motion pattern as "being in a hurry" and might decide not to bother the user. Another interesting aspect where KUI plays a role is when the user is expected to perform an action and this action does not occur. This is the case when, in our scenario, Steve forgot to put the milk in the fridge. The application subscribed to a motion event that does not occur within a time interval.

Safe-Critical Work Environments

Bill is a specialized worker in a chemical plant. He typically operates an industrial chemical reactor. He wears a head-mounted display and he is connected to the main control desk through wireless radio communication gears. While normally operating the reactor, suddenly Bill starts running (accelerates) toward the emergency exit. He is not able to alert the control desk about what is happening. The KUI interface detects this motion pattern as abnormal and figures out that the operator is trying to escape from a dangerous situation. The system then opens the doors on the pathway toward the exit of the reactor building and then immediately closes them after the operator is sensed to have passed through them.

In certain industrial settings such as chemical plants, it is important that the operator keeps his hands free in order to be able to do his usual manual work, while at the same time he/she accesses the automated commands and looks at the supervision information needed to complete the task. The role of KUI is apparent because it provides an additional implicit input modality that might serve to detect sudden instinctive reactions to dangerous situations.

The KUI Model

In this section, we present the main concepts of Kinetic User Interfaces that are implemented as software components in the KUI middleware architecture.

The KUI Conceptual Taxonomy

In KUI, motion is a main (or primary) interaction modality afforded by the physical space to users through the motion of *tracked entities*. Tracked entities are any objects or autonomous (possibly living) things for which we can provide location and motion information. Tracked entities are represented by KUI components called *Kuidgets*. Interaction with Kuidgets happens when users affect their motion properties or change spatio-temporal relationships among them (e.g., an object is entering into an area). For instance, when the user is driving a car, the motion properties of its corresponding Kuidget will be continuously updated with its current position, speed, acceleration, and direction.

The term "Kuidget" has been chosen to make the parallel with a GUI's widgets, that is, software components that provide public interfaces for a hardware sensor and whose interaction is implemented in terms of messages and call-backs (Winograd,

2001). Kuidgets are the software counterpart of some real world entities that can be used for interaction in KUIs. A KUI-enabled system is thus able to recognize the current location of Kuidgets, and makes sense of their motion parameters such as path, speed, acceleration, and direction. Location and motion sensors (e.g., GPS or other tracking devices, accelerometers, compasses, altimeters) typically provide three-dimensional location and motion information to Kuidgets. Kuidgets are classified according to four main dimensions: *geometry*; *kinetic properties; degree of autonomy*; and *type of motion*.

From the geometric point of view, Kuidgets can be arbitrary three-dimensional objects. However, it makes sense to distinguish between those objects whose size is not relevant and those for which it matters. Entities of the first type are considered as points while others are considered as geometric shapes. This distinction is application-dependent, because one entity can be considered a point in one application and a shape in others. For instance, a vehicle (a car, a train, a ship, a plane) is a point when considered as a moving object in the space, and it is a space when considered as a container of objects and people. In the KUI model, the same entity plays two roles at the same time and is linked to two distinct Kuidgets.

Kuidgets can be *fixed* or *mobile*. Fixed Kuidgets are typically places or landmarks in the physical space, while mobile Kuidgets are physical entities whose location and motion can be observed by tracking the entity or can be provided by their embedded location and motion sensors.

In modelling KUI's dynamics we adopt the *status-event semantics*, which means that KUI-based applications should be able to effectively deal both with the *status* of objects and with the *events* they generate. Thus, as an underlying model for dealing with Status-Event semantics in KUI, we adopt the Environment and Artefacts theory for multi-agent systems as proposed by (Ricci et al., 2006). Accordingly, we further classify Kuidgets along their degree of autonomy as *artefact Kuidgets* and *agent Kuidgets*. Artefact Kuidgets correspond to mobile physical objects that cannot move autonomously (e.g., a mobile phone, a car). The motion properties of an artefact Kuidget can be directly determined and communicated by the artefact itself (e.g., a GPS sensor + a mobile network connection) or observed by another entity (e.g., the infrastructure of the containing object, a nearby artefact, or an agent). The events of moving, grabbing, dragging, and dropping artefact Kuidgets are triggered by the detection of their current kinetic properties in the physical space and by the actions performed through their interfaces for direct manipulation (e.g., pressing a button on the object while moving it). Agent Kuidgets correspond to autonomous moving entities (people, animals, robots). Agent Kuidgets have a higher degree of autonomy, and they can induce motion to other artefact Kuidgets.

At the physical level, there is not much difference between artefacts and agent Kuidgets; they are essentially KUI's components, and as long as their corresponding physical objects are providing their location and motion information, they are treated equally in KUIs. At a conceptual level, however, they differ because agents can control and operate artefacts and have a higher degree of autonomy. This distinction is particularly useful when KUI-enabled applications need to determine the location and motion of Kuidgets in the absence of up-to-dated information. Motion of artefact Kuidgets typically has to be somehow causally linked to agent Kuidgets; sometimes artefacts cause the motion of agents, and sometimes it is the other way around.

Artefact Kuidget typically keeps its last observed (communicated) location if they are not linked to any moving entity (i.e., the law of inertia). Even in cases where no information can be obtained for an artefact Kuidget, its current location can be inferred by default just by knowing that it is unlinked from a moving Kuidget. Different from artefact Kuidgets, agent Kuidgets have more freedom. When unlinked from any moving artefact Kuidgets, their current location and motion status cannot be safely inferred; they can move without being tracked. Of course, there also might be the case that an artefact is no longer tracked, but this case is considered as an error condition rather than a choice selected by the user. In other words, in KUI agent Kuidgets can decide when they can be tracked, while artefacts cannot.

Two Kuidgets can be logically linked and they can provide location and motion information to each other. For instance, a car equipped with a GPS sensor (an artefact Kuidget) can provide location and motion information to its driver (an agent Kuidget). Conversely, a user carrying a GPS sensor can provide location and motion information to the car Kuidget by setting a logical link between the car and the user who is driving the car. It is important to notice that when the user leaves the car, even if the link is destroyed, the car Kuidget keeps its last location.

It is also our goal to make KUI as general as possible in order to uniformly cope with different geographical scales (e.g., tabletop, room, building, cities) and with different types of location-aware devices (e.g., GPS, RFID, Wireless cell triangulation, ultrasonic, ultra-wideband, infrared). For this purpose, we also distinguish between different *types* of physical space. Following (Dix et al., 2000), we consider *topological* and *symbolic* spaces[9]. In topological spaces, objects are localized by their exact position by means of an absolute coordinate system and through a notion of distance. In symbolic spaces, locations are considered as symbolic elements (e.g., rooms, buildings, cities), and object are localized through spatial relations with other objects (e.g., in the bedroom, near the red table). For topological spaces, the two basic types of references are *points* and *zones*, while for symbolic spaces, entities are explicitly connected through symbolic spatial relations such as containment, accessibility, and so forth. Different from (Dix et al., 2000), we do not make any distinction between real and virtual spaces. In our approach, virtual spaces are managed by applications and they do not need to be represented at the KUI level. However, KUI allows the geo-localization of virtual objects; these are entities of the computing space mapped to the geographical space (e.g., a geo-tag or a zone).

The detection of particular spatio-temporal relations between Kuidgets can trigger application-specific KUI events. There are several spatio-temporal relations that can be modelled. We propose here that a basic KUI should provide at least two types of spatio-temporal relations: *proximity* and *containment*. For these relations it is important to consider their temporal dimension, namely the start and end time, and the duration of the relation. For instance, if two mobile Kuidgets (e.g., two agents) are observed while moving together along the same path or into the same location, the application will be notified with a "joint motion" event by the KUI manager. Then, the application might make inferences, and as a result, establish an application-dependent relation between the two Kuidgets. For instance, when the two agent Kuidgets are moving together, the application can infer (with the help of other contextual information) that they might be friends. Similarly, when two Kuidgets that are supposed to jointly move cease to do so, an event could be triggered that in certain circumstances could denote an unusual situation. For instance, a car moving somewhere while its owner moves elsewhere else might denote that the car has been stolen.

The last dimension for our classification is the type of motion of mobile Kuidgets. In order to cope with most possible situations, we consider both *endogenous* and *exogenous* motion. Endogenous motion occurs when objects move without any change of location. For instance, a rotating object that remains in the same place counts as endogenous motion; another example is the sudden motion sensors embedded in Apple Macintosh[10] laptops that can be exploited as an input modality in games. Exogenous motion represents the familiar case in which objects are displaced in the space. However, even if an entity is affected by exogenous motion, this does not necessarily mean that the exact change of location is tracked. For instance, if motion is detected by an accelerometer, the interface can use this information to trigger an event. This is the case of a Nintendo Wii™ controller WiiMote that is used to interact with games without detecting the exact change of location of players. More precisely, endogenous motion pertains to the fact that the spatial coordinate system is centred on the moving object, while exogenous motion is referenced to an external coordinate system.

The KUI Middleware

The software architecture we propose for KUI is supposed to be integrated within a larger context-aware middleware for Ubicomp. As in GUI, KUI should be independent from the underlying OS, and should enable rich interaction for context-aware Ubicomp systems. For this reason, we do not commit ourselves to a specific middleware. Rather, we focus on a general "pluggable" software component, which would allow us to make KUI available in an arbitrary *context-aware middleware* (see (Baldauf et al., 2006) for a review). However, KUI can be used as a standalone

Figure 1. KUI Middleware

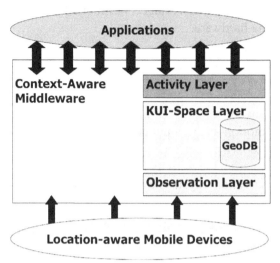

system if the interface between the KUI manager and motion-aware mobile devices is made through ad-hoc drivers.

The KUI middleware is made of three layers of abstraction (as shown in Figure 1). Below, we provide details about each layer:

- The *Observation Layer* is the lower level. Its role is to collect kinetic contexts from location and motion aware devices and from other hardware sensors.

- The *KUI-Space Layer* is an object-oriented environment that contains and manages Kuidgets state and their semantic relationships. Information flow coming from the observation layer is used to update the state of Kuidgets. Location information pertaining to Kuidgets is stored in a suitable data structure, the GeoDB (e.g. a GIS[11]), that is also used to store and manage physical space references of fixed and mobile Kuidgets for both topological and symbolic spaces.

- The *Activity Layer* manages the context history, and aggregates KUI events into higher-level semantic events (i.e., for the detection of specific interaction patterns) that are sent to the applications. In this layer, representations of *situations* will be constructed by aggregating kinetic information from Kuidgets and other contextual information. Moreover, models of activities will be matched with the spotted situations in order to determine the occurrence of anomalous behaviours.

More specifically, in the KUI software components location and motion information are linked to either fixed Kuidgets or mobile Kuidgets that are localizable by means of tracking hardware.

The KUI Components

The KUI Middleware can be seen as a user interface server that connects client applications to motion-aware input devices. In that sense, our model is similar to the X-Windows toolkit model. KUI provides an API to applications for subscribing aggregated events from the Activity Layer and encapsulates motion-aware devices through the Observation Layer. The main components of the KUI middleware are detailed in Figure 2.

A number of location and motion-aware devices can be connected to any Kuidget for which they cooperate in providing its kinetic information. Kuidgets are identified by universally unique identifiers (UUID), and are linked to entries in the GeoDB that provides both direct localization and indirect localization through explicit relationships with other Kuidgets not linked to directly localizable elements. When the Observation Layer produces fresh kinetic information for a given Kuidget, a callback is sent to KUI-Space manager component, which updates the correspond-

Figure 2. Sketch of the KUI Toolkit

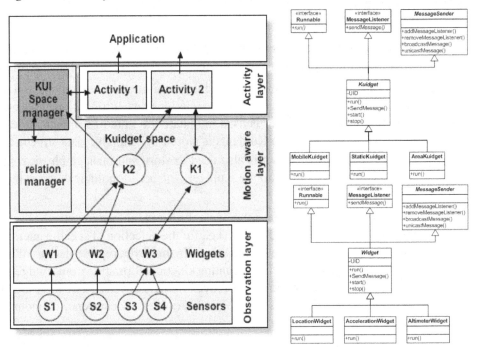

ing geographical information in the GeoDB and manages the relations between active Kuidgets.

The KUI-Space Manager is responsible for the aggregation and filtering of low-level events produced by the Observation Layer. Observations also can be obtained from the hosting context-aware middleware through *context widgets* (Dey et al., 2001). Context widgets are abstractions for different types of context sensors. They hide the complexity of the sensor communication protocols and offer a hot-plugging mechanism for dynamically adding and removing sensors to the system. As for GUIs, the application does not have to be modified when the pointing system changes, for instance, from mouse to pen. In our case, Kuidgets connected to location and motion Widgets do not know what kind of sensor is actually in use when they get kinetic information.

The Relation Manager receives location updates from the KUI-space and processes them according to the (programmable) relation rules. Relations between Kuidgets are created, deleted or updated and dispatched to the KUI-space manager, which then sends them to the upper Activity Layer through a notification mechanism. When some pre-defined geographical relationship change occurs (e.g., an object enters an active zone), the Relation Manager is responsible of notifying these events to the Activity Layer or directly to the subscribing Kuidgets. These events can be programmed as triggers that check conditions matched against the GeoDB, while aggregate events can be subscribed by objects in the upper Activity Layer. Relations between Kuidgets can be created either by the Kuidget's internal logic in response to Kuidget events triggered when retrieving information from the GeoDB, or explicitly by applications. The latter case is useful when we logically link agent and artefact Kuidgets together, allowing one of them to inherit motion properties from the other one.

The Activity Layer is responsible of aggregating motion information from one or several Kuidget, as well as dynamic information generated by the Relation Manager. Relations and Kuidgets status are used as the building blocks for the recognition of the previously described kinetic interaction patterns.

Enabling Technology

The KUI middleware can be implemented on top of a context-aware middleware such as the *Context Toolkit* (Dey et al., 2001) and it can be integrated within any enterprise architecture like J2EE or .NET. Kinetic-aware devices typically will be connected through wireless Internet so that client-server software architecture is apparently justified. Applications exploit localization infrastructures for indoor and outdoor tracking. Indoor localization technologies include RFID antennas, ultrasonic, ultrawide-band, and IR sensors. For outdoor localization and motion tracking, GPS offers the most available tracking solution, which, combined with wireless Internet communication (e.g., GPRS, EDGE or UMTS) is nowadays available on commercial mobile phone and handheld devices. Additionally, we expect to detect others (more local) motion parameters (such as acceleration and direction) by using wearable sensors like accelerometers and digital compasses. For this point, it is crucial for the Observation Layer to be capable of dealing with several location and motion tracking technologies at the same time and of easily associating them with Kuidgets. The accuracy of different localization devices and motion sensors is not considered to be an issue in this discussion that pertains to the conceptual framework for the development of user interfaces based on kinetic input. We expect, in any case, that motion tracking and wearable sensor technology will rapidly improve, as already has been the case for other enabling technology like, for instance, the diffusion of broadband Internet connection for the Web.

Conclusion

In this chapter, we explored the notion of *kinetic-awareness* in Ubicomp user interfaces by means of the seamless and transparent integration of objects motion detection in the physical space as a primary input modality. Kinetic User Interfaces enable the users of Ubicomp systems to establish an interaction through continuous tracking of kinetic-aware mobile devices at different spatial scales and by the acquisition of kinetic input through motion-aware embedded sensors. KUI interfaces allow the seamless integration of contextual (implicit) and intentional (explicit) interaction through motion. We presented a conceptual framework for KUI interfaces and a middleware as the basis for implementing the KUI component in standard Ubicomp architectures.

Kinetic-awareness in Ubicomp seems to take over simple location-awareness. Motion-based interaction is a complementary notion to context-awareness. It is not just a matter of acting while moving, but *acting by moving*. Motion is a great source of information that leverages new dimensions of user experience in Ubicomp systems. As noted in (Beaudouin-Lafon, 2004), in post-WIMP user interfaces, it will be necessary to shift towards a more holistic view of user interaction. Users are expected to interact through *activities* rather than single actions. Moreover, they will try to achieve higher-level goals through activities, rather than to accomplish tasks through planned actions. KUI provides a framework for designing Ubicomp applications with embodied interaction with a special focus on unobtrusiveness and fluidity.

References

Abowd, G.D., Mynatt, E.D., & Rodden. T. (2002, January-March). The Human Experience. *Pervasive Computing 1*(1), 48-57.

Abowd, G.D., & Mynatt, E.D. (2000). Charting Past, Present, and Future Research in Ubiquitous Computing. *ACM Transactions on Computer-Human Interaction, 7*(1), 29–58.

Addlesee, M., Curwen, R., Hodges, S., Newman, J., Steggles, P., Ward, A.., & Hopper, A. (2001). Implementing a Sentient Computing System. *IEEE Computer, 34*(8), 50-56.

Ashbrook, D., Lyons, K., & Clawson, J. (2006). Capturing Experiences Anytime, Anywhere. *IEEE Pervasive Computing 5*(2), 8-11.

Baldauf, M., Dustdar, S., & Rosenberg, F. (2007). A Survey on Context Aware Systems. *International Journal of Ad Hoc and Ubiquitous Computing*, Inderscience Publishers. forthcoming. Pre-print from: http://www.vitalab.tuwien.ac.at/~florian/papers/ijahuc2007.pdf

Banavar, G., & Bernstein, A. (2004). Challenges in Design and Software Infrastructure for Ubiquitous Computing Applications. *Communications of the ACM, 45*(12), 92-96.

Barfield, W., & Caudell, T. (Eds.). (2001) *Fundamentals of Wearable Computers and Augmented Reality*. LEA Books.

Beaudouin-Lafon, M. (2000). Instrumental Interaction: An Interaction Model for Designing Post-WIMP User Interfaces. In *Proceedings of ACM Human Factors in Computing Systems*, CHI 2000, La Haye (Pays-Bas), Avril 2000, CHI Letters 2(1):446-453, ACM Press.

Beaudouin-Lafon, M. (2004). Designing Interaction, not Interfaces. In Costabile, M.F. (Ed.), In *Proceedings of the working conference on Advanced visual interfaces AVI 2004*, (pp. 15-22). Minneapolis: ACM Press.

Bellotti, V., Back, M., Edwards, K., Grinter, R, Lopes, C., & Henderson, A. (2002). Making Sense of Sensing Systems: Five Questions for Researchers and Designers. In *Proceedings of CHI 2002* (pp. 415-422), Minneapolis: ACM Press.

Bleecker, J. (2006). *Why Things Matter: A Manifesto for Networked Objects — Cohabiting with Pigeons, Arphids and Aibos in the Internet of Things*. Retrieved from http://research.techkwondo.com/files/WhyThingsMatter.pdf

Brumitt, B., Meyers, B. Krumm, J., Kern, A.,. & Shafer, S. (2000). EasyLiving: Technologies for Intelligent Environments. In *Proceedings of Second International Symposium on Handheld and Ubiquitous Computing HUC2K*, (pp. 12-29). Bristol, UK, Springer Verlag.

Chen, G., & Kotz, D. (2000). *A Survey of Contex-Aware Mobile Computing Research.* (Tech. Rep. No. TR2000-381), Darthmouth Science Department.

Cheverst, K., Davies, N., Mitchell, K., Friday, A., & Efstratiou, C. (2000). Developing a Context-aware Electronic Tourist Guide: Some Issues and Experiences. In *Proceedings of CHI 2000* (pp. 17-24). The Netherlands.

Davis, M. King, S., Good, N., & Sarvas, R. (2004). From Context to Content: Leveraging Context to Infer Media Metadata. In *Proceedings of 12th Annual ACM International Conference on Multimedia MM2004* (pp. 188-195). New York, ACM Press.

Dey, A.K., & Abowd, G.D. (2000). CyberMinder: A Context-Aware System for Supporting Reminders. In *Proceedings of the 2nd International Symposium on Handheld and Ubiquitous Computing HUC2K* (pp. 25-27), Bristol, UK, Springer Verlag.

Dey, A.K., Salber, D., & Abowd, G.D. (2001). A Conceptual Framework and a Toolkit for Supporting the Rapid Prototyping of Context-Aware Applications (anchor article of the special issue on Context-Aware Computing). *Human-Computer Interaction Journal, 16*(2-4), 97-166.

Dix, A., Rodden, T., Davies, N., Trevor, J., Friday, A., & Palfreyman, K. (2000). Exploiting space and location as a design framework for interactive mobile systems. *ACM Transactions on Computer-Human Interaction, 7*(3), 285-321.

Dix, A. (2002a). Managing the Ecology of Interaction. In Pribeanu, C., & Vanderdonckt, J. (Eds.), *Proceedings of Tamodia 2002 - First International Workshop on Task Models and User Interface Design* (pp. 1-9). Bucharest, Romania: INFOREC Publishing House, Bucharest.

Dix, A. (2002b). Beyond intention - pushing boundaries with incidental interaction. In *Proceedings of Building Bridges: Interdisciplinary Context-Sensitive Computing*, Glasgow University, Sept. 9th 2002.

Dix, A., Finlay, J., Abowd, G., & Beale, R. (2004). *Human-Computer Interaction* (Third Edition). Prentice Hall. 2004.

Dourish, P. (2001). *Where the Action Is: The Foundations of Embodied Interaction.* Cambridge, MIT Press.

Fitzmaurice, G.W. (1996). *Graspable User Interfaces.* Unpublished doctoral dissertation, Department of Computer Science, University of Toronto.

Gaye, L., Mazé, R., & Holmquist, L.E. (2003). Sonic City: The Urban Environment as a Musical Interface. In *Proceedings of the Conference on New Interfaces for Musical Expression* NIME-03 (pp. 109-115), Montreal, Canada.

Greenfield, A. (2006). *Everyware: the dawning age of ubiquitous computing.* New Riders publishers, Berkeley. 2006.

Harter, A., Hopper, A., Steggles, P. Ward, A., & Webster, P. (2002). The anatomy of a Context-Aware Application. *Wireless Networks,* 8, 187-197.

Hightower, J., & Borriello, G. (2001). Location systems for ubiquitous computing. *IEEE Computer 34*(8), 57-66.

Holmquist, L., Schmidt, A., & Ullmer, B. (2004). Tangible interfaces in perspective: Guest editors' introduction. *Personal and Ubiquitous Computing 8*(5), 291-293.

Hong, D., Chiu, D.K.W., & Shen, V.Y. (2005). Requirements elicitation for the design of context-aware applications in a ubiquitous environment. In *Proceedings of ICEC'05* (pp. 590-596).

International Telecommunication Union (2005). *The Internet of Things: Executive Report*. Retrieved from http://www.itu.int/pub/S-POL-IR.IT-2005/e. Geneva, 2005

Kleinrock, L. (1997). Nomadic computing. *Telecommunication Systems 7*(1-3): 5-15.

Kidd, C.K., Orr, R.J., Abowd, G.D. Atkeson, C.G., Essa, I.A., MacIntyre, B., Mynatt, E., Starner, T.E., & Newstetter, W. (1999, October 1-2)). The Aware Home: A Living Laboratory for Ubiquitous Computing Research. Paper presented at *the Second International Workshop on Cooperative Buildings* CoBuild99, Pittsburgh, PA (LNCS 1670).

Koile, K., Tollmar, K., Demirdjian, D., Shrobe, H., & Darrell, T. (2003). Activity Zones for Context-Aware Computing. In *Proceedings of Ubicomp 2003,* (pp. 90-106).

Mackay, W.E. (1998). Augmented reality: linking real and virtual worlds. A new paradigm for interacting with computer. In *Proceedings of International Conference on Advanced Visual Interfaces* AVI'98, (pp. 13-21).

Meier, R., Harrington, A. Termin, T., & Cahill, V. (2006). A Spatial Programming Model for Real Global Smart Space Applications. In Eliassen, F. & Montresor, Al. (Eds.) *Proceedings of the 6th IFIP International Conference on Distributed Applications and Interoperable Systems* DAIS 06 (pp. 16-31). Bologna, Italy, 2006. Lecture Notes in Computer Science, Springer-Verlag.

Nardi, B.A. (Ed.) (1996). *Context and consciousness: activity theory and human-computer interaction*. Cambridge, MA: MIT Press.

Negroponte, N. (1995). *Being Digital*. Vintage Editions. 1996.

Norman, D.A. (1999). *The Invisible Computer*. Cambridge, MA. MIT Press.

Norrie, M.C., & Signer, B. (2005, January). *Overlaying Paper Maps with Digital Information Services for Tourists*, In proceedings of *The 12th International*

Conference on Information Technology and Travel and Tourism ENTER 2005, Innsbruck, Austria.

Nova, N., Girardin, F., & Dillenbourg, P. (2006, May 9-12)). The Underwhelming Effects of Automatic Location-Awareness on Collaboration in a Pervasive Game. In proceedings of *The International Conference on the Design of Cooperative Systems* COOP06 (pp. 224-238). Carry-le-Rouet, Provence, France.

Pallotta, V., Brocco, A., Guinard, D., Bruegger, P., & De Almeida, P. (2006, June 27). RoamBlog: Outdoor and Indoor Geoblogging Enhanced with Contextual Service Provisioning for Mobile Internet Users. In *Proceedings of the 1st International Workshop on Distributed Agent-Based Retrieval Tools* (pp. 103-121). Cagliari, Italy.

Rekimoto, J. (1997). Pick-and-Drop: A Direct Manipulation Technique for Multiple Computer Environments. In *Proceedings of International Conference on 10th annual symposium on User Interface Software and Technology* UIST'97 (pp. 31-39).

Ricci, A., Viroli, M., & Omicini, A. (2006, April 18-21). Construenda est CArtAgO: Toward an Infrastructure for Artifacts in MAS. In *Proceedings of the European Meeting on Cybernetics and Systems Research* EMCSR'06 (vol. 2 pp. 569–574). University of Wien, Vienna, Austria.

Román, M., Hess, C.K., Cerqueira, R., Ranganathan, A., Campbell, R.H., & Nahrstedt, K. (2002). GAIA: A Middleware Infrastructure to Enable Active Spaces. *IEEE Pervasive Computing, 1*(4), 74-83.

Rukzio, E. (2006). *Physical Mobile Interactions: Mobile Devices as Pervasive Mediators for Interactions with the Real World.* Unpublished doctoral dissertation, University of Munich.

Salkham, A., Cunningham, R., Senart, A., & Cahill, V. (2006). *A Taxonomy of Collaborative Context-Aware Systems* (Tech. Rep. No. TCD-CS-2006-30). Dept. of Computer Science, University of Dublin, Trinity College.

Shafer, S.A.N., Brumitt, B., & Cadiz, J. (2001). Interaction issues in context-aware intelligent environments. *Human-Computer Interaction, 16*(2), 363-378.

Schilit, B.N. (1995). *System architecture for context-aware mobile computing.* Unpublished doctoral dissertation, Columbia University, 1995. Retrieved from http://citeseer.ist.psu.edu/schilit95system.html

Sousa, J.P., & Garlan, D. (2002). *AURA: an Architectural Framework for User Mobility in Ubiquitous Computing Environments.* In *Proceedings of the IEEE Conference on Software Architecture* (pp. 29-43), Montreal.

Sparacino, F. (2005). Intelligent Architecture: Embedding Spaces with a Mind for Augmented Interaction. In Costabile, M.F. & Paternò, F. (Eds.): *Proceedings of the* INTERACT *2005 - Human-Computer Interaction* IFIP TC13 *International Conference* (pp. 2-3). LNCS 3585 Springer Verlag.

Spence, M., Driver, C., & Clarke, S. (2005). Sharing Context History in Mobile. Context-Aware Trails-Based Applications. Paper presented at the *1ˢᵗ international workshop on exploiting context histories in smart environments* ECHISE 2005, Part of PERVASIVE 2005, Munich, Germany, 2005.

Ullmer, B., & Ishii, H. (2000). Emerging Frameworks for Tangible User Interfaces. *IBM Systems Journal* 9(3-4), 915-931.

Want, R., Pering, T., Borriello, G., & Farkas, K.I. (2002). Disappearing Hardware. *IEEE Pervasive Computing 1*(1), 26-35.

Weiser, M. (1991). The Computer for the 21st Century. *Scientific American, 265*(3), 94-104.

Weiser, M. (1993). Hot topic: Ubiquitous computing. *IEEE Computer*, October 1993, 71-72.

Weiser, M. (1994). The world is not a desktop. *ACM Interactions, 1*(1), 7-8.

Weiser, M. & Seely Brown, J. (1996). *The Coming Age of Calm Technology* (Tech. Rep.) Xerox PARC.

Winograd, T. (2000). Towards a Human-Centered Interaction Architecture. In Carroll, J. (Ed). *Human-Computer Interaction in the New Millennium*. Addison-Wesley, Reading, MA.

Winograd, T. (2001). Architectures for context. *Human-Computer Interaction*, 16(2,3,4).

Endnotes

[1]   http://www.ubiq.com/hypertext/weiser/UbiHome.html

[2]   http://en.wikipedia.org/wiki/Web_2.0

[3]   http://www.socialight.com

[4]   http://www.ubisense.com

[5]   WIMP stands for "Windows, Icons, Menus, Popups".

[6]   The motion detection can be obtained either by the mobile device itself (e.g. a GPS-enabled handheld) or by external device or infrastructure (e.g. a badge tracked by a sensing space).

[7]   This interaction pattern is similar to the Teleport application (Addlesee et al., 2001), which allows users wearing ActiveBadges to move their desktop environments from a PC to another.

8   See (Salkham et al., 2006) for an overview.

9   We changed the names attributed to these types of space by (Dix et al., 2000). Our "topological" corresponds to their "cartesian" and our "symbolic" corresponds to their "topological".

10   http://www.apple.com/

11   Geographical Information Systems

Chapter IX

M-Traffic:
Mobile Traffic Information and Monitoring System

Teresa Romão, FCT/New University of Lisbon, Portugal

Luís Rato, Universidade de Évora, Portugal

Antão Almada, YDreams, Portugal

A. Eduardo Dias, YDreams, Portugal

Abstract

Traffic information is crucial in metropolitan areas, where a high concentration of moving vehicles causes traffic congestion and blockage. Appropriate traffic information received at the proper time helps users to avoid unnecessary delays, choosing the fastest route that serves their purposes. This work presents Mobile Traffic (M-Traffic), a multiplatform online traffic information system, which provides real-time traffic information based on image processing, sensor's data, and traveller behaviour models. This system has a modular architecture that allows it to easily be adapted to new data sources and additional distribution platforms. In order to estimate route delay and feed the optimal routing algorithm, a traffic microscopic simulation model was developed, and simulation results are presented. This mobile information service ubiquitously provides users with traffic information regarding their needs and preferences, according to an alert system, which allows a personalized pre-definition of warning messages.

Introduction

Current advances in mobile communications and positioning systems, as well as the broad use of mobile devices, with increasing functionalities in users' daily life represent new opportunities to extend traffic information systems beyond the traditional information delivered by radio, TV or the Web. Typically, this information is manually maintained by human operators and may not be appropriately updated. None of these information channels are permanently available to users at the moment and at the location they need them. Moreover, they do not provide quantitative data, only available by image or sensor data processing, and they only supply information regarding the current traffic situation; they do not predict traffic conditions for the future.

Mobile Traffic (M-Traffic) is a R&D project developed jointly by YDREAMS (www.ydreams.com), Universidade de Évora (http://www.uevora.pt), and Siemens AG (www.siemens.com), which proposes an advanced technological solution for providing street traffic information. M-Traffic focuses on providing traffic information where and when it is most necessary and making this information available on mobile devices. The proposed solution takes advantage of video cameras in places where traffic conditions are most difficult. Based on these images, the system will provide its functionalities, which go far beyond displaying video information in real-time. Images are processed in order to adapt to various types of devices, which in turn permit the extraction of quantitative and qualitative data about the traffic flow. All the information is geo-referenced in a geographical information system and can be visualised on different devices such as PCs, mobile phones, or PDAs.

Together with the streamed video, M-Traffic offers a set of functionalities suitable for different types of users and appropriate to diverse distribution devices. These functionalities rise from image processing, sensor data, and the use of traffic flow models, which simulate and predict traffic conditions. The purpose of traffic simulation models is twofold. First, it is to estimate the traffic flow and time delay in segments of street network which are not covered by sensors and second, to predict the evolution of traffic conditions. These estimates are the base to routing algorithm.

The system allows users to personalise the service, in order to easily access specific information and alerts. Users may create their own profile, which allows them to receive the information they need as soon as they enter the system.

In the beginning, M-Traffic was thought to be applied in the city of Lisbon, but its modular structure allows its adaptation to be used in any other city with a straight-forward task.

This document describes a concrete application of ubiquitous computing technologies to solve a frequent problem faced by users in their everyday life--finding their way through a crowded city.

Background

In addition to the traditional traffic information services available through radio and television, several Web sites offer online traffic information. Typically, this information is manually maintained by human operators and may not be appropriately updated. Usually, these services do not provide reliable estimations for the duration of trajectories; they consider just a few points of measure, and they only provide information concerning the current situation, not predicting traffic conditions. Moreover, these services do not ubiquitously provide the information to users, forcing them to search for the data they need.

TrafficMaster (http://www.trafficmaster.co.uk/) provides traffic information services for UK, including live traffic information on World Wide Web enabled devices, map-based congestion information, and a suite of personalised mobile telephone traffic information services, WAP traffic maps, and favourite journey reporting. Traffic information is also made available by AA (Automobile Association), (http://www.theaa.com), where users are able to plan routes, examine traffic conditions, and view incident reports.

Some systems also provide real-time traffic images for traffic conditions monitoring including video streaming. The site of the Instituto de Estradas de Portugal—IEP (Portuguese Road Institute) (http://www.estradasdeportugal.pt) allows the visualisation of streamed video captured by video cameras situated in relevant locations. Vodafone "Trânsito em directo" service (http://www.vodafone.pt/main/funandinfo/alertas/transito/default.htm) allows users to receive alert messages with links to updated images collected by cameras located in the spatial point of their interest. The advanced traveller information system (ATIS) of the New York City Department of Transportation (DOT) provides both streaming video and frequently updated still images from locations in the five city boroughs via the World WideWeb (http://nyc-tmc.org/) or the City Drive Live on NYC TV, the television network of the City of New York on Channel 74.

The AirVideo traffic service, available by TrafficLand Company, (http://www.trafficland.com/airvideo_intro.php), displays live views from several public traffic cameras on Web-enabled cellular phones. Users can customise cell phone presentations of camera views to display commonly used roadways, as well as alternative routes. TrafficLand currently provides access to over 3,500 live video cameras on its public Web site. More recently, Google Maps (http://www.google.com/gmm/index.html) allows users to search for directions, maps and satellite imagery, and to access real-time traffic information in over 30 major U.S. metropolitan areas directly from Palm OS 5 devices. However, these systems do not consider two main problems--the need for quantitative data, only available by image or sensor data processing, and the necessity of generating appropriate graphic output for the different types of client devices such as mobile phones or PDAs.

Traffic.com (http://www.traffic.com/index.html) provides users with traffic reports and hotspot alerts for the U.S. via the World WideWeb. Information is gathered from three types of sources: digital traffic sensors; commercial and government partners; and their traffic operations centre staff members, who consistently monitor traffic conditions.

The Mississippi Traffic Watch, powered by the Mississippi Department of Transportation (http://www.mstraffic.com), provides real-time traffic information in 24 of the largest metropolitan areas in the USA. It owns and continues to expand a wireless digital sensor network for collecting traffic and logistics data. From their Web site, users have access to city traffic reports or customise their own city traffic reports in order to receive traffic information by e-mail or telephone.

Inrix (http://www.inrix.com/default.asp) uses Bayesian machine learning algorithms to make statistical inferences and predictions about traffic, based on variables such as weather conditions, construction schedules, holidays, sporting events, and historical traffic patterns. Users will be able to access the technology via partner channels on a variety of devices including smart phones and personal navigation devices, in-vehicle devices, PC desktop applications, Web portals, destination sites, and fleet applications.

The systems mentioned above are mostly traffic information providers; they are not aware of the users' context and they may require the use of specific devices, which reduce their ubiquity.

Circumnav Networks project turns cars themselves into traffic data-collection devices, which then share data wirelessly with other Circumnav-powered cars (http://innovativemobility.org/research/ici/circumnav.pdf). This creates a "social network" of traffic information that all drivers in the network can use to select their routes. The Autoscope system by Image Sensing Systems, Inc., (http://www.autoscope.com/index.htm) provides wide area video vehicle detection by using a high performing microprocessor-based CPU with specialised image processing boards contained in either a camera, box or card format, and software to analyse video images.

Research undertaken at MIT prompted the development of DynaMIT system, which anticipates traffic flow using a database of past conditions and real-time speed measurements and vehicle counts (http://mit.edu/its/dynamit.html) (Ben-Akiva, 1996;

Ben-Akiva, 1997). The key to the functionality of DynaMIT is its detailed network representation, coupled with models of traveller behaviour.

Classic approaches to traffic modelling are based either on fluid flow model or on the microscopic behaviour of each car-driver system (Ahmed, 1999; Marques, 2005). Approaches based on cellular automata have also been successfully developed in traffic modelling (Nagel, 1992).

System Description

The Mobile-Traffic project comprises the conception, design, and validation of a geo-referenced multiplatform online traffic information system, which ubiquitously provides real-time traffic information based on image processing, sensor's data, and traveller behaviour previewing models. M-traffic main features include:

- Automatic detection of abnormal traffic conditions;
- Prediction of traffic conditions based on historical data and current conditions;
- Determination of the best route based on actual or predicted traffic conditions;
- Handling of heterogeneous sources of information;
- Easy customization of the output to different languages and devices;
- Generation of alert messages whenever a specific traffic condition occurs in a pre-defined area;
- Dissemination of traffic information among users by SMS or e-mail.

M-Traffic defines a framework that handles data collected by traffic sensors and turns it into usable information for the drivers. Real-time information conveyed by M-Traffic can be accessed any time through the use a large variety of mobile devices such as mobile phones or PDAs. The system is also able to determine the best route between two or more points (allowing the definition of several intermediate points) based on the actual or predicted traffic conditions.

M-Traffic also provides qualitative comparative data. For example, traffic jams are common on several roads in certain periods of time. Users that frequently take a specific route know it, so there is no novelty in telling them so. M-Traffic tells users how traffic conditions are compared with the usual traffic conditions they are familiar with. For each point in space, M-Traffic compares the current data with the

Figure 1. Example of an M-Traffic interface screen for mobile phones

data registered in similar conditions and reveals if traffic is more or less congested than usual in those same areas.

M-Traffic ubiquitously provides users with traffic information regarding their needs and preferences according to an alert system, which allows a personalized pre-definition of warning messages. Users can configure the system in order to receive alert messages whenever a specific traffic condition occurs in a pre-defined area. Users can also define a set of locations where they most frequently pass (hotspots), facilitating access to information related to those locations. Moreover, users inter-acting with the M-Traffic system through mobile phones are able to forward traffic information to other users sending SMS or e-mail messages. Figure 1 exemplifies the system's user interface for mobile phones.

Architecture

This system architecture follows the client-server model and is based on several structurally independent, but functionally interdependent modules. Therefore, the system can be easily adapted to new data resources and additional distribution platforms.

The most relevant modules composing M-Traffic system (Figure 2) are:

- **Sensor data processor:** This module is responsible for collecting the traffic information detected by the sensors.

Figure. 2. M-Traffic Architecture

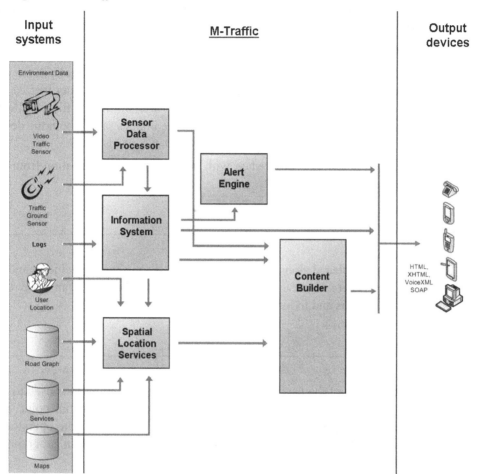

- **Information system:** This provides the system with statistical and historical traffic data, as well as rules, heuristics and simulation data used to assess and predict the traffic conditions. This module also includes the simulation models and the Traffic Status Generator that holds an updated data structure containing the traffic status information.

- **Alert engine:** This automatically detects abnormal traffic conditions and sends alert messages to the users.

- **Spatial location services:** The main objectives of this module are to allow the real-time determination of users' position, and to calculate the best route between two spatial points.

- **Content builder:** This delivers the information adjusted to the various types of distribution platforms. When this module receives a request, it sends a query to the Information System to select the data related to the area mentioned in the request, formatted according to the characteristics of the device that generated the request.

M-traffic framework was designed to be used by different client applications with their own structure and design. The framework produces XML data that can be transformed into any markup language using XSLT transformation files, while the image renders accept several parameters so that the images satisfy both the device and client application requirements.

The framework needs to be nourished with geo-referenced information from different sources, including:

Traffic Sensors

These are sensors placed along the roads to detect the presence of vehicles and the average speed. There are several types of sensors with the most commonly used being video cameras and loops placed on the asphalt.

User Location

This is the position of the user who is requesting the information. It is used to find the best route from the user's location to another designated spatial point. This data can be supplied by a GPS-enabled device, by the mobile phone operator, or simply typed by the user. The location can be an address or a point in geographical coordinates.

Road Graph

The road graph is a representation of the road system covered by the M-Traffic and includes all the information regarding the roads, such as category (e.g., highway, street, round-about), type (e.g., for pedestrians or vehicles), directions (one or two-way), door numbers, turn permissions, and length.

It is used for the calculation of the route between two or more points, to find the geographic position of a point given its address (geo-coding), or to find the closest address given a geographic position (reverse geo-coding).

Maps

Maps are graphical representations of the spatial area covered by the system, used for visualization purposes as the background to show output data to the users and guide them through the physical space. Maps can be aerial photographs or schematic.

Services

Services supply information about geo-located points like restaurants, hotels, gas stations, or pharmacies. The location of these points can be supplied as an address or in geographical coordinates, and can be represented over a map.

Sensor Data Processor

The objective of this module is to gather and process the data collected by sensors, and generate, in real-time, the information to nourish the system's database. It can access the sensors directly or query an existing system where this data is stored.

This module comprises several sub-modules, each one responsible for collecting data from one type of sensor (Figure 3). When video cameras are used, this module includes the Image Processor sub-module to extract quantitative and visual data from images captured by the video cameras. The Image Processor structure comprises the following sub-components (Figure 4):

Figure. 3. Sensor Data Processor module structure. This module can easily integrate several new sub-modules to process data collected by additional different types of sensor.

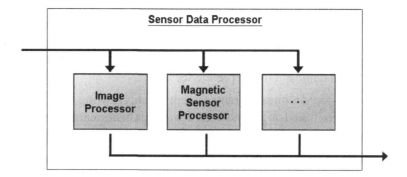

Figure 4. Image Processor components

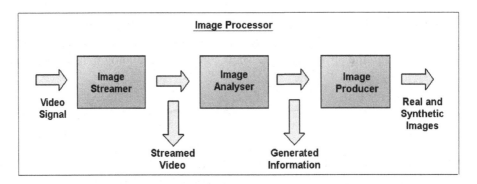

- **Image Streamer:** This receives the video signal or files and produces input streams for the Information System, the Image Analyser and Image Producer sub-modules.

- **Image Analyser:** This analyses the video streams produced by the Image Streamer and provides the resulting data to the Information System and the Image Producer sub-module.

- **Image Producer:** Based on the video streams received from the Image Streamer and the data arriving from the Image Analyser, generates images adjusted to the different devices served by the Content Builder, which are then sent to the Information System.

New sub-modules can easily be added to the Sensor Data Processor in order to allow the system to collect data from new types of sensors.

Information System Module

The M-Traffic information system stores, manages, and provides all the data related to the traffic and the users such as vehicle count, average speed, accident related data, weather conditions, data collected by the Sensor Data Processor module, statistic data, heuristics and simulation data used to assess and predict the traffic conditions, users' personal data, and users' preferences.

Traffic data is stored with an incremental approach, allowing the prediction of future traffic conditions based on the analysis of previous historical data, as well as weather conditions or the occurrence of events that affect the normal traffic flow.

This module includes the Traffic Forecast Engine that, using the collected traffic information and artificial-intelligence algorithms, can predict the traffic status at a

Figure 5. Information System module components

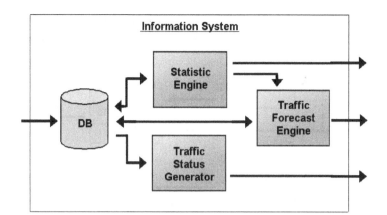

given time and place, based on the actual traffic status in the entire road network. It comprises a simulation model for the modelling and analysis of a traveller's behaviour and traffic conditions, which is presented later.

This module also includes the Statistic Engine that processes the real-time traffic data in order to generate statistical information of the traffic conditions. It classifies the traffic conditions according to the period of the day, day of the week, day of the month, and day of the year. Exceptional days like holidays and special event days are processed separately. These statistical data are used by other modules, and can also be displayed to drivers to better plan a trip.

Also, this module comprises the Traffic Status Generator that keeps an updated data structure containing the current traffic status information, which can be seen as a real-time snapshot of the traffic status in the whole area covered by the system.

Figure 5 depicts the structure of the Information System module.

Alert Engine

The Alert Engine allows the system to automatically detect abnormal traffic conditions. It periodically compares the traffic conditions to the statistical values kept by the Information system module and, given some heuristics, checks if the traffic is more or less congested than usual in the same conditions (e.g., same period of the day, same day of the week). If it detects abnormal traffic conditions, an event is generated and alerts are sent to the users according to their profiles and traffic status previews. This module can use the data generated by the Traffic Forecast Engine allowing alerts to be issued ahead of time.

Figure 6. Spatial Location Services module structure

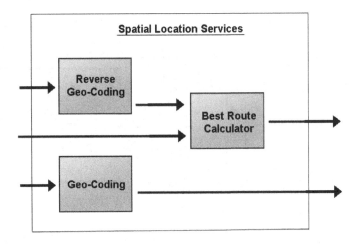

Spatial Location Services

The main objectives of this module are to allow the determination of a user's position in real-time, and calculate the best route between two spatial points. It includes several sub-components (Figure 6):

- **Geo-coding:** This determines the geographical coordinates of a given address and requires the road information data for the process.

- **Reverse Geo-coding:** This determines the closest address to a given geographical point and requires road information data for the process.

- **Best Route Calculator:** This determines the best route between two or more address points. The calculation depends on the data supplied. It can determine the shortest, the quickest, or the cheapest route and several intermediate stop points can be defined. When supplied with the traffic information, it determines the best route given the actual traffic conditions. When supplied with the traffic forecast information, it determines the best route given the traffic conditions for that moment in time.

Content Builder

This module should support the access to M-Traffic by different mobile devices with distinct characteristics and information processing power.

Figure 7. Augmented-Reality image on a mobile phone

Figure 8. Synthetic image of a complex cross showing the traffic intensity

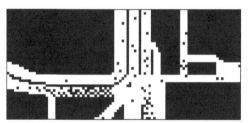

The ever increasing diversity of mobile devices with diverse technical and functional capabilities (CPU power, display size, interaction paradigms) brings further complications concerning the adaptation and dissemination of content. Content builder is designed to be easily extended to support the use of M-Traffic by additional mobile devices and to provide formatted content including:

- Images generated from a camera captured images overlaid with traffic data, using colour and text (Figure 7);
- Colour or black and white synthetic images that sketch the traffic conditions in a defined area (Figure 8);
- Real-time video captured by traffic cameras;
- Textual structured information formatted according to the characteristics of the requesting device.

The content builder structure can be visualized in Figure 9. It comprises several sub-components:

- **Augmented-Reality Image Render:** This generates augmented images from traffic camera captured images superimposed with traffic data, using colour and text. The render gets the current frame from the video system and draws the traffic conditions on it (Figure 7). The final image is also adapted to the driver's device constraints. For that reason, it is resized, and the number of colours is reduced, if needed.

- **Synthetic-Image Render:** This generates colour or black and white synthetic images that sketch the traffic conditions in a selected area. Synthetic images are simple diagrams that represent graphically the traffic conditions. These images are useful when there is no video system covering the area and can be displayed in the majority of devices.

- **Textual Information Generator:** This structures and formats textual information according to the characteristics of the requesting device.

Figure 9. Content builder module structure

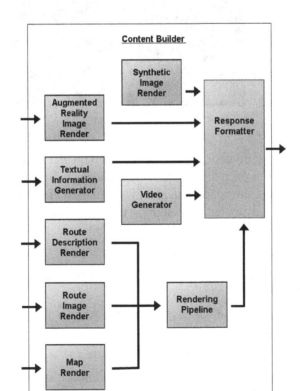

- **Video Generator:** This produces real-time video captured by traffic cameras.

- **Route Description Render:** This processes the best route result, provided by the Spatial Location Services, so that the name of the roads, direction changes, and other useful information are added to it. The output of this module is in XML and, for example, the direction changes are coded as tags instead of text so that it can later be translated into any language and into different output formats using XSLT rules.

- **Route Image Render:** This draws the route so that it can be super-imposed on a map. It gives total control over line colour, style, and width.

- **Map Render:** This generates the background map image, given the geographic coordinates, images size, and source.

- **Rendering Pipeline:** This allows the combination of several layers of images. It gives total control over the layer order, position, size, and opacity. This component also enables the addition of other elements to the image such as legend, copyright notice, and watermark.

- **Response Formatter:** This builds up the request reply according to the network connection and the requesting device.

Traffic Simulator

In order to reply to user requests, the routing service (sub-module of the Spatial Location Services module) must calculate the best route over the graph that represents the street's network in the area covered by the system. However, not every street has sensors (either image or ground sensors). Thus, in order to find minimum time routes, it is necessary to estimate the delay in each street from a simulation model. Apart from image and ground sensor data, the dynamic state of this model can be fed by statistical data and isolated event data. This model aims to describe the behaviour of each car-driver along a predefined route. Thus, a microscopic traffic simulation model was developed.

Model

Classical models for traffic simulation follow either a fluid flow (macroscopic) analogy or an individual car-driver description (microscopic) approach. In spite of being studied since the 50's, only recently the computational power allowed the microscopic simulation approach to emerge as an important tool to study traffic dynamic behaviour. This approach enables the modelling of driver and car characteristics variability.

The model presented in this work has two regimes--a car-following regime and a free-flow regime. These regimes are according to driver behaviours that try to follow the leading vehicle with safety space head way, if it is close enough (less than an upper threshold), or else will drive at a desired speed that depends on the street and the driver. From kinematics laws,

$$\frac{d^2 x_n}{dt^2} = acceleration$$

a car following acceleration dynamic model is defined taking into account: the characteristic street speed; vehicle characteristic parameters; driver perception pure delay; and the driver eagerness to follow the preceding car. The general form of the classical car-following acceleration is

$$action(t) = sensitivity(t - T) \times stimulus(t - T)$$

where t is the observation instant, T is the perception pure delay, $action(t)$ is the acceleration, $stimulus(t)$ is what thrives the driver decision, and $sensitivity(t)$ is a weight put in the stimulus. In this work, the sensitivity is unary and the stimulus is the space headway. Nevertheless, a safety distance d_s depending on the vehicle speed is considered,

$$d_s = \alpha \frac{dx}{dt} + d_v$$

where d_v is the vehicle size and α is a constant, which has an effect similar to the sensitivity term.

In this work to model the effect of traffic lights, a threshold distance d_l is considered. If the vehicle is further than d_l from the traffic lights, then those are ignored. Whenever the vehicle is in the traffic light influence area, it responds to the red lights generating a negative acceleration that is calculated such that the vehicle stops behind the traffic light position or another vehicle ahead.

Once the acceleration model depends on two events that may occur independently, the existence of a leading car and the presence of a traffic light, acceleration is the minimum of the two. This amounts to a safety conservative strategy. The final acceleration is saturated in minimum (maximum breaking) and maximum values that are characteristics of the car-driver model.

Simulator Implementation

The simulator is implemented in java. This choice has the advantage of producing portable applications, and the object oriented paradigm is very convenient to implement the main simulator components (vehicles, traffic lights, streets, and sensors) as classes. Furthermore, building a multithreaded implementation allows one to easily parallelise the execution of the simulation whenever multiprocessing may be available.

A configuration input file defines the street graph, the length of each street, the sensor's location, the traffic lights location and temporization cycles, and the car-driver system parameters. The initial conditions are also defined in this file and include a route for each vehicle.

The simulator outputs the position of each vehicle for every sampling time as well as sensor signals that give vehicle counts and average speed at a predefined time interval. These sensor signals correspond to those frequently given by the Traffic Management System. So, this makes it possible to load the traffic status database

Figure 10. Position of vehicles along the street with traffic lights at 100, 200 and 300 meters

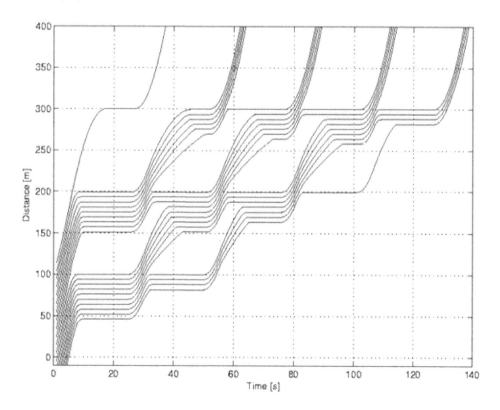

with data from the simulator and compare the simulator results to measured data. Another goal of the simulator is to test the precision of delay estimates based on average speed which is measured by sensors, though covering only a limited region of the graph.

Simulation Results

In this section, some results are presented that illustrate the macroscopic vehicle dynamic behaviour in a street segment. The parameters used in the simulations presented below result from a calibration made with just one driver-vehicle system and do not include a parameter variability study.

Simulations were performed using the Euler integration method with a fixed integration time of 1 second.

Figure 10 shows the positions vs. time for each vehicle in a street with three traffic lights. The congestion effect due to the traffic lights at 100, 200, and 300 meters is clear.

Simulation results may be used to test several decisions concerning the M-Traffic system, such as the best place to put the ground sensors or to validate the weighting factor in the graph used by the routing algorithm. The following example concerns the routing algorithm, a sub-module of the Spatial Location Services, which has

Figure 11. Estimated vehicle delay versus the delay in simulation

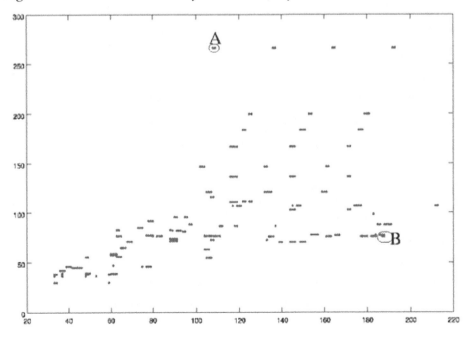

been implemented using a street's length as a weighting factor in the graph. This amounts to a minimum path criterium. One goal of the system being developed is to use a minimum time criterium in the routing module. Since there are some streets with sensors that count vehicles and measure speed, it is a natural choice to use the speed information in order to estimate street traffic delay T_{street} .

$$T_{street} = \frac{l_s}{\bar{v}}$$
(1)

where l_s is the street length, and $\bar{v}$ is the average speed over a predefined period.

Figure 11 shows the result of estimated delay vs. the simulation delay for a wide set of conditions. This simulation use 50 vehicles and covers situations with long queues near the traffic lights, which correspond to streets with high traffic intensity and a short green light period, as well as other situations with very short queues. The temporization cycles, and the location of sensors also vary, representing a broad range of situations. If the estimated time delay was perfectly correlated with the average speed, we would expect to observe a linear relation in Figure 11. It can be seen that when there are queues, the sensor position is critical, and the results have a large dispersion. Estimates that are not in agreement with the "true" delay are due to sensor position. Whenever there are queues near the traffic lights, a sensor located closer to the traffic light indicates a lower average vehicle speed than those located further.

Though there is a correlation between estimated delay and simulation, there are some results quite far from the ideal linear correlation. Results indicated with A in Figure 11 correspond to an over estimated delay. The sensor is located too close to the traffic light in the region that is most affected by the traffic light queue.

Results indicated with B in Figure 11 correspond to an under estimated delay. The sensor is located too far away from the traffic light in a region not affected by the traffic light queue.

This indicates that delay estimates as (1) are not enough to the routing algorithm. Thus, another algorithm should be used to estimate the delay. A more accurate estimate must include other sources of information besides the average speed such as vehicle count in a fixed period of time.

Conclusion

This chapter presents a multi-platform mobile traffic information and monitoring system, which provides real-time traffic information. M-Traffic service ubiquitously provides users with traffic information regarding their needs and preferences, according to an alert system, which allows a personalised predefinition of warning messages. The system is aware of the user's location, providing traffic information and alerts accordingly.

M-Traffic has a modular architecture based on several structurally independent, but functionally interdependent modules. Therefore, the system can easily be adapted to receive and allocate new types of data input (sensors, image, direct logs), and to output data to additional distribution platforms. New sub-modules can be easily added in order to allow the system to collect data from new types of sensors or to provide data to new client devices.

A simulation model is presented and some results are shown. One of the services in this system is a routing service based on a minimum path criterium. In order to change this criterium to minimum time, a delay estimate precision was studied against sensor location. To fully take advantage of the simulation model, it should be calibrated with a statistical sample of driver-vehicle systems, and a set of the most requested routes should be included in the simulator to model travellers' behaviour.

Future Research Directions

Processing power tends to become so distributed in the environment that computers as we see them today will disappear. New smaller, lighter, and more powerful mobile devices are constantly appearing in the market. These devices allow users to easily access all kinds of information wherever and whenever they need it.

During any decision making process, it is important to have access to relevant data and to be able to anticipate future scenarios. The prediction of future situations can guide users through more appropriate procedure that consequently allow them to achieve better results regarding their established goals. In our particular case of traffic information systems, it is important to accurately preview future traffic conditions, in order to provide users with the best route. Since routes can be large in duration and distance, it is important to know, in advance, how traffic will be in certain location when we will arrive there. It is also important to be able to access traffic information during the whole trip, since traffic conditions may change and we may want to change the route at a certain point.

In the future, we will explore new methods to accurately predict traffic conditions, and innovative visualization techniques and interface procedures that facilitate users' interactions with new mobile devices within a ubiquitous computing scenario.

Acknowledgment

The authors gratefully acknowledge the contribution of National Research Organisation, ADI—Agência de Inovação, project *M-traffic—POSI Action 1.3 Investigação em Consórcio*. Luís Rato has been supported by project FLOW—POSC/EEA-SRI/61188/2004.

References

Ahmed, K. (1999). *Modeling Drivers' Acceleration and Lane Changing Behavior.* Unpublished doctoral dissertation, MIT, MA.

Ben-Akiva, M., Bierlaire, M., Koutsopoulos, H. N., & Mishalani., R. G. (1996, September 9-11). *DynaMIT: Dynamic network assignment for the management of information to travellers.* Paper presented at the 4th Meeting of the EURO Working Group on Transportation, Newcastle, UK.

Ben-Akiva, M., Bierlaire, M., Bottom, J., Koutsopoulos, H.N., & Mishalani, R.G. (1997). *Development of a route guidance generation system for real-time application.* Paper presented at the 8th International Federation of Automatic Control Symposium on Transportation Systems, Chania, Greece.

Beymer, D., McLauchlan, P., Coifman, B., & Malik, J. (1997). *A Real-time Computer Vision System for Measuring Traffic Parameters.* In *Proceedings of Conference on Computer Vision and Pattern Recognition (CVPR '97)* (pp. 495-501). IEEE Computer Society.

Marques, M. C., & Silva, R. N., (2005). *Traffic Simulation for Intelligent Transportation Systems Development.* In *Proceedings of the 8th International IEEE Conference on Intelligent Transportation Systems*, Vienna, (pp. 320-325). IEEE Computer Society.

Nagel, K., & Schreckenberg, M. (1992). A cellular automaton model for freeway traffic. *Journal de Physique, I (2)*, 2221-2229.

Additional Reading

Drane, C. R. & Rizos, C. (1998). *Positioning Systems in Intelligent Transportation Systems.* London, UK: Artech House.

El-Rabbany, A. (2006). *Introduction to GPS: The Global Positioning System* (2nd Ed.). London, UK: Artech House.

Greenfield, A. (2006). *Everyware: The dawning age of ubiquitous computing.* Berkeley, CA: New Riders.

Marques, M.C. (2005). *Simulation and control methodologies for distributed traffic management systems.* Unpublished doctoral dissertation (in Portuguese), Faculdade de Ciências e Tecnologia da Universidade Nova de Lisboa.

Ogata, K. (2003). *System dynamics* (4th Ed). Prentice Hall.

Chapter X

Towards Ambient Business:
Enabling Open Innovation in a World of Ubiquitous Computing

Christian Schmitt, University of Cologne, Germany

Detlef Schoder, University of Cologne, Germany

Kai Fischbach, University of Cologne, Germany

Steffen Muhle, University of Cologne, Germany

Abstract

Ubiquitous computing enables the development of new innovative applications and services. Particularly influential on future business services will be the connection of the real with the virtual world by embedding computers or smallest processors, memory chips, and sensors into the environment and into physical objects, as well as using natural, multimodal customer interaction. Bearing in mind that ubiquitous computing entails the interaction of mobile smart objects and local smart environments hosted by different service providers, we propose an open approach to encourage the development of new and innovative smart applications and services. Considering the Open Source community, we assert that such an open approach reveals innovation potentials that cannot be achieved in proprietary information system environments. Most research projects, as well as commercial initiatives, however, focus mainly on specific, proprietary applications like smart shopping environments, and do not incorporate further prospects of using an open approach. Therefore, this chapter discusses as a first step the impact of Open Innovation in a world of ubiquitous computing from an economic perspective. Then, the design of an Open Object Information Infrastructure (OOII) that enables Open Innovation in the context of ubiquitous computing is presented. Finally, an innovative smart service called the Federative Library (FedLib), which represents a first instantiation of the OOII, is introduced to demonstrate the feasibility of the design.

Introduction

The connection of the real and the virtual world encourages the development of new and innovative applications and services. Google is a prominent case which distinctly underlines the creative power of combining both worlds (Roush, 2005). In June of 2005, Google released an official API for Google Maps and Google Earth. Through this, consumers and external developers now have access to detailed aerial and satellite maps and advanced geographical visualization tools that can easily be used to display data atop the Google maps. Almost immediately, a community of "geotagging" map makers was formed that ties information on the Web to geographical coordinates in order to build geospatial applications (examples of so-called "map mash-ups" can be found in Gibson, 2006). Geotagging means amplifying physical places with information so that, for instance, users of mobile devices with location technologies can retrieve additional information related to their current locations. This includes location-based ads and listings for nearby shopping, dining, entertainment, and business outlets or even photographs, videos, stories, and other personal information uploaded to the Internet and pinned to specific latitudes and longitudes. As a result, the community participates in the innovation process and in building "a browser for the earth," as John Hanke, general manager of Google's Keyhole Group, describes Google Earth (Roush, 2005). This could enable a new and natural means of accessing location-based information. Wade Roush (2005) describes this vision by drawing a comparison: "Every page on the Web has a location, in the form of a URL. Now every location can have a Web page [...] it means that navigating both the Web and the real geography around us is about to become a much richer experience, rife with occasions for on-the-spot education and commerce. It means that we will be able to browse the Web-and the virtual earth encompassed within it-simply by walking around." (p. 60)

As the Google case also illustrates, opening access to information systems and intellectual property (IP) to complementors, suppliers, users, and even to competitors encourages innovation, increases the attractiveness of platforms, and enriches service provision through the incorporation of external information sources. With the world evolving from Electronic Business to ubiquitous computing (Weiser, 1991) (and pervasive computing (Hansmann, 2003) or ambient intelligence (Aarts, 2001) respectively), even more comprehensive opportunities for implementing innovation are likely to arise. Innovative information gathering and access is enabled by the connection between the real with the virtual world by embedding computers or the smallest processors, memory chips, and sensors into the environment and into physical objects (Gershenfeld, 1999), as well as using natural, multimodal user interaction (Dam, 2001).

However, existing approaches frequently rely on rather proprietary information systems that reveal their data and services only partially or under certain conditions. Bearing in mind that ubiquitous computing entails the interaction of mobile smart objects and local smart environments hosted by different service providers, we propose using an open approach to encourage the development of new and innovative smart applications and services. Considering the Open Source community, we assert that such an open approach reveals innovation potentials that cannot be achieved in proprietary information system environments. Various developers with different perceptions can then search for relevant smart services, as well as information gathered by smart objects or environments, combine them freely, and hence create their own innovative services.

The rest of the chapter is structured as follows. The following section presents related work. Then, we first introduce our framework for ambient business. We then discuss the impact and potential of Open Innovation in a world of ambient business from an economic perspective. Next, we present the design of an architecture called the open object information infrastructure (OOII) that enables open innovation in the context of ambient business. To demonstrate the feasibility of the design, we introduce an innovative smart service called the Federative Library (FedLib) that will be the first instantiation of the OOII. The chapter concludes with a summary and further research questions.

Background

Several authors have considered the impact on business that comes with ubiquitous computing. Most work starts with a discussion of technological progress and the business impact arising from that progress. Roussos (2006) adopts this perspective. In his view, contingencies for ubiquitous commerce arise from emerging technologies which again have an impact on business innovation, as well as on society. Similar to that view, Mattern (2005) discusses technological progress that allows deploying smart objects in an informatized world around us. Within this world, informational counterparts of everyday objects and of people induce social and political challenges and pave the way to new applications. Fleisch and Tellkamp (2006) act on this assumption and provide a framework that helps to identify value-creating application areas and discuss challenges in implementing these applications. Whereas Fleisch and Tellkamp focus on processes within a company or between companies, Fano and Gershman (2002) consider the impact that smart services will have on relationships between customers and the service provider. These relationships will be profoundly affected by new classes of services emerging in smart environments. Based on the vision that a service provider will steadily be able to access customers, they make a set of assumptions about how services will be provided in a world of ubiquitous computing.

By discussing technology, smart environments and several business aspects, the present literature gives considerable insights into how ubiquitous computing will impact future business. However, current frameworks do not even consider the potentials for innovation. For example, the German Federal Office for Information Security provides a framework to discuss the socio-economic impact of ubiquitous computing (BSI, 2006). It considers "determining factors," "enabling technologies," "pervasive computing features," and "Impacts" without addressing innovation. Therefore, we propose in the following section our framework for ambient business before discussing the impact of ambient business on innovation.

The Framework for Ambient Business

The framework for ambient business divides the analysis of ubiquitous computing in the context of entrepreneurial activities into four perspectives (see Figure 1).

First, the emerging technologies layer focuses on advances in technology during the last few decades that allow the development of new types of IT-infrastructures. These emerging technologies present new qualities that open up new forms of IT usage covered in the smart environments layer. Thus, new applications (smart services layer) can be implemented within smart environments. Finally, the ambient business layer deals with the impact of these innovative smart services on economy, business environment, and society.

Emerging Technologies

Advances in networking as well as embedded technology, display technology, and nanotechnology have been driving the research on ubiquitous computing during recent past decades (Hilty, 2005). Smaller and more powerful, but less power-con-

Figure 1. The Framework for Ambient Business

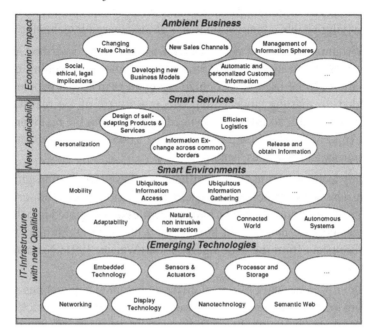

suming, information technology has facilitated the development not only of common IT-devices. Even objects such as coffee cups (Gellersen, 1999) and pens (Anoto, 2007) can be equipped with sensors, processors, storage capacity, and actuators. The objects can be connected with each other in order to "cooperate," thus forming joint embedded IT environments. As a result, new opportunities for applications scenarios arise.

Current progress in the layer of emerging technologies is indeed quite remarkable. An in-depth discussion of technologies, therefore, is beyond the scope of this chapter. The remainder of this chapter assumes a portfolio of technologies which designers and developers of applications and services can use as a basis for presenting technical solutions for application demands in a world of ubiquitous computing. In this context, Semantic Web (Berners-Lee, 2001) technologies are of particularly great relevance.

Smart Environments

In the second layer, the qualities of emerging technologies are explored. The role of these qualities is twofold. First, they are the means for revealing new applications and services based on the emerging technologies. Second, when analyzing the shortcomings of current applications and services, the qualities can pave the way for satisfying people's innovation needs at the emerging technologies level.

An environment equipped with an IT-infrastructure as described above is able to gather information about people, things, and other surrounding conditions. The information can be used to recognize the context in which people and things are embedded, so that the environment becomes aware of the real world. Thus, the environment is able to estimate the needs arising from the real world and to adapt itself to (mobile) users and situations (Coutaz, 2005), or may even act autonomously. The environment becomes "smart."

Emerging technologies not only facilitate extensive information gathering, but also provide new ways to interact with users. Information access and services presented by the smart environment can be almost seamlessly integrated into the user's world. Interfaces become natural and interaction with them subliminal. The technology even disappears from the user's perception (Weiser, 1991; Norman, 1998; Want, 2002).

Although different qualities reveal different potential applications, the qualities of emerging technologies are not independent from each other. In fact, like the emerging technology layer, only by analyzing the interplay of different qualities and by transferring them to the application domain, can the full breadth of application potentials be revealed. Accordingly, these qualities point to smart services that may be developed on top of smart environments.

Smart Services

Merging the real and the virtual world, every relevant object in the real world acquires an informational counterpart in the form of a data object (Mattern, 2005). Thus, a service that uses this informational counterpart may know the location and condition of a physical object. Such services are already applied to ensure efficient logistic processes (Angeles, 2005) and whenever assets have to been managed. Due to the decreasing costs of corresponding technology, services will not only be offered to companies, but a vast range of services is also conceivable for individuals. Books, clothes, and CDs may be managed in a similar manner in the future. By analyzing the current and past context of an object, which comprises additional information from outside the environment, appropriate supportive services can be developed and offered through a so called smart product (Maass, 2006). Additional services may be presented for use, for example, at a medicine cabinet when the medicine runs short (Floerkemeier, 2003). Such services can also be individualized, so that they adapt to the preferences, habits, and current situation of the user (Coutaz, 2005). When services become fully aware of their context, they could be invoked automatically, without explicit manual interaction by the user (Tennenhouse, 2000).

Ambient Business

The ability of smart services to adapt themselves to situations and provide a huge amount of information instantly not only supports current business processes and distribution channels, but it also opens new ways of doing business.

Services in the application domain of supply chain and asset management reveal opportunities for monitoring tangible assets more closely and thus creating a higher degree of control. Yet, the costs of control decline at the same time. Not only high-value products, but also lower-value ones can be managed by efficiently smart services. This results in a very tight mesh of control throughout the company (Fleisch, 2005). Through means of such control, processes can be adjusted to incidents that are internal or external to the processes. This may result in more efficient and reliable processes within an organization.

Inter-organizational processes that utilize smart services may also cut costs in the supply chain. Through crossing internal company borders, information flows that are highly aligned with the flow of physical goods reduce losses, and control overhead that frequently occur at such borders (Strasser, 2005). Furthermore by, opening up their data base, companies are able to offer smart services to each other, for example, control and information services (Fleisch, 2005). Functions that were previously closely linked to one's own organization can now be outsourced. It becomes feasible for companies to offer their outstanding capabilities that were previously bound to the organization to suppliers, customers, and even to competitors.

In the future, products may be provided more as a bundle of the physical product itself and the services linked to it. It may be sold as a platform for generating additional revenues by means of services in the after-sale phase. In this case, the vendor comes closer to the customer through two means. First, he is able to address a customer not only through traditional sales channels like a store. He can also address the customer at the preferred location (Fano, 2002), which may have an enormous impact on business models and sales channels. Second, information may flow in the other direction as well. Users can provide usage information to the vendor and receive special services or a monetary reward in return. The vendor can use this information to align R&D-efforts to users' needs. Going one step further, smart services can be used to involve users in the R&D-process, whether directly or via mediators like Innocentive (Innocentive, 2007).

It can be assumed that ambient business entrepreneurs will find themselves in markets with short innovation cycles. Like the internet, smart environments follow the end-to-end principle. This principle states that the intelligence of an information system rests, that is, in the end-user-devices, not in the network (Saltzer, 1984). Someone who can exercise control as a central authority typically owns the network. In contrast, the "ends" of the network are typically in user's control. The user is able to replace or enhance the ends and to deploy innovative applications and content.

Thus, Lessig (2002) argues, systems that put the end-to-end principle into practice encourage innovation. The short innovation cycles in the internet can largely be explained by the fact that they implement this principle. Smart environments are largely considered to be built out of smart devices and, therefore, follow the end-to-end principle as well. Users of smart environments can decide what device they want to use and what smart services they should deliver. Therefore, the innovation cycles in ambient business are likely to be at least as short as in Electronic Business. Moreover, consideration must be given to the fact that smart services can be invented around all instances of our life that allow the creation of manifold potential applications. New entrants may attend to these potential applications, enter existing markets, and shift competition (Watson, 2002). Companies have to reconsider how to cope with new competitors in a high-velocity market as well as what strategies and business models to apply.

Smart environments and services that are deployed in our everyday life may have considerable social, ethical, and legal implications which also have to be considered in the business perspective. Different studies reveal corresponding potentials and perils. Positive effects can be expected throughout all activities of daily life. In particular, elderly people and handicapped persons may benefit from supportive applications and natural interfaces (Coroama, 2003). These interfaces may also close the digital divide between those with and those without access to computing facilities (BSI, 2006). Hilty et al. (2005) raises the question whether positive effects resulting from efficiency enhancements may be partially undone by side effects, that is, by increasing people's stress level, and whether smart products may lead to pollution and health hazards. However, most concerns relate to the amount of gathered data and resulting privacy issues. History suggests that balancing companies' benefits and customers' privacy is crucial for the success of commercial smart environments (McGinity, 2004). Bohn (2005), Hilty (2005), Bizer (2006), and BSI (2006) provide an in-depth analysis of possible perils and give hints how to balance benefits and user's privacy. Lahlou (2003) proposes a set of privacy guidelines to cope with this challenge.

In addition to these social, ethical, and legal implications, the aim of this chapter is primarily to discuss the impact of open innovation in a world of ambient business from an economic perspective.

Open Innovation from an Economic Perspective

The idea of encouraging innovation throughout openness with regard to IS was widely discussed in the early 1980s when mainframe vendors started to restrict the use of object program and source code of formerly unrestricted software. As a countermove and in order to gain independence of the software industry, Richard Stallman (1999) propagated the idea of free software. This paradigm shift away from the conventional IP regime resulted in software that can be used, modified, and redistributed by everyone. Related movements like Open Source (Lerner, 2002; O'Reilly, 1999), Open Standards (Perens, 2006; West, 2004), Open Systems (Gabel, 1987), and Open Content (Ciffoilli, 2003; Wiley, 1999) all follow a similar idea: By modifying and recombining existing work, innovation can be collectively achieved. Thus, self-organized ecosystems of Open Innovation emerge when independent actors contribute to a product system (the product and its complementary assets). These Open Innovation ecosystems have proven that they are able to compete with companies that are reluctant to open up their systems and their IP. Software like Apache, Mozilla, and Linux has achieved a considerable market share, and Wikipedia comes close to the quality of the Encyclopaedia Britannica (Wales, 2005).

The idea of openness may contradict the common approach of value extraction of a kind of assets, that is, intellectual assets, in most societies. It is widely assumed that these assets can and should be owned by someone and hence are the IP of the creator or perhaps of the buyer. However, such IP shares the fate of most intangible assets. Once it is revealed and brought into the public domain, there is the risk that it becomes common. The creator and his competitors can use the asset to create value. The potential for the creator to differentiate his products from those of competitors is reduced. Hence, the use of the asset by competitors reduces the creator's return on the asset (Magee, 1977). In order to ensure compensation for the creators of innovative intellectual work, legislators enact laws to protect intellectual property rights (IPR). Creators and buyers of special rights are exclusively allowed to utilize property for a certain period of time. Through these laws, intellectual work should be rewarded and innovation stimulated (Chesbrough, 2006).

The management of intellectual assets often focuses on closing up companies' borders from the intellectual assets point of view in order to keep others from harvesting the fruit of their labor. However, legal instruments often cannot hinder third parties from gaining large shares of the profit arising from innovations: The protection mechanisms are often not enforceable. They are easy to bypass by using slight modifications of the IP in question, and this results in various forms of uncompensated adaptation (Teece, 1986). Under certain conditions, IPR can be ignored. The music and software industries are examples of this phenomenon. Thus, IPR are often not capable of protecting the owner from the exploitation of assets by others.

Closed companies' borders may not only frustrate the aim to protect assets; in fact, they may prevent companies from gaining profit from their assets at all. R&D departments regularly create intellectual assets that cannot be utilized within the company. Procter & Gamble, for example, estimated in 2002 that it only commercialized 10 % of its patents, whereas the remaining 90 % virtually gathered dust on shelves (Sakkab, 2002). Licensing may be a viable option to exploit unutilized patents (Rivette, 2000). However, potential licensees are often reluctant to adopt external technology (Chesbrough, 2006), and the legal protection of an IP is often too weak to make licensing a viable option.

Companies such as Google and Amazon turn in part away from the closed way of managing intellectual assets and appear to profit from opening up their information systems and, therefore, revealing some of their intellectual assets. As another example, IBM donated 500 patents to the Open Source community in 2005 instead of generating revenue by licensing it. Moreover, IBM spends $100 million each year in the development of Linux. IBM opens up these assets to regain a prominent role in the operating system market—a position it had lost beforehand with AIX (Chesbrough, 2006)—and is now able to use Linux as a platform to sell products and services around Linux (West, 2003).

Drivers for Open Innovation in Ambient Business

To reveal the drivers for making assets publicly available in a world of ubiquitous computing and the resulting potential benefits, the open approach can be discussed from a resource perspective (Barey, 1991; Penrose 1959; Wernerfelt 1984). This perspective reveals the possibilities arising from a resource exchange at the layers of the device infrastructure, the information infrastructure, and of the smart service.

Resources can be considered as tangible and intangible assets that are tied somehow semi-permanently to the firm (Wernerfelt, 1984). They compass all input factors that are needed to create value during a product life cycle. Companies can leverage the resource base to achieve a competitive advantage if these are valuable, rare, imperfectly imitable, and nonsubstitutable (Barney, 1991). As such, innovative related resources that fulfill these requirements can contribute to achieve an advantageous position in markets in which innovative products and services are valued by customers.

As argued before, in a world of ubiquitous computing, innovation life cycles may be short. From innovations in technologies and services often spring a disruptive force that leads to changes in the market environment: New innovators entering the market and unpredictable demand shifts may change the market structure. However, competitive advantage can only be achieved when the company's resources are in line with market conditions (Eisenhardt, 2000). Yet, in the changing markets of ubiquitous computing, frequent adaptation of the resource base is necessary. On the one hand, this is a major challenge for companies in UC markets. On the other hand, this should be seen as an outstanding opportunity to gain competitive advantage through superior capabilities in resource acquisition, namely adaptation, integration and reconfiguration of internal and external resources (Teece, 1997).

However, companies may not be able to alter their resource base on their own fast enough, and necessary resources may not be available for licensing. For example, when Microsoft released Windows NT and Windows 95, Apple had to innovate in its operating system to cope with Microsoft. However, Apple was not able to alter its resource base accordingly. It, therefore, published its source code partly as an open source and allowed external programmers to contribute to the software development process (West, 2003). Following this example, opening up a company's border and letting resources and, thus, intellectual assets pass through may be a viable strategy for acquiring new resources.

Open Innovation in Ambient Business Settings

In ambient business, diverse resources can be incorporated to enhance the innovative potential that is associated with a company's innovation processes and the innovation potential of its products. These resources can be obtained from all stakeholders of the company's products, especially customers, suppliers and manufacturers of complementary products, and also from competitors as well. Accordingly, a transfer can be conducted at every level of the proposed framework.

The device infrastructure builds up a smart environment and, hence, provides the foundation for smart services by gathering data and interacting with the user. Access to a device infrastructure is an essential asset for service providers. A tightly restricted and exclusive access to the IT-infrastructure through proprietary standards allows the creation of a monopoly position. This facilitates the monopolist to set rules which rivals must obey (Adams, 1982). Furthermore, the proprietary standards of the infrastructure create a barrier for new entrants because a change to another infrastructure is linked with incompatibility costs. However, providers of complementary devices and services are likely to be discouraged from using a tightly controlled IT-infrastructure (Farrell, 1985; Garud, 2002). Therefore, it may be impossible for a company that is playing the proprietary game to build up the full range of different devices of various application domains. Hence, if a company opens up its device infrastructure and relies on open standards, access to foreign innovative components may be gained by allowing them to become integrated into the company's own infrastructure.

Garud and Kumaraswamy (1993) showed through the Sun Microsystems case how companies could improve their strategic position by implementing an open system strategy. By relying on open standards and by liberally licensing some of its own know-how, Sun attracted capable complementors that helped to improve the overall systems performance. Sun ensured its head start in competition by conducting shorter innovation cycles then its competitors.

Another strategy to ensure returns is to retreat to a certain layers of the product architecture. Layers that do not contribute to a distinctive resource base generally do not help companies to gain a competitive advantage. By opening up these layers, an unrestricted foundation for higher layers may be laid that will be further developed by external innovators. Thus, the company may concentrate on extending its distinctive resource base on an upper layer, such as developing smart services. Apple, for example, published only source code of the operation system's lower levels. However, the Graphical User Interface and certain APIs, with which Apple can differentiate its operation system from its rivals, remained closed source (West, 2003).

As demonstrated earlier, the information infrastructure is the basis on which services are growing. It is, therefore, an important resource. The richer the information pool in terms of quality and quantity, the more services can be provided. These services will also be more reliable. For that infrastructure, the same principles apply as to the device infrastructure, since both are infrastructure layers. The information infrastructure that is available can be enhanced by opening it up and allowing other information infrastructures to interlink with it. Furthermore, companies may benefit from receding that layer and to commercialize the smart service layer. As distinct from the device infrastructure, when considering the information infrastructure, the user may play a more important role. Sensors deployed in the environment allow gathering data from a user's context without bothering the user, who may here fore willingly contribute this information to a company's information infrastructure assuming he trusts it. In this case, a services provider as well as a user may benefit from highly customized services. The user may play a more active role when it comes to semantically enriched data. Such enrichment can only be automatically conducted in exceptional cases.

Such tasks commonly require human judgment, for instance, to decide whether the Eiffel tower is ugly or beautiful. By opening up the base data, users can be encouraged to fulfill the tasks. Amazon's mechanical Turk is an example for a platform that brings together tasks that need human judgment to be solved and people that are willing to solve such tasks. Persons like students, housewives/ husbands, and pensioners may be attracted by being paid a small amount of money (Amazon, 2007). A voluntary participation, however, may be provoked whenever the user can benefit from an enriched information pool or consider his participation as an act of self-expression. Google Earth is a prime example of users being willing to contribute to a (partly) opened database (Roush, 2005). Other motivation mechanisms exist, such a mechanism, in which the work is disguised as a game (Ahn, 2006).

One of the major challenges of innovation—and therefore of creating smart services—is bringing together need information and solution information. These two types of information cannot usually be found at one and the same site (Hippel, 1994; Thomke, 2002). As a resource, solution information encompasses all information that provides a company with the technological competence and the potential that is necessary to supply customer needs and that resides traditionally in the company's site (Thomke, 2002; Thomke, 2003). Need information encompasses the user's preferences and requirements with respect to new products and services (Reichwald, 2006). It is generally in the user's domain. The innovator's lack of need information is a critical drawback for creating smart services. Thackara (2001) states that in the current ubiquitous computing research, developers know how to create amazing things with ubiquitous computing technology, but they lack in need information. They do not know how to use their knowledge to create solutions that benefit the user. However, obtaining this information is far from easy. Need information is somewhat "sticky," that is, it can only be conventionally revealed from potential users through costly and time consuming methods. Users often do not fully understand their needs or are not able to explicate them (Hippel, 1994). Smart environments can help to overcome this problem by studying contextual data gained from the user. Thus, it may be able to observe how a user behaves in using a smart service, which problems he encounters and what needs may remain unfulfilled.

Another way to overcome the problem is suggested by von Hippel (Hippel, 2002, 2005). By outsourcing need-related tasks to users, the problem of how to directly acquire sticky need information can be avoided. Thus, the user handles a task, which the company formally conducted, and returns a solution he is satisfied with. This solution is commonly less sticky than the need information itself. However, to fulfill the task, the user needs relevant solution-information that sticks with the company. Here, the company partly opens up its information pool by providing a design tool, called toolkit, to the user. This toolkit implements the company's solution information, which is provided in such a manner that the user can handle it easily. Smart Environment may broaden the facility of toolkits. Sophisticated toolkits may be able to be provided to the user at that point where his need generally occurs. Multimodal interfaces (Dam, 2001) may facilitate a richer interaction with the toolkit and, thus, allow solving complex tasks. Tangible interfaces can be used to let the user not only interact by "mediating" devices such as keyboard, mouse, and display, but to directly manipulate physical objects (Sharlin, 2004). An example of such a tangible interface is the "illuminating clay" from Piper et al. (2002). The computing system is able to gather the form of the clay the user works with and is able to augment it with additional information. Recent advancements in 3D-Printers may open up additional opportunities to integrate need information. The project Fab@ Home, for example, provides documentation about how to build a 3D-Printer for private purposes (Fab@home, 2006).

Enabling Open Innovation in a World of Ambient Business

As mentioned above, the information infrastructure is an important resource in ambient business settings. Accordingly, opening up ubiquitous computing systems enables innovation in a world of ambient business. If smart devices and smart environments are built on common standards and are opened up mutually, new possibilities for innovation arise through the combination of information pools, devices, and services. Furthermore, natural, multimodal, and tangible interfaces may simplify remote interaction within Open Innovation ecosystem (e. g., Pinhanez, 2004).

Xerox took the first steps to implementing smart environments in their research project Parctab (Want, 1995). Since then, many more research projects, as well as commercial initiatives, have appeared (for an overview of selected projects, see Endres, 2005). However, these initiatives focus mainly on specific, proprietary applications like smart shopping environments and do not incorporate further prospects of using an open approach (for an overview of smart environments in general, see Cook, 2005). Implementing an open approach as proposed in this chapter means, in essence, granting access to mobile smart objects and local smart environments hosted by different service providers, and to information gathered by them. To enable the reuse of smart environments and information gathered by smart objects, a common understanding of their semantics is essential to the recombination and to the creation of new smart applications and services. Accordingly, we propose the creation of an Open Object Information Infrastructure (OOII) as shown in Figure 2, which complies with the requirements to enable Open Innovation. The various components will be explained below.

Building up Smart Environments

The embedding of computers or smallest processors, memory chips, and sensors into physical objects, referred to as smart objects, constitutes a step toward connecting the real with the virtual world. Other examples are sensor networks—smallest sensors introduced into the environment, forming ad-hoc networks in order to recognize, for example, the whereabouts, speed, size, and form of objects and to observe them over a period of time (Culler, 2004). Sensors may perform an important role in the context of managing object information. This is particularly true for the use of sensors which permit a clear identification of smart objects by remote enquiry. With the assistance of Radio Frequency Identification (RFID), objects are identified automatically without line of sight, by transponders which are attached to them (Finkenzeller, 2003).

It has to be taken into account that the information content of sensor data is rather limited. Hence, the data must be gathered and formed into usable events by means of appropriate filter and aggregation procedures. Numerous projects for the development of suitable middleware have already commenced, but focus primarily on integration of sensor data in closed, business-related applications or communication between smart objects (for an overview of selected projects, see Henrickson, 2006 and Schoch, 2005). Most projects, however, ignore the further use of the information in other contexts or by external developers.

Figure 2. The Open Object Information Infrastructure (OOII)

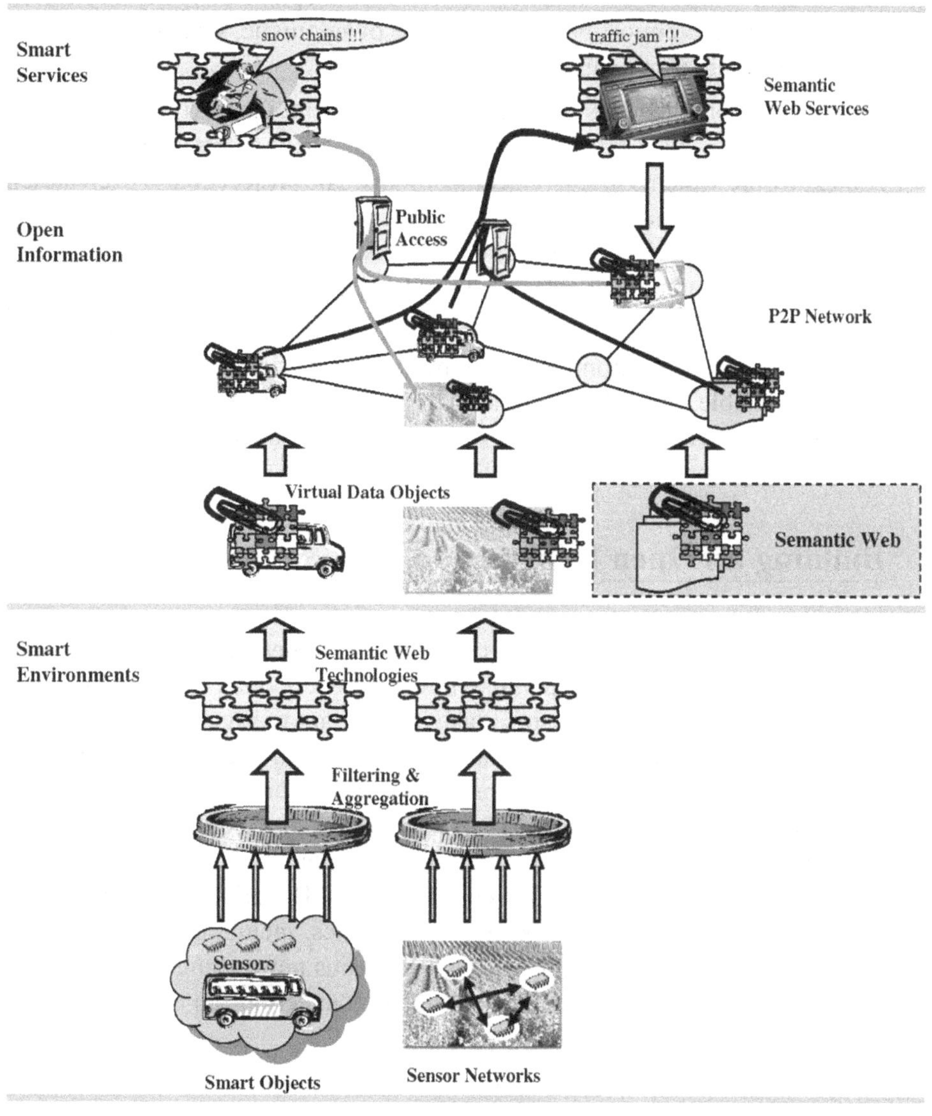

Ensuring the utilization of gathered data for external developers requires extending existing middleware technologies with mechanisms for the semantic markup of sensor data. Semantic Web standards such as Topic Maps (Durusau, 2006; Garshol, 2006; Pepper, 2001;), or RDF(S)/OWL (Brickley, 2004; McGuinness, 2004) can be employed for this purpose. Several middleware technologies have already been extended with mechanisms for the semantic markup of sensor data. SOAM (Smart Object Awareness and Adaptation Model) (Vazquez, 2006) is one initial approach. SOAM is a smart environment reactivity model in which user preferences are formalized using the Standard Ontology for Ubiquitous and Pervasive Applications (SOUPA)(Chen, 2005). These preferences lead to adaptation on smart objects without explicit user intervention, because of the use of automatic, semantic reasoning with respect to the environmental conditions.

An extended version of this ontology is also used by the Context Broker Architecture (CoBrA) (Chen, 2005). This is a broker-centric agent architecture for supporting context-aware systems in smart meeting rooms. The project goal is to create a meeting room that can facilitate typical activities as setting up presentations (allowing users to control services via speech), or adjusting lighting and background music in a room in a manner that is tailored for the specific meeting.

Even if these projects incorporate semantic technologies, they do not consider the reuse of their smart environments within external smart services. Nevertheless, they could be suitable for application within the OOII, as they enable the combination of ubiquitously gathered information with additional semantically-enriched information provided, for example, by the Semantic Web.

Building up Open Information

In developing smart environments, the large number of smart objects must be taken into account. Additionally, the prevailing energy and capacity limitations of embedded computers and sensors make it necessary to save accompanying virtual data objects and to process information on additional network nodes which have sufficient memory capacity and computer power. These prerequisites advise the implementation of peer-to-peer (P2P) networks that offer better scalability and a self-organized and decentralized coordination of unused or limited resources, compared to the alternative client/server architecture (Barkai, 2001; Milojicic, 2002; Oram, 2001; Schoder 2003). Other characteristics, including a higher fault tolerance and a more effective support of spontaneous networking of entities, may be advantageous as well, because no continuous connection can be ensured for smart objects, due to their mobility.

In order to enable Open Innovation, arbitrary access to the stored semantically enriched object information must be ensured for external developers. As the Napster case revealed, central approaches tend to limit access to the information offered or even deny it completely. However, P2P projects like Freenet (Clarke, 2000) and Free Haven (Dingledine, 2000) have demonstrated how an anonymous and censor-free information access can be made possible. Using P2P networks for storing and retrieving semantically enriched information requires an extension of possibilities to pose semantic queries. On the one hand, scientific research is pursuing scheme-based approaches, and, on the other hand, ontologies or P2P Semantic Web services are applied (for an overview of selected projects, see Staab, 2006).

Using semantic query facilities, various developers with different perceptions can search for relevant (object) information, combine the information freely, and, hence, create innovative services (as indicated in Figure 2). For example, information about the speed of vehicles (low speed for a number of cars) combined with their actual location (they are all in a certain area) and additional information (a road map) might indicate that they are stuck in a traffic jam on a highway. This information could then be provided to others as a traffic-information service. In order to facilitate even the reuse of this new smart service, the service has to be specified semantically and published in the OOII. Subsequently, other developers can reuse this service (and the connected smart environments and objects), combine services with information gathered by another local sensor network (the outdoor temperature in a certain area is below zero), and set up a warning system (you are traveling to a snowy area—do not forget your snow chains).

In order to discover and integrate semantically enriched information, a number of semantic web services (Alesso, 2004; Fensel, 2002) and smart agents (Konnerth, 2006; Lee, 2005;) have been developed. However, these projects mainly solve negotiation problems with respect to a common understanding of certain application contexts. The user-oriented framework of Task Computing (Masuoka, 2004) is a promising approach in the context of ubiquitous computing. It uses the Task Computing Environment Object Ontology (TCE, 2004) and is designed to operate dynamic ubiquitous environments in which a mobile computing user dynamically discovers the current set of available semantically defined services (Song, 2004). The end-user can easily and seamlessly integrate and manipulate services found on their own computer, the nearby devices and relevant remote Web services. However, Ben Mokhtar et al. (2006) claim that even this opportunity, or need to select the right composition among all the possible compositions suggested to the user, presents a major drawback of this framework. Accordingly, they developed a COnversation-based service Composition middleware (COCOA) that minimizes the necessary user interaction by enabling the automatic and transparent deployment and execution of user tasks.

Nevertheless, these approaches are limited to the discovery of smart services within smart environments in order to improve user interaction. They do not address global service discovery as needed within our OOII. METEO-S WDSI (Verma, 2005) and GloServ (Arabshian, 2005) are approaches that perform global service discovery through the use of P2P networks. METEO-S WDSI presents a scalable environment for Web service publication and discovery among multiple registries in general. It uses an ontology-based approach to organize registries into domains and enable domain based classification of all Web services. Each of these registries supports semantic publication and the discovery of Web services. GloServ is a global service discovery architecture that can be used to build a distributed context-aware service discovery system related to pervasive computing scenarios (Arabshian, 2006). Currently, we examine which one of these approaches would be applicable within the OOII.

Building Up Smart Services

Based on Open Information, innovative services can be developed. The Federative Library (FedLib) represents one first instantiation of our OOII (see Figure 3) and demonstrates the feasibility of the design. The FedLib is a library service for work groups that functions without the need for collecting books at a centralized location. In fact, the collection is held by the participants themselves. Book owners decide

Figure 3. The Federative Library (FedLib)

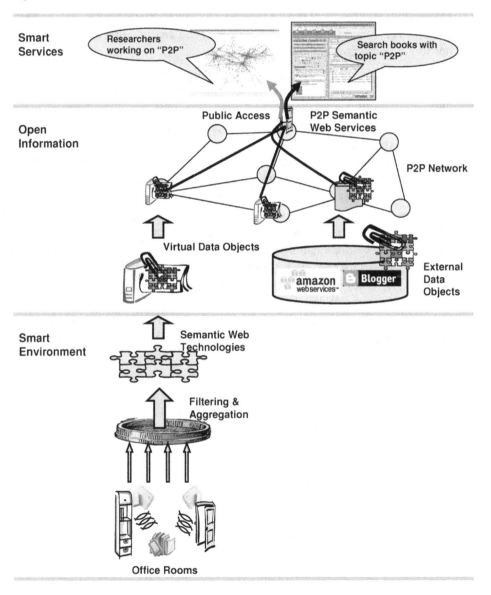

about making their books available for use by others. Thus, originally exclusive private collections of books that are common in organizations could be opened up to other would-be readers.

The pilot implementation of the FebLib will be realized within the Department of Information Systems and Information Management and includes our own office rooms and books, as well as books from the faculty library. We already built up the necessary smart environment and started to extend a reference information manager to the corresponding search-client in order to integrate the smart service into the daily workflow of a research assistant. Besides building up the smart environment, we focus on reviewing existing technology for further use within the FedLib and OOII.

Implementing the smart environment of the FedLib, bookshelves and doors of our office rooms are equipped with RFID readers (see Figure 4). Books labeled with RFID tags are distributed in the participants' offices. In order to enable ubiquitous information gathering about the presence of books, the detection of a book's current location must be combined with former "reads" to corresponding events. For instance, when the system detects a book at the door reader in Office 1, information must be available as to whether the book is leaving or entering the office. It is leaving if the book was previously detected on the bookshelf in Office 1. It is entering if the book was previously located at the door reader in Office 2.

By aggregating these semantically enriched events with additional information about the occupant of each office, the FedLib can track and allocate books automatically in terms of the current borrower. This minimizes administrative overhead, due to the ubiquitous integration of processes in the daily workflow of the research assistants. It therefore becomes possible to borrow books by collecting them directly from a colleague's shelf, taking them to one's own office, and placing them at the table

Figure 4. Smart Office Environment for the FedLib

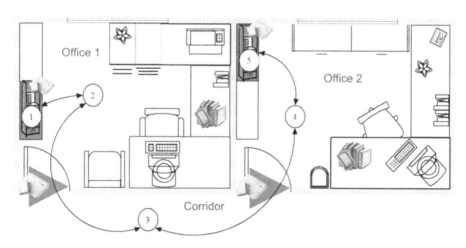

there. In order to return a book, it can simply be put back on one's own bookshelf. During that natural interaction with the Federative Library, the location and status of the book changes according to the events occurring (numbered 1 to 5 in Figure 4). In order to integrate even the management and the retrieval of books into the daily work of a research assistant, the corresponding search-client is integrated in a reference information manager. Furthermore, services like Amazon's Web Service (Levitt, 2005) and special semantically-annotated resources produced by Semblogging (Cayzer, 2004), are suitable for integration into the manager in order to provide additional useful information.

Conclusion

Previous research and the movement towards openness suggest that an opening of information systems may reveal new contingencies for innovation. In order to analyze these contingencies in a world of ubiquitous computing, we applied the framework of ambient business. We showed that opening up smart environments as well as smart services, reveals potentials for innovative services that can be created by external developers. Thus, the innovative strength of companies that act in open systems cannot be achieved by those that rely on rather proprietary information systems. However, most contemporary projects ignore the further use of the information in other contexts or by external developers.

By designing the Open Object Information Infrastructure, we showed how to open up ubiquitous computing systems. Within this infrastructure, information pools that emerge from smart devices are connected by existing Semantic Web standards. This allows developers to search for and combine information they need, create innovative services, and reuse and combine them in an innovative manner. By introducing the first instantiation of the OOII, we demonstrated the feasibility of our design. The Federated Library combines information from decentralized objects and external services to an innovative library services that cannot be realized in closed environments.

However, the open approach is not only applicable from the technological point of view. Economic rationality can argue similarly in favor of opening information systems and thus companies' intangible assets. In some instances, property rights cannot fulfill their aim of fostering innovation, but in fact encumber a further development that builds up on the protected assets. Therefore, in terms of economic and social welfare, the guarantee to freely use innovation as well as the incentive to commercialize innovations has to be perfectly balanced.

Additionally, a cross-border flow of intellectual resources can be beneficial. In high-velocity markets as can be expected in ambient business, the alignment of company resources to the corresponding market becomes critical. In particular, innovation-related resources have to cope with market developments. Opening up the company's borders can be a strategy for acquiring external innovation-related resources and, therefore, a head start in competition with closed innovators.

Future Research Directions

Questions arise regarding the willingness of market players to adopt the idea of Open Innovation. First, open smart environments may infringe privacy. Consequently, we may ask what information a user considers private and in what situations. What information should, therefore, *not* be freely available to service providers? How should laws be formulated in a world in which information is freely exchanged? The first studies have already appeared which analyze the dangers associated with the emergence of ubiquitous computing (Hilty, 2005; Bizer, 2006; BSI, 2006), but they are only the first steps towards answering the core questions.

Likewise, companies must consider which resources and information should be allowed to cross their borders. Sophisticated strategies have to be implemented to ensure the appropriability and, therefore, the return on the innovations. Thus, a manager may ask what products and resources should be opened and to what extent. What are the company's distinct resources that have to be maintained inside the company? What kind of resources can be utilized more effectively outside? Control of the resource transfer must be established.

Furthermore, organizational structures and processes have to be adapted to facilitate the adaptation of external resources, and employees have to be trained to interact with external stakeholders. Moreover, external innovators have to be attracted. When increasingly more companies try to harness users' resources and creative power, how will the users react? Will their attention and time become a limited resource so that companies have to compete for it?

References

Aarts, E., Harwig, R., & Schuurmans, M. (2001). Ambient intelligence. In P. Dennin (Ed.), *The invisible future-the seamless integration of technology in everyday life* (pp. 235-250). New York: McGraw-Hill.

Adams, W., & Brock, J. W. (1982). Integrated monopoly and market power: System selling, compatibility standards, and market control. *Quarterly Review of Economics and Business, 22*(4), 29-42.

Alesso, H., & Smith, C. (2004). *Developing Semantic Web Services*. Natick, MA.: Peters.

Amazon (2007). *Mechanical Turk*. Retrieved on April 10, 2007 from http://www.mturk.com/mturk/help?helpPage=whatis, 2007

Angeles, R. (2005). RFID Technologies: Supply-Chain Applications and Implementation Issues. *Information Systems Management, 22* (1), 51-65.

Anoto (2007). *Anoto Group AB, Lund, Sweden*. Retrieved on April 10, 2007 from http://www.anoto.com/

Arabshian, K., Schulzrinne, H., Trossen, D., & Pavel, D. (2005, June). *Global Service Discovery using the OWL Web Ontology Language*. Paper presented at the International Workshop on Intelligent Environments, Colchester, England.

Arabshian, K., & Schulzrinne, H. (2006). Distributed Context-aware Agent Architecture for Global Service Discovery. In *Proceedings of the 2nd International Workshop on the use of Semantic Web Technologies for Ubiquitous and Mobile Applications* (pp. 17-19).

Barkai, D. (2001). *Peer-to-peer computing. technologies for sharing and collaboration on the net*. (Technical Rep.). Hillsboro: Intel Press.

Barney, J. (1991). Firm Resources and Sustained Competitive Advantage. *Journal of Management, 17* (3), 99-120.

Berners-Lee, T., Hendler, J., & Lassila, O.: The Semantic Web. *Scientific American, 284*(5), 34-43.

Bizer, J., Dingel, K., Fabian, B., Günther, O., Hansen, M., Klafft, M., Möller, J., & Spiekemann, S. (2006). *TAUCIS: Technikfolgen-Abschätzung Ubiquitäres Computing und Informationelle Selbstbestimmung*. Retrieved on April 10, 2007 from https://www.datenschutzzentrum.de/taucis/ita_taucis.pdf

Bohn, J., Coroama, V., Langheinrich, M., Mattern, F., & Rohs, M. (2005). Social, Economic, and Ethical Implications of Ambient Intelligence and Ubiquitous Computing. In W. Weber, J. M. Rabaey, & E. Aarts (Ed.), *Ambient Intelligence* (pp. 5-29). Berlin, Heidelberg : Springer.

Brickley, D., & Guha, R. (2004). RDF Vocabulary Description Language 1.0: RDF Schema, Retrieved on April 10, 2007 from http://www.w3.org/TR/rdf-schema/ 2004

BSI, Federal Office for Information Security (2006). Pervasive Computing: Trends and Impacts. Retrieved on April 10, 2007 from http://www.bsi.bund.de/literat/studien/percenta/Percenta_elay.pdf

Cayzer, S. (2004). Semantic blogging and decentralized knowledge management. *Communications of the ACM, 47*(12), 47-52.

Chen, H., Finin, T., & Joshi, A. (2005). The SOUPA Ontology for Pervasive Computing. In T. Valentina (Ed.), Ontologies for Agents: Theory and Experiences,

Whitestein Series in Software Agent Technologies (pp. 233-258). Basel: Birkhäuser.

Chesbrough, H. (2006). *Open Business Models: How to Thrive in the New Innovation Landscape.* Boston, MA: Harvard Business School.

Ciffolilli, A. (2003). Phantom authority, self-selective recruitment and retention of members in virtual communities: The case of Wikipedia. *First Monday, 8*(12). Retrieved on April 10, 2007 from http://www.firstmonday.org/issues/issue8_12/ciffolilli/index.html, 2003

Clarke, E., Sandberg, O., Wiley, B., & Hong, T. (2000). Freenet: A distributed anonymous information storage and retrieval system. In H. Federrath (Ed.), *Proceedings of the ICSI Workshop on Design Issues in Anonymity and Unobservability.* Berlin: Springer.

Cook, D. J., & Das, S. K. (2005). *Smart Environments: Technology, Protocols, and Applications.* Hoboken, NJ: Wiley.

Coutaz, J., Crowley, J. L., Dobson, S., & Garlan, D. (2005). Context is Key. *Communications of the ACM, 48* (3), 49-53.

Coroama, V. et al. (2003). Leben in einer smarten Umgebung: Ubiquitous-Computing-Szenarien und −Auswirkungen. (Technical Rep. No. 431). *ETH Zurich.* Retrieved on April 10, 2007 from http://www.vs.inf.ethz.ch/publ/papers/szenarien-FINAL.pdf

Culler, D., Estrin, D., & Srivastava, M. (2004). Overview of sensor networks. *Computer, 37*(8), 41-49.

Dingledine, R., Freedman, M., & Molnar, D. (2000). The free haven project: Distributed anonymous storage service. In H. Federrath (Ed.), *Proceedings of the ICSI Workshop on Design Issues in Anonymity and Unobservability.* Berlin: Springer.

Durusau, P., Newcomb, S., & Barta, R. (2006). Topic Maps Reference Model, ISO 13250-5. Retrieved on April 10, 2007 from http://www.isotopicmaps.org/tmrm/

Eisenhardt, K., & Jeffrey, M. A. (2000). Dynamic Capabilities: What are they? *Strategic Management Journal, 21* (10/11), 1105-1121.

Endres, C., Butz, A., & MacWilliams, A. (2005). A Survey of Software Infrastructures and Frameworks for Ubiquitous Computing. *Mobile Information Systems Journal, 1*(1), 41-80.

Fab@Home (2007). *Fab@Home.* Retrieved on April 10, 2007 from http://www.fabathome.org/

Fano, A. & Gersham, A. (2002). The Future of Business Services in the Age of Ubiquitous Computing. *Communications of the ACM, 45* (12), 83-87.

Farrell, J., & Saloner, G. (1985). Standardization, compatibility, and innovation. *RAND Journal of Economics, 16* (1), 70-83.

Fensel, D. (2002). Semantic web enabled web services. In I. Horrocks, J. A. Hendler (Ed.), *Proceedings of the First International Semantic Web Conference on The Semantic Web* (pp. 1-2). London: Springer.

Finkenzeller, K. (2003). *RFID-Handbook*. Chichester, West Sussex : Wiley.

Fleisch, E., & Mattern, F. (2005). *Das Internet der Dinge Ubiquitous Computing und RFID in der Praxis*. Berlin: Springer.

Fleisch, E., & Tellkamp, C. (2006). The business value of ubiquitous computing technologies. In G. Roussos (Ed.), *Ubiquitous and Pervasive Computing New Frontiers for Electronic Business* (pp. 93-114). London: Springer.

Floerkemeier, C., Lampe, M., & Schoch, T. (2003). The Smart Box Concept for Ubiquitous Computing Environments. In *Proceedings of sOc'2003,* Grenoble, (pp. 118-121),

Gabel, H. L. (1987). Open Standards In Computers. In H. L. Gabel (Ed.), *Product Standardization And Competitive Strategy (*pp. 91-123). Amsterdam: Elsevier.

Garshol, L., & Moore, G, (2006). Topic Maps-Data Model. Retrieved on April 10, 2007 from http://www.isotopicmaps.org/sam/sam-model/

Garud, R., & Kumaraswamy, A. (1993). Changing Competitive Dynamics in Network Industries: An exploration of Sun Microsystems' Open Systems Strategy. *Strategic Management Journal, 14* (5), 351-369.

Garud, R., Jain, S., & Kumarswamy, A. (2002). Institutional entrepreneurship in the sponsorship of common technological standards: The case of Sun Microsystems and Java. *Academy of Management Journal, 45*(1), 196-274.

Gellersen, H., Beigl, M. & Krull, H. (1999). The MediaCup: Awareness Technology embedded in an Everyday Object. In H.-W. Gellersen (Ed.), *Proceedings of the Handheld and ubiquitous computing first international symposium, (HUC'99)* (pp. 308-310). Heidelberg: Springer.

Gershenfeld, N. (1999). *When Things Start to Think*. London: Hodder & Stoughton.

Gibson, R., & Schuyler, E. (2006). *Google Maps Hacks*. Sebastopol, CA: O'Reilly.

Hansmann, U. (2003). *Pervasive Computing*. Berlin: Springer.

Henrickson, K., Robinson, R. (in press). A survey of Middleware for Sensor Networks: State-of-the-art and future Directions. *Proceedings of the International Workshop on Middleware for Sensor Networks*.

Hilty, L., Behrendt, S., Binswanger, M., Bruinink, A., Erdmann, L., Fröhlich, J., Köhler, A., Kuster, N., Som, C., & Würtenberger, F. (2005). *The Precautionary Principle in the Information Society.* Retrieved on April 10, 2007 from http://www.ta-swiss.ch/a/info_perv/2005_46e_pervasingcomputing_e.pdf

Innocentive (2007). *Innocentive Inc., Andover, USA.* Retrieved on April 10, 2007 from http://www.innocentive.com

Konnerth, T., Hirsch, B., & Albayrak, S. (2006). Jadl: An agent description language for smart agents. In *Proceedings of Declarative Agent Languages and Technologies* (DALT06).

Lahlou, S., & Jegou, F. (2003). *European Disappearing Computer Privacy Design Guidelines V1.0. Ambient Agoras Report D15.4. Disappearing Computer Initiative.* Retrieved on April 10, 2007, from http://www.ambient-agoras. org/downloads/D15%5B1%5D.4_-_Privacy_Design_Guidelines.pdf

Lee, W. (2005). An intelligent agent for rfid-based home network system. In Yang, L. (Ed.), *EUC 2005, LNCS 3824* (pp. 499-508), Berlin: Springer.

Lerner, J., & Tirole, J. (2002). Some Simple Economics of Open Source. *The Journal of Industrial Economics, 52* (2), 197-234.

Lessig, L. (2002). The Architecture of Innovation. *Duke Law Journal, 51*(6), 1783-1801.

Levitt, J. (2005). *The Web Developer's Guide to Amazon E-Commerce Service: Developing Web Applications Using Amazon Web Services.* Lulu Press.

Maass, W., & Filler, A. (2006). Towards an Infrastructure for Semantically Annotated Physical Products. In C. Hochberger, R. Liskowsky (Ed.), *Proceedings Informatik 2006* (pp. 544). Bonn: Gesellschaft für Informatik.

McGinity, M. (2004). RFID: Is This Game of Tag Fair Play? *Communications of the ACM, 47*(1), 15-18.

Magee, S. P. (1977). Multinational Corporations, the Industry Technology Cycle and Development. *Journal of World Trade Law, 11,* 287-321.

Masuoka, R., Labrou, Y., & Song, Z. (2004). Semantic Web and Ubiquitous Computing-Task Computing as an Example. *AIS SIGSEMIS Bulletin, 1*(3), 21-24.

Mattern, F. (2005). Ubiquitous computing: Scenarios from an informatised world. In A. Axel Zerdick, A. Picot, K. Schrape, J. Burgelman, R. Silverstone, V. Feldmann, C. Wernick, & C. Wolff (Ed.), *E-Merging Media-Communication and the Media Economy of the Future* (pp. 145-163). Berlin: Springer.

McGuinness, D.,& van Harmelen, F. (Ed.) *OWL Web Ontology Language Overview. W3C Recommendation.* Retrieved on April 10, 2007 from http://www. w3.org/TR/owl-features/

Milojicic, D., Kalogeraki, V., Lukose, R., Nagaraja, K., Pruyne, J., Richard, B., Rollins, S., & Xu, Z. (2002) *Peer-to-peer computing.* (Technical Rep), HP Laboratories Palo Alto.

Mokhtar, S. B., Georgantas, N., & Issarny, V. (2006, June). *COCOA: COnversation-based Service COmposition in PervAsive Computing Environments.* Paper presented at the IEEE International Conference on Pervasive Services (ICPS'06), Lyon, France.

Norman, A. D. (1998). *The Invisible Computer.* Cambridge, MA: MIT Press.

Oram, A. (2001) *Peer-to-Peer: Harnessing the Benefits of a Disruptive Technology.* Sebastopol: O'Reilly.

O'Reilly, T. (1999). Lessons from open-source software development. *Communications of the ACM, 42* (4), 32-37.

Penrose, E. T. (1959). *The Theory of the growth of the firm.* Oxford: Blackwell.

Pepper, S., & Moore, G. (2001) *XML Topic Maps (XTM) 1.0.* Retrieved on April 10, 2007 from http://www.topicmaps.org/xtm/

Perens, B. (2006). *Open Standards Principles and Practice.* Retrieved on April 10, 2007 from http://perens.com/OpenStandards/Definition.html

Pinhanez, C., & Pingali, G. (2004). Projector-camera systems for telepresence. In G. Pingali, F. Nack, H. Sundaram (Ed.), *Proceedings of the 2004 ACM SIGMM workshop on Effective telepresence* (pp. 63-66). New York, NY: ACM Press.

Piper, B., Ratti, C., & Ishii, H. (2002). Hands-On Interfaces: Illuminating Clay: a 3-D tangible interface for landscape analysis. In Wixon, D. (Ed.), *Proceedings of the SIGCHI conference on Human factors in computing systems: Changing our world, changing ourselves* (pp. 355-363). New York, NY: ACM Press.

Reichwald, R., & Piller, F. (2006). *Interaktive Wertschöpfung: Open Innovation, Individualisierung und neue Formen der Arbeitsteilung.* Wiesbaden: Gabler.

Rivette, K. G.,& Kline, D. (2000). *Rembrandts in the attic.* Boston, MA.: Harvard Business School Press.

Roush, W. (2005). Killer Maps. *Technology Review, 108* (10), 54-60.

Roussos, G. (2006). Ubiquitous computing for electronic business. In G. Roussos (Ed.), *Ubiquitous and Pervasive Computing: New Frontiers for Electronic Business* (pp. 1-12). London, Springer, 2006.

Saltzer, J. H., Reed, D. P., & Clark, D. D. (1984). End-to-end arguments in system design. *ACM Transactions on Computer Systems, 2* (4), 277-288.

Sakkab, N. Y. (2002). Connect & Develop Complements Research & Development at P&G. *Research-Technology Management, 45*(2), 38-45.

Schoch, T. (2005). Middleware für Ubiquitous-Computing-Anwendungen. In E. Fleisch, F. Mattern (Ed.), *Das Internet der Dinge Ubiquitous Computing und RFID in der Praxis* (pp. 119-140). Berlin: Springer.

Schoder, D., & Vollmann, C. (2003). Value Scope Management-Beherrschung der Wertschöpfungskette im M-Commerce am Beispiel ''i-mode''. *Mobile Commerce : Gewinnpotenziale einer stillen Revolution* (pp. 125-143). Berlin: Springer.

Sharlin, E., Watson, B., Kitamura, Y., Kishino, F., & Itoh, Y (2004). On tangible user interfaces, humans and spatiality. *Personal and Ubiquitous Computing, 8*(5), 338-346.

Song, Z., Labrou, Y., & Masuoka, R. (2004). Dynamic Service Discovery and Management in Task Computing. In *MobiQuitous 2004* (pp. 310-318). Boston: IEEE.

Staab, S., & Stuckenschmidt, H. (2006). *Semantic Web and Peer-to-Peer*. Berlin: Springer.

Stallman, R. (1999). The GNU Operating System and the Free Software Movement. In C. Di Bona (Ed.), *Open sources: voices from the open source revolution*. Sebastapol, CA: O'Reilly.

Strasser, M., Plenge, C., & Stroh, S. (2005). Potenziale der RFID-Technologie für das Supply Chain Management in der Automobilindustrie. In. E. Fleisch, F. Mattern (Ed.), *Das Internet der Dinge Ubiquitous Computing und RFID in der Praxis* (pp. 177-196). Berlin: Springer.

Thackara, J. (2001). The design challenge of pervasive computing. *Interactions, 8*(3), 46–52.

TCE, Task Computing Environment Object Ontology (2004). Retrieved on April 10, 2007 from http://www.flacp.fujitsulabs.com/tce/ontologies/2004/03/object.owl

Teece, D. J. (1986). Profiting from technological innovation: Implications for integration, collaboration, licensing and public policy. *Research Policy, 15* (6), 285-305.

Teece, D. J., Pisan, G., & Shuen, A. (1997). Dynamic Capabilities and Strategic Management. *Strategic Management Journal, 18* (7), 509-533.

Tennenhouse, D. (2000). Proactive computing. *Communications of the ACM 43*(5), 43-50.

Thomke, S., & von Hippel, E. (2002). Customers as Innovators: A New Way to Create Value. *Harvard Business Review, 80* (4), 74-81.

Thomke, S. (2003). *Experimentation Matters: Unlocking the Potential of New Technologies for Innovation.* Boston, MA: Harvard Business School Press.

Van Dam, A. (2001). User interfaces: Disappearing, dissolving, and evolving. *Communications of the ACM, 44*(3), 50-52.

Vazquez, J. Delpiña, D. & Sedans, I. (2006). SoaM: An envisonment adaption model for pervasive Semantic Web. (LNCS 3983, 108-117.

Verma, K., Sivashanmugam, K., Sheth, A., Patil, A., Oundhakar, S., & Miller, J. (2005). METEOR-S WSDI: A Scalable Infrastructure of Registries for Semantic Publication and Discovery of Web Services. *Journal of Information Technology and Management, Special Issue on Universal Global Integration, 6*(1), 17-39.

Von Ahn, L. (2006). Games with a Purpose. *IEEE Computer, 39*(6), 92-94.

Von Hippel, E. (1994). "Sticky Information" and the Locus of Problem Solving: Implications for Innovation. *Management Science, 40*(4), 429-439.

Von Hippel, E., & Katz, R. (2002). Shifting Innovation to Users via Toolkits. *Management Science, 48*(7), 821-833.

Von Hippel, E. (2005). *Democratizing Innovation.* Cambridge, MA: MIT Press.

Wales, J. (2005). Internet encyclopaedias go head to head. *Nature 438*(15), 900-901.

Want, R., Schilit, B., Adams, N., Gold, R., Petersen, K., Ellis, J., Goldberg, D., & Weiser, M. (1995). *The PARCTAB ubiquitous computing experiment* (Technical Rep. No. CSL-95-1). Palo Alto, CA: Xerox Palo Alto Research Center.

Want, R., Borriello, G., Pering, T., & Farkas, K. I. (2002). Disappearing Hardware. *IEEE Pervasive Computing 1*(1), 36-47.

Watson, R. T., Pitt, L. F., Berthon, P., & Zinkhan, G. M. (2002). U-Commerce: Expanding the Universe of Marketing. *Journal of the Academy of Marketing Science, 30*(4), 333-347.

Weiser, M. (1991). The computer of the 21st century. *Scientific American, 256*(3), 94-104.

Wernerfelt, B. (1984). A Resource-based View of the Firm. *Strategic Management Journal, 5*(2), 171-180.

West, J. (2003). How open is open enough? Melding proprietary and open source platform strategies. *Research Policy, 32*(7), 1259-1285.

West, J. (2004, May). *What are Open Standards? Implications for Adoption, Competition and Policy.* Paper presented at the Standards and Public Policy Conference, Chicago, Illinois.

Wiley, D (1999). Open Content. Open Publication License. Retrieved on April 10, 2007 from http://www.opencontent.org/openpub/

Additional Reading

Aarts, E., Harwig, R., & Schuurmans, M. (2001). Ambient intelligence. In P. Dennin (Ed.), *The invisible future-the seamless integration of technology in everyday life* (pp. 235-250). New York ;London: McGraw-Hill.

Benkler, Y. (2006). *The Wealth of Networks: How Social Production Transforms Markets* and *Freedom*. New Haven, CT.: Yale Univ. Press.

Chesbrough, H. (2006). *Open Business Models: How to Thrive in the New Innovation Landscape*. Boston, MA: Harvard Business School.

Chesbrough, H. W., Vanhaverbeke, W., & West, J. (2006). *Open innovation: researching a new paradigm.* Oxford: Oxford University Press.

Fano, A., & Gersham, A. (2002). The Future of Business Services in the Age of Ubiquitous Computing. *Communications of the ACM, 45* (12), 83-87.

Fleisch, E., & Mattern, F. (2005). *Das Internet der Dinge Ubiquitous Computing und RFID in der Praxis*. Berlin: Springer.

Fleisch, E., & Tellkamp, C. (2006). The business value of ubiquitous computing technologies. In G. Roussos (Ed.), *Ubiquitous and Pervasive Computing New Frontiers for Electronic Business* (pp. 93-114). London: Springer.

Gershenfeld, N., Krikorian, R. & Cohen, D. (2004). The internet of things. *Scientific American*, 291(4), 76-81.

Lessig, L. (2002). The Architecture of Innovation. *Duke Law Journal, 51*(6), 1783-1801.

Mattern, F. (2005). Ubiquitous computing: Scenarios from an informatised world. In A. Axel Zerdick, A. Picot, K. Schrape, J. Burgelman, R. Silverstone, V. Feldmann, C. Wernick, & C. Wolff (Ed.), *E-Merging Media-Communication and the Media Economy of the Future* (pp. 145-163). Berlin: Springer.

Reichwald, R., & Piller, F. (2006). *Interaktive Wertschöpfung: Open Innovation, Individualisierung und neue Formen der Arbeitsteilung*. Wiesbaden: Gabler.

Thomke, S., & von Hippel, E. (2002). Customers as Innovators: A New Way to Create Value. *Harvard Business Review, 80* (4), 74-81.

Von Hippel, E. (2005). *Democratizing Innovation*. Cambridge, MA: MIT Press.

West, J. (2003). How open is open enough? Melding proprietary and open source platform strategies. *Research Policy, 32*(7), 1259-1285.

Chapter XI

Activity-Oriented Computing

João Pedro Sousa, George Mason University, USA

Bradley Schmerl, Carnegie Mellon University, USA

Peter Steenkiste, Carnegie Mellon University, USA

David Garlan, Carnegie Mellon University, USA

Abstract

This chapter introduces a new way of thinking about software systems for supporting the activities of end-users. In this approach, models of user activities are promoted to first class entities, and software systems are assembled and configured dynamically based on activity models. This constitutes a fundamental change of perspective over traditional applications; activities take the main stage and may be long-lived, whereas the agents that carry them out are plentiful and interchangeable. The core of the chapter describes a closed-loop control design that enables activity-oriented systems to become self-aware and self-configurable, and to adapt to dynamic changes both in the requirements of user activities and in the environment resources. The chapter discusses how that design addresses challenges such as user mobility, resolving conflicts in accessing scarce resources, and robustness in the broad sense of responding adequately to user expectations, even in unpredictable situations, such as random failures, erroneous user input, and continuously changing resources. The chapter further summarizes challenges and ongoing work related to managing activities where humans and automated agents collaborate, human-computer interactions for managing activities, and privacy and security aspects.

Introduction

Over the past few years, considerable effort has been put into developing networking and middleware infrastructures for ubiquitous computing, as well as in novel human-computer interfaces based on speech, vision, and gesture. These efforts tackle ubiquitous computing from two different perspectives—systems research and HCI research—hoping to converge and result in software that can support a rich variety of successful ubiquitous computing applications. However, although examples of successful applications exist, a good understanding of frameworks for designing ubiquitous computing applications is still largely missing.

A key reason for the lack of a broadly applicable framework is that many research efforts are based on an obsolete application model. This model assumes that ubiquitous computing applications can support user activities by packaging, at design time, a set of related functionalities within a specific domain, such as spatial navigation, finding information on the Web, or online chatting. However, user **activities** may require much diverse functionality, often spanning different domains. Which functionalities are required to support an activity can only be determined at runtime, depending on the user needs, and may need to evolve in response to changes in those needs. Examples of user activities targeted by ubiquitous computing are navigating spaces such as museums, assisting debilitated people in their daily living, activities at the office such as producing reports, as well as activities in the home such as watching a TV show, answering the doorbell, or enhancing house security.

This chapter introduces activity-oriented computing (AoC) as a basis for developing more comprehensive and dynamic applications for ubiquitous computing. Activity-oriented computing brings user activities to the foreground by promoting models of such activities to first class primitives in computing systems.

In the remainder of this chapter, the section on background presents our vision for activity-oriented computing and compares it with related work. Next we discuss the main challenges of this approach to ubiquitous computing. Specifically, we discuss user mobility (as opposed to mobile computing), conflict resolution and robustness, mixed-initiative control, human-computer interaction, and security and privacy.

The main body of the chapter presents our work towards a solution. Specifically, we discuss software architectures for activity-oriented computing and how to address the challenges of mobility and robustness, as well as the options to model user activities. The chapter ends with a discussion of future directions concerning human-computer interactions, and the tradeoff between ubiquity and security and privacy.

Background

The vision of AoC is to make the computing environment aware of *user activities* so that resources can be autonomously managed to optimally assist the user. Activities are everyday actions that users wish to accomplish and that may be assisted in various ways by computing resources in the environment. Done right, AoC will allow users to focus on pursuing their activities rather than on configuring and managing the computing environment. For example, an AoC system could reduce overhead by automatically customizing the environment each time the user wishes to resume a previously interrupted long-lived activity, such as preparing a monthly report, or organizing a party.

To help make this vision concrete, the following examples illustrate possible applications of AoC:

- **Elderly care:** Rather than relying on hardcoded solutions, AoC enables domain experts such as doctors and nurses to "write prescriptions" for the activities of monitoring the health of the elderly or outpatients. Such descriptions enable smart homes to take charge of those activities, collaborating with humans as appropriate. For example, the heart rate of an elderly person may be monitored by a smart home, which takes responsibility to alert family members when alarming measurements are detected. Who gets alerted and the media to convey the alert may depend on contextual rules, such as the seriousness of the situation, as prescribed by the doctor; the elder's preferences of who to contact, who is available, who is closer to the elder's home, whether sending an SMS appropriate, and so forth.

- **Entertainment:** While others have explored the vision that music, radio, or television can follow occupants as they move through the house, activity-oriented computing enables a more general approach. Entertainment can be defined as an activity, allowing preferences and constraints to be specified, and underlying **services** to be shared, such as tracking people, identifying and using devices in various rooms. For example, the same location services used for home security activities can be used for entertainment; the television that can be used for entertainment can also be used for displaying images of a visitor at the front door.

- **Home Security:** Many homes have a security system that uses sensors to detect burglary attempts and fires. They are standalone systems with limited capabilities; for example the system is typically either on or off and control is entirely based on a secret code. If the security system were built as an activity service, it could be an open system with richer functionality. For example:

  o   A richer set of control options, for example, based on fingerprint readers or voice recognition. These methods may be more appropriate for children or the elderly.

  o   More flexibility (e.g., giving neighbors limited access to water the plants when the homeowners are on vacation, the ability to control and interact with the system remotely, or incorporate cameras that ignore dogs).

  o   Remote diagnosis, for example, in response to an alarm, police or fire responders may be able to quickly check for false alarms through cameras.

- **Doorbell:** A very simple activity is responding to somebody ringing the doorbell. Today's solution is broadcast; the doorbell is loud enough to alert everybody in the house and then people decide independently or after coordination (through shouting!) how to respond. In activity-oriented computing, a doorbell activity carried out by the hallway selects a person, based on their current location, current activity, and age. If the visitor can be identified, it might be possible to have the person who is being visited respond. Also, the method of alerting the person can be customized, for example, using a (local) sound, displaying a message on the television screen, or flashing the lights. Finally, if nobody is home, the doorbell service can take a voice message or, if needed, establish a voice or video link to a house occupant who might be available in their office or car. Activities such as answering the phone could be handled in a similar way, that is replace the broadcast ringing by a targeted, context-aware alert.

What is Activity-Oriented Computing

Activity-oriented computing adopts a fundamental change of perspective over traditional applications in that **activities** take the main stage and may be long-lived, whereas the agents that carry them out are plentiful and interchangeable; how activities are best supported will evolve over time, depending on the user's needs and context. In AoC, activities are explicitly represented and manipulated by the computing infrastructure. Broadly speaking, this has two significant advantages.

First, it enables explicit reasoning about user **activities**: which activities a user may want to carry out in a particular context; what functionality (**services**) is required to support an activity; what are the user preferences relative to quality of service for each different activity; which activities conflict; which have specific privacy or security concerns, and so forth.

Second, it enables reasoning about the optimal way of supporting activities, through the dynamic selection of service suppliers (agents) that implement specific functions relevant to the activity. Thanks to the explicit modeling of the requirements of activities and of the capabilities of agents, the optimality of such assignment may be addressed by quantitative frameworks such as **utility** theory. Also, by raising the level of abstraction above particular applications or implementations, activity models make it easier to target a broad range of concrete implementations of similar services in different devices, in contrast to solutions based on mobile code (more in the Challenges section, below).

Related Work

Early work in ubiquitous computing focused on making certain applications ubiquitously available. For that, it explored OS-level support that included location sensing components to automatically transfer user interfaces to the nearest display. Examples of this are the work on teleporting X Windows desktops (Richardson, Bennet, Mapp, & Hopper, 1994) and Microsoft's Easy Living project (Brumitt, Meyers, Krumm, Kern, & Shafer, 2000). This idea was coupled with the idea of desktop management to treat users' tasks as sets of applications independent of a particular device. Examples of systems that exploit this idea are the Kimura project (MacIntyre et al., 2001), which migrates collections of applications across displays within a smart room, and earlier work in aura that targets migration of user tasks across machines at different locations (Wang & Garlan, 2000). Internet Suspend-Resume (ISR) requires minimal changes to the operating system to migrate the entire virtual memory of one machine to another machine (Kozuch & Satyanarayanan, 2002). These approaches focus on making applications available ubiquitously, but do not have a notion of user activity that encompasses user needs and preferences, and therefore do not scale to environments with heterogeneous machines and varying levels of service.

More recent work seeks to support cooperative tasks in office-like domains, for example ICrafter (Ponnekanti, Lee, Fox, & Hanrahan, 2001) and Gaia (Román et al., 2002); as well as domain-specific tasks, such as healthcare (Christensen & Bardram, 2002) and biology experiments, for example, Labscape (Arnstein, Sigurdsson, & Franza, 2001). This research shares with ours the goal of supporting activities for mobile users, where activities may involve several services in the environment, and environments may contain heterogeneous devices. However, much of this work is predicated on rebuilding, or significantly extending, operating systems and applications to work over custom-built infrastructures. In contrast the work described in this chapter supports user activities with a new software layer on top of existing operating systems, and accommodates integration of legacy applications.

Focusing on being able to suspend and resume existing activities in a ubiquitous environment does not go all the way toward the vision of providing ubiquitous assistance for user activities. Such support can be divided into two categories: 1) helping to guide users in conducting tasks; and 2) performing tasks, or parts of tasks, on behalf of users. An early example of the first category is the Adtranz system (Siewiorek, 1998), which guides technical staff through diagnosing problems in a train system. More recent work concentrates on daily life, often for people with special needs, such as the elderly, or those with debilitated health (Abowd, Bobick, Essa, Mynatt, & Rogers, 2002; Intille, 2002).

Research on automated agents takes assistance one step further by enabling systems to carry out activities on behalf of users. Examples of this are the RETSINA framework (Sycara, Paolucci, Velsen, & Giampapa, 2003), with applications in domains such as financial portfolio management, e-commerce and military logistics; and more recently the RADAR project (Garlan & Schmerl, 2007), which focuses on the office domain, automating such tasks as processing e-mail, scheduling meetings, and updating Web sites.

Consumer solutions for activities in the home are beginning to emerge, mainly from the increasing complexity of configuring home theater equipment. Universal remote controls, such as those provided by Logitech, allow users to define activities such as "Watch DVD," which choose the input source for the television, output of sound through the home theater system, and choosing the configuration of the DVD player (Logitech). However, in these solutions, activities are bound to particular device and device configurations—the activities themselves must be redefined for different equipment, and it is not possible for the activities to move around different rooms in the home, or to allow different levels of service for the same activity.

In this chapter, we discuss the potential and the challenges of having software systems using activity models at runtime. Specifically, we focus on the benefits of using activity models for enabling users to access their activities ubiquitously, and for delegating responsibility for activities to automated agents.

Challenges

Activity-oriented computing raises a number of challenges that must be addressed by any adequate supporting infrastructure and architecture.

- **User mobility:** As users move from one environment to another—for example, between rooms in a house—activities may need to migrate with the users, tracking their location and adapting themselves to the local situation. A key distinction between user mobility in AoC and previous approaches is that no assumptions are made with respect to the users having to carry mobile devices, or to the availability of a particular kind of platform at every location. Since different environments may have very different resources (devices, services, interfaces, etc.) a critical issue is how best to retarget an activity to a new situation. For example, an activity that involves "watching a TV show" can be changed into "listening" when the user walks through a room that only offers audio support. Solving this problem requires the ability to take advantage of context information (location, resource availability, user state, etc.), as well as knowledge of the activity requirements (which services are required, fidelity tradeoffs, etc.) to provide an optimal use of the environment in support of the activity.

- **Conflict resolution:** Complicating the problem of automated configuration and reconfiguration is the need to support multiple activities—both for a single user and between multiple users. If an individual wants to carry out two activities concurrently that may need to use shared resources, how should these activities simultaneously be supported? For example, if the user is engaged in entertainment, should the doorbell activity interrupt that activity? Similar problems exist when two or more people share an environment. For example, if two users enter the living room hoping to be entertained, but having different ideas of what kind of entertainment they want, how can those conflicts be reconciled? Solving this problem requires (a) the ability to detect when there may be conflicts, and (b) the ability to apply conflict resolution policies, which may itself require user interaction.

- **Mixed-initiative control:** The ability to accomplish certain kinds of activities requires the active participation of users. For example, the door answering activity, which might be associated with a house, requires occupants of the house to respond to requests from the house to greet a visitor. Since humans exhibit considerably more autonomy and unpredictability than computational elements, it is not clear how one should write the activity control policies and mechanisms to allow for this. Standard solutions to human-based activities (such as work-flow management systems) are likely not to be effective, since they assume users will adhere to predetermined plans to a much higher degree than is typically the case in the kinds of domains targeted by ubiquitous computing.

- **Security and privacy:** Some security and privacy issues can be solved through traditional mechanisms for security, but others are complicated by key features of ubiquity; they include rich context information, and user mobility across public or shared spaces such as a car, or an airport lounge. In a multi-user environment with rich sources of context information (such as a person's location), an important issue is how to permit appropriate access to and sharing of that information. Furthermore, which guarantees can be made to a user that wishes to access personal activities in a shared space? What mechanisms can back such guarantees? Are there deeper issues than the exposure of the information that is accessed in a public space? Is it possible that all of a user's information and identity may be compromised as a consequence of a seemingly innocuous access at a public space?

- **Human-computer interaction:** Many of the activities that a ubiquitous computing environment should support will take place outside of standard computing environment (such as a networked office environment). In such environments, one cannot assume that users will have access to standard displays, keyboards, and pointing devices. How then can the system communicate and interact with users effectively? What should be the role of emerging technologies such as augmented reality and natural interaction modalities such as speech, gesture, and ambient properties such as light and smell?

While the challenges above stem from the problem domain, we now turn to the challenges associated with building a solution for AoC.

- **Activity models.** The first challenge is to define what kinds of knowledge should be imparted in systems to make them aware of user activities. Specifically, what should be the contents and form of activity models? What should be the semantic primitives to compose and decompose activities? At what level of sophistication should activity models be captured? Presumably, the more sophisticated the models, the more a system can do to assist users. For example, to help users with repairing an airplane or with planning a conference, a significant amount of domain knowledge needs to be captured. But obviously, capturing such knowledge demands more from users (or domain experts) than capturing simple models of activities. Is there an optimal level of sophistication to capture activity models—a sweet spot that maximizes the ratio between the benefits of imparting knowledge to systems and the costs of eliciting such knowledge from users? Or is it possible to have flexible solutions that allow incremental levels of sophistication for representing each activity, depending on the expected benefits and on the user's willingness to train the system?

- **System design.** Systems that support AoC should be capable of dynamic reconfiguration in response to changes in the needs of user activities. Ideally, such systems would also be aware of the availability of resources in the environment and respond to changes in those. The questions then become: What is an appropriate architecture to support activity-oriented computing? What responsibilities should be taken by a common infrastructure (middleware) and which should be activity- or service-specific? What are the relevant parameters to guide service discovery (location, quality of service, etc.) and how should discovery be geographically scoped and coordinated? Can activity models be capitalized to handle the heterogeneity of the environment, self-awareness and dynamic adaptation? Furthermore, what operations might be used to manage activities: suspend and resume, delegate, collaborate, others? What should be the operational semantics of each of these operations?

- **Robustness.** In AoC, robustness is taken in the broad sense of responding adequately to user expectations, even in unpredictable situations, such as random failures, erroneous user input, and continuously changing resources. First of all, should adequacy be a Boolean variable—either the system is adequate or it is not—or can it be quantified and measured? Specifically, are there system capabilities and configurations that are more adequate than others to support a user's activity? If so, can measures of adequacy be used to choose among alternatives in rich environments? For example, is the user better served by carrying out a video conference on a PDA over a wireless link, or on the wall display down the hall?

Towards a Solution

To address the challenges identified above, we decided to start with relatively simple models of activities and address concrete problems where the advantages of AoC could be demonstrated. This section summarizes our experience of about six years at Carnegie Mellon University's project **aura**. Initially, this research targeted the smart office domain, and later extended to the smart home domain (more below).

Designing systems for AoC brings up some hard questions. What makes those questions especially challenging, is that to answer them, we need to reexamine a significant number of assumptions that have been made about software for decades. Not surprisingly, our own understanding of how to answer those questions continues to evolve. This section is organized around the set of solution-related challenges identified above; namely, system design, activity models, and robustness.

System Design

The first research problem we focused on, starting around the year 2000, was user mobility in the smart office domain. Here, activities (or tasks) typically involve several applications and information assets. For instance, for preparing a presentation, a user may edit slides, refer to a couple of papers on the topic, check previous related presentations, and browse the web for new developments. An example of user mobility is that the user may start working on the presentation at his or her office, continue at the office of a collaborator, and pick the task up later at home.

The premise adopted for user mobility is that users should not have to carry a machine around, just as people normally don't carry their own chairs everywhere. If they so desire, users should be able to resume their tasks, on demand, with whatever computing systems are available. This premise is neither incompatible with users carrying mobile devices, nor with mobile code. Ideally, the capabilities of any devices or code that travel with the user contribute to the richness of the environment surrounding the user, and therefore contribute to a better user experience. A discussion of why solutions centered on mobile devices, mobile code, or remote computing (such as PC Anywhere) are not entirely satisfactory to address user mobility can be found in (J.P. Sousa, 2005).

Designing a solution to support user mobility is made harder by the heterogeneity of devices where users may want to resume their activities, and by dynamic variations in the resources and devices available to the user. Even in a fairly restricted office domain, it is common to find different operating systems, offering different suites of applications (e.g., Linux vs. PC vs. Mac). In a broader context, users may want to carry over their activities to devices with a wide range of capabilities, from handhelds to smart rooms. In addition to heterogeneity, mobile devices are subject to wide variations of resources, such as battery and bandwidth. Ideally, software would automatically manage alternative computing strategies based on user requirements and on the availability of resources. Moreover, in heavily networked

Table 1. Terminology

task	An everyday activity such as preparing a presentation or writing a report. Carrying out a task may require obtaining several *services* from an *environment*, as well as accessing several *materials*.
environment	The set of *suppliers*, *materials* and *resources* accessible to a user at a particular location.
service	Either (a) a service type, such as printing, or (b) the occurrence of a service proper, such as printing a given document. For simplicity, we will let these meanings be inferred from context.
supplier	An application or device offering *services* – for example, a printer.
material	An information asset such as a file or data stream.
capabilities	The set of *services* offered by a *supplier*, or by a whole *environment*.
resources	Are consumed by *suppliers* while providing *services*. Examples are: CPU cycles, memory, battery, bandwidth, and so forth.
context	Set of human-perceived attributes such as physical location, physical activity (sitting, walking...), or social activity (alone, giving a talk...).
user-perceived state of a task	User-observable set of properties in the *environment* that characterize the support for the task. Specifically, the set of *services* supporting the task, the user-level settings (preferences, options) associated with each of those services, the *materials* being worked on, user-interaction parameters (window size, cursors...), and the user's preferences with respect to quality of service tradeoffs.

Table 2. Summary of the software layers in aura

layer	mission	roles
Task Management	*what* does the user need	monitor tasks, contexts and preferences
		map tasks to needs for services in an environment
		for complex tasks: decomposition, plans, context dependencies
Environment Management	*how* to best configure the environment	monitor environment capabilities and resources
		map service needs and user-level state of tasks to available suppliers
		ongoing optimization of the utility of the environment relative to user task
Env.	support the user tasks	monitor relevant resources
		fine grain management of QoS/resource tradeoffs

environments, remote servers may constantly change their response times and even availability. Ideally, users should be shielded as much as possible from dealing with such dynamic variations.

Before describing an architecture for supporting user mobility as outlined above, Table 1 clarifies the terminology used throughout this chapter, since although the terms are in common use, their interpretation is far from universal.

Our starting point for supporting user mobility was to design an infrastructure, the **aura** infrastructure, that exploits knowledge about a user's tasks to automatically configure and reconfigure the environment on behalf of the user. Aura is best explained by a layered view of its infrastructure together with an explanation of the roles of each layer with respect to task suspend-resume and dynamic **adaptation**.

First, the infrastructure needs to know *what* to configure for; that is, what a user needs from the environment in order to carry out his or her tasks. Second, the infrastructure needs to know *how* to best configure the environment; it needs mechanisms to optimally match the user's needs to the capabilities and resources in the environment.

In our architecture, each of these two sub-problems is addressed by a distinct software layer: (1) the *Task Management* layer determines *what* the user needs from the environment at a specific time and location; and (2) the *Environment Management* layer determines *how* to best configure the environment to support the user's needs.

Table 2 summarizes the roles of the software layers in the infrastructure. The top layer, *task management* (TM), captures knowledge about user needs and preferences for each activity. Such knowledge is used to coordinate the configuration of the environment upon changes in the user's task or context. For instance, when the user attempts to carry out a task in a new environment, TM coordinates access to all the information related to the user's task, and negotiates task support with environment management (EM). Task Management also monitors explicit indications from the user and events in the physical context surrounding the user. Upon getting indication that the user intends to suspend the current task or resume some other task, TM coordinates saving the user-perceived state of the suspended task and recovers the state of the resumed task, as appropriate.

The *EM layer* maintains abstract models of the environment. These models provide a level of indirection between the user's needs, expressed in environment-independent terms, and the concrete capabilities of each environment.

This indirection is used to address both heterogeneity and dynamic change in the environments. With respect to heterogeneity, when the user needs a service, such as speech recognition, EM will find and configure a supplier for that service among those available in the environment. With respect to dynamic change, the existence of explicit models of the capabilities in the environment enables automatic reasoning when those capabilities change dynamically. The Environment Management adjusts such a mapping automatically in response to changes in the user's needs (adaptation initiated by TM), and changes in the environment's capabilities and resources (adaptation initiated by EM). In both cases adaptation is guided by the maximization of a **utility function** representing the user's preferences (more in the section on Robustness, below).

The *environment layer* comprises the applications and devices that can be configured to support a user's task. Configuration issues aside, these suppliers interact with the user exactly as they would without the presence of the infrastructure. The infrastructure steps in only to automatically configure those suppliers on behalf of the user. The specific capabilities of each supplier are manipulated by EM, which acts as a translator for the environment-independent descriptions of user needs issued by TM. Typically, suppliers are developed by wrapping existing applications. Our experience in wrapping over a dozen applications native to Windows and Linux has shown that it is relatively easy to support setting and retrieving the user-perceived state (Balan, Sousa, & Satyanarayanan, 2003; J.P. Sousa, 2005).

This layering offers a clean separation of concerns between what pertains to user activities and what pertains to the environment. The knowledge about user activities is held by the TM and travels with the user to each environment in which he or she wishes to carry out activities. The knowledge about the environment stays with the EM and can be used to address the needs of many users.

A significant distinction of this approach to user mobility is that it does not require code or devices to travel with the user. A generic piece of code, Prism, in the TM layer *becomes* an **aura** for a user by loading models of user activities. Those models are encoded in XML for convenience of mobility across heterogeneous devices (more in the section on Activity Models, below).

Extending to the Home Environment

Although the layered perspective played an important role in clarifying the separation of concerns and protocols of interaction, it captures only the case where users consume services, and software components provide them.

In the smart home domain, software could take responsibility for activities, and users might be asked to contribute services for those activities. For example, a smart home might take charge of the home's security and ask a human to lock the windows when night falls. Other examples of activities include a user watching a TV show, a user checking on a remote family member, the main hallway facilitating answering the door, and the home keeping a comfortable temperature. These examples prompted us to realize that any domain entity could have an aura, and that an aura might find itself on either the supplying or the consuming side, or both. Specifically, **auras** can be associated with:

- People including individual residents, or groups, such as a resident's parents, or the entire family.

- Spaces, such as the main hallway, living room or the entire home. Spaces of interest are not necessarily disjoint.

- Appliances, such as a TV, phone, table or couch. Appliances have a well-defined purpose and may have a range of automation levels, from fairly sophisticated (a smart refrigerator), to not automated at all (an old couch).

- Software applications, such as a media player, a video conferencing app, or a people locator. Applications run on general purpose devices, and which applications are available on one such device define the purpose that the device may serve.

Figure 1 shows the run-time architectural framework for an activity-oriented system. The boxes correspond to types of components, and the lines to possible connectors between instances of those types.[1] Part (a) shows our initial understanding based on the smart office domain, and part (b) shows the more general framework. Contrasting the two, it is now clear that the TM corresponded to an aura (of users) that consumed services but supplied none; and suppliers corresponded to auras of software that supplied services, but consumed none.

In the new architectural framework, when an aura boots up, it first locates the EM (see the section on Service Discovery, below) and then may engage on the service

Figure 1. Architectural framework

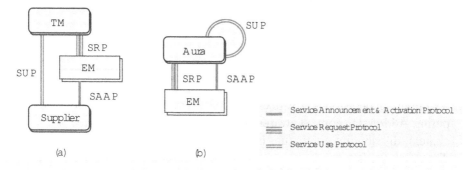

Figure 2. Snapshot of the architecture of one system

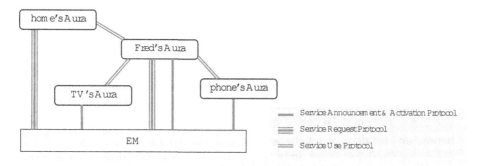

announcement & activation protocol (SAAP) to announce any services that its entity provides, as well as on the service request protocol (SRP) to discover services that are relevant to support the entity's activities. Once the services in other auras are actually recruited by the EM, using the SAAP, the consumer aura and the supplier auras interact via the service use protocol (SUP) to reconstruct the user-perceived state of the activity.

Figure 2 shows an example of an architecture that was dynamically created to respond to the needs of a user, Fred, at a particular place, Fred's home. The boxes correspond to run time components (autonomous processes that may be deployed in different devices) rather than denoting code packaging, and the lines correspond to connectors, that is, actual communication channels that are established dynamically as the components are created. The diagram represents two kinds of components: auras, with rounded corners, and the EM, and it visually identifies the different kinds of interaction protocols between the components (see Figure 1).

The instance of the architecture in the example is the result of Fred's aura interacting with the EM to recruit two suppliers: the TV and the phone's auras, after interpreting

Fred's needs for the desired activity. This architecture may evolve to adapt to changes in Fred's needs, and in the figure, Fred's aura is also shown as being recruited by the home's aura to get Fred to open the front door.

Context Awareness

An important decision is how to enable context awareness in activity-oriented computing. Addressing context awareness can be decomposed into three parts—sensing context, distributing contextual information, and reacting to context. We start by discussing the latter.

Potentially, all domain entities, and therefore their auras, might want to react to context. A user's aura may change the requirements on an activity, or change which activities are being carried out depending on context such as user location, or whether the user is sitting alone at the office, driving a car, or having an important conversation with his or her boss. Suppliers contributing services to an activity may want to change modalities of those services based on context. For example, an application that shows confidential information may hide that information automatically if someone else is detected entering the room; or an application that requires text or command input may switch to speech recognition if the user needs to use his or her hands, say, for driving a vehicle. The EM may change the allocation of suppliers for a given activity based on user location. For example, if the user is watching a TV show while moving around the house, different devices may be allocated: the TV in the living room, the computer monitor at the home office, etc. The upshot of this is that contextual information should be accessible to all the boxes in the architecture.

Initially, we thought that a dedicated part in the infrastructure would be in charge of gathering and distributing contextual information; there would be a Context Management component/layer in each environment, just like there is an Environment Management. However, both the contextual information and the policies for distributing such information are associated with each user and not really with the environment where that user happens to be. Therefore, auras are the hub of knowledge about the entities they represent.

Whenever a component wishes to obtain contextual information about entity X, it will ask X's aura. X's aura itself may use a variety of mechanisms to gather information about X. For example, since physical location of a space is normally a non-varying property, the aura for a home can read the home's location from a configuration file. In contrast, the aura for an application running on a cell phone equipped with GPS might obtain the application's location from the device's GPS. The aura for a person P typically obtains P's contextual information via contextual information services (CIS).

Unlike sensors specific to devices or spaces, CIS's are fairly generic. Specifically, devices such as a thermometer attached to a wall, or a window sensor for detecting whether *that* window is open or closed, are accessed only by the auras of the corresponding physical spaces. In contrast, given a training set with a person's face, a generic face recognizer may be able to track that person's location inside an office building by using cameras spread over rooms and halls.

CISs are integrated into the architecture using the same protocols for discovery and activation as other services, which allows for gracefully handling of activity instantiation in both sensor-rich environments, such as a smart building, and in depleted environments, such as a park.

While CIS components release information based on generic premises such as the rule of law (e.g., only an authenticated aura for X or a law enforcement agent with a warrant can obtain information about X), the auras themselves are responsible for knowing and enforcing their entity's privacy policies regulating whom to release which information. As an example of distribution policy, a user may authorize only a restricted group of friends to obtain his or her current location.

Service Discovery

In the initial architectural framework (Figure 1.a), **service** discovery is coordinated by the environment management layer. When we expanded the focus of our research to the smart home domain, around the year 2004, we revisited the problem of service discovery. Among the questions that prompted this revisiting are: are there real advantages in brokering discovery? What are the relevant parameters to guide service discovery (location, quality of service, etc.)? How can discovery be geographically scoped? Would some measure of physical distance be enough for such scoping? Can discovery be scoped by geographical areas that are meaningful to the user? We elaborate on these below.

This first question is what should be the strategy for discovery. Many activities in the smart home domain involve entities performing services for other entities, and it is up to auras to find and configure the services required by their entities. For example, for watching a TV show, Fred will need some entity to play the video stream for him. Fred's aura takes care of finding and configuring such an entity in Fred's vicinity (for instance the TV in the living room,) and to change the video stream to other convenient entities whenever Fred moves around the home (a TV in the kitchen, a computer in the office, etc.).

One candidate solution would be to have auras broadcast service availability and/or service requests. However, service discovery in ubiquitous computing involves not just matching service names or capabilities but, ideally, it would find *optimal* services in terms of attributes such as desired levels of quality of service, user preferences, proximity, and so forth. Furthermore, scoping the search would be constrained by network administration policies regarding broadcast (see below). Also, it is hard to establish trust based on broadcast mechanisms.

Because finding the optimal entities to perform services is both a non-trivial problem and common across auras, there are clear engineering advantages in factoring the solution to this problem out of individual auras and into a dedicated piece of the infrastructure. Specifically, the benefits of introducing Environment Managers (EMs) as discovery brokers include:

- **Separation of concerns:** It is up to specialized service brokers to know *how* to find the optimal entities to provide services, while each aura retains the responsibility of knowing *what* services are required by their entity's activities at each moment. By providing a separate locus for optimal discovery in EMs, auras can focus on the task-specific knowledge required to interact with other auras, once they are identified.
- **Efficiency:** EMs can cashe service announcements, thereby improving the latency of processing a service request, and reducing the network traffic required to locate a service, whenever one is requested.

auras register the services offered by the entity they represent with an EM. Each service posting includes the type of service and all attributes of the offering entity that characterize the service. For example, Fred's aura announces that Fred is capable of *answering the door* (service type,) along with Fred's contextual attributes pertaining to his current *location* and whether he is *busy*. Although Fred's aura might know about Fred's blood pressure, that wouldn't be directly relevant for his ability to answer the door. As another example, the aura for a printer announces its ability to *print documents*, along with the printer's *location*, *pages per minute* and *queue length* (contextual and quality of service attributes).

auras may request an EM to find services, as needed by the activities of the entities they represent. Service discovery is guided by optimality criteria in the form of **utility** functions over the attributes of the service suppliers and of the requesting entity. Specifically a service request is of the form:

```
find x : service | y • max u(p_x, p_y)
```

This means: find a set of entities $\underline{x}$, each capable of supplying a `service`, given the requestor entity y, such that a utility function u over the properties of y and of the elements of $\underline{x}$ is maximized. The following are examples with simple utility functions:

Track Fred's location. Upon startup, Fred's aura issues:

```
find x₁:people-locating | Fred
```

That is, find x_1 capable of providing a people locating service for Fred.

Follow-me video. When Fred wishes to watch a soccer game while moving around the house, his aura issues:

```
find x₁:video-playing | Fred · min x₁.location - Fred.lo-
cation
```

That is, find a video player closest to Fred. In this case, maximizing the utility corresponds to minimizing the physical distance between Fred and the video player.

Doorbell. When the doorbell is pressed by someone, the aura for the main hallway issues:

```
find x₁:door-answering, x₂:notifying | hallway
    · x₁.busy = no & min (x₁.location - hallway.location
                      + x₁.location - x₂.location)
```

That is, find a notifying mechanism and a door answerer that is not busy and both closest to the hallway and to the notifying mechanism.

Utility functions are quantitative representations of usefulness with respect to each property. Formally, selecting a specific value of a property, such as x_1.busy = no, is encoded as a discrete mapping, specifically:

$$u_{x_1 \cdot busy}(yes) \mapsto 0, \ u_{x_1 \cdot busy}(no) \mapsto 1$$

For properties characterized by numeric values, such as the distance to the hallway, we use utility functions that distinguish two intervals: one where the user considers the quantity to be good enough for his activity, the other where the user considers the quantity to be insufficient. *Sigmoid* functions, which look like smooth step functions, characterize such intervals and provide a smooth interpolation between the limits of those intervals. Sigmoids are easily encoded by just two points; the values corresponding to the knees of the curve that define the limits *good* of the good-enough interval, and *bad* of the inadequate interval. The case of "more-is-better" qualities (e.g., *accuracy*) are as easily captured as "less-is-better" qualities (e.g., *latency*) by flipping the order of the *good* and *bad* values (see (Sousa, Poladian, Garlan, Schmerl, & Shaw, 2006) for the formal underpinnings).

In the case studies evaluated so far, we have found this level of expressiveness for utility functions to be sufficient.

Scoping Service Discovery

The second question is how service discovery can be scoped in a way that is meaningful to the user. Specifically, many searches take place in the user's immediate vicinity, such as the user's home.

However, neither physical distance nor network range are good parameters to scope discovery. For example, if the user's activity asks for a device to display a video, the TV set in the apartment next door should probably not be considered, even though it might be just as close as other candidates within the user's apartment, and be within range of the user's wireless network as well. To be clear, once a set of devices is scoped for discovery, physical distance may be factored in as a parameter for *optimality* (see above).

Furthermore, sometimes users may want to scope discovery across areas that are not contiguous. For example, suppose that Fred is at a coffee shop and wants to print an interesting document he just found while browsing the internet. Fred may be willing to have the document printed either at the coffee shop, or at Fred's office, since Fred is heading there shortly. A printer at a store down the street may not be something that Fred would consider, even though it is physically closer than Fred's office.

The question about scoping service discovery can then be refined into (a) if not by distance or network boundaries, how can the range of one environment be defined? and (b) how to coordinate discovery across non-contiguous environments?

When an aura directs a discovery request to an EM, by default, discovery runs across all services registered with that EM. That is, the range of an environment is defined by the services that registered with its EM. The question then becomes, how does an aura know with which EM it should register its services? For example, how would the aura for the TV set in Fred's living room know to register its services with the EM in Fred's apartment, and not with the neighbor's?

Auras resolve their physical location into the network address of the appropriate EM by using the environment manager binding protocol (EMBP).[2] This service plays a similar role to the domain naming service in the internet, which resolves URI/URLs into the network address of the corresponding internet server. Physical locations are encoded as aura location identifiers (ALIs), with structure and intent similar to universal resource identifiers (URIs) in the internet. Like URIs, ALIs are a hierarchical representation meant to be interpreted by humans and resolved automatically. For example, *ali://pittsburgh.pa.us/zip-15000/main-street/1234/apt-6* might correspond to Fred's apartment; and *ali://aura.cmu.edu/wean-hall/floor-8/8100-corridor* to a particular corridor on the 8th floor of Wean Hall at Carnegie Mellon University.

Requests for discovery across remote and/or multiple environments can be directed to the local EM, which then coordinates discovery with other relevant EMs (more below). The following are examples of such requests. When Fred is at home and wishes to print a document at the office, his aura would issue a request like:

```
find x:printing | Fred • u(…)
       @ ali://aura.cmu.edu/wean-hall/floor-8/8100-corridor
```

Or, if Fred wanted to consider alternatives either at home or at his office:

```
find x:printing | Fred • u(…)
       @ ali://aura.cmu.edu/wean-hall/floor-8/8100-corridor,
       ali://pittsburgh.pa.us/zip-15000/main-street/1234/apt-6
```

Or, if Fred wanted to search a number of adjacent environments, such as all the environments in his office building:

```
find x:printing | Fred • u(…)
       @ ali://aura.cmu.edu/wean-hall
```

Any such requests are directed by the requestor aura to the local EM, which then resolves such requests in three steps:

1. Use the EMBP to identify the EMs that cover the desired region.
2. Obtain from such EMs all the service descriptions that match the requested service types.
3. Run the service selection algorithms over the candidate set of services.

Activity Models

What to include in activity models is ultimately determined by the purpose that those models are meant to serve. In some applications of activity models the goal is to assist users with learning or with performing complex tasks. Examples of these are applications to automated tutoring, expert systems to help engineers repair complex mechanisms, such as trains and airplanes, and automated assistants to help manage complex activities such as organizing a conference (Garlan & Schmerl, 2007; Siewiorek, 1998). For these kinds of applications, models of activities may include a specification of workflow, as a sequence of steps to be performed, and cognitive models of the user.

In the smart office domain, we experimented with enabling users to suspend their ongoing activities and resume them at a later time and/or at another location, possibly using a disjoint set of devices. For that purpose, the models capture user needs and preferences to carry out each activity. Specifically, such models include of a snapshot of the services and materials being used during the activity, as well as utility theory-based models of user preferences (for details on the latter, see (Sousa et al., 2006)).

Figure 3 shows a grammar for modeling **activities**, or tasks, as a set of possibly interconnected services. This grammar follows a variant of the Backus-Naur Form (BNF, see for instance (ISO, 1996)). To simplify reading the specification, we drop the convention of surrounding non-terminal symbols with angle brackets, and since the task models are built on top of XML syntax, we augment the operators of BNF with the following:

```
E ::= t: A; C
```

defines a type E of XML elements with tag t, attributes A, and children C, where t is a terminal symbol, A is an expression containing only terminals (the attribute names), and C is an expression containing only non-terminals (the child XML elements). In this restricted use of BNF, whether a symbol is a terminal or non-terminal is entirely established by context. So, for instance the rule:

```
Book = book: year ISBN; Title {Author}
```

allows the following as a valid element:

```
<book year="2004" ISBN="123">
    <title>...</title>
```

Figure 3. Grammar for specifying task models

```
Task        ::= auraTask: id;
Prefs {ServiceSnapshot | MaterialSnapshot | Config}

ServiceSnapshot ::= service: id type;
    Settings
MaterialSnapshot ::= material: id;
    State

Config ::= configuration: name weight;
    { Service | Connection }

Service ::= service: id;
    {Uses}
Uses        ::= uses: materialId;

Connection ::= connection; id type;
    Attach QoSPrefs
Attach ::= attach: ;
    From To
From        ::= from serviceId port;
To ::= to: serviceId port;
```

```
    <author>...</author>
    <author>...</author>
</book>
```

Specifically, in Figure 3, a task (model) is an XML element with tag `auraTask`, with one `id` attribute, and with one `Prefs` child, followed by an arbitrary number of `ServiceSnapshot`, `MaterialSnapshot`, and `Config` children. A task may be carried out using one of several alternative service configurations of services.

Services stand for concepts such as *edit text*, or *browse the web*, and materials are files and data streams manipulated by the services. A service may manipulate zero or many materials; for instance, text editing can be carried out on an arbitrary number of files simultaneously. That relationship is captured by the `Uses` clauses within the `Service` element.

The snapshot of the user-perceived state of the task is captured in the *Settings* and *State* elements. The *Settings* element captures the state that is specific to a service, and shared by all materials manipulated by that service, while the *State* element captures the state that is specific to each material. A detailed discussion of this grammar can be found in (Sousa, 2005).

Figure 4. Example task model for reviewing a video clip

```
<auraTask id="34">
  <preferences>
    <service template="default" id="1"/>
    <service template="default" id="2"/>
  </preferences>
  <service type="playVideo" id="1">
    <settings mute="true"/>
  </service>
  <material id="11">
    <state>
      <video state="stopped" cursor="0"/>
      <position xpos="645" ypos="441"/>
      <dimension height="684" width="838"/>
    </state>
  </material>
  <service type="editText" id="2">
    <settings>
      <format overtype="0"/>
      <language checkLanguage="1"/>
    </settings>
  </service>
  <material id="21">
    <state>
      <cursor position="31510"/>
      <scroll horizontal="0" vertical="7"/>
      <zoom value="140"/>
      <spellchecking enabled="1" language="1033"/>
      <window height="500" xpos="20" width="600" mode="min" ypos="100"/>
    </state>
  </material>
  <configuration name="all" weight="1.0">
    <service id="2">
      <uses materialId="21"/>
    </service>
    <service id="1">
      <uses materialId="11"/>
    </service>
  </configuration>
  <configuration name="only video" weight="0.7">
    <service id="1">
      <uses materialId="11"/>
    </service>
  </configuration>
</auraTask>
```

Figure 4 shows one example of a task model for reviewing a video clip, which formally is a sentence allowed, or generated, by the grammar in Figure 3. This example was captured while running the infrastructure described in the section on System Design. The user defined two alternative configurations for this task: one including both playing the video and taking notes, the other, playing the video alone. Both services use a single material: *play video* uses a video file, with material id 11, and *edit text* uses a text file, with material id 21. The user-perceived state of the task is represented as the current service settings, under each service, and the current state of each material. For instance, the state of the video includes the fact that the video is stopped at the beginning (the cursor is set to 0 time elapsed), and it indicates the position and dimensions of the window showing the video.

Extending to the Home Environment

In the smart home domain, in addition to supporting suspend/resume of activities, we wanted to enable users to delegate responsibility for some activities to **auras**. Examples of the latter activities include managing intrusion detection for the home, finding a person to answer the door for a visitor, or assisting with monitoring elder family members.

The research questions then become: is the services and materials view of activities adequate in the smart home domain? For enabling auras to take responsibility for activities, which concepts should activity models capture?

The usefulness of capturing the services needed for an activity seems to carry over well into the smart home domain. For example, in the case of the doorbell scenario, the activity of answering the door requires finding services such as notification can be supplied by devices such as a telephone, a TV, a buzzer, etc., and *door answerer*, which can be supplied by a qualified person (e.g., not a toddler). Selecting the suppliers for such services is guided by the home owner's preferences encoded in the activity model, which may include things such as the door needs to be answered within a certain time, and that the notification service should be in close proximity to the candidate door answerer.

A prototype of this case study has shown that these models can handle sophisticated policies of configuration (e.g., excluding children from answering the door, or specifying criteria for proximity) and that they trivially accommodate the dynamic addition of new notification devices.

This prototype also highlighted two fundamental differences between the kinds of activities supported in the smart-office domain and the ones we target in the smart-home domain. The first difference is that, while in the office domain services were only provided by automated agents (software), now people may also be asked to provide services. This has implications on how auras control service supply, since people are much more likely than software to do something totally different than what they are being asked. In the example, after being notified to answer the door, a person may get sidetracked and forget about it. It is up to the responsible aura to monitor whether or not the service is being delivered, and react to a "fault" in a similar way as it would in the case of faulty software: by seeking a replacement (more in the section on Robustness).

The second difference is that, in the smart home domain, auras may take the responsibility for activities; this is related to the question above of which concepts to capture in activity models to enable that to happen. In the smart office domain, when a fault cannot be handled, for example, if a suitable replacement cannot be found for a faulty supplier, the problem is passed up to the entity responsible for the activity, that is, the user. If an aura is to be truly responsible for an activity, it must be take charge of such situations as well.

One way of addressing a hurdle in one activity, is to carry out another activity that circumvents the hurdle. In the example, if the hallway aura cannot find a person to answer the door, it may take a message from the visitor, or initiate a phone call to the person being visited.

A simple enhancement of activity models to allow this is to support the specification of conditions to automatically resume or suspend activities. Such conditions are expressed as Boolean formulas over observation of contextual information. For example, if everyone left the house, resume the intrusion detection activity.

For these models to cover situations as the one where a person could not be found to answer the door, contextual information needs to be rich enough to include semantic observations, such as "the door could not be open for a visitor."

Another scenario where we tested this approach is the elder care scenario. The aura for Susan, Fred's grandmother, runs a perpetual task that recruits a heart monitor service for her. Susan defined under which conditions her aura should trigger the task of alerting the family. When defining such conditions, Susan takes into consideration her physician's recommendations, but also conditions under which she may desire privacy. Fred's aura runs a perpetual task of monitoring contextual postings by Susan's aura. It is up to John to (a) define that posting such a notification should trigger the task of alerting him, and (b) define the means employed by his aura to carry out such a task. For example, if Fred is at the office, his aura sends an instant message to Fred's computer screen; otherwise, it sends a text message to Fred's cell phone.

While these are simple scenarios, they illustrate the ability to chain activities, and to direct the exact behavior of activities, by capturing conditions on contextual information in the models of activities. Such conditions are associated to the operations of either resuming or suspending activities, and can be monitored by auras to automatically initiate the corresponding operation.

Formally, condition-action primitives can be used to express the same space of solutions than other more sophisticated approaches, such as models of activities based on workflow notations, or on hierarchical decomposition of activities. Which approach would be more suitable for end-users to express and understand such models is an open research problem.

Robustness

The term *robustness* in activity-oriented computing is interpreted very broadly: is the system's behavior consistent with the users' expectations, even under unanticipated circumstances. In this section, we first use the examples in the Background section to identify key robustness requirements. We then look at the challenges associated with supporting robust operation, distinguishing between general challenges and challenges that are specific to the home environment. Finally, we summarize some results showing how we support robust tasks in an office environment and discuss how these results can be extended to support activities in the home.

Properties

In daily use, the system should correctly identify the users' intent and should support a wide variety of activities in a way that is consistent with their preferences and policies. If users observe unexpected behavior, the system should be able to explain its behavior. This will increase the users' confidence in the system and will allow the system to improve over time. For example, by adjusting preferences and policies, either manually by the user or automatically by the system (case-base reasoning) the system's future behavior can be made to better match user intent. Similarly, the system should be able to engage users if input is confusing or unexpected. Ideally, the system would be able to recognize undesirable or unsafe actions, for example, a child opening the door for a stranger.

The above properties must also be maintained as the system evolves and under failure conditions. For example, when new services or devices are added (e.g., camera and face recognition software is added to support the doorbell scenario) or become unavailable (e.g., the license for the face recognition software expired), the system should automatically adapt to the available services.

Challenges

When we looked at how to support user activities and tasks in different environments (e.g., work in an office, daily activities in the home, or guiding visitors in a museum), we found that several key challenges are shared across these environments. These generic challenges include capturing and representing user intent, discovering and managing services and devices (suppliers), and optimizing resources allocation to maximize overall system utility. All these functions should be adaptive, that is, automatically adapt to changes in the computational and physical environment and to changes in the goals and preferences of users.

Each environment also adds its own challenges. For example, activities in homes are device-centric (e.g., displays, sound) or include physical actions that involve people (e.g., opening doors). Managing and allocating such "resources" is very different from an office environment, where tasks are computer-centric and are supported by executing applications that use a variable amount of resources (network bandwidth, CPU, battery power). Similarly, the interactions with users are very different in the home (discreet interface for non-experts) and the office (keyboard/mouse/display used by computer knowledgeable users).

Robustness in an Office Environment

In order to achieve robustness in a smart-office environment, we have designed, implemented and evaluated an infrastructure that uses utility theory to dynamically select the best achievable configuration of services, even in the face of failures and coming online of better alternatives (Sousa et al., 2006).

Robustness is achieved through self-**adaptation** in response to events ranging from faults, to positive changes in the environment, to changes in the user's task. Self-adaptation is realized through a closed-loop control system design that senses, actuates, and controls the runtime state of the environment based on input from the user. Each layer reacts to changes in user tasks and in the environment at a different granularity and time-scale. Task Management acts at a human perceived time-scale (minutes), evaluating the adequacy of sets of services to support the user's task. Environment Management acts at a time-scale of seconds, evaluating the adequacy of the mapping between the requested services and specific suppliers. Adaptive applications (fidelity-aware and context-aware) choose appropriate computation tactics at a time-scale of milliseconds.

Let us illustrate the behavior of the system using the following scenario. Fred is engaged in a conversation that requires real-time speech-to-speech translation. For that task, assume the aura infrastructure has assembled three services: speech recognition, language translation, and speech synthesis. Initially both speech recognition and synthesis are running on Fred's handheld. To save resources on Fred's handheld, and since language translation is computationally intensive, but has very low demand on data-flow (the text representation of each utterance), the translation service is configured to run on a remote server. We now discuss how the system adapts in response to faults, variability in resource and service availability, and changes in the user's task requirements:

- **Fault tolerance**. Suppose now that there is loss of connectivity to the remote server, or equivalently, that there is a software crash that renders it unavailable. Live monitoring at the EM level detects that the supplier for language translation is lost. The EM looks for an alternative supplier for that service, for example, translation software on Fred's handheld, activates it, and automatically reconfigures the service assembly.

- **Resource and fidelity-awareness**. Computational resources in Fred's handheld are allocated by the EM among the services supporting Fred's task. For computing optimal resource allocation, the EM uses each supplier's spec sheet (relating fidelity levels with resource consumption), live monitoring of the available resources, and the user's preferences with respect to fidelity levels. Resource allocation is adjusted over time. For example, suppose that during the social part of the conversation, Fred is fine with a less accurate translation, but response times should be snappy. The speech recognizer, as the main driver of the overall response time, gets proportionally more resources and uses faster, if less accurate, recognition algorithms (Balan et al., 2003).

- **Adaption.** Adaptation is also needed to deal with changes in resource availability. Each supplier issues periodic reports on the Quality of Service (QoS) actually being provided—in this example, response time and estimated accuracy of recognition/translation. Suppose that at some point during the conversation, Fred brings up his calendar to check his availability for a meeting. The suppliers for the speech-to-speech translation task, already stretched for resources, reduce their QoS below what Fred's preferences state as acceptable. The EM detects this "soft fault," and replaces the speech recognizer by a lightweight component, that although unable to provide as high a QoS as the full-fledged version, performs better under sub-optimal resource availability. Alternatively, suppose that at some point, the language translation supplier running on the remote server (which failed earlier) becomes available again. The EM detects the availability of a new candidate to supply a service required by Fred's task, and compares the estimated utility of the candidate solution against the current one. If there is a clear benefit, the EM automatically reconfigures the service assembly. In calculating the benefit, the EM factors in a cost of change. This mechanism introduces hysteresis in the reconfiguration behavior, thus avoiding oscillation between closely competing solutions.

- **Task requirements change**. Suppose that at some point Fred's conversation enters a technical core for which translation accuracy becomes more important than fast response times. The TM provides the mechanisms to allow Fred to quickly indicate his new preferences; for instance, by choosing among a set of preference templates. The new preferences are distributed by the TM to the EM and all the suppliers supporting Fred's task. Given a new set of constraints, the EM evaluates the current solution against other candidates, reconfigures, if necessary, and determines the new optimal resource allocation. The suppliers that remain in the configuration, upon receiving the new preferences, change their computation strategies dynamically, for example, by changing to algorithms that offer better accuracy at the expense of response time.

Suppose that after the conversation, Fred wants to resume writing one of his research papers. Again, the TM provides the mechanisms to detect, or for Fred to quickly indicate, his change of task. Once the TM is aware that the conversation is over it coordinates with the suppliers for capturing the user-level state of the current task, if any, and with the EM to deactivate (and release the resources for) the current suppliers. The TM then analyses the description it saved the last time Fred worked on writing the paper, recognizes which services Fred was using and requests those from the EM. After the EM identifies the optimal supplier assignment, the TM interacts with those suppliers to automatically recover the user-level state where Fred left off. See Sousa and Garlan (2003) for a formal specification of such interactions.

Extending to the Home Environment

We are currently enhancing this solution to provide robust support for activities in the home. While the key challenges are the same (e.g., optimizing utility, adapting to changes, etc.), extensions are needed in a number of areas.

First, activities in the home are very different from tasks in the office. For example, since some activities in the home involve physical actions, people must be involved (e.g., to open a door), that is, people become suppliers of services. Moreover, some tasks are not associated with individuals, but with the home itself (e.g., responding to the doorbell or a phone call). This change in roles means that it is even more critical to make appropriate allocations since the cost of mistakes is much higher; for example, people will be much less willing to overlook being personally inconvenienced by a wrong decision, than when a suboptimal application is invoked on their computer.

Second, many activities in the home involve the use of devices that are shared by many people, or involve deciding who should perform a certain action. This means that the Task Manager will typically need to balance the preferences and goals of multiple users. An extreme example is conflicts, for example, when multiple users would like to use the same device. In contrast, tasks in the office typically involve only personal resources (e.g., a handheld) or resources with simple sharing rules (e.g., a server).

Third, the methods for interaction with the system will be much different in the home. Even on a handheld, Fred had access to pull down menus and a keyboard to reliably communicate with the system. For the home environment, we are exploring natural modalities of interaction, which are less intrusive, but more ambiguous (more in the section on Future Research).

Finally, uncertainty will play a more significant role in the home, for example, because of unpredictable behavior when people are asked to perform services, or due to ambiguity caused by primitive I/O devices. Work in progress is extending the utility optimization components to explicitly consider uncertainty.

Future Research

Some of the challenges identified in this chapter are the topic of undergoing and future work, such as research on the kinds of knowledge to capture in activity models so to support mixed-initiative control, including delegation and collaboration among human and automated agents. Below we summarize our current work on human-computer interaction and on security and privacy for AoC systems.

User Interfaces for Managing Activities

Human-computer interaction in the office domain currently uses one de-facto standard modality, based on keyboards, pointing devices, and windows-based displays. In a more general ubiquitous computing setting, natural modalities such as speech and gesture may be highly desirable, but they also may lead to ambiguity and misunderstanding. For example, if Fred points at a TV where a soccer game is playing and leaves the room, does that mean that Fred wants to keep watching the game while moving around the house, that the TV should pause the game until Fred returns, or that the TV should be turned off?

Rather than trying to pick a privileged modality of interaction, we take the approach that interactions between humans and auras may have many channels that complement and serve as alternatives to each other. For example, users might indicate their intention to suspend an activity verbally, but might sometimes prefer a graphical interface to express a sophisticated set of contextual conditions for when an activity should be automatically resumed. The research questions then become: what are appropriate modalities for each kind of interaction? Is there a role for explicit interactions, as well as for implicit interactions based on sensing and inference? Can different modalities be coordinated, contributing to disambiguate user intentions? What mechanisms can be used to detect and recover from misunderstandings? What are specific technologies that can be harnessed in the home?

To support explicit interactions, we started exploring technologies such as Everywhere Displays and RFID. The Everywhere Displays technology uses a digital camera to track down the location of a user, and then uses a projector to project an image of the interface onto a surface near the user (Kjeldsen, Levas, & Pinhanez, 2004). The feedback loop through the camera allows the image to be adjusted for certain characteristics of the surface, such as color and tilt. The user interacts with this image by performing hand motions over the image, which are then recognized via the camera. This technology supports a metaphor similar to the point-and-click metaphor, although fewer icons seem to be feasible relative to a computer screen, and a rich set of command primitives, such as double clicking or selecting a group of objects, seems harder to achieve.

RFID technology supports a simple form of tangible interfaces (Greenberg & Boyle, 2002). For example, RFID tags can be used to create tangible widgets for activities. In the example where Fred is watching the game on TV, Fred may bind an activity widget with the show playing on the TV by swiping the widget near the TV. That activity may be activated in other rooms by swiping the activity widget by a reader in the room, or deactivated it by swapping the widget again, once activated (see demo video at (Sousa, Poladian, & Schmerl, 2005)).

Tradeoff between Ubiquity and Security

The big question to be answered is: can ubiquity be reconciled with goals of security and privacy? There seems to be a tradeoff between the openness of ubiquitous computing and security assurances. The very meaning of *ubiquity* implies that users should be enabled to use the services offered by devices embedded in many different places. But how confident can users be that those devices, or the environment where they run, will not take advantage of the access to the user's information to initiate malicious actions?

Rather that taking an absolute view of security and privacy, we argue that there are different requirements for different activities. For example, the computing environment at a coffee shop could be deemed unsafe to carry out online financial transactions, but acceptable for sharing online vacation photos with a friend.

In essence, this is a problem of controlling access; ideally, a ubiquitous computing environment would gain access only to the information pertaining to the activities that a user is willing to carry out in that environment, and none other.

Unfortunately, existing solutions for controlling access are not a good fit to this problem because they make a direct association between identity and access. Specifically, once a user authenticates, he gains access to *all* the information and resources he is entitled to, and so does the computing environment where the user authenticated.

A candidate solution would be to associate access control to the cross-product of users and environments; in the example, user Fred at the coffee shop would get access to a limited set of activities, but user Fred at his office would get access to a wide range (possibly all) of Fred's activities. A serious problem with this solution is that it would require the pre-encoding of all the types of environments where the user might want to access his or her activities.

Another candidate solution would be for users to have multiple identities; Fred at the coffee shop would use an identity that has access to the vacation photos, but not to online banking. This solution has two obvious problems; first, separating the activities and associated information for the different identities may not be clear cut, and may quickly become cumbersome for moderately high numbers of activities. Second, if users are given the freedom to define new identities and the corresponding access controls, does that mean that every user should be given security administration privileges?

We are currently investigating an access control model centered on the notion of *persona*. A user is given one identity and may define multiple personae associated with that identity. The user may freely associate activities with personae in a many-to-many fashion, and may also define which credentials are required to activate each persona. This model has a number of benefits, as follows.

First, it allows users to manage which activities are seen by an arbitrary environment (by authenticating specific personae) while drawing a clear boundary on the administrative privileges of each user.

Second, users may draw on rich forms of authentication to make the overhead of authentication proportionate to the security requirements. For example, for activating Fred's financial persona, Fred may require two forms of id to be presented, such as entering a password *and* scanning an id card, while for his social persona, a weak form of authentication, such as face or voice recognition, will suffice.

Third, the model offers users a coherent view of the personal workspace centered on their identity, while enabling users to expand the set of accessible activities at will, by providing the credentials required to activate the desired personae.

Conclusion

The key idea of Activity-oriented Computing (AoC) is to capture models of user activities and have systems interpret those models at run time. By becoming aware of what user activities entail, systems can do a better job at supporting those activities, either by facilitating access to the activities while relieving users from overhead such as configuring devices and software, or by taking responsibility for parts or whole activities.

This chapter described the authors' work on building systems to support AoC. It discussed how those systems may address challenges inherent to the problem domain, such as user mobility and conflict resolution, as well as challenges that are entailed by building the systems themselves. Specifically, (a) defining what to capture in activity models (b) designing systems that do a good job at supporting user activities while addressing the challenges in the problem domain, and (c) making those systems robust, self-aware, self-configurable, and self-adaptable. The chapter dissected those challenges, identified specific research questions, and described how the authors answered these questions for the past six years, as their understanding of the issues improved.

The main contributions of this work are as follows:

- Pragmatic models of user activities that enable mobile users to instantiate activities in different environments, taking advantage of diverse local capabilities without requiring the use of mobile devices, and retaining the ability to reconstitute the user-perceived state of those activities

- Mechanisms that enable scoping service discovery over geographical boundaries that are meaningful to users, and which can be specific to each activity and be freely defined

- A utility-theoretic framework for service discovery that enables optimization of sophisticated, service-specific models of QoS and context properties

- A robustness framework, based on the same utility-theoretic framework, that departs from the traditional binary notion of fault and uniformly treats as an optimization problem faults, "soft faults" (unresponsiveness to QoS requirements,) and conflicts in accessing scarce resources

- Closed-loop control that enables systems to become self-aware and self-configurable, and to adapt to dynamic changes in both user/activity requirements and environment resources

- A software architecture that harmoniously integrates all the features above, additionally (a) integrating context sensing according to the capabilities of each environment, and (b) coordinating adaptation policies with applications that may contain their own fine-grain mechanisms for adaptation to resource variations

This chapter also summarized ongoing and future work towards addressing other challenges, namely, supporting activities where human and automated agents collaborate (mixed-initiative activities), exploring human-computer interaction modalities for AoC in ubiquitous computing environments, and investigating models for security and privacy.

Acknowledgment

This material is based upon work supported by the National Science Foundation under Grant No. 0615305

References

Abowd, G., Bobick, A., Essa, I., Mynatt, E., & Rogers, W. (2002). *The Aware Home: Developing Technologies for Successful Aging.* Paper presented at the AAAI Workshop on Automation as a Care Giver, Alberta, Canada.

Arnstein, L., Sigurdsson, S., & Franza, R. (2001). Ubiquitous Computing in the Biology Laboratory. *Journal of Lab Automation (JALA), 6*(1), 66-70.

Balan, R. K., Sousa, J. P., & Satyanarayanan, M. (2003). *Meeting the Software Engineering Challenges of Adaptive Mobile Applications* (Tech. Rep. No. CMU-CS-03-111). Pittsburgh, PA: Carnegie Mellon University.

Brumitt, B., Meyers, B., Krumm, J., Kern, A., & Shafer, S. (2000). EasyLiving: Technologies for intelligent environments. In Gellersen, Thomas (Eds) *Proceedings of the 2nd Int'l Symposium on Handheld and Ubiquitous Computing* (HUC2000), LNCS 1927, (pp. 12-29), Bristol, UK: Springer-Verlag.

Christensen, H., & Bardram, J. (2002, September). Supporting Human Activities – Exploring Activity-Centered Computing. In Borriello and Holmquist (Eds.) *Proceedings of the 4th International Conference on Ubiquitous Computing* (UbiComp 2002), LNCS 2498, (pp. 107-116), Göteborg, Sweden: Springer-Verlag.

Garlan, D., & Schmerl, B. (2007). The RADAR Architecture for Personal Cognitive Assistance. *International Journal of Software Engineering and Knowledge Engineering, 17*(2), in press.

Greenberg, S., & Boyle, M. (2002). Customizable physical interfaces for interacting with conventional applications. In Proceedings of the *15th Annual ACM Symposium on User Interface Software and Technology* (UIST 2002) (pp. 31-40). ACM Press.

Intille, S. (2002). Designing a home of the future. *IEEE Pervasive Computing, 1*(2), 76-82.

ISO. (1996). *Extended Backus-Naur Form* (No. ISO/IEC 14977:1996(E)). Retrieved on from http:// www.iso.org: International Standards Organization

Kjeldsen, R., Levas, A., & Pinhanez, C. (2004). Dynamically Reconfigurable Vision-Based User Interfaces. *Journal of Machine Vision and Applications, 16*(1), 6-12.

Kozuch, M., & Satyanarayanan, M. (2002). *Internet Suspend/Resume.* Paper presented at the 4th IEEE Workshop on Mobile Computing Systems and Applications, available as Intel Research Report IRP-TR-02-01.

Logitech, I. Logitech Harmony Remote Controls. Retrieved on from http://www.logitech.com

MacIntyre, B., Mynatt, E., Voida, S., Hansen, K., Tullio, J., & Corso, G. (2001). Support for Multitasking and Background Awareness Using Interactive Peripheral Displays. In *ACM User Interface Software and Technology* (UIST'01), pp. 41-50, Orlando, FL.

Ponnekanti, S., Lee, B., Fox, A., & Hanrahan, P. (2001). ICrafter: A Service Framework for Ubiquitous Computing Environments. In Abowd, Brumitt, Shafer (Eds) *3rd Int'l Conference on Ubiquitous Computing* (UbiComp 2001), LNCS 2201, pp. 56-75. Atlanta, GA: Springer-Verlag.

Richardson, T., Bennet, F., Mapp, G., & Hopper, A. (1994). A ubiquitous, personalized computing environment for all: Teleporting in an X Windows System Environment. *IEEE Personal Communications Magazine, 1*(3), 6-12.

Rochester, U. The Smart Medical Home at the University of Rochester. Retrieved on from http://www.futurehealth.rochester.edu/smart_home

Román, M., Hess, C., Cerqueira, R., Ranganathan, A., Campbell, R., & Narhstedt, K. (2002). Gaia: A Middleware Infrastructure for Active Spaces. *IEEE Pervasive Computing, 1*(4), 74-83.

Siewiorek, D. (1998). Adtranz: A Mobile Computing System for Maintenance and Collaboration. In *Proceedings of the 2nd IEEE Int'l Symposium on Wearable Computers* (pp. 25-32). IEEE Computer Society.

Sousa, J. P. (2005). *Scaling Task Management in Space and Time: Reducing User Overhead in Ubiquitous-Computing Environments* (Tech. Rep. No. CMU-CS-05-123). Pittsburgh, PA: Carnegie Mellon University.

Sousa, J. P., & Garlan, D. (2003). *The aura Software Architecture: an Infrastructure for Ubiquitous Computing* (Tech. Rep. No. CMU-CS-03-183). Pittsburgh, PA: Carnegie Mellon University.

Sousa, J. P., Poladian, V., Garlan, D., Schmerl, B., & Shaw, M. (2006). Task-based Adaptation for Ubiquitous Computing. *IEEE Transactions on Systems, Man, and Cybernetics, Part C: Applications and Reviews, Special Issue on Engineering Autonomic Systems, 36*(3), 328-340.

Sousa, J. P., Poladian, V., & Schmerl, B. (2005). Project aura demo video of the follow me scenario. Retrieved from http://www.cs.cmu.edu/~jpsousa/research/aura/followme.wmv

Sycara, K., Paolucci, M., Velsen, M. v., & Giampapa, J. (2003). The RETSINA MAS Infrastructure. *Joint issue of Autonomous Agents and MAS, Springer Netherlands, 7*(1-2), 29-48.

Wang, Z., & Garlan, D. (2000). *Task Driven Computing* (Tech. Rep. No. CMU-CS-00-154). Pittsburgh, PA: Carnegie Mellon University.

Endnotes

[1]   For generality, the protocols of interaction were renamed from previous architecture documentation (e.g. Sousa & Garlan, 2003, Sousa, 2005). For instance, the EM—Supplier protocol is now the Service Announcement and Activation Protocol (SAAP). Since these protocols were already based on peer-to-peer asynchronous communication, no changes were implied by the transition to the new perspective of the architectural framework.

[2]   As discussed in the subsection on context awareness, there is a variety of mechanisms for auras to obtain their physical location, or more precisely, the location of their corresponding entities.

Chapter XII

Privacy Threats in Emerging Ubicomp Applications:
Analysis and Safeguarding

Elena Vildjiounaite, VTT Technical Research Centre of Finland, Finland

Tapani Rantakokko, Finwe LTD, Finland

Petteri Alahuhta, VTT Technical Research Centre of Finland, Finland

Pasi Ahonen, VTT Technical Research Centre of Finland, Finland

David Wright, Trilateral Research and Consulting, UK

Michael Friedewald, Fraunhofer Institute Systems and Innovation Research, Germany

Abstract

Realisation of the Ubicomp vision in the real world creates significant threats to personal privacy due to constant information collection by numerous tiny sensors, active information exchange over short and long distances, long-term storage of

large quantities of data, and reasoning based on collected and stored data. An analysis of more than 100 Ubicomp scenarios, however, shows that applications are often proposed without considering privacy issues, whereas existing privacy-enhancing technologies mainly have been developed for networked applications and, thus, are not always applicable to emerging applications for smart spaces and personal devices, especially because the users and their data are not spatially separated in such applications. A partial solution to the problem of users' privacy protection could be to allow users to control how their personal data can be used. The authors' experience with mobile phone data collection, nevertheless, suggests that when users give their consent for the data collection, they don't fully understand the possible privacy implications. Thus, application developers should pay attention to privacy protection; otherwise, such problems could result in users not accepting Ubicomp applications. This chapter suggests guidelines for estimating threats to privacy, depending on real world application settings and the choice of technology; and guidelines for the choice and development of technological safeguards against privacy threats.

Introduction

After having read a large number of scenarios of emerging Ubicomp applications (found in project deliverables and research publications which describe prototypes of smart spaces, smart personal devices, objects and their functionalities) and visionary future Ubicomp scenarios (found mainly in roadmaps), we concluded that most scenarios present a sunny, problem-free vision of our future. With the exception of the surveillance problem in some cases, most scenarios do not consider the privacy issues that the new technologies are likely to raise. For example, they do not discuss possible privacy problems due to conflicts between people's interests or personal curiosity.

The discovery that Ubicomp technologies raise privacy problems is not new; and research into privacy protection is actively going on, but after a state-of-the art review of work on privacy protection, we have come to the conclusion that most of this work deals with privacy protection in such network applications as m-commerce, Web browsing, virtual meetings, location-based services, and so forth, where users can be physically separated from their personal data. Even in these applications, no scalable solutions fully applicable in real life exist, and this lack of protection allows large-scale eavesdropping, as we know from the news (Web site of the American Civil Liberties Union and the ACLU Foundation, 2006).

The work on privacy protection in smart spaces and in connection with personal devices is even less mature than that concerned with network applications, while visionary Ubicomp scenarios suggest many situations in which confidential data and secrets occasionally can be discovered. When reading Ubicomp scenarios, however, we rarely found any discussions about the possible implications of a new technology for privacy, and even fewer descriptions of privacy protection measures. M. Langheinrich has collected a list of excuses why privacy protection is rarely embedded in new applications (Langheinrich, 2006), but such a practice can lead to the danger that problems appear after an application has already been developed and installed, and then either the users are left to suffer from privacy violation problems, or application developers are faced with the negative reactions of the users and the need to update the application. One recent example is a bus ticketing application in Helsinki which was storing data about travellers' routes. The application received bad publicity (criticism in the newspaper *Helsingin Sanomat* (Koponen, 2002)), and updating an already installed application would obviously be a costly operation. In cases where users' criticism is directed against an already installed application, which runs on non-reprogrammable microcontrollers (a common situation in the case of a commercial application), an application update can be very costly. Thus, embedding privacy protection in Ubicomp applications at the development stage would be beneficial for application developers.

The main emphasis in this chapter will be on possible problems rather than the benefits of new technologies and applications, because readers of Ubicomp papers usually encounter descriptions of benefits rather than descriptions of problems. The success of Ubicomp development also requires the understanding of possible problems, however, and safeguarding against them, including safeguarding against possible privacy implications. There is no doubt that the notion of privacy alters with time, so that with the invention of phones (and especially mobile phones), for example, physical distance from other people can no longer guarantee privacy. Similarly, with the development of cameras (especially digital cameras, with their capability for recording more views than their owners can sort through carefully), people have become used to seeing more details of other people's lives than was ever possible before.

There are very important differences between past and future technologies, however, which could change our lives more quickly than we could possibly adapt our understanding of the world, human behaviour, ethics and laws to the new technologies: first, past technologies were largely controlled by a human, whereas future technologies will be capable of automatic actions. Since it is much easier to notice a human observer than a tiny sensor, it will be possible to collect much more data without people being aware of it. Second, large-scale accumulation of data in a digital form will no longer require manual (slow) human work in order to connect information from different sources, so that it may be easier to assemble the full life story of a person in the future than it was to find scattered pieces of information in the past. Third, modern devices are smaller in size, more reliable and move closer to the human body than was the case in the past, and it is proposed that these could be embedded into clothes, watches or jewelry. Consequently, it will become easier to have always-on mobile devices, but more difficult to switch them off. Our perception of the privacy aspect known as the "right to be left alone," for example, has changed significantly with the invention of stationary phones and especially mobile phones, but it has still been preserved by the possibility for switching the phone off or not hearing it ringing when taking a shower or walking in a noisy place (and it is not easy to check whether a person did not hear a phone call or was simply not in the mood to answer it). Will one still be able to avoid undesired conversation in the Ubicomp future of embedded connectivity, or will society change so that people will not be offended or angry when their children, relatives or subordinates do not answer a call that they have evidently heard? How society will adapt to the capabilities of new technologies is an open question, but we think that technology developers should not rely on human nature changing quickly, and the results of deploying new technologies in computer-supported collaborative work (Bellotti, 1993) support this opinion.

This chapter first summarises the views of different researchers on what privacy is, after which it will briefly describe how Ubicomp researchers see the world of the future and what possible implications for users' privacy may not be safeguarded in the scenarios. After that, the chapter will present the authors' experiences of mobile phone data collection and users' opinions regarding their privacy expectations before and after data collection, which suggest that the privacy implications were underestimated before data collection. It will then present the state of the art in privacy-enhancing technologies and highlight the gaps that create privacy risks. After that it will suggest guidelines for estimating the threats to privacy, depending on real world application settings and on the choice of technology, as well as guidelines for the choice and development of technological safeguards against these threats.

Privacy Expectations in the Real World

It is suggested in the work of Lahlou et al. (Lahlou, 2003), that privacy protection requires an understanding of how new technologies change the ways that have developed in the physical world, where personal privacy is protected by the following borders (Bohn, 2005):

- **Natural Borders:** physical borders of observability, such as walls, clothing, darkness, facial expression (a natural border protecting the true feelings of a person)
- **Social Borders:** expectations with regard to confidentiality in certain social groups, such as family members, doctors and lawyers, for example, the ex-

pectation that your colleagues will not read personal fax messages addressed to you

- **Spatial or Temporal Borders:** expectations by people that parts of their lives can exist in isolation from other parts, both temporally and spatially, for example, a previous wild adolescent phase should not have a lasting influence on the current life of a father of four, or a party with friends should not affect relations with colleagues
- **Borders due to Ephemeral or Transitory Effects:** expectations that certain action or spontaneous utterances will soon be forgotten or simply unnoticed because of limitations on people's attention and memory

These borders are bi-directional, that is, people expect these borders not only to protect the person's feelings, appearance, actions, and so forth from the outside world, but also to protect the person from intrusions by the outside world. Physical borders are perhaps perceived as most reliable, as can be illustrated by how poker players control their faces, for instance, or by the custom of knocking on the closed door of somebody's private room or office. People also have a well-developed mental model of the limits of their own or others' ability to notice and remember details of what is going on around them. For example, people in a conference room usually expect that others' attention and memory will be devoted to the content of a presentation rather than to the auditory aspect. Concerning social and spatial borders, people perceive them as not so strong; for example, the likelihood of encountering the same people in different circumstances or of broken confidentiality is not negligible. In general terms, the stronger is the personal belief that a certain border is reliable, the more difficult it will be to adapt to its violation by a new technology. Experiments in the research area of computer-supported collaborative work suggest one example of the adaptation difficulty. In order to facilitate awareness and communication between colleagues, video cameras were installed in the offices of participants. Although this awareness proved to be useful, the experiments showed that people often act according to the "old" mental model of being reliably hidden by office walls (Bellotti, 1993).

Future Vision of the Ubicomp World and Problems with Privacy

A joint vision of Ubicomp researchers regarding the future world was formulated after reading more than 100 roadmap scenarios and research publications. This vision presents a world in which everything is connected and where any activity is possible in any place, supported by applications installed in the environment and in personal devices. Research activities have been devoted to supporting communications between family members and colleagues in different locations (e.g., between workplaces and homes (Aschmoneit, 2002; Dukatel, 2001; Jansson, 2001) and between moving people (Aschmoneit, 2002; Dukatel, 2001; ITEA, 2004), often via video links), and to supporting remote shopping (Dukatel, 2001), learning (Dukatel, 2001), and even remote health care (Bardram, 2004; ITEA, 2004). The future vision also pictures a very safe world, in which technologies ensure safe driving (ITEA, 2004; Masera, 2003) and safe control of home appliances (e.g., locking and unlocking of doors at home (Masera, 2003)), and help in finding keys (Orr, 1994) and toys (Ma, 2005). Technologies are also expected to help people to remember past events, both personal (Gemmel, 2004; Healey, 1998) and work-related (Aschmoneit, 2002), and to give reminders regarding current and future activities and duties (Kim, 2004).

A typical vision of the Ubicomp future involves technology caring for a person, correctly identifying that person's wishes and environment, and reacting to them appropriately. An attractive example of such a vision can be found in the Flying Carpet "Daily Life" visionary scenarios of the Mobile IT forum (Kato, 2004). It is worth noting, however, that the Flying Carpet scenario differs from many others in the sense that its interaction is human-initiated, whereas many other scenarios are more privacy threatening because they suggest that technology will be able to anticipate a person's needs and to act on behalf of that person (e.g., Ducatel, 2001).

There are many positive sides to the Ubicomp vision of future, but it does not seem realistic to assume that Ubicomp technologies will be problem-free. It is thus important to understand the possible problems and to safeguard against them whenever possible. In some cases, achieving safety is more important than protecting privacy. It has been observed, for example, that elderly people can trade their privacy for support and safety (Mynatt, 2000), and that the saving of people's lives through improvements in health care or detection of the location of emergency calls requires

Figure 1. Mobile IT forum, part of a "Daily Life" scenario from FLYING CARPET, Version 2.00 (Kato, 2004), page 4

the storage of personal data which could potentially lead to violations of privacy. In such applications, the most important measure of privacy protection is first to store as little data as are needed for the application to function properly, and second, to ensure that the data cannot be easily accessed by unauthorised people. In many other applications, however, it is important not to trade off privacy for convenience in a blind fashion; for example, the personalisation of recommender systems or location-based services can be designed in more or less privacy-protecting ways. The main goal of this chapter is to point to certain important problems and to suggest methods for improving privacy protection in various Ubicomp applications, so that application developers can choose the most suitable methods.

For example, when reading Ubicomp scenarios one can rarely find a description of how access to personal data or to actuators can be controlled, whereas user-friendly access control is one of crucial factors determining the success of the Ubicomp concept. The example of mobile phones shows that personal data in a phone (such as photos, an address book, or a calendar) will in practice be available to anybody who picks up the phone, due to the inconvenience of password authentication, which takes place once, when the phone is being switched on, after which the phone remains in the "on" state for many days or weeks, unprotected. Although it has always been possible to look through somebody's address book, diary or photo albums in order to find the desired information, this has usually required visiting that person's room and searching through the items there, which may be difficult, at least for a person living in another place. Nowadays, personal mobile devices can store as much in the way of information and photos as several old-style address books, diaries, and photo albums (and will store even more when Personal Lifetime Store application scenarios (Gemmel, 2004) become a reality and when mobile payment logs can also be stored), but they are far less well protected, because they are not locked inside a house or a drawer. Personal mobile devices accompany their owners everywhere and can reveal large quantities of stored personal data, because the users often bypass the inconvenient security measures available for data protection (such as entering a password or rolling a finger across a fingerprint sensor). Since no convenient, user-friendly authentication has yet been developed, personal Ubicomp devices and non-personal smart spaces are likely to disclose their users' data and secrets, and we are now obliged to suggest how to reduce this risk.

The threats to privacy presented in this chapter are not really new, because the reasons for their existence (including conflicts of interest between people and organisations, human curiosity, envy, greed, and beliefs in one's own right to control others) are age-old problems. On the other hand, technology has changed the ways in which personal data can be disclosed.

The components of a typical Ubicomp application are shown in Figure 2. Each component can cause problems in its own way.

Figure 2. A generic view of an Ubicomp application: the thin arrows indicate infor-mation collection, transmission and storage; the thick arrows indicate information push.

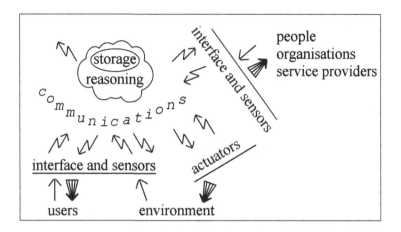

Privacy problems essentially fall into three major groups, the best-known of which concerns problems associated with information flow from the user, that is, due to the acquisition, transmission, and storage of personal data in large quantities. Most privacy-enhancing technologies (PETs) are being developed for the protection of personal data in networked applications, but new Ubicomp applications present new challenges. It has often been proposed, for example, that awareness between family members and colleagues should be supported via the transmission of video data, which violates traditional personal expectations regarding the notion that "if I am hidden behind a wall, I am invisible." Memory aids (personal (Gemmel, 2004; Healey, 1998) and recordings of work meetings (Aschmoneit, 2002)) imply the storage of raw video data, which violates personal expectations regarding the limits of human's attention and memory. There are two reasons for these problems. First, as work in the computer-supported cooperative activity domain has shown (Bellotti, 1993), humans are not accustomed to environments full of sensors, and continue to behave according to their expectations regarding their privacy in the real world. The second reason is the blurring of boundaries between "traditional" application domains. For example, work-related communications from home can intrude into one's personal life, and conversations on private matters from smart workplaces can be recorded automatically along with work-related conversations. In addition, sensors, which were traditionally used only in certain domains (e.g., physiological sensors associated with health care, video cameras for security pur-poses) have been suggested for use in other domains, such as entertainment. Since the traditional view of the entertainment domain assumes that its data are not very confidential (and consequently do not require strong protection measures), there is a danger of the disclosure of health problems detected by physiological sensors in the entertainment domain.

The second group of privacy problems concerns those caused by linkages between different kinds of data (mainly stored data). For example, it has been proposed that a personal memory aid should not record everything, but instead, it should measure the personal arousal level via skin conductivity sensors and other physiological sensors and record only the exciting scenes (Gemmel, 2004; Healey, 1998). Since none of proposed memory aid prototypes has good access control over stored data, these would allow a young boy's parents, for example, to find out easily which girl their son is most interested in. Physiological sensors also have been proposed for measuring the degree of approval of TV programmes (Nasoz, 2003; Palmas, 2001). In this case, the linking of personal physiological responses to information on TV programmes can facilitate the surveillance of citizens from the point of view of whether they support government decisions or not. The linkability problem is in general acknowledged, and PETs in networked applications aim at protection from such data linkability. In such applications as smart spaces and personal devices, however, the problem of data linkability has received less attention, and privacy problems with memory aids, for example, are usually discussed from two points of view: first, how to achieve agreement with the people recorded; and second, whether the police could search through the recorded data or not. The problem of avoiding the curiosity of family members is usually ignored. The dangers of data linkages are in general underestimated by researchers, as we have observed in the example of our own data collection system (see next chapter).

The third group of privacy problems comprises those caused by information flow towards the users, either because technology-initiated communication intrudes into personal life, because the content of the information can disclose private information, or because actuators fail (e.g., to open or close a door at home). Intrusions of technology into personal life can happen when an application interacts with people (e.g., reminds someone to do something) or when an application does not allow people to escape communication with others. Currently, it is easy for a person to say that he missed a phone call because the battery in his mobile phone was empty, or because of street noise, and so forth, but will it be as easy to avoid undesirable communications in the future, when communication is embedded in clothes and battery life is longer? Most parents have observed how their children miss phone calls or "forget" mobile phones at homes when they want to escape from their parents' control; and although such situations are harmful for the parents' nerves, it seems that in most cases, it is necessary for children to make their own decisions and take risks.

The content of information can disclose personal data in two possible ways: if it is delivered in the presence of other people and they hear (or see) the message (e.g., if a movie recommender application suggests that the users should watch adult videos in the presence of their children), or if the information contains data about people other than the user (as one can notice more details during the playback of a memory aid than during a live conversation).

This group of problems is the least studied of all, and PETs dealing with these problems are almost non-existent. What is also important about this group of problems is that technology-initiated communications can reduce user acceptance (users do not always like it when the technology makes the decisions) or hinder personal development. As the work of Nissenbaum (2004) shows, "the right to be left alone" is very important for personal development because people need relative insularity to develop their goals, values, and self-conceptions. Furthermore, if technology cares about personal safety and comfort and relieves people from many responsibilities (such as remembering to take one's keys or to close a door), it becomes more difficult to develop responsibility in children. Children traditionally learn to be responsible for not losing keys, for doing their homework, for taking the right books to school, and for other small everyday tasks, but if all these responsibilities are shifted to Ubicomp technologies, what will replace them in growing children? To the best of our knowledge, the scenarios do not suggest any replacement. Instead, the role of children in many Ubicomp scenarios is limited to playing computer games. Research into computer-supported learning is an exception, but even there learning is mainly supported by augmented reality (Price, 2004), which is also a kind of game. One example of Ubicomp scenarios regarding children is the ITEA roadmap (ITEA, 2004) screenplay of "the Rousseaus' holiday"-- holidays spent by a family consisting of a mother, father, and two children (10 and 13 years old). The screenplay describes how the family goes to a summer cottage "at the seaside on Lonely Island off the Mediterranean coast of France" and that "the kids are unhappy to leave home … because of the high-end, virtual reality video and gaming entertainment equipment, which was recently installed … in their house" (p. 134). If the roadmap leads us to a world in which school children are not interested in Lonely Islands, will we want such a world?

An Example of Unexpected Privacy Problems in Mobile Phone Data Collection

In our case study, the mobile phone usage data were collected with the goal of personalisation and context adaptation of mobile phone applications. The data gathered were a rough location estimate based on phone cell ID (granularity of cell ID-based positioning in our case ranged from several hundred metres to several kilometres), and phone usage data comprised of the duration of incoming and user-made phone calls and usage of different phone applications such as SMS typing, games, a calendar, whether the keyboard was in use or not, and so forth. No phone numbers were logged, nor any SMS contents or application entries, just the start and end of phone calls, the opening and closing of an application, the keyboard being in use, and so on. In addition, logs of Bluetooth activity were collected; each phone that participated in data collection was recording the IDs of all Bluetooth devices in its communication range. All the data items were time stamped with absolute time. Data were collected with respect to five users around the clock for five-seven days.

It is important to note that the users who participated in the data collection were informed about what data were being collected and gave their consent, largely because they did not expect any privacy problems. The users did not want precise location tracking (by GPS, for example) and did not want the content of their actions to be logged, but they allowed logging of the simple facts of actions taking place. It is also important to note that all our users were application developers in the field of context-aware computing, with several years of experience in developing Ubicomp applications. Thus, one would expect them to give their consent to data collection with a much better understanding of the consequences than the average person.

After the data had been collected and analysed, however, we found that when all the seemingly harmless components were linked together, they revealed a lot about the users. They actually allowed us to figure out what kind of person each user was: how communicative they were; whether they usually initiated communications or just received calls and SMS from others and reacted to them; whether or not they had regular routines in their life; whether they were hard-working people; whether they had an active night life; and so on. After discovering that the data told us a lot about the users, we asked them whether they expected such a result, and whether they like this result. For all the users but one, the result was quite surprising, and only one of them told us that he did not care whether other people could gain such information about him. Thus, the power and the unpleasant consequences of information linkage are largely under-estimated even by developers of Ubicomp applications.

We also asked the users to mark which parts of the information (not speculations regarding the user's personality, but lower-level data components) they could make available to their family members, which parts to colleagues and which parts they would not like to become available to a stranger who happened to access the information accidentally. Most of the users did not care much whether their family members or colleagues could access the data or not (although all but one user marked some information as "if family members knew it, it might occasionally be unpleasant" and some other information as "if colleagues know it, the situation might occasionally be unpleasant"). Only one user would allow strangers to access this information, however, and none of them wanted it to appear on the Web.

After that we asked the users' opinion regarding where more personal secrets can be discovered: in public places, at home or at work. Four users told us that a Ubicomp application installed in a home environment had high chances of discovering personal secrets, applications in a work environment and location tracking applications had medium chances, and applications installed in public places had the lowest chances. One user (the only person in our study who had an active night life) named location tracking as the most privacy-threatening, Ubicomp applications in public places (such as streets) and at home as moderately dangerous and those at work as the least dangerous. We realize that five users in a study is not a significant number, but we think that the results are interesting because all the subjects were well acquainted with the Ubicomp concept.

Our own data analysis confirms the users' opinions, because most of our conclusions were made after processing the data acquired in a home environment. We also observed that if the time stamps had not revealed absolute times, it would have been more difficult to analyse the data. For example, if the time stamps and location stamps had been encrypted or relative to certain application-dependent events, it would have been difficult to distinguish between the home and work environments and to make deductions about users' personalities. In our case location was shown only as a cell ID, so it was not very informative, but a very curious person would nevertheless be able to "decode" it.

The experiences with collecting IDs of Bluetooth devices in the communication range were also very interesting, as it was possible to find out from the phone logs when the neighbours of a test subject came home and when they went to sleep and to deduce something about their personalities.

The State of the Art in Privacy Protection

The term "privacy enhancement" has been used for more than a decade to represent technologies concerned with various aspects of Internet security. Privacy protection in Internet applications should be based on the main principles of privacy protection as listed in the Common Criteria for Information Technology Security Evaluation (anonymity, pseudonymity, unlinkability, and unobservability). A survey of privacy-enhancing technologies in the HiSPEC report of 2002 stated, however, that more effort had been invested in protecting user identities than personal data in the previous years (HiSPEC, 2002). Similarly, the PISA project in 2003 concluded that previous research efforts had mainly been concerned with the protection of users' identities, but not very much with users' actions (Blarkom, 2003). Since then, research efforts regarding the protection of personal data and user actions have increased, but they have mainly been concentrated on Internet applications.

Nevertheless, the PRIME study on the state of the art regarding privacy protection in network applications, carried out in 2005, has pointed out many performance problems and security weaknesses, and reached the conclusion that even the most recent techniques and tools are still far from providing a holistic approach to usable and secure anonymizing networks (Camenisch, 2005). It is worth noting that the conclusion refers to the current technology settings, not to future technology settings such as smart environments and personal memory aids. The goal of the PRIME project is to develop a framework for privacy and identity management in electronic information networks given current settings, and the project has made significant efforts in the areas of access control (the term "access control" in PRIME stands mainly for the access / release / processing of data by software methods, unlike the more traditional understanding of the term as the granting of access rights to a person), cryptography, communication infrastructure and user-side (allowing users to specify how their personal data can be used), and service-side (management of obligations) identity management. Access control research is concerned with developing policies for access control and a language for their description, in order to allow users to control the use of their personal information and to allow negotiations between different counterparts without revealing sensitive information.

The PAW project is a continuation of the privacy protection research with regard to the use of software agents and is working on cryptographic techniques and licensing languages (a description of what one is allowed to do with data during processing and what not). Licensing languages and machine-readable privacy policies are an active research area in which most of the research is concerned with the privacy policies of Web sites. A recently developed platform for privacy preferences (P3P) (Cranor, 2003) allows Web sites to convey their policies in machine-readable form, so that they can be checked on the user side and compared with user preferences. P3P does not actually force Web sites to stick to their promises, however.

The goal of the FIDIS project (Bauer, 2005) is to develop privacy-preserving methods of identity management for mobile wireless applications in current technology settings. The project has proposed a privacy diamond model for these settings, the main components in which are user, device, location and action, and has suggested that user privacy should be protected by hiding some of the links between these components of the model. The FIDIS project has also presented a classification of identity management systems (IMS), first as systems for account management (pure IMS, where the main goal is authentication, authorization, and accounting), second as systems for personalized services which need both user identity and profiles or log histories, and third as systems for pseudonym management, for example, in web services. Good practices for these systems were proposed, including separate access to the user authentication data, user account data and personal data (addresses, etc.) in identity management systems of the first type; and an architecture was developed for a mobile device security tool for creating partial identities and using them in wireless and wired networks.

To summarize, the projects listed above, and some others, mainly deal with privacy protection in network applications and, to some extent, with protecting personal data stored in personal devices. It is mainly proposed that the data stored in personal devices should be protected by means of encryption, but the inconvenience of the related security measures creates "large holes in security and privacy" (Caloyannides, 2004, p. 85), which is very dangerous considering the huge increase in the amount of personal data stored in modern mobile phones. Security and privacy problems affecting personal devices constitute a very challenging problem in general terms; on the one hand, the limited computational capabilities, battery life and screen size of mobile devices pose problems for developers of security methods, while on the other hand, the main burden of configuring and updating security settings and anti-virus software is being placed on the owners of these personal devices, who often have neither the necessary special education, nor the time or enthusiasm to do that.

Research into privacy protection in such emerging domains as smart environments and smart cars is in its infancy, and only generic guidelines have been developed. The work of Langheinrich et al. (2001), for example, suggests how the fair information practices (listed in current data protection laws) can be applied to Ubicomp applications, and shows how difficult it might be to apply them. The fair information practices state, for instance, that the user must have access to the data about him that has been stored, and the right to change details that are wrong. In a Ubicomp future, however, it will not be easy for users to find all the items of data about them that are stored in the network and in the personal devices of surrounding people (let alone check them). Moreover, some data processing techniques (such as neural networks) store user models in a form that is difficult to interpret.

The work of Hong et al. (2004) proposes high-level privacy risk models based on two aspects: first, the social and organisational context in which an application is embedded (Who are the data sharers and observers? What kinds of personal information are shared? What is the value proposition for information sharing, its symmetry, etc.?), and second the technological aspect (How is the collection, storage and retention of personal data organized? Who controls the system? Is there any possibility to opt out?). This is close to our understanding of privacy threats, but we suggest that other aspects should also be taken into account, especially the probability of accidental information flow (not intended by the designers). Furthermore, this work mainly suggests guidelines for risk estimation, not for safeguards.

The work of Lahlou et al. (2003) focuses "on the specific issues of the data collection phase" (Forward, p. 2) and proposes high-level guidelines. One of the most important guidelines is to minimize data collection. Such generic design guidelines as "think before doing" and "understand the way in which new technologies change the effects of classic issues" (i.e., existing solutions in the physical world) (p.3) can be applied in other spheres as well as data collection, but these are very generic design guidelines.

To summarize, most of the research into privacy protection is concerned with protection of the information flow from users, whereas other privacy aspects have not received much attention from researchers.

Gaps in Privacy Enhancing Technologies

For most Ubicomp scenarios to work well, advanced privacy-protecting safeguards, which do not yet exist (although research into them has started), will be required. We suggest that the most important safeguards are the following:

- **Intelligent Reasoning Capabilities**: advanced artificial intelligence algorithms capable of recognizing sensitive data in order to avoid recording or publishing it, for example, algorithms capable of intelligent online summarizing of audio recordings (online conversion of a meeting audio stream into a text document, including only working discussions), algorithms capable of detecting that persons in a video or photo are naked or kissing, algorithms capable of adaptation to the user's ethics and culture (a photo of a Muslim woman with her head uncovered is private, while for the majority of Finnish women this would be nothing special) and so on. To some extent these capabilities can be implemented as common-sense rules, such as "if a person is alone, or if there are only two persons in a room, the probability of discovering confidential data is higher than if there are a larger number of people." In addition, algorithms for detecting unusual patterns of copying and processing of personal data are needed (e.g., if a new back-up is made soon after the previous back-up it may indicate data theft, and an alarm should be given), because these would also be of help when a person authorized to work with the data is dishonest, unlike other access control methods, which work mainly against outsiders.

- **User-Friendly Security**: advanced access control and security methods, such as frequent unobtrusive context-aware authentication of users. Different user verification methods should be chosen, for example, depending on the application that a user wants to access, or on the user's location and behaviour; access to a calculator application should not require user effort (Stajano, 2004), whereas access to personal memory aid data should be allowed only to the data owner. Thus, the current "once and forever" password-based user verification on mobile phones, which facilitates unauthorised use when the owner is in another room, for instance, should be replaced with continuous unobtrusive user verification, for example, based on user behaviour or voice recognition, and on stronger authentication methods if unobtrusive authentication fails but access to sensitive data continues to be requested. In general terms, we suggest that security should be a fairly effortless matter for users (e.g., updates of anti-virus software should be system-initiated and happen at convenient times) and should be enforced. We suggest this by analogy with control over technical conditions in personal cars and the security enforced with regard to financial operations, because future Ubicomp scenarios envision personal devices that perform life-critical tasks (health monitoring and health care (Bardram, 2004; ITEA, 2004), financial tasks, and identity management (Ducatel, 2001). A malfunctioning personal device could fail to notice a health crisis on the part of the device owner, or fail to communicate this to the doctors, for example, and it could also create threats to other people; for instance, if it sends a lot of spam and malware to surrounding personal devices it can significantly slow down their operation and hinder their performing of the tasks required of them. Work on user-friendly authentication is an emerging research area. Current work is mainly concerned with biometrics, which is not a perfect solution, because of possibility of spoofing biometric sensors. Thus, we suggest that biometric modalities which carry a high danger of identity theft (e.g., fingerprint and iris) should be used cautiously and only with aliveness detection, and that a fusion of several not so privacy-threatening biometric modalities (such as voice, gait, or behaviour) should be used as a primary or complementary means of authentication.

- **Communication protocols which do not use Unique Device Identifiers**: it is easy to link a device ID or a smart object ID to a user and to track the user's actions. Communication protocols which hide the very fact of communication would be an ideal case, because a lot of information can be acquired by tracking who communicates with whom. For example, it can be concluded from the fact that a person has started to visit the Web page of a certain bank that that person has opened an account at this bank, and a false request to update a recently created account in this particular bank has higher chances of succeeding than when sent to an established client of the bank, or to a client of another bank. This safeguard has the drawback that it would hinder the discovery of users with malicious intentions or with malfunctioning personal devices sending out spam and viruses, but this problem can be partially solved by means of good firewalls and anti-virus software, which would protect against malware (see "user-friendly security" bullet). In cases where the detection of users' IDs is important, these communication protocols cannot be used (e.g., some applications can require the using of IDs in communication protocols), but their usage should not be a common practice because large-scale logging of everybody's actions is not likely to improve security in society, as the famous security expert Bruce Schneier pointed out (Schneier, 2005, 2007).

- **Secure ad-hoc communications:** if a device owner enables ad-hoc Bluetooth communications, for example, the sending of a large number of requests to this device can slow down its operation or even exhaust the battery. This is not a direct threat to privacy, but it might engender privacy if the encryption of personal data becomes delayed, and it is definitely a violation of the "right to be left alone" in cases where the user cannot simply ignore incoming spam because he is expecting an important message.

- **Encryption for untrustworthy platforms**: not all functions can be executed in encrypted form. Instead, it is common to decrypt the code and the data before execution, which allows spying.

- **Unified, concise user interface methods of maintaining user awareness** about the functionality of the application and its privacy threats, possibly in graphical form (e.g., similar to road signs). A warning about video cameras is currently placed on the doors of shops (although with no information as to whether video data is stored or not, or for how long), but other Ubicomp technologies would require similar icons.

- **More detailed transparency tools for awareness in average non-technical users** regarding security risks, the correct usage of anti-virus and firewall applications, the dangers of data collection and the accepting of ad-hoc messages from unknown devices, and so on. Since users do not want to spend much time on security education, these tools and their user interfaces should be really intelligent and work "just in time." Currently, it is too easy for users to make mistakes (it is often too easy to ignore important questions that all look the same, and click yes without even reading a security-related question). For example, the current practice of asking users whether they agree to "accept temporarily, for this session," a security certificate regarding a certain Web site is not really helpful, because the same question is used for all Web sites, and it is not linked to other data regarding the website in question.

- **Recovery means**: first, if somebody's personal data was compromised (e.g., a fingerprint was forged), it is necessary to switch quickly and easily to a new authentication procedure in all applications (home, work, smart car, banking, etc.), unlike the current situation, in which recovery from an identity theft requires significant efforts on the part of the victim and can harm that person's reputation. Second, if a personal device is lost, the personal data contained in it can be protected from strangers by security measures such as data encryption and strict access control. However, it is important that the user does not need to spend time customising and training a new device (so that denial of service does not occur). Instead, the new device should itself load user preferences, contacts, favourite music, and so forth, from a back-up service, probably a home server. We suggest that ways be developed to synchronize data in personal devices with a back-up server in a way that is secure and requires minimal effort from the user.

Dimensions of Privacy Threats Analysis

Privacy risks fall into two major groups, the first of which is application domain-dependent risks, which depend on the personal or organizational activity being supported. Health data, for example, are considered sensitive, and designers of applications for hospitals are obliged to follow corresponding privacy protection regulations. Second, privacy risks are caused by a mismatch between personal expectations regarding current privacy levels and reality, which do not depend on the application domain. If a person perceives his current situation to be a private one (e.g., being alone at home) but in fact is being monitored, the chances that personal secrets will be discovered are higher than if the person perceives the current situation as public (e.g., giving a talk at a large meeting) and takes care of his own privacy.

Consequently, we suggest the following dimensions for the analysis of privacy threats:

- Real-world dimensions:
  - People's personalities
  - People's activities
  - The environment where an activity takes place
- Dimensions of technology functionality:
  - Information flow
  - Computer control level vs. personal control level
  - Balance between technology aspects (storage and communication vs. reasoning capabilities and control level)

Real World Dimensions

People's personalities are important because the notion of what is considered private and what is not depends on the person and the situation (context) (Nissenbaum, 2004). For example, the chances that a married man's personal data will accidentally be accessed by his wife or children are fairly high, even though secrets withheld from family members are not unusual; for example, parents often prefer to keep children unaware of the existence of adult videos at home, in order to prevent them from watching these while the parents are away. Personal activity is obviously an important dimension for privacy risk analysis because an activity consumes and produces a flow of information; for instance, large quantities of financial data are involved in paying bills, and health and identity data are involved in a call to a doctor. The environment is an important dimension (one which unfortunately is not always considered) because people's mental models of current privacy levels are based on traditional perceptions of their environment (e.g., "now I am alone in my office, so that nobody can see me") and people behave more or less freely depending on their estimation of current privacy levels. We suggest that applications should take the following into account:

- **traditional perceptions of the environment** (e.g., perception of the home as a private environment; perception of a wall as a non-transparent object, perception of a street as a public place)

- **common activities in the environment** (e.g., in an office people usually work)

- **other probable activities in the environment** (e.g., calling a doctor or flirting with a colleague in an office environment). Previous guidelines for the estimation of privacy threats (Hong, 2004) took account of the activity dimension mainly in the sense of the primary user activity supported by the application, but secondary activities are also very important.

Privacy threats coming from real-world settings can be roughly categorized as high, medium, and low in intensity. We suggest that application developers should always consider the privacy risk to be high when the application can run in the presence of children (which concerns most home-domain applications). Furthermore, we suggest that application developers should not give parents unlimited power to check and control what their children are doing. Instead, the children's privacy should be protected carefully, because they need this privacy for their personal development (Nissenbaum, 2004).

We suggest that high-intensity threats exist in connection with activities dealing with health care, finance, and communication between family members and close friends. High threats appear in the home environment, first because people perceive it as private and behave freely, and second because the security of home computers and personal devices is to a large extent the responsibility of their users, whereas many people (elderly people and children especially) do not have the education, skills or in many cases the desire to take care of the security of personal Ubicomp applications, which makes them vulnerable to all kinds of security faults. High-intensity threats also exist in an office environment, because on the one hand people cannot avoid dealing with private issues at work and are highly dependent on their work, and on the other hand, they are not free to decide on the environment in which they have to work, whereas organizations invest a lot of money in the development and installation of Ubicomp applications in workplaces. It is, thus, quite probable that Ubicomp applications will be deployed in workplaces sooner than in homes.

Figure 3. Guidelines for evaluation of real-world privacy threats caused by certain environments and activities

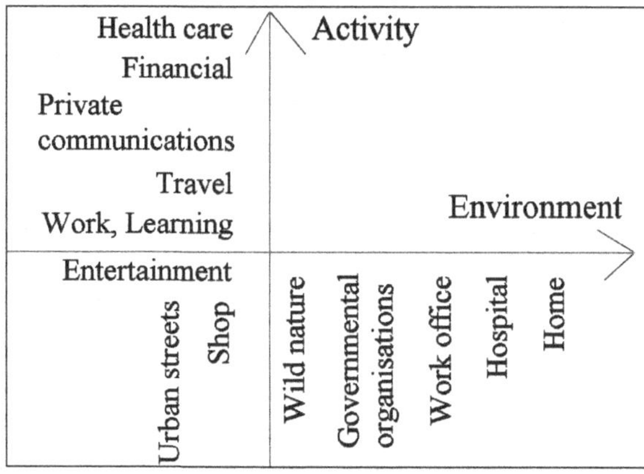

Medium threats to privacy appear in connection with shopping (increasing competition between retailers can lead to advertisements that are targeted at personal preferences and to hunting for personal data), learning and mobility activities (by mobility we mean travelling within a city as well as on holiday or for one's work), and relatively low-level threats are associated with entertainment activities.

Our informal grading of the dimensions of the privacy threats caused by real-life activities and the environment is presented in Figure 3.

Technology Choice Dimensions

Information flows start from data collection performed by sensors. The most popular sensors in Ubicomp scenarios are audio, video, positioning, physiological, safety, and comfort sensors, together with those used for logging human-computer interactions.

Physiological sensors are most dangerous from the privacy point of view, because they detect what is inside a person's body, that is, they "break into" the most private sphere. These sensors are the basis for building health care applications, where strict rules for the protection of health data exist. Ubicomp scenarios, nevertheless, suggest that these sensors could be used for purposes other than health and fitness. Detection of a person's mood and emotions is an active research area (Nasoz, 2003), and suggested applications include the detection of interesting scenes for automatic audio and video capture for lifetime personal stores (Gemmel, 2004; Healey, 1998) and the estimation of a user's preferences for TV programmes (Palmas, 2001). If physiological data are linked to the content of TV programmes and to the presence of other people, however, personal feelings become dangerously "naked" and can reveal to parents such facts as who their child is in love with, or else they can be used by governments for monitoring the loyalty of citizens. Physiological sensors can also detect health problems, but such data will not be properly protected, because the data protection requirements in the domain of TV personalization are not very strict.

Video and audio sensors violate natural privacy-protecting borders such as walls, and video cameras can reveal a lot more than audio sensors. In Ubicomp scenarios, they are suggested for use in real-time communication between people and for helping parents to monitor their children, for instance, by logging potentially dangerous situations (Ma, 2005). Second, such sensors have been suggested for memory augmentation, for example, the recording of work meetings (Aschmoneit, 2002) or personal memory aids (Gemmel, 2004; Healey, 1998). The first type of application "breaks the walls," while the second type violates people's belief in the limits of others' attention and memory.

Biometric sensors have mainly been suggested for access control, and carry a danger of identity theft. Safety and comfort sensors (temperature, light, car acceleration etc.) can reveal users' personalities and often initiate information push; for example, they may issue reminders to switch the stove off or employ actuators to do it automatically. This is beneficial for people suffering from dementia or for families with babies, but if teenagers are assumed to be as irresponsible in caring about home safety as babies, there may be little opportunity left for them to develop a sense of responsibility.

The application control level denotes how much technology does on behalf of its users. An application that reminds its user to take pills in the event of high blood pressure, for example, has a high control level because it initiates the measuring of blood pressure and a dialogue with the user. Such a dialogue may annoy the individual or reveal personal health details if it happens at the wrong moment or in public. An application which filters shopping advertisements according to user preferences also has a high control level, because the user can never know about certain shopping alternatives if they are filtered out. (An important question for such applications is who sets the filtering rules and how they can be prevented from favouring a particular shop.)

With more extensive information collection, transmission and storage capabilities and higher control levels, technology poses more privacy threats. Most Ubicomp scenarios involve application-dependent information storage and a lot of wireless communication (between objects, people, and organizations). We suggest that significant threats to privacy can arise if technology penetrates walls and the human body, for instance, by using physiological, video and/or audio sensors. Significant threats are also likely to be caused by high control levels (i.e., the capability of a technology to act on behalf of a person, e.g., to call an ambulance in an emergency) or by biometric sensors (due to the possibility of identity theft).

Figure 4. Guidelines for evaluating privacy threats caused by technology choices

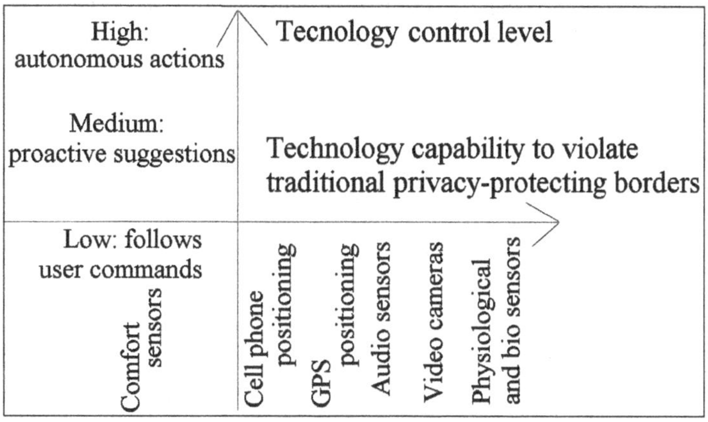

We also suggest that privacy threats should always be regarded as high when the linkage of data from several sources is possible, for example, when either of a lot of data about one person can be aggregated (as in most personal devices), or certain data about a large number of people. We suggest that the dangers of information linkage are often under-estimated, as we have observed in the case of our data collection system.

Medium threats are associated with positioning sensors (without time stamps they provide location data, but not much activity data, whereas location plus time information is a much greater threat to privacy) and with a medium level of technology control (the capability to make proactive suggestions, e.g., to issue reminders). Fairly low threat levels are associated with a low level of control (e.g., ranking advertisements according to criteria explicitly set by the user) and with comfort sensors (lighting, heating, etc.).

We would like to emphasize that threats to personal privacy are very often caused by mismatches between the application control level and application intelligence, and particularly by the fact that the technology is already capable of storing and transmitting a lot of data, but is not capable of detecting which data it should not store or transmit (with the exception of predefined data categories such as health and finance). In order to ensure "the right to be left alone," however, and to prevent the accidental disclosure of confidential data, for example, via an audio reminder to take medicine when the user is in somebody's company, it is very important that the intelligence of an application should correspond to its level of control (in other words, to its level of autonomy: what technology can do on its own initiative). Another example can be found in (Truong, 2004), which presents scenarios of Ubicomp applications made by end users, where one of the users suggested automatic recordings of parties in his home. If such an application is deployed in a large home and records two persons discussing personal matters in a room without any other guests, for example, it can lead to privacy problems. These would not appear if the application were intelligent enough not to record such a scene.

Guidelines for Safeguarding Against Privacy Threats

Estimates of the threats to privacy created by the combining of real-world settings and technology choices in certain popular Ubicomp scenarios are presented in Figure 5. Since the scenarios do not describe implementation details, the estimates are only approximate. The threats in the "safe driving" application scenario, for example, depend on data storage (e.g., whether a time-stamped log of speed, acceleration etc. is stored or not) and data exchange (e.g., between cars driving behind the other),

Figure 5. Examples of levels of privacy threats in popular scenarios

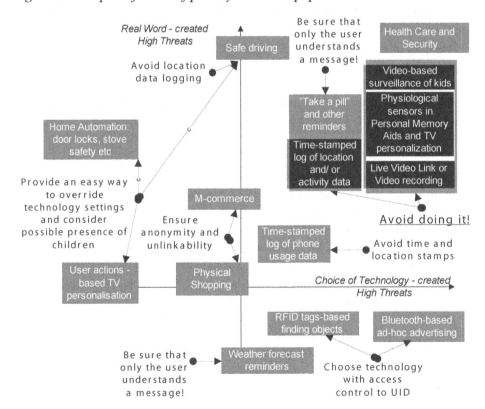

but a high application control level is in any case a threat to privacy, because the technology might be wrong, and because the users don't always accept its superiority. Similarly, "issuing reminders about the weather forecast for the destination when on a journey" presents privacy threats because it is a form of technology-initiated interaction. What if the reminder is given when the user is in the company of a person whom he would prefer to be unaware of his journey?

When reading Ubicomp scenarios, we have not found any for applications which do not have either high technology risks, or high real-world risks, or both. In fact, most scenarios fall into the category of high technology risks. We suggest that if an application implies high technology risks, these should be reduced by lowering the control level of the technology, choosing the sensors differently and reducing the linkability of the data and by other applicable methods (see below).

By lowering the control level of technology, we mean that applications should ask the user's permission before taking potentially privacy-threatening actions, for instance, for video and audio recording. By a different choice of sensors, we mean that same kind of data can often be acquired in many ways, each of them presenting different privacy threats. Movie recommendation applications, for example, need user feedback data, and the ways of obtaining it include the use of physiological sensors, the analysis of facial expressions, speech recognition, monitoring of the noise level in a room, and monitoring user actions such as fast forward scrolling (which is the safest in terms of privacy). Even if fast forward scrolling and noise level monitoring might not give as good results as physiological sensors (which have not actually been tested), they should be preferred because they pose less of a threat to privacy. From our data collecting experiences, we would argue that what we can tell about a person through the linkage of different kinds of data it is frequently under-estimated. We regard reducing data linkage as very important, and suggest that absolute time stamps should be avoided; that is, data should be stamped with the time relative to the application and as much real-time data processing should be done as possible.

Furthermore, we suggest that since applications with both high threats due to real-world settings and high threats due to technology settings require advanced safeguards (such as intelligent reasoning capabilities or user-friendly security), which do not yet exist, such applications should be deployed only in domains with strict legal regulations, such as healthcare or banking, and then only with a fairly low level of technology control. In other domains we suggest that the deployment of such applications should be postponed until the technology becomes more intelligent. For example, we suggest that the use of physiological and video sensors and data stamped with absolute times should be avoided unless it is critical for the preservation of life and security. The suggestions made above do not apply to cases where the technology performs its tasks reliably and the users do not perceive the privacy problems as being important; for example, elderly people may be willing to trade off privacy against the gaining of support in time, and babies do not care about privacy at all.

In addition, we suggest the following good practices:

- **Real-time data processing**: select algorithms and hardware capable of processing data immediately in real time (performing real-time feature selection, or finding answers to predefined "pattern exists or not" queries), so that the storage of raw data (even temporarily) is avoided;

- **Encrypted or relative location stamping and time stamping:** For example, instead of investigating the dependence of high blood pressure on absolute time, an application should stamp the data relative to the moment of taking a pill or calculate the average time when the user's blood pressure was above a given threshold;

- **Data deletion or editing after an application-dependent time**: For example, when a user buys clothes, all information about the material, price, designer, and so forth, should be deleted from the clothes' RFID tags. For applications that require active RFID tags (such as finding lost objects (Orr, 1999), the RFID tag should be changed so that no links are left between the shop database and the personal clothes. Similarly, the location of an emergency call does not require the storage of long-term location data, so that this should be avoided;

- **Data processing in a personal device instead of sending data to the environment**: Instead of submitting a query with personal financial preferences to a shop in order to find suitable products, for example, the application should submit a more generic query, even at the cost of an increase in data filtering in personal devices, and anonymous payment procedures should be used whenever possible.

- **Choice of communication technologies which do not use permanent hardware IDs in their protocols, or at least have control over access to these IDs,** and which allow the communication range to be controlled. The current situation with Bluetooth communication, for example, is that if a device owner enables ad-hoc communication (in order to use the full range of possible applications), the device responds to each request with its ID, allowing user tracking even over walls, due to the fairly large communication range that is beyond user control.

- **Detection of hardware removals and replacements**: Users are currently not warned about replacements/ removal of attached sensors or memory cards when devices are in the "off" state, thus making physical tampering easier (Becher, 2006). Since personal devices will be monitoring a user's health in the future (Bardram, 2004; ITEA, 2004), unauthorized replacement of sensors could result in a death if they failed to detect a health crisis.

- **Transparency tools**: These are user-friendly ways to warn users about possible privacy violation problems which might result from the technologies deployed around him/her and ways to configure technology settings easily. For example, users might prefer to sacrifice some of the benefits of an application for the sake of anonymity, to reduce the level of control of applications or adjust the way in which incoming advertisements are filtered (if advertisements which are considered uninteresting by the application are completely removed, this carries a danger that the user will never hear about some options). One solution could be to have several "privacy profiles" in devices, so that each profile defines which groups of applications and means of communication are enabled and which not in different settings. Users would then just need to switch between profiles instead of dealing with a bundle of options with the risk of forgetting some of them. Our own experiences with data collection have shown that since even Ubicomp application developers do not fully understand the possible consequences of their data collection, transparency tools should be really carefully designed.

- **Means of disconnecting** gracefully: Users should be able to switch an application or device off completely, or to switch off some of its functionalities in such a way that other people do not take it as a desire by the user to hide, and in such a way that the device is still usable (e.g., users should be able to check calendar data while having the communication functionality switched off).

Conclusion

We have presented here an analysis of Ubicomp scenarios from the point of view of possible implications regarding privacy and have considered the state of the art in research into privacy protection, which does not allow safeguards to be provided against all possible problems. Recent news reports suggest that large-scale surveillance by means of ubiquitous technologies (the Internet and phones) has already started (Web site of the American Civil Liberties Union and the ACLU Foundation, 2006). The analysis of Ubicomp scenarios does show, however, that privacy protection is not yet considered a necessary design requirement, which can lead to a lack of user acceptance.

A typical approach to privacy threat analysis is to estimate the sensitivity of data that have been collected and stored, which depends on the application domain (e.g., health care data are considered sensitive) and on the consumers of the information (Hong, 2004). We suggest that privacy protection should also depend on which borders of real-life privacy are violated by the technology, because the likelihood of acquiring sensitive data accidentally is high if the technology penetrates through supposedly reliable physical borders. Furthermore, we suggest that privacy protection should consider not only information flows from users, but also information flows towards users.

The design guidelines for the estimation of privacy threats and for privacy protection in emerging Ubicomp applications have been proposed after a thorough analysis of Ubicomp scenarios, observations made during long-term runs with Ubicomp applications in a work environment (Bellotti, 1993) and our own experiences. Our guidelines are intended to protect individuals both from regular leakage of confidential data (such as location tracking data) and from the accidental discovery of sensitive data, for example, the discovery that two guests at a party had a heated discussion on a balcony. The effectiveness of such guidelines is very difficult to evaluate, due to the rare occasions on which such events happen and the fact that attempts to "capture" them would be unethical. We are not aware of any work presenting results on how certain privacy-protecting guidelines actually protect or disclose real secrets.

Our experiment with phone data collection, nevertheless, convinced us that since it is difficult to over-estimate what kind of discoveries an application can make, developers should be very cautious and take care to protect users against infringement of their privacy by various categories of interested persons and organizations ranging from the limited number of experienced hackers up to the large numbers of curious family members, relatives, colleagues, neighbours and so on, who luckily are most probably not endowed with such advanced computer skills. The guidelines and safeguards are proposed in order to help application developers decide which problems they should pay attention to and choose the most appropriate safeguards in relation to the application and the device capabilities. Implementation of some of the proposed safeguards would require a significant increase in the computational capabilities of personal devices, but such notable hardware improvements have been achieved recently, that it is likely to become possible in the near future to dedicate more memory to data processing algorithms instead of only to data storage. In cases where the capabilities of personal devices are insufficient for the desired safeguards, we suggest that users should be made aware of the possible problems (proper transparency tools should be developed for non-technical users) and allowed to choose a trade-off between the benefits and problems of the applications.

Ubicomp technologies can help to make life better if they are accepted by users, but this acceptance will be jeopardized if the problems created by the new technologies are not analysed and minimized. One of the important benefits of Ubicomp technologies will be to increase the security of individuals and society as a whole, for instance, making it possible to locate an emergency phone call, which could help to save the users' lives, or to access descriptions of crimes in remote locations and to compare them, which could help to find criminals. Similarly, access to a patient's lifelong health record could help to reveal an allergy and save the person's life. In general, new technologies provide support for a safer and more convenient life and for communications, so that it would be possible to access everybody and everything (family members, doctors, services, etc.) from any place and any time. The current situation is, nevertheless, such that the benefits are emphasized more than the possible problems, and thus we would like to emphasize the problems in this paper. New technologies can have implications for privacy with respect to the surveillance of citizens by governments and surveillance between people, for example, control exercised by parents or spouses over the activities of their family members. Although in some cases surveillance is clearly undesirable (e.g., parents do not want their children to be able to discover the prices of their purchases easily, to know which videos they watch or to see all their photos), it is an open question whether the surveillance of citizens by a government and the surveillance of children by their parents can increase the safety of society as a whole. The surveillance of children can help to save them from abuse, traumas or drug addiction, but in many cases such surveillance is not likely to do any better than the old-style trust and love in a family. Thus, it may be better when developing new technologies to aim at detecting when children are in real danger rather than at simply providing their parents with means of control all their actions? Although it is easier to develop technology by which parents can monitor their children, it might lead to their growing into irresponsible or helpless people.

Regarding whether the surveillance of citizens by a government can increase safety in society as a whole, we would like to cite the opinion of the famous security expert Bruce Schneier, who says in his essay "Why Data Mining Won't Stop Terror" (2005) that "we're not trading privacy for security; we're giving up privacy and getting no security in return." Schneier continues to debate over the idea of trading off privacy for extra security in later articles. For example, in "On Police Security Cameras: Wholesale Surveillance" (2007), he says that "the effects of wholesale surveillance on privacy and civil liberties is profound; but unfortunately, the debate often gets mischaracterized as a question about how much privacy we need to give up in order to be secure. This is wrong." Schneier suggests that, although the police should be allowed to use new technologies to track suspects, data on people who are not currently under suspicion should not be stored. The decision of the society regarding the bus ticketing application in Helsinki was in line with this opinion, that is, society decided against trading off privacy for security. In many cases, however, new technologies can help to increase safety without threatening privacy. The possibility to locate an emergency phone call can help to save the users' lives, for example, but the threats to users' privacy can be minimized first by keeping only short-term, recent location data, and second by strict control over access to this data.

We suggest that the most important safeguards are an appropriate balance between the level of technology control and its level of artificial intelligence (how advanced the reasoning is and how the access control methods are implemented), an appropriate choice of sensors (sensors with powerful capabilities for violating natural privacy-protecting borders should not be used wantonly), and other hardware (such as communication chips with a configurable communication range and access control to their ID), the prevention of data linkability by avoiding absolute time stamps and location stamps, especially in applications which cannot provide user anonymity (such as smart spaces and personal devices), user-friendly security and user-friendly system configuration methods. The list of the proposed safeguards is not exhaustive and could well change with the development of new technologies. Novel application scenarios or the unpredictable use of new technologies, for example, could introduce new threats to privacy, which could require more safeguards. On the other hand, if methods of reliable unobtrusive biometric recognition with aliveness detection can be developed for mobile devices in the near future, this will significantly improve the protection of personal data and make some of our recommendations outdated. However, since our analysis is based on application scenarios and roadmaps for Ubicomp technology development and for the development of privacy-enhancing technologies, we believe that our recommendations for the evaluation of privacy threats and safeguarding against them will be valid for as long as the scenarios analysed here are valid, and for as long as gaps in privacy-enhancing technologies pointed out here continue to exist. Since one fairly common reason for privacy problems in these scenarios is an insufficient level of system intelligence for the complexity of the tasks, and since computer capabilities for data collection, storage and transmission are growing faster than the intelligence of data processing algorithms, protection against privacy violations is likely to remain an important problem in the future.

Acknowledgment

This Article is based on research supported by the EU project SWAMI: Safeguards in a World of Ambient Intelligence (IST-2004-006507)

References

Aschmoneit, P., & Höbig, M. (Ed.) (2002). *Context-aware collaborative environments for next generation business networks: scenario document* (COCONET deliverable D2.2). Telematica Institute.

Bardram, J. E. (2004). The personal medical unit - a Ubiquitous Computing infrastructure for personal pervasive healthcare. In T. Adlam, H. Wactlar, I. Korhonen, (Ed.), *UbiHealth 2004 - The 3rd International Workshop on Ubiquitous Computing for Pervasive Healthcare Applications*.

Bauer, M., Meints, M., & Hansen, M. (2005). *Structured overview on prototypes and concepts of identity management systems* (FIDIS Deliverable D3.1). Retrieved on March 15, 2006, from http://www.fidis.net/fileadmin/fidis/deliverables/fidis-wp3-del3.1.overview_on_IMS.final.pdf

Becher, A., Benenson, Z., & Dornseif, M. (2006). Tampering with motes: real-world physical attacks on wireless sensor networks. In J. A. Clark, R. F. Paige et al. (Ed.), *The Third International Conference* on *Security in Pervasive Computing* (pp. 104-118).

Bellotti, V., & Sellen, A. (1993). Design for privacy in Ubiquitous Computing environments. *Proceedings of the The Third European Conference on Computer Supported Cooperative Work (ECSCW'93)* (pp. 77-92). Kluwer.

Blarkom, G. W. van, Borking, J. J., & Olk, J. G. E. (Ed.). (2003). *Handbook of privacy and privacy-enhancing technologies: the case of intelligent software agents*, TNO-FEL, The Hague.

Bohn, J., Coroama, V., Langheinrich, M., Mattern, F., & Rohs, M. (2005). Social, economic, and ethical implications of Ambient Intelligence and Ubiquitous Computing. In W. Weber, J. Rabaey, E. Aarts (Eds.), *Ambient Intelligence* (pp. 5-29). London: Springer-Verlag.

Caloyannides, M.A. (2004). The cost of convenience: a Faustian deal, *IEEE Security & Privacy, 2*(2), 84 – 87.

Camenisch, J. (Ed.). (2005). *First annual research report* (PRIME deliverable D16.1). Retrieved on March 12, 2006, from http://www.prime-project.eu.org/public/prime_products/deliverables/rsch/pub_del_D16.1.a_ec_wp16.1_V1_final.pdf

Cranor, L. F. (2003). P3P: making privacy policies more useful. *IEEE Security and Privacy, 1*(6), 50-55.

Ducatel, K., Bogdanowicz, M., Scapolo, F., Leijten, J., & Burgelman, J.-C. (2001). *Scenarios for Ambient Intelligence in 2010*. Institute for Prospective Technological Studies (IPTS), EC-JRC, Sevilla.

Gemmel, J., Williams, L., Wood, K., Lueder, R., & Bell, G. (2004). Passive capture and ensuing issues for a personal lifetime store, In *Proceedings of the First ACM Workshop on Continuous Archival and Retrieval of Personal Experiences* (pp. 48-55).

Healey, J. & Picard, R.W. (1998). StartleCam: a cybernetic wearable camera. In *The Second International Symposium on Wearable Computing* (pp. 42-49).

HiSPEC project (2002), *Privacy enhancing technologies: state of the art review, version 1*. HiSPEC Report. Retrieved on March 1, 2006, from http://www.hispec.org.uk/public_documents/7_1PETreview3.pdf

Hong, J., Ng, J, Lederer, S., & Landay, J. (2004). Privacy risk models for designing privacy-sensitive Ubiquitous Computing systems. In *Proceedings of the Conference on Designing Interactive Systems* (pp. 91-100).

Information Technology for European Advancement (2004), *ITEA Technology Roadmap for Software-Intensive Systems* (2nd ed.). Retrieved on March 1, 2006, from www.itea-office.org

Jansson, C. G., Jonsson, M., Kilander, F. et al. (2001). *Intrusion scenarios in meeting contexts* (FEEL Deliverable D5.1). Royal Technical University. Retrieved on March 1, 2006, from http://dsv.su.se/FEEL/zurich/Item_3-Intrusion_scenarios_in_meeting_contexts.pdf

Kato, U., Hayashi, T., Umeda, N. et al. (Ed.). (2004). *Flying Carpet: Towards the 4th Generation Mobile Communications Systems*, Version 2.00. 4th Generation Mobile Communications Committee. Retrieved on March 2, 2006, from http://www.mitf.org/public_e/archives/index.html

Kim, S. W., Kim, M. C., Park, S. H. et al. (2004). Gate reminder: a design case of a smart reminder. In D. Benyon, P. Moody et al. (Ed.) *Conference on Designing Interactive Systems* (pp. 81-90).

Koponen, K., Matkakorttien käytöstä syntyy valtava tietokanta matkustajista, *Helsingin Sanomat* (Finnish newspaper), 19.9.2002.

Lahlou, S. & Jegou, F. (2003). *European disappearing computer privacy design guidelines v1* (Ambient Agora Deliverable D15.4), Retrieved on March 2, 2006, from http://www.ambientagoras.org/downloads/D15%5B1%5D.4_-_Privacy_Design_Guidelines.pdf

Langheinrich, M. (2001). Privacy by design – principles of privacy-aware Ubiquitous Systems. In G. D. Abowd, B. Brumitt et al. (Ed.) *Proceedings of the Third International Conference on Ubiquitous Computing (UbiComp 2001)* (pp. 273-291). Springer-Verlag (Lecture Notes in Computer Science).

Langheinrich, M. (2006). *Personal privacy in Ubiquitous Computing*. Presentation in UK-Ubinet Summer School 2004. Retrieved on March 2, 2006, from http://www.vs.inf.ethz.ch/publ/slides/ukubinet2004-langhein.pdf

Ma, J., Yang, L. T., Apduhan, B. O. et al. (2005). Towards a smart world and ubiquitous intelligence: a walkthrough from smart things to smart hyperspaces and UbicKids. *International Journal of Pervasive Computing and Communications* 1(1), 53-68.

Masera, M., & Bloomfeld, R. (2003). *A Dependability Roadmap for the Information Society in Europe* (AMSD Deliverable D1.1). Retrieved on March 2, 2006, from https://rami.jrc.it/roadmaps/amsd

Mynatt, E., Essa, I., & Rogers, W. (2000). Increasing the opportunities for aging in place, In *Proceedings of the ACM Conference on Universal Usability* (pp. 65-71).

Nasoz, F., Alvarez, K., Lisetti, C., & Finkelstein, N. (2003). Emotion recognition from physiological signals for user modelling of affect. In *Proceedings of the Third Workshop on Affective and Attitude User Modelling*. Retrieved on March 3, 2006, from http://www.cs.ubc.ca/~conati/um03-affect/nasoz-final.pdf

Nissenbaum, H. (2004). Privacy as Contextual Integrity. *Washington Law Review, 79*(1), 101-139.

Orr, R. J., Raymond, R., Berman, J., & Seay, F. (1999). *A system for finding frequently lost objects in the home* (Tech. Rep. 99-24), Graphics, Visualization, and Usability Center, Georgia Tech.

Palmas, G., Tsapatsoulis, N., Apolloni, B. et al. (2001). *Generic Artefacts Specification and Acceptance Criteria*. (Oresteia Deliverable D01). Retrieved on March 2, 2006, from http://www.image.ntua.gr/oresteia/deliverables/ORESTEIA-IST-2000-26091-D01.pdf

Price, S., & Rogers, Y. (2004). Let's get physical: the learning benefits of interacting in digitally augmented physical spaces. *Computers and Education 43*(1-2), 137-151.

Schneier, B. (2005). Why Data Mining Won't Stop Terror. *Wired News*, March 9, 2005. Retrieved on April 19, 2007, from http://www.schneier.com/essay-108.html

Schneier, B. (2007). On Police Security Cameras: Wholesale Surveillance. *San Francisco Chronicle*, January 2007. Retrieved on April 19, 2007, from http://www.schneier.com/essay-147.html

Stajano, F. (2004). One user, many hats; and, sometimes, no hat – towards a secure yet usable PDA. In *Proceedings of the Security Protocols Workshop 2004* (pp. 51-64).

Truong, K. N., Huang, E. M., Stevens, M. M., & Abowd, G. D. (2004). How do users think about Ubiquitous Computing. In *Proceedings of CHI '04 extended abstracts on Human factors in computing systems* (pp. 1317 – 1320).

Web site of the American Civil Liberties Union and the ACLU Foundation (2006). *Eavesdropping 101: What Can The NSA Do?* 31.01.2006, Retrieved on March 2, 2006, from http://www.aclu.org/safefree/nsaspying/23989res20060131.html

Wright, D., & Gutwirth, S. (2008). *Safeguards in a world of ambient intelligence*. Springer

About the Contributors

Pasi Ahonen graduated at 1994 as PhLic in industrial physics from the Dept. of Physics at the University of Helsinki. During that time, he learned in practise how to measure the physical environment (building sensors, etc.). Ahonen also has 10 years of recent industrial experience in mobile system research topics such as VPN networks and clients, WLAN, push-to-talk, video and audio compression, mobile operating systems, system architectures and performance analysis and so forth. IP network security protocols, in particular, have been a focus area for him a long time. His industrial experience also includes telecommunications networks design, digital exchanges, network architectures and ethernet networks.

Petteri Alahuhta is technology manager in the Mobile Interaction Knowledge Centre of VTT Technical Research Centre of Finland (VTT). He is leading R&D concentrating on mobile system and ambient intelligence technologies. He holds an MSc in computer science and engineering and an eMBA title, both from the University of Oulu. He has over 12 years of experience in the research and development of advanced information technologies including artificial intelligence, software technologies, context-aware systems, mobile information processing, and technologies and user interaction technologies. He has worked on a number of international research projects in the field of ambient intelligence and advanced information technology.

Antão Almada has a degree in computer science. He has worked at several startups, both in Silicon Valley and in Portugal. At Sense8, he developed real-time 3D graphics applications for several Fortune 500 companies. At Paraform, he was the main architect and user interface developer for the company's award-winning software. Paraform's software has been used worldwide, namely on automotive industrial design and special effects production at major movie studios. Currently, at YDreams, he is the main architect at the R&D department. He also defines methodologies and procedures for company's software development.

Yacine Atif received the PhD in computer science from Hong Kong University of Science and Technology (HKUST) (1996). He worked as a post-doc at Purdue University, and then accepted a faculty position at Nanyang Technological University (NTU) in Singapore. Since 1999 he has been with the UAE University. From 2005 to 2006, he was at Massey University in New Zealand. Dr. Atif has made a number of research contributions, particularly in the areas of Internet computing and multimedia communication with applications in e-commerce and e-learning. He is also involved in the technical programs of several research forums such as program co-chair for WCNC 2007 (Wireless Communications and Networks Conference) and Innovations 2006 (Innovations in Information Technology).

Marco Avvenuti is an associate professor with the Dipartimento di Ingegneria dell'Informazione of the University of Pisa. He graduated in electronic engineering (1989) and received his PhD in information engineering from the University of Pisa (1993). In 1992 and 1996 he was a visiting scholar at the Berkeley's International Computer Science Institute (ICSI). He is a member of the IEEE Computer Society. His current research interests are in the areas of mobile and pervasive computing and wireless sensor networks. He has been involved in several projects on distributed systems funded by the European community, the Italian Ministry of Education and Research and the Italian National Council of Research (CNR).

Rachid Benlamri is an associate professor in the Department of Software Engineering at Lakehead University in Canada. He received the PhD degree in computer science from the University of Manchester in the United Kingdom (1990). His research interests are in the areas of Semantic Web, mobile learning, and Internet computing. Dr. Benlamri is involved in the technical programs of several research forums such as program co-chair for CMMSE 2007 (Context Modeling and Management for Smart Environments Workshop) and IWML 2006 (International Workshop on Wireless and Mobile Learning). His contribution to research projects in industry and academia led to the publication of papers in numerous reputable journals and conferences.

Jawad Berri received the PhD degree in computer science from Paris-Sorbonne University in France (1996). Before joining Etisalat University College, he was a researcher at the Institute of Computer Science at the University of Zurich in Switzerland. Jawad's research interests focus on e-learning, and Web-based applications. He has been involved in many projects related to e-learning, m-learning, Semantic Web, learner modelling, automatic summarization, web information filtering, information extraction from on-line documentation, Arabic language processing and mobile agents for web information discovery. His contributions to research projects in industry and academia led to the publication of papers in numerous reputable journals and conferences.

Pascal Bruegger is PhD student at the Computer Science Department of University of Fribourg and member of the PAI research group. He joined the University of Fribourg in 2003 as master student. Pascal Bruegger's main background is in electronics and software engineering. He spent more than 10 years as an IT specialist in several companies in many countries worldwide. His main focus of research is the study of a new interaction paradigm in ubiquitous computing and human computer interaction (HCI). He is interested in extend ing standard models of HCI by integrating physical motions as a primary input modality.

João Álvaro Carvalho is full professor at Department of Information Systems, School of Engineering, University of Minho, Portugal. He is the head of the Department of Information Systems. He holds a PhD in information systems from the UMIST (University of Manchester Institute of Science and technology), UK (1991). His research and teaching interests include the foundations of information systems, information systems development, meta-modelling, requirements engineering and knowledge management. He is the national representative of Portugal in IFIP TC 8 since 1996 and the President of the Portuguese Association for Information Systems (APSI—Associação Portuguesa de Sistemas de Informação).

Tiziana Catarci received her PhD in computer science from the University of Rome where she is currently a full professor. She has published over 100 papers and 10 books on a variety of subjects comprising user interfaces for databases, 2D and 3D data visualization, adaptive interfaces, visual metaphors, usability testing, data quality, cooperative database systems, database integration, web access. Dr. Catarci is regularly in the programming committees of the main database and human-computer interaction conferences and is associate editor of *ACM SIGMOD Digital Symposium Collection (DiSC)*, *VLDB Journal*, *World Wide Web Journal*, and *Journal of Data Semantics*.

Sajal K. Das is the founding director of UTA's Center for Research in Wireless Mobility and Networking (CReWMaN). He received his PhD in computer science from the University of Central Florida (1988) and his MS in computer science form the Washington State University (1986). He received his BTech in computer science form the University of Calcutta (1983). Das has published over 170 research papers in journals and conference proceedings in the areas of wireless networks and protocols, mobile computing, parallel/distributed processing, performance modeling, applied graph theory and interconnection networks. He has also directed numerous funded projects in these areas. Das serves on the editorial boards of the *Journal of Parallel and Distributed Computing* (as the subject area editor of mobile computing), *Parallel Processing Letters*, and the *Journal of Parallel Algorithms and Applications*. He has guest-edited special issues for many leading journals. He has served on the program committees of numerous conferences including IEEE IPDPS, ICPP, IEEE INFOCOM, and ACM MobiCom. He was general vice-chair of the IEEE International Conference on High Performance Computing (HiPC2000), program vice chair of HiPC'99, and the Founding Program Chair of WoWMoM'98 and WoWMoM'99. Dr. Das also serves on the ACM SIGMOBILE and IEEE TCPP executive committees. He is a member of the IEEE and ACM.

A. Eduardo Dias has a PhD in ubiquitous computing and contextual information and has been an assistant professor at the University of Évora since 1999, teaching ubiquitous computing, HCI, information systems, CG and software engineering. His R&D work has been published in books, journals and renowned conferences like ACM's CHI, GIS and AVI, SPIE, JEC-GI, EUROGRAPHICS. He is a member of the ACM and of the New University of Lisbon's research group on multimedia information processing and interaction (CITI-FCT/UNL). He co-founded YDreams and has been a company VP since then. Under his direction YDreams established global partnerships with market leaders in several areas.

Alan Dix is professor of computing at Lancaster University, UK and a director of the University's exploitation company LUBEL. He has worked in human-computer interaction research since the mid-1980's and is the author of one of the main textbooks in the area. He has also been a founding director of two Internet start-up companies focused on intelligent agent technology and web community building. Alan's earliest work in HCI focused on using formal techniques. However, recent work includes random sampling for visualisation of very large data sets; mobile interfaces, ubiquitous computing, situated display, designing user experience, and understanding physicality and creativity.

José Eduardo Fernandes is an assistant teacher at Department of Computer Science at Bragança Polytechnic Institute, Bragança, Portugal. He holds a master in information systems from Department of Information Systems, University of Minho, Portugal. Currently, he is a PhD student at the Department of Information Systems, University of Minho, researching on model-driven development for pervasive information systems. His current research interests include software engineering, pervasive information systems, and development of information systems.

Kai Fischbach is a research associate at the University of Cologne (Department for Information Systems and Information Management), Germany. His current research interests include social networks, knowledge networks, the economics of ubiquitous computing and peer-to-peer computing. He is the co-chair of the "Ubiquitous Computing" mini-track at AMCIS 2007.

Michael Friedewald is a senior scientist and consultant for information and communication technology, foresight and technology assessment at the Fraunhofer Institute for Systems and Innovation Research in Karlsruhe, Germany. In recent years he has conducted numerous studies on ambient intelligence on behalf of the European Commission and the German Federal Parliament. He has coordinated the EC-funded study, *Safeguards in a World of Ambient Intelligence* (SWAMI). Prior to SWAMI he did research on mobile communications, software patents and innovation patterns in the German hardware and software industry for various public clients.

Silvia Gabrielli received a PhD in cognitive sciences from the University of Padova (I) and since 1994 has been working in the field interaction design and usability evaluation of ICT. In recent years, her research focus has been on methodologies for usability and accessibility evaluation of mobile applications, as well as on the design and evaluation of educational environments. Silvia is currently working as a research fellow at HCI Lab (University of Udine, Italy).

David Garlan is a professor of computer science at Carnegie Mellon University. His research interests include software architectures, formal methods, self-healing systems, and task-based computing. He received his PhD in computer science from CMU.

Béat Hirsbrunner is full professor and leader of the Pervasive and Artificial Intelligence Research Group at the University of Fribourg. He holds a diploma and PhD in theoretical physics from ETHZ Zurich and University of Lausanne. He has been postdoc, visiting researcher and professor at the universities of Rennes and Berkeley, EPFL Lausanne, and IBM Research Labs San José. He has conducted research works on topics of parallel, distributed and pervasive computing, coordination languages, and human-computer interaction. He has been involved in several Swiss, European and U.S. research projects. He served as Dean of the Faculty of science of the Unversity of Fribourg, and is since 2001 a member of the Swiss NSF Council and Vice-President of SARIT.

Rui Huang received the PhD in computer science from The University of Texas at Arlington (2006), and the BS degree in computer science from Texas Christian University (1998). He has held a number of positions in software industry. His research interests include wireless networks, sensor networks, network protocols and algorithms. He is a member of the IEEE and its Communications Society.

Christine Julien received the BS degree in computer science and biology (2000) from Washington University in Saint Louis. She continued at Washington

University for her graduate degrees, where she received the MS degree (2003) and the DSc degree (2004), both in computer science. She is currently an assistant professor on the faculty of the Department of Electrical and Computer Engineering at the University of Texas at Austin, where she is a member of the Center for Excellence in Distributed Global Environments. She has published papers in varying areas including mobile computing, software engineering, group communication, and formal methods. Her current research interests involve communication and software engineering issues related to mobile and pervasive computing environments.

Sanem Kabadayi received her BS in electrical engineering and BS in physics degrees from the University of Texas at Austin (2000). She received her MSEECS from Sabanci University (2002). She is currently a PhD student in the Department of Electrical and Computer Engineering at the University of Texas at Austin and a member of the Mobile and Pervasive Computing Group. Her current research focuses on middleware for immersive sensor networks and pervasive computing environments.

Dimitrios C. Karaiskos holds a bachelor degree in informatics and telecommunications from the National and Kapodistrian University of Athens, Greece. He has also been awarded with an MSc in information systems from the Athens University of Economics and Business, Greece. He is currently studying towards his PhD in pervasive information systems in Athens University of Economics and Business, Greece. His main research interests lie in the area of pervasive IS, RFID technology and sensor networks. He also has much experience regarding programming on both desktop and mobile devices in various platforms and programming languages.

Stephen Kimani is currently an academic and research member of Jomo Kenyatta University of Agriculture and Technology (Kenya) and is affiliated with the University of Rome "La Sapienza" (Italy). He has been a post-doctoral researcher with the University of Rome "La Sapienza" (2004-2006). Dr. Stephen Kimani holds PhD in computer engineering (University of Rome "La Sapienza", Italy, 2004) and MSc in advanced computing (University of Bristol, UK, 1998). His main research interest is in human-computer interaction (HCI), in particular, as HCI relates to areas/aspects such as user interfaces, usability, accessibility, visualization, visual information access, visual data mining, digital libraries, and ubiquitous computing. He has published widely including book chapters, journal articles, and at international conferences and workshops in computer science. He is serving and has served in various program committees of and reviewing for journals, conferences and workshops. Furthermore, he is and has been involved in organizing sessions at international conferences and workshops. He has been involved in proposing and running projects in computer science, including Italian and European research projects. He is actively involved in leading, developing and coordinating research teams; teaching classes at undergraduate and postgraduate levels; and overseeing/ supervising postgraduate student projects.

Panayiotis E. Kourouthanassis is adjunct lecturer at the University of the Aegean and Senior Research Officer in the Wireless Research Center of the Athens University of Economics and Business. He is co-editor of an edited volume on pervasive information systems and member of the executive board of the AIS special interest group on Mobile and Ubiquitous Information Systems (SIGMUBIS). He has also co-organised three research tracks on pervasive information systems at international conferences.

Ricardo J. Machado is an assistant professor of software engineering and coordinator of the Software Engineering and Management Research Group (SEMAG) at the Department of Information Systems, University of Minho, Guimarães, Portugal. He is the R8 Coordinator (Europe, Middle East and Africa) of IEEE Computer Society. He is founder of the IFIP WG10.2 Working Group on Embedded Systems and founder of the international workshop series MOMPES (International Workshops on Model-Driven Methodologies for Pervasive and Embedded Software). His current research interests include software engineering, embedded software, and pervasive information systems. For more information, consult his website at http://www.dsi.uminho.pt/~rmac.

Steffen Muhle is a research associate at the University of Cologne (Department for Information Systems and Information Management), Germany. His main research interests include the strategic implications of open innovation and the economics of ubiquitous computing and ambient business.

Vincenzo Pallotta is a senior research associate and lecturer at the Computer Science Department of University of Fribourg and a member of the Pervasive and Artificial Intelligence research group. He holds a MSc and a PhD in computer science respectively from University of Pisa, Italy, and from the Swiss Federal Institute of Technology in Lausanne (EPFL), Switzerland. Vincenzo Pallotta's main background is in formal models for artificial intelligence and human-computer interaction through natural language interfaces. He has been involved in several Swiss and European research projects. His current research focus is the development of new interaction paradigms for ubiquitous computing. Based on his previous work on knowledge representation and reasoning, he is aiming to create a comprehensive theory of cognitive agency, which includes, among other aspects, the models of interaction with the physical environment (i.e. embodied cognition).

Tapani Rantakokko is a researcher and mobile software developer. After graduating from University of Oulu (2003), he specialized in context awareness, sensors and mobile user interfaces as a research scientist at VTT. In 2006 he left

VTT to co-found Finwe, a mobile software company with expertise in context awareness and recognition algorithms. Currently, he holds a position at Finwe as a senior software designer and partner, and is excited about making context awareness a reality in mobile terminals.

Luís Rato holds a PhD on electrotecnic engineering in the area of control systems; he is a professor at the University of Évora, Portugal where he teaches operating systems, information theory, computer architecture and computer networks. He is member of the research group on Computer Science and Information Technologies at the University of Évora (CITI-UE). He has been involved in several research projects related with control systems, modelling and simulation.

Teresa Romão is an assistant professor at the University of Évora, Portugal, where she teaches computer graphics, decision support systems, system analysis and digital systems. Her PhD thesis focuses on multidimensional visualisation of spatial information. She is member of a research group on multimedia information processing and interaction (CITI-FCT/UNL). She has been involved in several research projects related to augmented reality, mobile storytelling and ubiquitous computing. Her research work has been presented and published in renowned conferences, journals and books, such as ACM GIS, ACM ACE, EUROGRAPHICS, ELSEVIER, TAYLOR & FRANCIS and SPIE. Teresa is member of the EUROGRAPHICS.

Bradley Schmerl is a senior systems scientist at Carnegie Mellon University. His research interests include dynamic adaptation, software architectures, and software engineering environments. He received his PhD in computer science from Flinders University in South Australia, and has held faculty positions at both Flinders University and Clemson University in South Carolina.

Christian Schmitt is a research associate at the University of Cologne (Department for Information Systems and Information Management), Germany. His main research interests include the enhancement of (decentralized) information management using new technologies such as ubiquitous and peer-to-peer computing.

Detlef Schoder is a professor at the University of Cologne, Germany where he is presiding over the Department for Information Systems and Information Management. He is the author of more than 140 reviewed publications including journal articles in leading international and German outlets, such as *Communications of the ACM, International Journal of Technology Management, Information Economics and Policy, Journal of Electronic Commerce Research, Zeitschrift für Betriebswirtschaft (ZfB)*, and *Wirtschaftsinformatik*. Schoder is on various editorial boards including *Information Systems and eBusiness Management, International Journal of Electronic Business, International Journal of Internet* and *Enterprise Management*. He is co-chair of the "Ubiquitous Computing" mini-track at AMCIS 2007.

João P. Sousa is an assistant professor of computer science at George Mason University. His research interests include applications of software architecture and artificial intelligence to ubiquitous computing and self-aware and self-adaptive distributed systems; as well as improving the user's leverage and experience with such systems. João received an electrical and computer engineering degree at the Technical University of Lisbon (IST,) worked for 10 years for the financial industry in Portugal, and then obtained his PhD in computer science at Carnegie Mellon University, where he also held a post-doctoral fellowship.

Peter Steenkiste is a professor of Computer Science and of Electrical and Computer Engineering at Carnegie Mellon University. His research interests include networking, distributed systems, and pervasive computing. He received an MS and PhD in electrical engineering from Stanford University and an engineering degree from the University of Gent, Belgium. You can learn more about his research from his home page http://www.cs.cmu.edu/~prs

Alessio Vecchio received his PhD in information engineering from the University of Pisa (2003). Currently, he works as a researcher at the Department of Information Engineering, where his activity is related to pervasive and mobile computing. His research interests also include distributed object systems, network emulation, and wireless sensor networks.

Elena Vildjiounaite received MSc from St-Petersburg Polytechnic University. Since 2001 she works at the Technical Research Centre of Finland (VTT) on projects for Ubicomp development. Her research interests include artificial intelligence, human-technology interaction, context awareness, user modelling and biometric authentication.

David Wright is managing partner of Trilateral Research & Consulting LLP based in London, which specialises in ambient intelligence, risk communication and security policy issues. He initiated the consortia and wrote much of the proposals for two successful EC-funded, Sixth Framework Programme projects, namely SWAMI (Safeguards in a World of Ambient Intelligence) and STARC (Stakeholders and Risk Communication). Prior to those projects, he researched and wrote reports on organisational scenarios and the civil protection sector under the EC's GMES programme and on public-private partnerships and dual-use technologies under the Galileo satellite navigation programme.

Gergely V. Záruba is an assistant professor of computer science and engineering at The University of Texas at Arlington (CSE@UTA). He received the PhD degree in computer science from The University of Texas at Dallas (2001) and the MS degree in computer engineering from the Technical University of Budapest, Department of Telecommunications and Telematics (1997). Záruba's research interests include wireless networks, algorithms, and protocols, performance evaluation, current wireless and assistive technologies. He has served on many organizing and technical program committees for leading conferences and has guest edited journals. He is a member of the IEEE and its Communications Society.

Index

A

abstraction dimension 70, 72, 74

access control 322, 324, 328, 330, 332, 336, 343, 344

activity-oriented computing (AoC) 281, 282, 283, 286, 287, 288, 309, 311, 312

activity theory model 177, 178, 182

advanced traveller information system (ATIS) 231

ambient business 253, 254, 257, 258, 261, 263, 270

ambient intelligence 253. *See also* ubiquitous computing (ubicomp)

angle of arrival (AoA) 86, 90, 92, 93, 94, 95, 101, 103, 105, 106, 107, 109, 110, 112, 114

ANOVA tests 150, 162, 163

application scenario 338

artificial intelligence (AI) 330, 343

attractiveness of alternatives (AA) 161, 162

augmented reality , 242

aura location identifiers (ALIs) 299

auras 284, 288, 290, 291, 292, 293, 294, 295, 296, 297, 298, 299, 303, 304, 306, 309, 314, 315

authentication 322, 328, 330, 331, 332

B

behavioral intention of use (BI) 161, 162, 163

C

camera-phones 2, 15

classes dimension 70, 74

context 173, 194, 195, 197, 198

context, definition of 173

context, five W's of 174

context-aware computing 207

context-awareness 205, 222

context-awareness, location-awareness 205, 208

context management 24

contextual information services (CIS) 294, 295

Cramer Rao bound (CRB) 86, 107, 108, 109, 111

Crossbow platform 137, 147

D

DataGlyphs technique 6

Data Matrix symbology 6, 8, 13, 14, 15, 18, 19

data processing 329, 339, 340, 342, 344

declarative applications in immersive sen-

sor networks (DAIS) 117, 118,
134, 135, 136, 137, 138, 141,
142,144, 145
decoders 3, 15, 18
development dimensions 70
development framework 76
device-agnostic 121
distributed cognition model 177, 178,
180, 181, 189, 193, 195, 198

E

embodied interaction
203, 204, 205, 208, 222
emerging technologies
253, 254, 255, 256
end-user applications 120
environment management (EM) 291, 292,
293, 294, 296, 298, 299, 306,
307, 308, 315
environment manager binding protocol
(EMBP) 298, 299
extensible markup language (XML)
236, 243

F

federative library (FedLib)
252, 253, 268, 269
feedback management 211
functional dimension 70, 71, 74

G

geographical adaptive fidelity(GAF) algorithm 84, 89
GeoGRID algorithm 84, 88
global positioning system (GPS) 84, 90,
92, 109, 113, 116
GOAFR+ algorithm 84, 87
graphical user interfaces (GUIs) 203, 204,
205, 211, 212, 221
GRID algorithm 84, 87, 88, 114, 116

H

human-computer interaction (HCI)
203, 204, 205

human computer interface (HCI) 177, 182
192, 194, 195, 196, 197, 198

I

image processing 229, 230, 232, 233
immersive environments 144. *See* immersive sensor networks
immersive sensor networks 119, 120,
122, 123, 125, 126, 144
in-network aggregation 122
in-network processing 121
in-network query resolution 145
information infrastructure
253, 260, 262, 263
innovation diffusion theory 150, 164
instrumented environment 118
interferometric ranging 86, 90, 93, 94,
95, 103, 107, 109, 110, 111,
112, 113

J

Java platform micro edition(JME)
3, 11, 12, 13, 21

K

kinetic-awareness 205
kinetic-aware systems 206
kinetic user interfaces (KUI) 210
kinetic user interfaces (KUI), interaction
patterns 204, 212, 213, 219, 221
kinetic user interfaces (KUI), interaction patterns, continuous tracking
212, 222
KUI widget (Kuidgets)
215, 216, 217, 220, 221

L

learner modeling 24, 28, 29
learning, context-aware 23, 24, 40, 23,
24, 25, 26
learning, mobile (m-learning) 23, 24, 25,
26, 27, 28, 29, 32
learning, personalized 24, 25

learning context 25, 23, 24, 25, 23, 25, 26, 27, 28, 29, 31, 32, 35, 36, 38, 39, 40, 42
learning object metadata (LOM) 27, 31, 32
learning objects (LOs) 25, 29, 31, 32, 39
learning Web (LW) 30, 38, 40
localization 83, 85, 86, 87, 88, 90, 91, 93, 94, 95, 96, 97, 98, 99, 100 101, 103, 104, 105, 106, 107, 108, 109, 110, 111, 112, 113, 114, 115, 116
location-aware services 207
location-based multicast (LBM) algorithm 84, 88
location aided routing (LAR) algorithm 84, 87, 88, 113, 116

M

MaxiCode symbology 6
middleware 117, 118, 120, 121, 124, 125, 126, 129, 132, 134, 136, 137, 141, 142, 143, 144, 145, 147, 149, 201, 209, 210, 212, 215, 218, 219, 220, 221, 222
MIDlets 11, 13, 15, 17
mobile ad hoc network (MANET) 84, 87, 89
mobile computing 202, 211, 226
mobile traffic (M-Traffic) system 229, 230, 231, 233, 234, 235, 238, 240, 241, 246, 247, 248, 236
model-driven architecture (MDA) 52, 53, 54, 55, 81
model-driven development (MDD) 46, 52, 53, 56, 57, 58, 59, 67, 68, 69, 70, 77, 78
model human processor model 177
motion as an input modality 206, 211
multilateration 91, 97, 99, 100, 115, 116. *See also* triangulation

N

nesC 124, 137, 138, 141, 147
nomadic computing 203. *See* ubiquitious computing

O

on-demand loading 3
ontologies 24, 25, 28, 29, 30, 31, 32, 33, 34, 35, 36, 37, 38, 39, 42
open innovation 253, 258
open object information infrastructure (OOII) 252, 253, 264, 265, 266, 267, 268, 269, 270
over-the-air provisioning (OTA) 11, 13

P

perceived ease of use (PEOU) 158, 160, 161, 162, 164, 165
perceived risk (PR) 161, 162
perceived usefulness (PU) 150, 158, 160, 161, 162, 163, 164
personal device 331, 332, 340
pervasive computing 46, 47, 48, 49, 51, 52, 79, 80, 81, 117, 118, 119, 121, 129, 148, 151, 253, 254, 267, 277. *See* ubiquitous computing (ubicomp)
pervasive information systems (pervasive IS) 150, 151, 164
pervasive information systems (PISs) 45, 46, 49, 52, 67, 68, 69, 70, 72, 74, 76, 77, 78
position-based multicast (PBM) algorithm 84, 88, 89
privacy 316, 317, 318, 319, 321, 322, 323, 324, 326, 327, 328, 329, 330, 331, 332, 333, 334, 335, 336, 337, 338, 339, 340, 341, 342, 343, 344, 345, 346
privacy-enhancing technologies (PETs) 323, 324, 325
project aura 288

Q

QR Code symbology 6, 8

R

RADAR project 285
radio frequency identification (RFID) 4, 5 22, 150, 151, 152, 153, 155, 156 157, 158, 159, 160, 162, 163,

164, 165, 167, 168, 169, 264, 269, 272, 274, 275, 277, 279
real-time 229, 230, 231, 232, 233, 235, 237, 239, 240, 243, 247, 249
received signal strength indication (RSSI) 85, 90, 91, 92, 93, 94, 95, 96, 98, 100, 101, 103, 104, 105, 106 107, 109, 110, 112
RETSINA framework 285
routing 83, 84, 86, 87, 88, 89, 97, 111, 113, 114, 115, 116

S

scenarios 213
Semantic Web 23, 24, 25, 26, 28, 32, 34, 40, 41, 42, 43, 255, 265, 266, 270, 272, 274, 275, 277
sensors 229, 230, 232, 233, 237, 243, 245, 247, 248
service announcement & activation protocol (SAAP) 293, 315
service request protocol (SRP) 293
service use protocol (SUP) 293
situated action model 177, 179, 180
situated interaction paradigm 181
smart environments 251, 253, 254, 256, 257, 258, 263, 264, 266, 267, 270, 271
smart services 253, 254, 256, 257, 258, 261, 262, 263, 266, 267, 270
spatio-temporal relations 218
strategy patterns 136, 141, 143

T

tangible user interfaces (TUI) 204, 227
task management (TM) 290, 291, 292, 307, 308
technology, user acceptance of 150, 157, 158, 159, 164, 168, 170
technology acceptance model (TAM) 150, 158, 165
ticketing systems 152, 153, 155, 156, 159, 162, 163, 164
time of arrival (ToA) 90, 91, 92, 95, 98, 100, 101, 103, 107, 109, 110 112

TinyOS 124, 137, 142
traffic information system 229, 233
traffic simulator 243–247
triangulation 101. *See also* multilateration

U

ubicomp applications, characteristics of 173
ubiquitous applications, design of 172, 173, 180, 182, 191, 193
ubiquitous commerce 253
ubiquitous computing (ubicomp) 23, 24, 25, 46, 47, 48, 79, 80, 81, 82, 118, 119, 120, 121, 122, 123, 125, 128, 134, 144, 145, 146, 148, 151, 171, 172, 173, 177, 178, 179, 180, 181, 182, 183, 185, 186, 187, 188, 80, 125, 183, 189, 43, 182, 174, 175, 177, 178, 190, 183, 189, 190, 191, 192, 193, 194, 197, 199, 201, 202, 203, 204, 211, 223, 224, 225, 226, 251, 252, 253, 254, 255, 260, 263, 267, 270, 271, 274, 278, 279, 316, 317, 318, 319, 320, 321, 322, 323, 325, 326, 327, 329, 330, 332, 334, 335, 336, 337, 338, 339, 341, 342, 344. *See* pervasive computing
ubiquitous solutions for pain monitoring and control in post-surgery patients (uPAIN) 59, 60, 61, 62, 63, 64, 66, 67, 68, 71, 74
universal product codes (UPCs) 5
universal resource identifiers (URIs) 299
unobtrusive interfaces 205, 211
user activities 280, 281, 282, 283, 284, 285, 286, 287, 288, 289, 291, 292, 293, 294, 295, 296, 300, 303, 304, 305, 306, 308, 310, 311, 312
user interface 172, 182, 192, 332

V

video streams 238
virtual sensors 126, 129, 130, 131, 132

133, 134, 139, 141, 143, 144, 146
visual tag 2, 3, 4, 7, 8, 9, 10, 14, 16, 17, 19

W

Web services 26, 32, 34, 41
Weiser, Mark 47, 48, 49, 82
wireless technologies 151